Freedom Is an Endless Meeting

FREEDOM IS AN ENDLESS MEETING

DEMOCRACY IN AMERICAN SOCIAL MOVEMENTS

Francesca Polletta

THE UNIVERSITY OF CHICAGO PRESS / CHICAGO AND LONDON

Francesca Polletta is associate professor of sociology at Columbia University.
She is the coeditor of *Passionate Politics: Emotions in Social Movements,*
published by the University of Chicago Press.

The University of Chicago Press, Chicago 60637
The University of Chicago Press, Ltd., London
© 2002 by The University of Chicago
All rights reserved. Published 2002
Printed in the United States of America

11 10 09 08 07 06 05 04 03 02   1 2 3 4 5

ISBN: 0-226-67448-7 (cloth)

Library of Congress Cataloging-in-Publication Data

Polletta, Francesca.
  Freedom is an endless meeting : democracy in American social
movements / Francesca Polletta.
      p.   cm.
  Includes bibliographical references and index.
  ISBN 0-226-67448-7 (cloth : alk. paper)
  1. Social movements—United States.   2. Community organization—
United States.   3. Political participation—United States.   4. Group
decision making—United States.   I. Title.

HN57 .P65   2002
303.48′4′0973—dc21

                                        2002020615

♾ The paper used in this publication meets the minimum requirements
of the American National Standard for Information Sciences—Permanence
of Paper for Printed Library Materials, ANSI Z39.48-1992.

Contents

Preface

Democracy has always been a concept at once radical and ambiguous. Ambiguous because *demos* could mean either the citizens of a city-state or the lower orders—"the rabble"—and *kratos* could mean either "power" or "rule." *Government by the people* could mean decisionmaking by elites in the name of the citizenry or direct deliberation by the masses themselves. In Athens after 461 B.C., it meant the latter. The most important political institutions of the city-state were filled by lot, and the ruling assembly was attended by six thousand or more citizens who made decisions by acclamation rather than voting. Until Athens fell to the Macedonians in 322 B.C., democracy *was* participatory democracy. To be sure, such egalitarianism flourished against the backdrop of strong inequalities. Women, the foreign born, and slaves were categorically excluded from the citizen body. But this was not the reason for Athenian democracy's condemnation by Plato, Socrates, and, more circumspectly, Aristotle. When "the State is faced with some building project, I observe that the architects are sent for," Socrates pointed out. "And when it is a matter of shipbuilding, the naval designers." Yet, when it was "something to do with the government of the country that is to be debated, the man who gets up to advise them may be a builder or equally well a blacksmith or a shoemaker, merchant or ship-owner, rich or poor, of good family or not."[1]

Left unclear in Socrates' complaint was whether democracy threatened the dictates of reason or the prerogatives of those in power. The question remains a live one. If social movement activists have been the last century's "rabble," then their bids to style themselves participatory democracies have been viewed by commentators with a mixture of respect and bemusement. If conservatives are struck by participatory democrats' dangerous disrespect for authority, even sympathizers have worried about their indifference to the demands of effective political action. Participatory democracy is fine for those with the time and the taste for endless meetings, they argue. But, for the powerless or those convinced that change is made by securing tangible concessions from intransigent authorities, it is surely an indulgence that they can ill afford.

I take issue with that conclusion. Far from being at odds with the demands of political effectiveness, participatory decisionmaking can help activists build solidarity, innovate tactically, secure the leverage of political opinion, and develop enduring mechanisms of political accountability. These can, in turn, contribute to making changes in the institutional political arena. Participatory democracy's benefits, in other words, should not be restricted to the realms of "cultural" or "personal" change. Recognizing these benefits requires a broader view of how social movements effect change than is current in the literature, however. Without efforts to develop leaders outside existing elites, narrow criteria for leadership are left unchallenged; without enduring organizations, concessions are easily lost; without mechanisms of accountability, representatives are often co-opted. But there is a catch. What makes it possible for people to capitalize on participatory democracy's developmental benefits is not the strict equality that participatory democrats have sometimes insisted on, but a more complex equality in which different skills, talents, and interests are seen as equally valuable. Ironically, that kind of equality has thrived in the same relationships—friendship, for example—that in other ways have undermined participatory democratic projects.

If, as Lawrence Goodwyn suggests, our misguided view of history as the march of progress has blinded us to the fact that we have few models for actually achieving democracy, this book can be taken as an effort to recuperate possibilities from over a hundred years' and seven movements' worth of experiments in democracy.[2] Perhaps, however, the story that I tell *is* a progressive one. Or perhaps academics have not caught up with the insights that activists have garnered in the field. As I was writing this book, I was struck by two sets of comments. In a story on activists' preparations for protests against the International Monetary Fund in Washington, D.C., in April 2000, a *New York Times* reporter noted the extraordinary coalition of groups that had come together to challenge corporate globalization. To explain why the coalition held, he quoted Njoki Njoroge Njehu, "a Kenyan who serves as one of the movement's key 'facilitators.' (Participants say there are no generals, only lieutenants and ground troops.)" According to Njehu, "the coalition has managed to bridge different purposes because it operates strictly by consensus."[3]

A second interesting comment came in a meeting of labor organizers that I attended that same month. Representatives of AFSCME (the American Federation of State, County, and Municipal Employees),

UNITE (the Union of Needle Trades, Industry, and Textile Employees), and SEIU (the Service Employees International Union) were in disagreement, and sometimes defensive, about the merits of their different unions' organizing strategies. But they were unanimous about the need for what they called a "consensus" process. To vigorous nods around the room, one organizer said, "Think about how we organize now. We parachute in, stay in a hotel, organize leaders, probably not the ones who were there before, and leave. And then we probably have to do the same thing all over again in a few years." He and other participants repeatedly invoked instrumental rationales for participatory decisionmaking: it was a way to build rank-and-file commitment, to target the issues that would speak to people where they were, to build coalitions with groups outside labor's traditional ambit.

Union organizers do not fit the standard image of democratic radicals, of ideological purists who refuse to engage in the bargaining required by mainstream politics and who would sacrifice political opportunities rather than cut short a discussion. Direct actionists probably fit the image better, and press accounts of the IMF protests did emphasize their expressive, sometimes downright silly character. But the Kenyan facilitator's view of consensus as a means to preserve differences while working through to common purposes suggests something different. Contemporary activists may simply be less constrained by the strategy/democracy conundrum than are their academic observers.

I have been writing this book for a long time and have incurred numerous debts. My first is to the activists who gave so generously of their time in interviews that lasted hours and sometimes days. They skillfully unpacked complex organizational dynamics, reframed my often fuzzy questions, and willingly evoked painful memories. They wanted, they said, to get the story right. I want to make special acknowledgment of Chude Pamela Allen, Elaine Baker, Ivanhoe Donaldson, Marshall Ganz, Casey Hayden, Mike Miller, and Mike Thelwell. Initial interviews with each of them evolved into conversations that have been going on for years now—and into friendships that I hope will last for years more. Two of the people I interviewed, Kwame Ture (Stokely Carmichael) and Stanley Wise, died before I completed the book. In recording my debt to them, I also want to celebrate their memory.

This book depends on a great deal of archival and oral-history material. My thanks to archivists at Columbia University's Oral History Collection, Howard University's Moorland-Spingarn Center, the Martin Luther King

Jr. Center for Nonviolent Social Action, New York University's Tamiment Center, the Swarthmore College Peace Collection, the Wisconsin State Historical Society, and the Chicago Historical Society. Support for the project came from the Bunting Fellowship Program of the Radcliffe Institute for Advanced Study, the Individual Fellows Program of the Open Society Institute, the National Endowment for the Humanities, and the Columbia University Council for Research in the Social Sciences.

I found terrific critics in the Great Barrington Theory Group, the Columbia Contentious Politics Seminar, the Boston College Media Research and Action Project, the Harvard Hauser Center Workshop, the Harvard Social Movements Seminar, the Bunting Fellowship Program, and the New York University Politics, Protest, and Power Workshop. Talks at Rutgers University, the Radcliffe Institute for Advanced Study, New York University, and the City University Graduate Center provided valuable opportunities to present portions of the book.

Colleagues and friends have commented on numerous versions of the arguments that I present here. Thanks especially to Chude Pamela Allen, Edwin Amenta, Alvin Atkins, Robert Benford, Mary Bernstein, Robb Bloom, Lynn Chancer, Elisabeth Clemens, Patricia Clough, Ivanhoe Donaldson, Kai Erikson, William Gamson, Herbert Gans, Marshall Ganz, Helen Garvy, Chad Goldberg, Jeff Goodwin, Jennifer Gordon, Casey Hayden, Richard Healey, Joseph Jackson, James Jasper, Michael Kramer, John Krinsky, Charles Lemert, Paul Lichterman, Jane Mansbridge, Mike Miller, Ann Mische, Kelly Moore, Jeffrey Olick, Robert Pardun, Adolph Reed Jr., Charlotte Ryan, John Skrentny, Marc Steinberg, Wayne te Brake, Chuck Tilly, and Elizabeth Wood. Miriam Bearse deserves special thanks. She conducted some of the interviews with women's liberationists that formed the backdrop to chapter 6, and she and I collaborated in developing the arguments made in that chapter. Linda Catalano, Isabell Moore, Greg Smithsimon, and Lesley Wood provided valuable research assistance and commentary.

Debra Minkoff and an anonymous reviewer for the University of Chicago Press offered suggestions for revision that were right on the mark. Of course, they bear no responsibility for my failure to take all of them. Executive Editor Doug Mitchell "got" the project from my first stumbling précis of it and has been a joy to work with ever since, as have Robert Devens, Mark Heineke, and Joseph Brown.

James Jasper's combination of intellectual creativity and analytic rigor pushed me to pursue entirely new directions while keeping my feet firmly on empirical ground. Kelly Moore's passionate commitment to both activism and scholarship buoyed me when the thickets of activist politics seemed daunting. Gregory, Maddalena, and Gabriella Polletta offered wise counsel and their unflagging confidence. Finally, Edwin Amenta served uncomplainingly as sounding board, editor, champion, and supplier of a steady stream of ice-cream sandwiches. Perhaps I would have finished this even without him. But there would have been much less to look forward to when it was done.

1

STRATEGY AND DEMOCRACY

Talk helps people consider the possibilities open for social change. . . . One person said, "freedom is an endless meeting."

SDS MEMBER (1965)

Conventional wisdom has it that participatory democracy is worthy in principle but unwieldy in practice. For groups devoted to social change, sustaining a decentralized, nonhierarchical, and consensus-based organization seems to mean sacrificing the quick decisions and clear lines of command necessary to winning concessions in a hostile political climate. When confronted with a sudden opportunity—say, authorities agree to a more moderate version of your group's demands—can you afford to have all your members discuss its potential benefits and liabilities, along with anything else anyone wants to talk about, until everyone agrees on every clause and caveat? How can you even plan a concerted effort like a march or a legislative campaign when you have devolved authority to numerous independent local groups? Can you risk vesting power in novices when engaged in the tricky infighting so characteristic of institutional politics? And can you transform society when busy transforming yourselves? If the appropriate metaphor for a social movement organization is an army, it is hard to think of an army that has won any battles by favoring community over hierarchy, freedom over discipline, and self-expression over effectiveness.

True, hundreds of social movement groups have tried. From pacifists' here-and-now revolution, to the beloved community of the Southern civil rights movement and the new left's participatory democracy, up to today's radically democratic antiglobalization groups, activists have sought to live the better community as they built it, to enact in their own operation the values of equality, community, and democracy that they wanted on a large scale. The chroniclers of these experiments have been sympathetic, but not overly optimistic. Over and over again, they have described progressive groups such as the pacifist Peacemakers, the Student Nonviolent

Coordinating Committee (SNCC), Students for a Democratic Society (SDS), and the women's liberationist collectives that proliferated in the late 1960s struggling to square commitments to radical egalitarianism and political efficacy—with creative results, but with the denouement all too often the group's collapse, as competing factions pressed for more radically democratic or more visibly effective actions. The very labels that analysts have used to describe such organizations—"expressive" rather than "instrumental," "prefigurative" rather than "strategic," "redemptive" rather than "adversary"—give away the stories they tell. Once participatory democrats enter the realm of contentious politics, their indifference to strategy seems to doom them to failure.[1]

This book tells a different story. Activists in every major movement of the last hundred years have found strategic value in participatory democratic decisionmaking. They have had many reasons for adopting the form, of course, and they have practiced it in different ways. But, over and over again, activists have been drawn to the *solidary*, *innovatory*, and *developmental* benefits of participatory democracy—benefits that are practical and political. When I ask Tom Hayden, the new leftist perhaps most responsible for popularizing the slogan "participatory democracy," why a group should strive for consensus, his answer is straightforward: because you need to count on other people putting their bodies on the line with you. Giving people a stake in the decision gives them a stake in the success of the action and in the survival of the group. Generations of direct action protesters have shared this view. For the radical pacifists whose opposition to war earned them public hostility and harassment, their egalitarian organizations did even more than that, helping them withstand their terrible isolation and sustaining the movement until the political climate had changed enough to garner them a new audience.[2]

In the conditions of uncertainty and relative powerlessness in which movement groups have so often operated, participatory democracy's innovatory and developmental benefits have been as important as its solidary ones. The sheer diversity of input into tactical choice that participatory democracy makes possible has enabled activists to outpace their opponents in generating novel tactics. In the Southern civil rights movement, organizers used participatory democracy to school local residents in the practice of politics, thus exploiting the developmental benefits of the form. Far from opposed to leadership, they aimed to create political leaders—and to create the mechanisms that would keep leaders accountable to their constituents. In other movements too, especially those that have depended on people with little experience of routine politics, making decisions by consensus and rotating leadership has helped create a pool of activists capable of enforcing the gains made by this movement and launching new rounds of activism. Participatory democracy's potential benefits, in sum, cannot be reduced to "personal" or "cultural" changes. They go to the heart of political impact.

If closer examination of activists' experiments with participatory democracy reveals neglected benefits of the form, however, it also suggests that we must look deeper than the supposedly intrinsic conflict between democracy and efficacy to account for its liabilities. For it is undeniable that most participatory democratic groups have struggled to survive past their founding, let alone realize politically transformative aims. The challenges that they have faced in coordinating large numbers of people with little preparation time and scarce resources have been daunting, and the economic and legal pressures on them to mimic conventional organizations equally so. But participatory democrats have also been thwarted by their very understandings of equality and democracy and efficiency. Equality has sometimes been interpreted as prohibiting any differences in skills or talents. What group members have viewed as effective leadership at one point has come later to be seen as manipulation. Democratic "purists" and "pragmatists" have battled for control of organizations, with each side claiming its own version of what truly democratic deliberation requires. How activists have defined participatory democracy has made practicing it as easy as four friends deciding where to go to dinner—and as difficult as negotiating a treaty among superpowers.

To say that activists' definitions of democracy have affected their ability to put the form to good use, in other words, that culture constrains strategy, will raise a red flag for sociologists. We tend to be wary of culturalist arguments, concerned that their after-the-fact quality gives us little leverage in understanding other cases. So what, we might ask, if we can show that a group's rigid understanding of democracy made it difficult actually to practice democracy? What does that tell us about the next group that adopts the form? Can we extract a generalizable argument from the myriad influences on a group's cultural understandings? We can—by investigating the observable social relationships in which activists' understandings of participatory democracy have been grounded.

Social relationships have shaped participatory democracy in two ways. One is that familiar relationships have provided normative frameworks for deliberation. Participatory democrats have treated each other as family members, as colleagues, and as business partners but especially, in the twentieth century at least, as religious fellows, as teachers and learners, and as friends. These relationships structured deliberative interactions by providing not only broad injunctions against competition and manipulation but also microinteractional rules about how to raise issues, frame disagreement, formulate (and even feel about) dissent.

In some ways, this was to good effect. As friends, learners, and religious fellows, participatory democrats in the movements that I studied treated differences in skills and preferences as sources of mutual learning rather than as obstacles to equality. They were able to make decisions without protracted negotiation and challenge. But each relationship also threatened the group's capacity to make decisions fairly and effectively. For instance, friendship's tendency to exclusivity and its aversion to difference made it difficult for 1960s activists to expand their groups beyond an original core. When they tried to implement mechanisms designed to equalize power, friendship's resistance to formalization impeded their efforts. When newcomers protested their outsider status, or when disagreement was experienced as betrayal, deliberation broke down. Just as pacifists had earlier confronted the limits of the associational model of religious fellowship on which they had based their deliberations and civil rights organizers struggled with the contradictions inherent in the notion of teaching democratic leadership, so friendship in some ways undermined a participatory democratic organization.

Social relationships have underpinned the practice of participatory democracy in a second sense. Activists' assessments of particular deliberative forms—of how egalitarian or efficient or radical they are—have been based in part on the social groups with which they have been identified. For example, what radical democracy meant and what it was good for changed for white student activists in the early 1960s when they began to associate it not with rural communards, Quakers, and pacifists but with black Southern students fighting white supremacy. Its value for black radicals changed a few years later when they came to see it, along with a paralyzing moralism and a self-indulgent penchant for individual freedom, as white. Top-down decisionmaking and a hardheaded instrumentalism, in contrast, came to be seen as black. Today, direct action activists embrace consensus but disdain the deliberative styles that they associate with "new agey" or "Californian" protest—self-oriented, they seem to mean, and unconcerned with practical politics. As a result, however, they have eschewed deliberative procedures that actually might make their decisionmaking more efficient. In each case, movement groups have defined themselves in imitation of, or opposition to, their higher-profile counterparts and have thereby foreclosed strategic possibilities as well as opening them up.

By illuminating the relationships that have underpinned activists' practice of participatory democracy, the story that I tell should revise our understanding of the vulnerabilities as well as the promise of the form. But another aim should be evident in the foregoing, which is to probe the role of culture in strategic action. One can think about the issues that I have raised so far in terms of a different question: Why do activists style their deliberations the way they do? More broadly, why do they decide to adopt a particular tactic, target, ideological frame, or way of making decisions—and decide later to modify or abandon it? Sociologists' ability to answer these questions has been compromised by the narrow conceptual categories on which they have relied. On the dominant theoretical models of strategic choice, movement leaders choose among competing options either by rationally assessing their potential to further such instrumental tasks as winning allies, avoiding repression, and sustaining rank-and-file enthusiasm or by determining how well particular options match their prior ideological commitments. Or else they try to juggle ideological considerations and instrumental ones. It is easy, from this vantage point, to see activists choosing a participatory democratic structure because they want to be true to their democratic ideals. And it is easy to see them abandoning it in favor of a more hierarchical and centralized structure when they realize that their organization's survival depends on putting instrumental concerns above ideological ones.[3]

I raised the possibility earlier, however, that participatory democratic forms might be adopted for strategic reasons rather than ideological ones. Conversely, might not hierarchical forms be adopted for ideological reasons: because they *connote* efficiency and seriousness, say, or connote masculinity or blackness? Might not activists choose an option or a way of interacting because it is powerfully identified with another group viewed as especially effective, radical, or principled—independent of any proof of its capacity to effect change, its unconventionality, or its normative integrity? Tracing the career of a single organizational form through seven movements allows us to investigate this possibility. More broadly, it can help us rethink how groups select from among the strategic options available to them—but without restricting our analytic options to strategy and ideology.[4]

THE STRONG CASE FOR PARTICIPATORY DEMOCRACY

When participatory democratic organizations exploded on the American scene in the late 1960s, scholarly observers were skeptical, sometimes downright dismissive. Student protesters were driven by a "romantic primitivism" that was irrational, incoherent, and susceptible to demagoguery. They demanded of their politics a "totality of undifferentiated perfection," according to sociologist Edward Shils, and, in their own deliberations as well as their relations with authorities, they displayed a dangerous unwillingness to compromise, the latter the sine qua non of democratic politics. More sympathetic observers saw in the desire to create democratic alternatives mainly expressive and therapeutic rationales. Activists sought "liberated selves in a loose community of equals," in historian Peter Clecak's not untypical formulation. Next to the possibility of "personal salvation," Clecak was convinced, politics "existed fitfully, even secondarily."[5]

In recent years, analysts have been much more willing to credit participatory democrats with explicitly political purposes. Experiments with egalitarian and cooperative decisionmaking are a kind of politics—just not the politics of parliamentary maneuver and bureaucratic manipulation. Rather, as sociologist Wini Breines put it in *Community and Organization*, her seminal study of the 1960s new left, by "prefiguring" within the current practices of the movement the values of freedom, equality, and community that they wanted on a grand scale, activists were helping bring them about. Their dilemma—and it was a dilemma, not a mistake—was that they wanted to effect political change without reproducing the structures that they opposed. To be "strategic" was to privilege organization over personhood and political reform over radical change, and this they would not do.

The label *prefigurative* has remained popular as a way to describe movement groups whose internal structure is characterized by a minimal division of labor, decentralized authority, and an egalitarian ethos and whose decisionmaking is direct and consensus oriented. SNCC, SDS, the Clamshell Alliance, 1970s feminist groups like Redstockings, and numerous environmental and anti–corporate globalization groups today fit the model. They can be compared to the National Association for the Advancement of Colored People (NAACP), the Sierra Club, and the National Organization for Women, all of which put the achievement of their goals, whether desegregation, securing environmental legislation, or getting women into elected office, above their still deeply held commitments to democracy. Accommodating the demands of funders may mean implementing bureaucratic allocative procedures; winning legislation or policy change may require centralized authority; responding quickly to the aggressive action of movement opponents may require leaders' unilateral action. Groups privileging democratic principles, by contrast, are unwilling to bow to the demands of political efficacy.[6]

Does this mean that groups privileging democratic principles cannot be politically effective? The concept of prefiguration was intended to capture the political seriousness of such groups, but also their potential for political impact. However, analysts have been less clear about how such impact occurs. Is building the new society within the shell of the old aimed at persuading people outside the movement of the desirability and viability of radically democratic forms, or is its purpose to transform participants' relationships with each other? Or do activists see themselves as preserving a democratic impulse until a more receptive era? Absent any attempt to distinguish among these and other possibilities and to define what counts as success, prefigurative goals risk sounding very much like expressive ones—defined only by their opposition to considerations of strategy. Moreover, even as they have championed prefigurative efforts *as* politics, analysts have sometimes restricted the reach of such efforts to the realms of cultural and personal change. Changing laws, policies, and political structures is the kind of "strategic politics" that is contrasted, a priori, to prefigurative politics. This misses altogether the possibility that participatory democracy in movements can advance efforts to secure institutional political change, that participatory democracy can be strategic. As I will show in a moment, it also makes it difficult to understand the conflicts that participatory democratic groups have faced—since their trajectories are reduced to the tensions between prefigurative and strategic commitments supposedly at their core.[7]

So the concept of prefiguration may in some ways limit our ability to assess the viability and strengths of participatory democratic forms. Sociologists of social movements have not neglected these strengths altogether. Sociologist Suzanne Staggenborg especially, but other authors too, have drawn attention to participatory democracy's tactical benefits. Decentralized and informal organizational structures can generate innovative tactics by encouraging group input. In combination with a group's cooperative ethos, they also strengthen the supportive bonds among members that make for political solidarity now as well as the likelihood that participants will continue active in later movements. Like these analysts, I describe benefits of innovation and solidarity. But I pay most attention to another category, that of developmental benefits. And I attribute all three kinds of benefits to features of participatory democracy that coexist alongside its informality, decentralization, and cooperative ethos.[8]

In the organizations that I studied, I was struck by participants' emphasis on *deliberative talk*. They expected each other to provide legitimate reasons for preferring one option to another. They strove to recognize the merits of each other's reasons for favoring a particular option, even though they did not necessarily rank those reasons in the same order. The point was to make each person's reasoning understandable: the goal was not unanimity so much as discourse. But it was a particular kind of discourse, governed by norms of openness and mutual respect. In talking through different options and reasons for choosing them, participants gained strategizing skills. They also had the opportunity to articulate, question, and sometimes redefine their own preferences. Participatory democracy in this incarnation thus differs from adversary democracy, which assumes that people know their preferences before deliberation begins, and from nondemocratic systems, which assume that leaders know their followers' interests better than the followers themselves do. But it also differs from the kind of strict consensus that provides little room for differences among participants. Unlike a Rousseauian "general will" reflecting the wills of noncommunicating individuals, the emphasis here is on communicative give-and-take.[9]

The second recurrent feature of the democracies treated in this book was a commitment on the part of members to generating new bases for legitimate authority. In principle, authority rested with the entire group. But, of course, no group makes every single decision by consensus, and no group offers equal power to *anyone* who wants it. The critical question is whether the grounds for authority are specified and, when appropriate, reformulated. Activists in many of the organizations that I studied sought to create new kinds of legitimate power. Their experimentalism was partly born of necessity: with few models of collectivist decisionmaking, they were forced to invent new ones. But it also reflected a view that the decisions that affected people's lives had been made only by the "qualified"—the credentialed, the moneyed, the powerful. Although activists sometimes slipped into renouncing authority altogether—"No Leaders" the cry—the more powerful thread in their deliberative ethos sought not to dispense with authority but to base it on more sensible criteria.

Of course, just as decentralized decisionmaking can become synonymous with uncoordinated decisionmaking and informality can conceal the operation of unaccountable power, so too the deliberative and experimental elements of participatory democratic decisionmaking sometimes backfired, the former dissolving into endless and action-stymieing talk, the latter into a castigation of any exercise of leadership or initiative. But I emphasize these features because they point to ways that participatory democratic decisionmaking can help movement groups effect institutional political change. Let me outline them briefly.

First, when people share *ownership* of decisions—activists frequently used that term—their sense of solidarity and commitment is heightened. Movement organizations can offer people little in the way of selective incentives to participate, and the long-term rewards are often unclear. People are less likely to participate if they are ambivalent about or opposed to the group's decisions or if they suspect that others may not be fully committed to what is supposed to be a group decision. The requirement that all members of the group voice their positions and commit to a line of action makes it likely that people will actually act to further the group's goals.

The trouble with majority voting, say its critics, is that every decision made leaves losers in its wake. The next time a decision must be made, those who lost this time may forge the alliances and strike the bargains necessary to win, thus subordinating the aim of making a good decision to their own desire to gain position. Or they may withdraw altogether from an organization part of whose appeal has been the opportunity to act with common purpose. Groups that put a premium on the possibility of consensus help that not to happen, thus generating important *solidary* benefits.

More important than an orientation to consensus, however, what I am calling the deliberative aspects of participatory democratic decisionmaking can build solidarity by pressing participants to recognize the legitimacy of other people's reasoning. The *process* of decisionmaking makes for a greater acceptance of the differences that coexist with shared purposes. In fact, consensus often aims not to arrive at a position or policy agreed to unanimously in all its particulars but to delineate a range of individual positions that are consistent with a group position. By requiring that participants take seriously each other's concerns and priorities, the process balances individual initiative with solidarity, both of which are critical to successful collective action. This may be the case as much during the doldrums of political quiescence as in the thick of mobilization. While a bureaucratic structure may be better able to preserve an organization in name during fallow periods, a participatory democratic one is more likely to preserve strong bonds among a group of movement stalwarts. When political conditions make wider mobilization possible again, these sustaining organizations offer a pool of activists capable of training new leaders and providing strategic and tactical advice.[10]

True, there are other organizational mechanisms for securing solidarity within a group. The authority of a charismatic leader may be enough to ensure participation even in the absence of collective decisionmaking. However, this may jeopardize the public perception that participants are committed to the cause because it is a worthy one rather than because they are in thrall to a charismatic leader. Movement groups are often attacked by their opponents for being controlled by "outside" forces or by a movement demagogue. One way to avoid or to counteract such charges is to demonstrate the group's—the *whole* group's—involvement in decisionmaking.[11]

A second set of strategic benefits of participatory decisionmaking can be labeled *innovatory*. The fact that movement groups rely at least in part on noninstitutionalized means forces them to operate in the realm of the uncertain. They may combine marches, boycotts, and civil disobedience with more conventional strategies like legislative lobbying, and some tactics have become so widespread as to be quasi-institutionalized. Still, activists' success usually depends on their tactical innovation. Since they have little evidence on what is effective in particular situations, seeking numerous points of view helps gain strategic information. Students of economic innovation have made a similar point: the flexibility of decentralized and informal organizations opens up room for multiple lines of input and communication. Participatory democrats' belief that good ideas can come from those not conventionally credentialed—again, the experimental character of the form—can also facilitate tactical experimentation.[12]

I want to discuss the *developmental* benefits of participatory democracy in more detail. For those who have been systematically excluded from political participation, participatory decisionmaking provides skills in negotiating agendas and engaging with political authorities. It trains people to present arguments and to weigh the costs and benefits of different options. It develops their sense of political efficacy. The point is not that powerless people lack agency. Political scientist James Scott has demonstrated that, if we look closely, we can always see an infrapolitics of dissent, a variety of sophisticated techniques for resisting and subverting the powerful. But to move from there to making an overt and organized challenge to authorities takes the kind of confidence that people inexperienced in the rules of engagement with the state may not have. Rotating leadership, establishing a norm of participation, and working to consensus trains people to *do* contentious politics. But why not train them to logroll, trade votes, caucus, and lobby? Why is participatory democracy any better equipped to foster the kind of learning that translates into effective action? Or, put the other way around, why do adversary or nondemocratic forms not promote such development?[13]

For one thing, in other systems, the decisionmaking process is less transparent. If a leader or an elite makes the decision—even if the input of members has been solicited—there is no obligation to reveal the reasoning behind the decision. Indeed, there is some incentive not to do so since exposing a decision as ill informed or one-sided might heighten members' frustration. If the group votes, no one is encouraged to make transparent her thinking process, that is, how she defined the grounds for making her decision. Balloting is often secret. In the debate before the vote, each side may be required to present its position. But efforts to persuade others are usually preceded by a calculation of likely yes and no votes and a concentration on swing voters. Neither the formally nondemocratic nor the adversary-democratic process gives people much exposure to new models for weighing options or the opportunity to frame and justify their positions publicly.

Thus far, my argument for the developmental virtues of participatory democracy will be familiar to students of J. S. Mill and John Dewey as well as to readers of contemporary democratic theorists like Carol Gould, Carole Pateman, C. B. Macpherson, Benjamin Barber, and Joshua Cohen and Joel Rogers. Participatory deliberation yields citizens who are more knowledgeable, public spirited, better able to see the connections between their own interests and those of others, and more willing to reevaluate their own interests. These theorists rarely talk about social movements, however. Most either describe an ideal participatory polity, with little attention to how we might get from here to there, or locate the potential for change in the voluntary associations of "civil society," defining such associations as nonpolitical. But, when we move from idealized polities or voluntary associations to social movement organizations, the developmental argument seems at first glance to fail. Besides the fact that it is hard to imagine movement organizations spending time perfecting democratic processes whose relation to achieving reforms is unclear, collective actors presumably already know what their interests are. Precisely what has brought them together as a group is the fact that their interests are currently unrepresented in the formal arena of political bargaining. Then why the necessity of deliberative processes intended to help them discover their common interests?[14]

Where this formulation fails is in missing the fact that no group is completely excluded from the political process. Male legislators claimed to represent women's interests before women gained the vote. Black Americans were always "represented" in local (white) power structures. The question was whose interests black leaders authorized by whites represented. Efforts within movement organizations to question group interests help assess whether the political changes that the movement is bringing about should count as victory and whether the ostensible representatives of the group—self-dubbed or newly recognized by authorities—in fact represent its interests. Participatory democracy is a way to craft new mechanisms of accountability and new norms of leadership. This is not to say that participatory democracy practiced within the movement can be transposed to government functions, that it can simply be writ large. Rather, activists can use their organizations to experiment with mechanisms of citizen input. When their own leaders or candidates they support gain political office, they can be made accountable to their constituencies in ways not encompassed by current conventions of representation. The latter has been more imagined than acted on in the movement groups that I studied since few of them lasted long enough to get their candidates into political office, let alone exercise some control over them. But, at various points, it has been advanced as a rationale for participatory democracy.[15]

The other elements of a developmental project have been uppermost for participatory democrats working within a tradition of political organizing. With roots in early labor organizing, that tradition flourished in the Southern civil rights movement and went on to inspire activists' practice of participatory democracy in the new left and the early women's liberation movement. That its role has been largely overlooked since then is a result of scholars' tendency to project later aspirations back onto earlier versions of participatory democracy and their general neglect of a form of collective action that tends to be low profile, local, and long-term. Recuperating a tradition of political organizing for a genealogy of participatory democracy is one of the central aims of this book.

In sum, then, participatory democracy's solidary benefits counteract movement groups' inability to offer much in the way of selective incentives to participate; its innovatory benefits counteract the fact that movements operate in a context of high uncertainty; and its developmental benefits counteract movement participants' political inexperience and the fact that any political gains they make are fragile. But there is a potential objection to be raised here. Have I risked seeing instrumental purposes where there are none? Do we lose something by treating participatory democracy as practical when, in adopting the form, many activists are trying precisely to dislodge the reign of the practical over that of the virtuous? I have two responses to this objection. One is that people's rationales for adopting any practice or arrangement are always multiple, ambiguous, and changing. I was surprised to find practical purposes where previously most analysts had seen only principled ones. Without diminishing the latter, I have tried to recover the former. My second response is that recognizing practical benefits alerts us to different dilemmas than we might otherwise recognize, ones that cannot be characterized in terms of the clash between moral principle and political reality.

DEMOCRATIC DILEMMAS

Participatory democracy, no surprise, usually takes longer than adversarial decisionmaking. It demands more patience, energy, and time on the part of its participants. People without much free time are at a disadvantage. In movements, opportunities are almost always fleeting, and fast responses are of the essence. Organizational theorists tell us that multiple lines of input in problem-solving and agenda-setting discussions are useful; the same cacophony of voices when solutions are being implemented is less so. Without a formal division of labor, activists may find it difficult to mobilize resources behind a chosen solution. Like its other benefits, participatory democracy's innovatory benefits may be more evident at some times than at others and may be undermined by features of the form that coexist alongside its participatory character.[16]

Another kind of problem that activists often confront is that maximizing one set of participatory democracy's benefits may come at the expense of maximizing another, say, solidarity at the expense of modeling alternatives or innovation at the expense of developing people's leadership skills. By reducing activists' efforts to create participatory democracies to their "prefigurative" purposes, analysts have missed not only the very different projects to which participatory democracy can be harnessed but also the sources of potential conflict among those projects. For example, politically isolated groups that are committed to participatory democracy are especially likely to insist on rigor in their practice of it as a way to justify members' continued participation. Such groups see themselves as islands of democracy in a sea of political conformity; to moderate their commitment to strict equality would be a first step down the slippery slope toward compromising other principles. Absolutism in the practice of participatory democracy may be one of the "commitment mechanisms" described by sociologist Rosabeth Kanter that sustain people's participation and loyalty. By contrast, making democracy seem viable and desirable to a broader nonmovement public would likely require efforts to make it seem easy to practice. But insisting on procedural rigor and refusing to do much to make its deliberative forms available and appealing to a broader public may help an isolated activist group survive in the long-term. Another problem: developing people's leadership capacities usually requires a complex equality in which some within the group are permitted more authority than others in areas in which they have special expertise— provided that they progressively cede that authority by training others, and provided that their authority in one area does not spill over into other areas. But that kind of complex equality may be perceived by outsiders as inequality, thus countering the group's claim to be exemplifying a true democracy.[17]

Paying attention to the contexts in which participatory democrats are operating raises one more set of questions. If, as I have suggested, participatory democracy has practical benefits where the routes to success are uncertain, where there are scant means for ensuring members' compliance, and where members have had few opportunities to exercise political leadership, then what happens when groups are not operating under such conditions? Is participatory democracy less valuable when there are preexisting bonds among members that give them a sense of ownership of the organization without the need to participate as fully in its operation? Where group members have had numerous opportunities to exercise leadership, will having the opportunity to do so in group deliberations be less educational? Where movement organizations occupy a stable position in the structure of political bargaining, will they benefit less from multiple lines of tactical input?

The answer to each question is yes, and I will return to these points in the chapters that follow. For now, I want to raise an issue that is further reaching in its implications for how we understand the fates of movement organizations. Groups have often abandoned or moderated participatory democratic forms or collapsed altogether in the wake of crises pitting democratic purists against self-styled pragmatists. What seems clear in the cases that I have studied is that there was more at stake in the disputes over decisionmaking than some members' absolutism with respect to democratic principles or others' willingness to abrogate those principles for short-term political gain. Instead, decisionmaking that was once easy became newly difficult. People began to distrust each other's motives, to see loquacity in meetings as egocentrism, silence as evidence of intimidation, and agreement as a product of manipulation. Deliberative talk no longer served to build respect for people's differences, and efforts to establish grounds for legitimate authority were impugned as self-serving. People insisted on the requirements of full democracy—decentralization, absolute equality, consensus—when relations among the group stopped seeming fair, mutually respectful, and emotionally satisfying.[18]

At issue, it seems, was less a conflict between principle and pragmatism than participatory democracy's inability to resolve interpersonal conflicts. Some have argued that the problem is fundamental to the form. The political scientist Jane Mansbridge puts it this way. When a group has common interests, consensus-based, face-to-face, and egalitarian deliberation can deliver good decisions. Consensus reinforces members' solidarity, helps them clarify their preferences, and brings fragmentary information to bear on joint problems. When members' interests diverge, however, practices that were intended to express and strengthen the group's shared purpose must protect individual interests against those of the majority or the powerful, and this they cannot do. If groups in this situation do not bring in some features of conventional adversary forms, they end up simply pressuring people into line. In this view, the weakness of participatory democracies is not their inconsistency with the demands of effective action but their inability to handle conflicting interests. The participatory democratic dilemma is how to choose a "group" interest from among competing individual ones.[19]

The flaw in this line of argument lies in its conception of interests. Mansbridge defines them as "'enlightened preferences' among policy choices, 'enlightened' meaning the preferences people would have if their information were perfect, including the knowledge they would have in retrospect if they had had a chance to live out the consequences of each choice before actually making a decision." Her point is to avoid both subjectivist and objectivist definitions, in other words, interests as personal preferences (which are unreflective and fleeting) and interests as identifiable through some universal yardstick or outside authority. Her definition is not an "operational" one, she notes: no one can ever have full information. But the mental experiment of imagining what it would be like to live out two or more choices can help identify what people's circumstances indicate their enlightened preferences might be.[20]

The problem is that it is very difficult to determine what constitutes a conflicting set of underlying interests rather than a more superficial difference that can be resolved through the consensus process. Moreover, an even cursory examination of past experiments in radical democracy shows that the battles that have divided groups have often had their origins in minimal differences of interest and principle—this in the retrospective views of those who fought them. What seems to have stymied participatory democratic deliberations in numerous cases has been disagreement over what properly democratic decisionmaking should entail. The contending views cannot be so easily mapped onto a prior set of interests or allegiances. The more important question, then, may be when people *perceive* their interests as diverging.[21]

That does not give us much to go on, however. If we depended solely on people's perception of conflicting interests to explain the breakdown of consensual deliberative forms, it would be difficult to generalize beyond the case. The challenge, then, is to identify other, less subjective sources of potential conflict in participatory democratic groups. Are some kinds of difference more likely to produce deliberative standoffs than are others? Can we trace these to characteristic features of the relationships among members of a participatory democracy? We can, I believe, if we take seriously the *relational* bases of decisionmaking.

THE SOCIAL RELATIONS OF DEMOCRACY

How do people make decisions in a participatory democracy? There may be formal rules. Major decisions are made by the group as a whole; when an issue is brought to the table, concerns are voiced until someone, formally designated or self-selected, asks whether people are in agreement on a line of action. In some systems, people can "stand aside" if they cannot commit fully to the group's decision but do not want to block it. But formal rules by themselves provide insufficient guidance actually to deliberate. In any system, whether participatory, adversarial, or some nondemocratic form, countless issues are not covered by the formal rules: what kinds of concerns can be brought up, how they should be framed, what kinds and degree of emotions should be displayed in debates, how breaches in the formal rules should be dealt with, and so on. Every system thus depends on a sophisticated set of normative understandings that accompany the formal rules, a kind of etiquette of deliberation. Such an etiquette does more than keep things civil. By routinizing interaction and domesticating attendant emotions, it generates trust in the process, its outcomes, and its participants. Trust, in turn, is vital to the institution's survival. Without it, say organizational theorists, decisionmaking is likely to become rigid, and the decisions that result are unlikely to be good ones.[22]

The normative underpinnings of deliberative systems can be taught. Congressional representatives are instructed in the arcane forms of address ("I yield to the gentleman from Virginia") that demonstrate the speaker's willingness to abide by the unwritten rules of the institution. But radical versions of democracy have been enacted chiefly in social movements. The fact that movements are oppositional and impermanent has made it difficult to institutionalize *any* of their tactics or deliberative forms. For this reason alone, "each new generation of incipient democrats finds itself beginning its social journey from, so to speak, square one," historian Lawrence Goodwyn writes. But Goodwyn is not quite right. Activists have never really started from square one. In every generation, veteran activists have given novices tips on how to structure their organizations and justifications for doing so democratically. Even more than that, however, in their efforts to craft new deliberative forms, American activists have drawn on familiar modes of decisionmaking from outside the sphere of protest politics, often from outside politics altogether.[23]

That this has been the case should not be surprising. After all, some relationships outside the political sphere are marked by the care and solicitousness that activists have seen as woefully lacking in political life. It makes sense that activists would innovate on the basis of the familiar, deriving from the nonpolitical relationships that they knew frameworks for new modes of political interaction. Still, it took me some time to recognize that the differences I was seeing in how participatory democratic organizations operated matched differences in how people generally interact as friends, teachers and students, and religious fellows. In studying tape recordings, transcripts, and minutes of deliberations in participatory democratic organizations, I began to trace patterns in how topics were introduced for discussion, how tasks were allocated, how participants reached compromises and won concessions from each other, how they preempted or resolved disputes, and how they dealt with members' unilateral actions, that is, actions not democratically approved by the group. Activists' personal correspondence, containing detailed commentaries about the internal life of the group, gave further indication of patterns in groups' operating styles. And interviews with former members of the groups in which I was interested—120 interviews in all, most lasting several hours, and some extending over the course of days—put flesh on the bones of the associational models that I was finding. Some of the people I interviewed had been active in two and even three of the organizations in question, and they provided finely grained comparisons of how the organizations worked. All the people I interviewed gave detailed portraits of how their groups were both like and unlike other groups in and outside the movement. And, with unyielding candor, they strove to make sense of the tensions and disputes that had sometimes overwhelmed their democratic efforts.[24]

Together, these materials and conversations pointed to the operation of three main deliberative styles (see table 1). Participatory democrats in the pacifist movement tended to rely on norms characteristic of religious fellowship in their decisionmaking. Some groups, such as the Fellowship of Reconciliation, were explicitly religious. Others, especially the radical pacifist groups that emerged after World War II, sought to create a secular alternative to faith-based opposition to war. However, in their reliance on the absolutism of personal conscience, they, like religious pacifists, located the ultimate authority for the rightness of a decision outside the group. As a result, decisionmaking often had what I call a *deferential* character. With important exceptions, participatory democrats did not spend much time negotiating democratic authority within the group. What made their decisionmaking *experimental*, as I have used the term, was their insistence on the primacy of the moral in political decisionmaking. Beyond that, however, provided that a decision did not violate a member's personal ethical standards, he or she tended to be comfortable deferring to those in the group with expertise on an issue. Tasks, too, were allocated in general

	Features of decisionmaking	How groups mitigate ineffectiveness	How groups mitigate inequality	Examples of movement groups	Potential sources of conflict	When conflict is likely to emerge
Religious fellowship	Deferential	Acceptance of authority within the group	Participants are equal before God	Pre– and post–World War II pacifist organizations	Resistance to forging new bases of authority	When dissenters invoke the dictates of conscience
Tutelage	Guided	Trust in organizer/tutor	Inequality is sphere specific and diminishing	SNCC, SDS's ERAP, faith-based organizing	Resistance to specifying the ends of action	When movement goals are unclear
Friendship	Informal and intimate	Mutual knowledge and trust	Inequality is counterbalanced by participants' potential, as well as real, skills in other spheres	SDS, SNCC, women's liberation collectives	Exclusiveness and resistance to formalization	When new members join or friendships are otherwise threatened

TABLE 1 THE RELATIONAL UNDERPINNINGS OF TWENTIETH-CENTURY AMERICAN MOVEMENT DEMOCRACIES

along the lines of expertise, with little debate. When disputes did threaten, or when individuals seemed reluctant to compromise on a decision, members sometimes explicitly invoked the demands of religious fellowship to secure unity, for example, calling on a speaker to "withdraw his motion in the spirit of good fellowship." Decisionmaking was formal but solicitous.[25]

Participatory democracy as it operated in the community organizing projects of the Southern civil rights movement and the Northern new left and in some contemporary community organizing efforts looked different. It resembled more a tutorial in leadership. Records of project meetings show that an organizer often introduced a problem for discussion and encouraged participants to discuss the issues involved, available options, and their relation to the movement's longer-term agenda. Participants were encouraged to volunteer or were asked to take responsibility for particular tasks by the organizer, and the process was often accompanied by praise for those who did. Organizers never directed anyone to do anything, however, nor did they argue for particular deliberative options, and they often encouraged residents to lead discussions. Still, they not uncommonly arranged the time and place of meetings, introduced topics, posed questions, and periodically drew participants' attention to the decisionmaking process. Discussions thus had a *guided* character.

Finally, friendship was the main interactional model for participatory democracy in SDS, in early women's liberation collectives, and among SNCC staff. The striking thing in these democracies was the *informal* quality of decisionmaking and its *intimacy*. Discussions were long and spilled out of formal deliberative settings. Decisions were made by informal consensus, and tasks were allocated or volunteered for on the basis of a combination of participants' preferences and skills. Often, there was no clear line between allocating and volunteering for tasks. "You do this, I'll do that"—that was the standard approach. Disputes were heated but rarely lasted from one meeting to another. And unilateral action by individuals in the group was either justified by the triviality of the issue or excused as a well-intentioned blunder rather than a bid for control.

These snapshots only hint at what decisionmaking was like in the organizations that I studied, and, in the following chapters, I will provide much fuller pictures. It is important to note, too, that each associational model reflects only one version variously of fellowship, tutelage, and friendship: a concept of fellowship rooted in Quakerism and the Protestant Social Gospel; a model of adult rather than children's education; and a mid-twentieth-century American understanding of friendship. Moreover, activists modified each of these models as they turned them into organizational norms. They extended Christian fellowship and friendship to a wider circle than people usually do, made political discussion and action an expectation of what friends do together, and emphasized the mutual dependence—and therefore equality—of organizer and residents. Still, delineating the normative expectations characteristic of each relationship helps make sense of differences in how groups have practiced participatory democracy. For groups whose associational model was one of friendship, having a formal leader conflicted with the informality that is one of friendship's defining features. For those whose associational model was one of tutelage, the existence of a leader was acceptable, provided that she was trusted and demonstrably committed to training others to be leaders. For those whose associational model was Christian fellowship, restrictions on membership or a required probationary period were not seen to be inappropriate, especially by people who had gone through a period of religious training themselves. Familiar associational models shaped people's conceptions of what was and was not democratic—even as they all agreed on the value of democracy.[26]

Delineating the associational models underpinning activists' practice of participatory democracy also helps explain why activists sometimes avoided the inefficiencies, inequities, and stalemates that critics have seen as intrinsic to the form. As interactional frameworks, fellowship, tutelage, and friendship enabled people to decide jointly in ways that they experienced as relatively fast and fair. Fast, because the mutual respect and solicitousness characteristic of each relationship supplied a general stability of behavioral expectations and the mutual trust that made it possible to depart occasionally from the routine. Fair, because inequalities in speaking time, authority, and skills were counterbalanced by equalities that are characteristic of each relationship. Friends' status in each other's eyes is based not only on their visible skills and talents but on their potential ones. Religious fellows see each other as equals in the eyes of God. And teachers see students' status gradually equaling their own. Finally, decisionmaking was relatively nonconflictual because, to phrase it in the language of individual and group interests, each relationship generated interests in its sustenance that trumped or recast individuals' interests outside the relationship.

However, familiar modes of association have also been the pressure points along which participatory democracies have fractured. For example, pacifist groups' respect for religious conviction made it difficult to argue against members who invoked the dictates of personal religious conscience to act in unilateral ways. To mediate such conflicts would have required them to go outside the normative framework within which their activism made sense. In SNCC, a commitment to "letting the people decide" failed to specify how much the people should decide and which people should decide. Since new people threaten old friendships, SDS was thrown into disarray by the entrance of new members—even though newcomers and veterans had largely similar ideological commitments. And women's liberationists had difficulty adhering to the procedures that they had set up to ensure egalitarian group relations since they seemed to violate the resolute informality characteristic of friendship.

More broadly, the familiarity of particular organizational forms and deliberative styles makes them easy to practice and easy to recommend to people with a similar background. But "the way we have always done things" is often rife with unexamined inequalities and exclusions. Participatory democracy's critics have tended to focus on its inefficiency and its inability to resolve conflicting interests. I see a different vulnerability, thornier because it is the flip side of one of participatory democracy's strengths. The same social relations that have sometimes made it easy to practice have also made it difficult to sustain.[27]

STRATEGY AND IDENTITY

The foregoing suggests that familiarity may be a more powerful basis for strategic choice generally than we recognize. In other words, when activists decide how to conduct their deliberations, how to structure their organization, how to communicate their message, how to advance their agenda, and all the other strategic and tactical choices that they make, they may be influenced not only by what is likely to be instrumentally effective and what is likely to be ideologically consistent but also by what is familiar. This seems fairly straightforward, yet it has not been much discussed in the scholarship on social movements. Scholars have tended to account for movements' trajectories either in terms of classically rational models of strategic choice or by representing activists struggling to balance their ideological principles with the demands of effective action. But there is much more to strategic choice than that.

Neither explanation grasps the fact that a tactical option or an organizational form may be appealing because it is similar to what we are used to. Lawyers are likely to see benefits in a legal strategy that non-laywers in similar situations might not. Ministers in movements may be more comfortable being advised by a circle of trusted colleagues than by a raucous meeting of the rank and file. One can see choices like these in instrumental terms. People are good at what they know. But the familiar option sometimes proves not to be the most effective.

There are still other bases for strategic choice. An option may be appealing to activists because it accords with their view of who they are. They may be loath to abandon a tactic—even when their strategic good sense tells them that it is not working any longer and that its connection to their formal beliefs is slim—because they have come to see it as central to their identity. Finally, activists may find some options more appealing than others because of the groups with which particular options are symbolically associated. The tactics used by a group widely viewed as on the cutting edge may be attractive to imitators regardless of any proof that those tactics are actually responsible for radical change. Those used by a group seen as having secured a pipeline to power may be attractive irrespective of their demonstrated political influence. For Eastern European feminists after the fall of Communism, for example, political parties and bureaucratic organizations were rendered unappealing by their firm association with Communist rule.[28]

Besides tactical choices, our very criteria for assessing what is instrumental, strategic, efficient—our conceptions of instrumental rationality— are based on the social associations underpinning those conceptions. For example, as numerous scholars have pointed out, Western notions of rationality have long been defined in implicit contrast to *female* and *nonwhite*. Although they are usually taken for granted, associations like these can be contested. Movements may be prime vehicles for such reassessment. Radical feminists, for instance, challenged the claimed neutrality of bureaucracy by showing how it reflected and rewarded masculinist values. They insisted on collectivist forms as a feminist alternative. Once institutionalized, such forms came to be seen as an essential component of what being a feminist was. For a feminist group *not* to implement participatory democratic practices required justification—and threatened to lose it legitimacy and support.[29]

Feminists' challenge to the conventional association between bureaucracy and masculinity was deliberate and self-conscious. Movements may also revise the identities built into particular practices, procedures, and arrangements less deliberately. A group may adopt a tactic for mainly instrumental or ideological reasons and then become powerfully associated with that tactic in the eyes of other organizations. The tactic becomes appealing or unappealing for that reason. The same thing can happen within a movement group, with an option assessed according to the fate of the subgroup with whom it is identified, say, militants or newcomers or women. Associations may be not so much with a particular strategy or tactic as with a recognizable orientation, an approach to strategic choice, say, participatory or autocratic, calm or impassioned. Once made, however, these associations may become part of the organization's deliberative calculus, ruling in and out strategic options. And if the organization is seen as a model for others, particular symbolic associations may become part of enduring repertoires, shaping subsequent decisionmaking in this movement organization and in others.

In SNCC, for example, the same deliberative practices that had been seen as practical, political, and "black" came to be seen as ideological, impractical, and "white." Because SNCC was widely viewed as the cutting edge of the black movement, moreover, its recoding of participatory democracy as ideological rather than instrumental, principled but impractical, and oriented toward transforming selves rather than toward gaining power came to be broadly embraced by black and white activists alike. The symbolic associations that accompanied a deliberative form thus shaped its subsequent value for and use by later activists.

The idea that one might predict the symbolic loading of particular options is appealing. We probably cannot do this, however, since which groups even appear on activists' radar screen reflects a combination of popular perceptions and media images as well as group members' individual contacts. But the point I want to make is that the association of a deliberative option with a particular group affects whether it is perceived as sufficiently radical or ideologically consistent and whether it is seen as practical, political, and efficacious. I will show, at different points in the following chapters, how symbolic social associations shaped what counted as strategic. In the concluding chapter, I will hazard some guesses as to how such associations develop.

OVERVIEW OF THE BOOK

My treatment of participatory democracy in social movements is both comparative and historical. I look for commonalities and differences in why groups strove to operate democratically and in the obstacles they encountered. I pay special attention to the political contexts in which activists operated and to the sources of the deliberative etiquettes that guided their decisionmaking. And I examine in detail the causes, stakes, and consequences of the conflicts over decisionmaking that they experienced. By tracing the practice of participatory democracy over time, I show how political purposes and possibilities were successively attached to and detached from it. The following chapters proceed chronologically, moving from the early-twentieth-century labor movement and pre– and post–World War II pacifism (chap. 2) to the Southern civil rights movement (chaps. 3 and 4), the new left (chap. 5), the women's liberation movement (chap. 6), and contemporary direct action and community organizing (chap. 7). In each one, I probe the purposes and constitutive bonds of democratic movement groups. Then I show how paying attention to these features explains the deliberative crises that they experienced better than do existing analyses, which have tended to focus either on tensions between democratic principle and practical effectiveness or on the conflicting prior interests of group members.

History has tended to reproduce the perspectives of those who pushed for structure and more conventional organizational forms rather than those who argued against them. We tend to hear more from the SNCC hardliners than from the SNCC "freedom highs," more from the SDS old guard than from the SDS new guard, more from the radical feminists who were muzzled by the antipathy to leadership than from the "quiet women." What struck me in talking to people among the freedom highs, the SDS new guard, and the quiet women was that the organizational conflicts that pitted them against the defenders of structure were never so simple as a battle between ideologues and pragmatists. Rather, the battles were between different ideologies, and, just as frequently, they were about other things—about friendship, and race, and the limits of liberalism.

I was persuaded to try to better integrate factors like those into our explanations for the fragility of participatory democratic organizations. But I was also persuaded to probe more deeply into the reasons that activists had for wanting participatory democracy, for arguing fiercely at times in favor of decisionmaking that was nonhierarchical, decentralized, and participatory. What became clear to me was that practical and political reasons coexisted with more expressive ones. And that a developmental rationale—the opportunity to learn by deciding jointly—figured in many activists' accounts, and more so than published treatments would have led me to believe. I was continually struck, however, as is anyone who has studied the internal life of a group, by how much was going on at any given moment, how many cross-cutting alliances and multisided conflicts, external considerations, and internal dramas were shaping decisions. It should go without saying that what I present in each case is just one slice of the reality of life in a movement group.

Together, the chapters tell another story, about how activists' changing understandings of equality and efficacy have both opened up strategic possibilities and derailed them. What the movements of the 1960s introduced into the lexicon of movement democracy was a powerful populist impulse. The point of participatory democracy was to surmount differences in skills and educational background, not by denying them, but by reasoning and learning together on the basis of mutual respect. This was a complex equality, in which people's lack of skills in one area was counterbalanced by their skills or dedication in another and in which pedagogy was valued as a way to reduce current imbalances in power. But complex understandings of equality would contend with and eventually cede to simpler ones in the 1960s, in which equality demanded identical treatment and equal time. There were some good reasons for that shift, among them that complex equality could too easily be invoked to justify imbalances that were neither limited in their scope nor temporary. But the explicitly political and developmental benefits of participatory democratic forms were undermined in the process. Today, activists are moving once again toward complex understandings of equality. But they are more alert to the inequalities that are built into conventional understandings of equal treatment, more sensitive to the liabilities of informality in relations among those unequal in status, and, at the same time, more attuned to the necessity of forging egalitarian relationships as well as rules. Therein lies great possibility.

2

ARMY, TOWN MEETING, OR CHURCH
IN THE CATACOMBS? THE ORGANIZATION
OF AMERICAN PROTEST, 1900–1960

The union must remain both an army and a town meeting. It must at the same time both
fight and discuss.

A. J. MUSTE, "FACTIONAL FIGHTS IN TRADE UNIONS" (1928)

It seems altogether likely that building a radical pacifist movement of any size will be a
tougher and slower job in the U.S. than anywhere else.... [W]ill reaction prove so strong
in the U.S. that we have to keep a small remnant alive... a church in the catacombs
pattern?

A. J. MUSTE, SPEAKING AT A PEACEMAKERS EXECUTIVE COMMITTEE MEETING (22 FEBRUARY 1952)

Ask a member of a group run on radically democratic principles why it
is important to strive for full participation and consensus, and she may
respond to the effect that "it's right" or that "any other way wouldn't be
respectful of our members," her tone suggesting that the better question
would be why a progressive group would *not* adopt such practices. Press
further, and she is likely to mention the importance of sustaining the
solidarity of the group and of acting on one's principles. Ask our participatory democrat about the political provenance of such ideas, and she may
well invoke the women's liberation movement and its legacy of "feminist
process." Or she may talk about Students for a Democratic Society's 1962
Port Huron Statement, with its inspirational vision of a "democracy of individual participation," or Martin Luther King Jr.'s "beloved community."
She may be familiar with the tradition of Gandhian nonviolent resistance
associated with radical pacifism. Or she may not have thought much at all
about the genealogy of participatory democracy, that in itself testimony to
its institutionalization in some segments of the contemporary movement
field.[1]

Pacifists were not the first American activists to use collectivist deliberative forms or the first to use such forms in the service of political reform rather than moral self-improvement. Nineteenth-century American utopians tended to see their communal experiments more as an alternative to the competitive self-striving of the modern world than as an intervention in it, but some communities had connections to abolitionist and women's suffrage movements. Between two and three hundred socialist and anarchist communities were founded in the second half of the nineteenth century. Anarchists, socialists, populists, and unionists all experimented with democratic forms, seeing them not as a retreat from political action but as a vital resource in their battles with employers, authorities, and public indifference.[2]

American pacifists were distinctive, however, in joining commitments to internal democracy with the strategies of nonviolent direct action that would become the hallmark of 1960s American protest. Indeed, pacifists' well-known commitment to making "the means reflect the ends" has been cited as inspiration for the utopian character of 1960s movements generally and, in particular, their commitment to participatory democracy. "The pacifist believes," Episcopal minister and Fellowship of Reconciliation (FOR) member Paul Jones wrote in 1928, "that the means and the end are so intimately related that it is impossible to get a coordinated and co-operative world by destructive methods that violate personality and increase antagonism and distrust." War for pacifists is not only wrong but also futile, since violent means cannot create a peaceful world. Pacifists have opposed war both by refusing personally to fight and by organizing collective resistance to war and militarism. Striving to create the Kingdom of God has also meant working to bring about social justice, and pacifists since World War I have been active in causes ranging from civil rights and civil liberties to labor organizing and environmentalism. Finally, the injunction, "Do now what thou wouldst do then," has issued in organizational experiments aimed at embodying the cooperative society of the future, furthering the "here-and-now revolution," by living it in co-ops, communes, and exemplary organizations.[3]

Pacifists played key roles in the civil rights movement: founding the Congress of Racial Equality (CORE) and the Southern Christian Leadership Conference (SCLC), training Martin Luther King Jr. in methods of nonviolent resistance, and organizing the 1961 freedom rides. Pacifists' writings in the 1940s and 1950s anticipated many of the concerns and commitments of new leftists in the 1960s. In magazines like *Politics*, *Direct Action*, and *Liberation*, pacifists developed critiques of technocracy and orthodox Marxism and championed the rights of racial minorities.

Early writers like A. J. Muste, David Dellinger, and Bayard Rustin were later joined by new leftists Tom Hayden, Carl Oglesby, Todd Gitlin, and Mario Savio. These connections have led historians to see in pacifism forebears of new left agendas and strategies of protest. And it is easy to trace a straight line of prefigurative commitment from the ashrams and intentional communities of 1950s radical pacifists to the new left's experiments in participatory democracy.[4]

Too straight a line would obscure other important influences on the organizational repertoire of the 1960s, however. In this chapter, I explore a surprising one: the early-twentieth-century labor movement. It is surprising because organized labor, with its labyrinthine bureaucracy and autocratic bosses, would hardly seem a model for anyone's radical democracy. Indeed, it was organized labor's narrow-minded pragmatism that new leftists defined themselves against in developing their own organizational forms and broader political vision. As new leftists saw it, labor, liberals, and the left were all guilty of elevating realpolitik to a guiding passion, and they refused to do the same. But, in creating participatory democracies, 1960s activists also built on a tradition of workers' education that was largely unknown to them—and has been largely ignored by genealogists of participatory democracy since then. In the 1920s, labor educators in union education departments, independent labor colleges, and university-affiliated summer schools set out to create a generation of union leaders capable of moving beyond the prevailing business unionism to agitate for more fundamental change. To do so, they developed a radical pedagogy that emphasized self-directed learning and experiments in collectivist decisionmaking. Three decades later, veterans of those efforts taught the democratic pedagogy that they had learned to young civil rights organizers. The result was a strategy of political organizing that treated participatory decisionmaking as a way to create indigenous leaders and radical aspirations. That strategy, in turn, shaped new leftists' understanding and practice of participatory democracy.

To grasp participatory democracy 1960s style, in other words, requires adding to the pacifist tradition of moral witness another tradition, one rooted in the labor movement and oriented less toward symbolic acts of nonviolent resistance than toward building enduring organizations. The two traditions came together in the activism of the early 1960s, along with something else: the discovery that people acting together without centralized command could have a dramatic impact. This discovery came with the 1960 student sit-ins, when tens of thousands of black Southern students bucked what they saw as the timidity of the "adult" civil rights organizations to launch dozens of autonomous local movements. The sit-ins transformed students' sense of political possibility in both the South and the North and gave them new ideas about how to organize to create radical change. In this chapter, then, I trace both the older traditions and the contemporaneous events that shaped 1960s activists' organizational repertoire.

Of course, pacifists and unionists meant very different things when they called for a more democratic movement. For pacifists, true democracy required group leadership and consensus; for unionists, it required regular elections and decisions made by majority vote rather than by administrative fiat. But both argued that democracy was their best hope for making practical gains: respectively, for building effective unions and for preserving a pacifist movement in a hostile political setting. This suggests that we need to look elsewhere than the supposedly intrinsic tension between democracy and efficacy to explain fully the struggles that pacifists and unionists faced in sustaining democratic organizations. I focus on two tensions that have characterized other movements as well. First, movement organizations often face competing demands to minister to the needs of their own membership and to build a broader constituency. Both tasks are eminently practical, but they are served by different styles of group interaction and decisionmaking. Second, activists have often been drawn to familiar forms of organization and deliberation even at the expense of the gains made through organizational innovation. The question for those wanting to create workable movement democracies is whether one can build a democratic movement culture on the basis of preexisting identities and familiar ways of interacting—and whether one can afford the time that it takes to craft new ones.

AN ARMY AND A TOWN MEETING: AMERICAN UNIONISM

What models of internal governance did the American labor movement offer later generations of activists? American labor leaders in the early twentieth century frequently emphasized the connections between an organized workers' movement and a strong American democracy. They exhorted each other to build "the new society within the shell of the old." Longtime American Federation of Labor (AFL) president Samuel Gompers, hardly known as a radical, called himself "three-quarters anarchist." But these statements should not be taken as a brief for radical democracy in the movement. Gompers's "business unionism"—it would become AFL policy—centralized funds and authority in powerful national unions. In calling himself anarchist, Gompers signaled, not his dislike of bureaucracy, but his belief that government was weak protection against the depredations of employers' power. Unions, not government, would be the institutions of working people's welfare in the future, and unions that avoided political involvement would prefigure that society, that is, would be the new within the shell of the old. To secure decent conditions for American workers required strong unions—guided by strong leaders.[5]

The other giant of the American labor movement, the tough-talking and charismatic United Mine Workers (UMW) president, John L. Lewis, was open in his disdain for internal democracy. Whether to structure a union democratically or autocratically, he put it bluntly to a UMW convention in 1936, "is a question of whether you desire your organization to be the most effective instrumentality or whether you prefer to sacrifice the efficiency of your organization in some respects for a little more academic freedom." For Gompers, Lewis, and others, democracy was impractical. Facing employers endowed with outsized financial reserves, legal resources, and political clout, and in periods when sudden economic downturns could affect millions, unions simply had to be disciplined, centralized machines. Movement leaders probably saw some merit in the labor educator A. J. Muste's argument that a union was both "army" and "town meeting," contending with employers, but also trying to provide workers some escape from the soul-deadening conditions of their work. Given what American labor was up against, they would undoubtedly argue, the balance between army and town meeting could not but be lopsided.[6]

Yet this common sense about union democracy never went unopposed. Before Gompers won the AFL presidency in 1886, he had to put down a democratic challenge in his own Cigar Makers local. When a slate of "Progressives" calling for more union democracy won the local's key offices from Gompers and his associates, the latter were reduced to withholding the union treasury to retain their power. Antipathies toward centralized union bureaucracy, both for its curtailment of locals' autonomy and for its exclusivist character, continued strong among American workers. Long after the AFL's creation, many unions organized along industrial rather than craft lines and rejected a centralized structure and the high dues that made it difficult for unskilled workers to join. The Industrial Workers of the World (IWW)—the Wobblies—prided itself not only on its penchant for direct action but also on its inclusive ethos and the policies that guaranteed that ethos: low dues, foreign-language sections, and a prohibition on organizers earning more than factory workers.[7]

Indeed, the major line of contention among unionists in the early part of the century centered on just how inclusive unions should be. Craft unions—"labor's aristocracy"—fought to control the production process and to restrict the hiring of unskilled workers. Their opponents argued for bigger and more inclusive unions benefiting skilled and unskilled workers alike. In the 1880s, the Knights of Labor went even further, opening district assemblies to all wage earners except professional gamblers, stockbrokers, bankers, lawyers, and those who profited from the sale of liquor. At its height, the Knights organized across race, industry, and gender lines and claimed over 700,000 members. Craft unionists had to fight off the Knights' challenge. They faced a similar challenge less successfully four decades later when industrial unionists demanded industry-wide organizing and overtly political activism. Eventually, John Lewis led industrial unionists out of the AFL and into the new Congress of Industrial Organizations (CIO). To whom the republic of labor should be extended was a question that exercised American unionists.[8]

How much control rank-and-file workers should have in that republic also continued an object of contention, if less often played out on a national stage. Surprising given their own subordination to Communist Party dictates from Moscow, American Communists were sometimes a voice for democratic reform in unions. Calling for more democracy made sense as a bid for popular support—the rank and file apparently *wanted* union democracy. Socialists, too, fought for more democracy in unions as well as contending in electoral politics. Other bids for democratic union reform came from the grass roots. Some historians have seen a veritable "alternative unionism" in federal labor unions and ad hoc factory committees in the 1930s: locally autonomous, organized across industries, and deeply democratic. In Austin, Minnesota, for example, the Independent Union of All Workers (IUAW) approached its goal of 100 percent unionization, with units of meatpackers, waitresses, barbers and beauticians, mechanics, construction workers, and municipal employees. Rank-and-file members of each unit set policy in weekly meetings and elected delegates to represent them in unionwide policymaking; weekly mass meetings brought together workers from all industries to develop solidarity campaigns. Union locals spread from Austin to South Dakota, North Dakota, Wisconsin, and Iowa.[9]

IUAW leaders greeted the formation of the CIO eagerly, as did unionists around the country. Many unionists believed that affiliation with a national movement would give them the strength in numbers that they lacked. They also believed that strong unionism was compatible with grassroots organization. Their optimism proved misplaced. None of the veteran union men who founded the CIO dissented from the AFL's tradition of centralized and authoritarian union leadership, as the CIO historian Robert Zieger points out. Their subordination of independent unions was entirely predictable. The experience for many workers, however, was demoralizing. For Chicago steelworker George Patterson, his independent union's affiliation with the CIO-founded Steel Workers Organizing Committee brought into the local officials who increasingly ran the show: "Anybody that could stand and talk and didn't bow to their thinking was gradually eliminated."[10]

That it could have been otherwise is unlikely, say the CIO's historians, and that it *should* have been otherwise is also doubtful. Industrial unionism in the mid- and late 1930s still battled powerful employers as well as fending off attacks by the AFL. American workers, for their part, remained ambivalent about unions. Neighborhood, ethnic, and religious allegiances competed with those of class solidarity, and organizers often confronted what seemed a solid wall of indifference. Episodes of worker militancy were far more the exception than the rule. Organizers of the famous 1937 Flint, Michigan, sit-down strike chose that tactic simply because it did not require many people—and they did not have many people. Building a national movement in these circumstances required professional staff leadership and centralized control, labor leaders argued. If, in the process, some officials developed a style that was autocratic, surely what counted was what they could get for their membership.[11]

But this view was not universal even among labor's officialdom. Rose Pesotta was a Russian émigré and a shirtwaist worker in New York who rose through the ranks of the International Ladies Garment Workers Union (ILGWU). After helping set up the ILGWU's first Education Department, she was elected to her local's Executive Board, then hired as a staff organizer by the international union, and eventually made the only woman vice president on the union's General Executive Board. In her attempts to organize women clothing workers, Pesotta experienced firsthand the local allegiances, especially to the church, that militated against the development of worker militancy. People used to the paternalism of church, family, and employers were uncomfortable with union organizers' confrontational strategies and egalitarian rhetoric. The solution, Pesotta believed, lay in treating workers' needs for recreation, education, health care, and housing as on a par with their needs for higher wages. This was the "social unionism" promoted by the ILGWU, and Pesotta saw it as a way to make the union a real competitor for workers' loyalty. Turning the union into a "year-round organization for citizenship, education, and culture," she wrote, would encourage workers to develop new solidarities and build the confidence that they needed to act on behalf of the group. Internal democracy was the best preparation for militant union leadership, Pesotta believed, but it required a foundation in new relationships.[12]

Pesotta's success in building such relationships was perhaps most obvious when workers at a Los Angeles factory that she organized vigorously protested her forced resignation from the union staff. Long a critic of the union's treatment of its women officers, she had been forced out after demanding for herself the managerial authority routinely granted men. In a petition to David Dubinsky, the head of the ILGWU, calling for Pesotta's reinstatement, workers wrote that Pesotta had "inspired us with a love of unionism and democracy." They were adamant: they would "not stand for dictatorship from Mr. Levy"—the ILGWU West Coast vice president who had fought for Pesotta's ouster—"any more than from Hitler or the Japs."[13]

Was Rose Pesotta's quest to build a democratic union admirable but unrealistic and—if the goal was to secure favorable contracts—possibly even counterproductive? Evidence suggests not. In a study of 236 contracts negotiated by CIO locals in California between 1938 and 1955, Judith Stepan-Norris and Maurice Zeitlin found that the contracts won by highly democratic unions were more likely to favor labor's interests.[14] Stepan-Norris and Zeitlin's explanation for democracy's efficacy is simple. Democratic unions kept their officials accountable to members' interests rather to those of employers. Comparing the agreements won by the CIO's "Big 3"—the United Automobile Workers (UAW), the United Steel Workers of America (USWA), and the United Electrical, Radio and Machine Workers of America (UE), which together accounted for 46 percent of the CIO's membership in 1944—Stepan-Norris and Zeitlin found that each union's success in winning pro-labor contracts matched its degree of internal democracy. UE was "one of the most democratically-run unions": its negotiating committees were elected, and all agreements required member referenda, as did calling and ending strikes. In the USWA, by contrast, power was firmly concentrated in the organization's top officers. Both the local and the national contracts signed by UE were more systematically pro-labor than were those of the USWA. The UAW was somewhere in between these two, in terms of both its degree of internal democracy and the strength of the contracts that it won.

If democracy was politically effective, then why did so many unions remain autocratically controlled, with centralized power, longtime appointed officials, and little internal contention? In a related study of thirty-five CIO unions, Stepan-Norris and Zeitlin found that a union's level of internal democracy reflected the extent to which it had been built from the ground up. Unions that had shifted their loyalties from the AFL to the CIO as the result of a revolt by the rank and file rather than action by union leaders were more likely to be internally democratic, as were those organized by their own organizers rather than a CIO organizing committee, those

amalgamated into a union whose structure was worked out through negotiation rather than absorbed into a unitary and centralized structure, and
those in an industry where Communists were active. Communists were
staunch believers in the rights that protected them as a political minority.
In addition, some had a commitment to democratic process (a commitment
that coexisted uncomfortably with their allegiance to the Party hierarchy).
In sum, if there was a tendency in union organizations to a suppression of
democratic processes, it stemmed less from the dictates of organizational
efficiency than from battles, more or less overt, between the rank and file
and their leaders.[15]

WORKERS' DEMOCRACY

By the 1950s, the leaders had, as some saw it, won the battle and were becoming less and less distinguishable from corporate executives. The union
president's lifestyle, the sociologist C. Wright Mills wrote, "is like that of
any middle-class businessman in an urban area." This is the image that
student activists in the early 1960s would have of the labor movement,
and it is one that they would find repugnant. But student activists failed
to acknowledge a very different legacy of the early labor movement, one
that would prove important to their own understanding of participatory
democracy. In the union education programs, independent labor colleges,
and university-affiliated summer schools that thrived in the early 1920s,
educators operated on the belief that a democratic pedagogy could bring
about radical social change. The ILGWU's Education Department, which
Rose Pesotta helped build, was a pioneer. The social sciences dominated
the curriculum, and problem-solving discussion was emphasized. By 1922,
over three thousand students attended ILGWU "Unity Centers" in and
around New York City. In the early 1920s, Pesotta took time out from organizing to study at the Bryn Mawr Summer School for Women Workers
and Brookwood Labor College.[16]

Bryn Mawr offered young working-class women eight weeks of liberal
arts education along with field projects, forums, discussion workshops,
and experiments in self-government intended to train them in the arts
of democratic participation. "It was interesting to me, this tremendously
strong, democratic process," Esther Peterson, the program's recreation director, said later. "Having grown up in a more authoritarian background, I
couldn't see how you could suddenly give power to people like that." But she
changed her mind: "You really have to begin to have faith and trust in people. It was a great experience for the young women to think that they had
a say in shaping the school's policies. I think it was rough, but it worked."[17]

Brookwood, founded in 1921 by pacifists and labor progressives, initially defined its mission modestly. It sought to "serve American labor with trained, responsible, liberally educated men and women from the ranks of the workers." This circumspection kept it in the good graces of the AFL, but, over time, it developed a more radical vocation. The timidity of the labor movement was no match for the pervasiveness of "capitalistic culture," the Brookwood teacher and economic historian David Saposs wrote in 1929. "The worker in the United States is surrounded with a point of view that is antilabor, or at best nonlabor. . . . This situation holds true of his political party, church, athletic club, fraternal and benefit society, press, theater and so on." Building an oppositional "labor culture" that would serve as the foundation of an effective labor movement required a pedagogy that was critical, cooperative, and thoroughly democratic. John Dewey was a staunch supporter of the college, and Brookwood teachers drew on his methods, emphasizing student-directed learning, unstructured discussions, and fieldwork. Students and teachers treated each other informally, and there were no grades, tests, or diplomas. As Brookwood lecturer Broadus Mitchell wrote of the approach, "Labor education is to be as nearly as possibly self-education, with the instructor acting chiefly as a guide. He must not hand down information. . . . If he is going to make thought organic with his students, he must make them think for themselves." In Brookwood's administration as well as its pedagogy, democracy was the governing ideal. School policies were made in joint faculty/student committees, and students had veto power over faculty appointments. Work tasks were shared.[18]

Seeking neither to educate people "out of their class" nor to create union functionaries, these programs and others like them—the University of Wisconsin's School for Women Workers, Work People's College in Minnesota, and Commonwealth College (the "Brookwood of the Southwest")—envisaged a generation of union leaders who would break out of the narrow business unionism of the AFL. They faced formidable obstacles. In the late 1920s, labor educational institutes were weakened by funding shortages and by sectarian conflicts on the left. Scarred by battles with Communists in the 1920s, the ILGWU stripped its educational activities of political content and emphasized instead cultural activities and narrow skills training for labor staff. The AFL had initially been supportive of workers' education but became increasingly anxious about the radical direction that that education was taking. After systematically curtailing the activities of the Workers' Education Bureau, an organization established to coordinate workers' education programs, the AFL censured Brookwood College in 1928 for alleged Communist tendencies. In spite of a spirited defense, the college never really recovered from the splits among the faculty created by the controversy. It disbanded in 1933. New Deal educational programs picked up where union-sponsored and independent ones left off, but usually without the radical aspirations of the earlier efforts.[19]

Still, the earlier efforts had lasting impact. Graduates went on to leadership roles in national unions and in countless locals. Among CIO leaders, for example, were to be found numerous Brookwood alumni. Teachers, too, went on to careers as union vice presidents as well as federal officials and academics. Those involved in workers' education also carried its vision and methods to other movements. Bryn Mawr's Colston Warne founded the Consumers' Union, and Esther Peterson was the first chair of the President's Commission on the Status of Women in 1961. A. J. Muste, former director of Brookwood, returned to the pacifist movement in 1936 after a demoralizing effort to organize a democratic workers' party. He would prove a staunch advocate for a pacifism that was both principled and pragmatic. While a student at the Union Theological Seminary, Myles Horton visited Brookwood in 1930 and found its program too rigidly structured for his taste. But the experience strengthened his commitment to launch a Southern alternative, and, in 1932, he created the Highlander Folk School in Monteagle, Tennessee, to train activists and educators in the labor movement. Highlander was racially integrated from the beginning, and it would have its greatest impact training leaders in the civil rights movement. The year after Horton came to Brookwood, Ella Baker did. Cofounder with George Schuyler of the Young Negroes' Cooperative League of America, Baker was in 1931 the league's national director and received a fellowship for a year at Brookwood. After her stint there, she helped found the National Negro Congress, worked as youth director and then director of branches for the National Association for the Advancement of Colored People (NAACP), and helped found the SCLC and then the Student Nonviolent Coordinating Committee (SNCC). Her career would be marked by continual struggles to expand the leadership of the civil rights movement to ordinary people.[20]

Baker and Horton would continue to practice and disseminate the radical pedagogy of early workers' education efforts. Participatory decisionmaking should both train ordinary people in the skills needed for political leadership and develop their broadest aspirations for the movement, they believed. They would treat participatory decisionmaking as a critical tool in organizing, and the young civil rights workers whom they trained would do the same. But Baker and Horton's influence on participatory democracy 1960s style was quiet. Few 1960s activists would identify them as sources

A. J. Muste, New York, 1950. (Photo courtesy of Swarthmore College Peace Collection, Fellowship of Reconciliation Papers)

for their understandings of how movement organizations should operate, and even fewer would cite the tradition of workers' education on which they built.

ALTERNATIVE MODELS

For the student authors of the 1962 Port Huron Statement, the new left's manifesto, the labor movement's glories were in the past. Over the years, the labor movement had, as they saw it, "succumbed to institutionalization, its social idealism waning under the tendencies of bureaucracy, materialism, business ethics." "Even the House of Labor has bay windows," they sniffed. But they reserved their fury for the narrow pragmatism that united left, labor, and liberals in unqualified admiration of "method, technique— the committee, the ad hoc group, the lobbyist, the hard and soft sell, the make, the projected image." "To be idealistic is to be considered apocalyptic, deluded," they wrote. "To have no serious aspiration, on the contrary, is to be 'tough-minded.'" What activists opposed was more a mind-set than concrete policies: more labor's loss of "idealism" than the content of its politics.[21]

That the radical left was so little source of democratic inspiration was especially galling to student activists. They could sympathize with the factors behind the left's decline: the political repression, pervasive cold war ideology, and revelations of Soviet atrocities committed in the name of a workers' utopia that had decimated the ranks of the committed. Journals like *Dissent* continued to take issue with the cold war orthodoxy, and some left writers like Michael Harrington spoke to a wide American audience. But, for students in the 1960s, the left was truly "old"—garrulous in its recounting of battles long over, suspicious of new ideas, and lodged in familiar organizational forms and political styles. Leftists' preoccupation with avoiding the taint of communism was hard for younger activists to understand. So was their predilection for making organizational combat into art.

Progressive activism as students encountered it in 1960 was not without an alternative to the hard-boiled rhetoric and narrow vision of the left. American pacifists had always insisted on the importance of the moral in politics. In the 1940s and 1950s, pacifists extended their critique of militarism to a society in which the economic bottom line, the bureaucratic ethos, and the logic of instrumental rationality passed as morality. "Power is everywhere and openly idolized," the editors wrote in the inaugural issue of *Liberation* in 1956. The left was as guilty as the center in mistaking gaining power for making change. "Allowing for exceptions," a *Liberation* contributor wrote, "radicalism stands in the tradition of power, of dominion and empire, of ruthless force, of 'practicality,' of 'realism.'"[22]

An honest utopianism, pacifists argued, had to be a part of a radical politics worthy of the name—but a utopianism that refused to withdraw from the political world. In intentional communities like Koinoia, Macedonia, and Glen Gardner, pacifists experimented with alternative forms of economic and social organization, but they also extended their democratic commitments to the direct action organizations that they formed. Groups like the Committee for Non-Violent Revolution (CNVR) (formed in 1946), the Peacemakers (formed in 1948), and the Committee for Nonviolent Action (CNVA) (formed in 1957) engaged in civil disobedience and daring acts of personal witness against the draft, war taxes, segregation in the federal prison system, and, eventually, atomic-weapons testing. These organizations were small, egalitarian, and collectivist. Inner revolution was not at odds with external change, pacifists were convinced. The movement would "escape th[e] megalomania" of a power-seeking left by extending "its idealism to its methods," one pacifist put it. "This means that the movement must live its principles. It must live cooperation."[23]

Statements like the latter strikingly anticipated new leftists' views of organization as well as their commitment to a politics that enacted its aims in the here and now. Yet radical pacifists cannot be said to have trained 1960s activists in participatory democracy. Staughton Lynd, pacifist, SNCC adviser, and antiwar activist, says that he has often wondered why "everyone in the 1960s suddenly started making decisions by consensus. Where did that come from?" He goes on: "There weren't enough Quakers and pacifists around to teach them." When I ask Tom Hayden what influence pacifists had on the organizational and deliberative style of Students for a Democratic Society (SDS), his answer is emphatic. "None." SDS modeled its meetings on SNCC's, Hayden says—it was the Southern civil rights movement, not pacifism, that shaped SDS founders' deliberative style.[24]

Hayden's is probably an overstatement. New leftists were eager readers of *Liberation*, and some would publish there themselves. For the early SDS leader Richard Flacks, A. J. Muste's skepticism of centralized organizations and his refusal to administer loyalty oaths and political litmus tests were influential in his own thinking about organization. Flacks's wife, Mickey, was a member of the pacifist Women Strike for Peace, an organization that was decentralized and participatory. Activists in Ann Arbor who had been involved with CORE—an organization founded by pacifists—ran their SDS chapter as a participatory democracy early on and well before national SDS did. Even before SDS existed, James Lawson, the FOR field secretary, trained the Nashville student activists who would become SNCC's leaders in Gandhian nonviolence and consensus decisionmaking. So there were lines of influence. Still, pacifists generally publicized their egalitarian organizational forms and deliberative styles less aggressively than they did their nonviolent methods. What accounts for their diffidence? Quakers and those familiar with their methods had never promoted consensus decisionmaking, longtime pacifist George Lakey says now. "You rely on consensus when you have a shared understanding of the theology. It is not to be imposed on people.... Quakers, at least in the 1950s, were antiproselytizing. We were reluctant to impose our methods."[25]

Pacifists' diffidence was also a consequence of their political marginality. Their absolute opposition to war had long denied them anything like a broad constituency, and, except during wartime, the memberships of their organizations remained tiny. Sophisticated in the methods of nonviolence, however, pacifists were periodically able to mobilize thousands of people around single issues, for example, the arms race in the late 1950s. They also offered their services to other movements both as trainers in nonviolence and as skilled strategists. A. J. Muste and other FOR members played that role in the labor struggles of the 1910s—until Muste, for one, found his allegiances conflicting and left the pacifist movement altogether (he returned to it later). In the interwar period, pacifists also formed coalitions with farm, women's, and labor groups to press for legislation and broad educational campaigns. Campaigns like the Committee on Militarism in

Education, the National Peace Conference (formed in 1932), the National Council for Prevention of War (1921), and the Emergency Peace Campaign (1936–37) gave pacifists access to broad publics outside their own small constituencies. For farm, labor, and women's groups, meanwhile, such agencies voiced a liberal consensus on foreign policy.[26]

After the Second World War, pacifists drew on their growing expertise in Gandhian nonviolence to play critical roles in the civil rights movement. Pacifists already had their own organization to battle racial discrimination with Gandhian principles of nonviolent resistance: CORE, founded in 1942 by the FOR field secretaries James Farmer and George Houser. But CORE's Northern base and mainly white membership restricted its size and influence for most of the 1940s and 1950s. Pacifists would have much greater impact in the South. When Montgomery activists used Rosa Parks's arrest for defying city segregation laws to launch a bus boycott in 1955, the FOR's Glenn Smiley and the War Resisters League's Bayard Rustin were immediately on the scene to counsel Martin Luther King Jr. and other boycott leaders in techniques of nonviolence. Rustin would continue an adviser to King. With Ella Baker and the leftist lawyer Stanley Levinson, he proposed the Southern mass-based direct action organization that became the SCLC. Smiley, for his part, ran workshops on nonviolence around the South and worked closely with leaders in black Southern communities to develop local coalitions for civil rights.[27]

Smiley emphasized to his FOR employers his view that the FOR's job was not to attempt to lead the civil rights movement but to "service" it. Pacifists' role here, as in the other movements that they "serviced," was a delicate one. Movement leaders were often wary of their intentions and skeptical of their motives. To gain their trust, pacifists were extraordinarily careful not to overstep the bounds of their advisory role. For example, when Bayard Rustin helped found the SCLC, he seems to have made no effort to push for a nonhierarchical structure. But he was later critical of the structure that the SCLC adopted. "Like the black church, the structure of the SCLC was autocratic," he wrote. "Major decisions rested with Dr. King. He determined when and where an action would take place, what tactics would be employed, when a campaign should be accelerated, and when compromises should be made." Although the familiarity of a ministerial leadership role legitimated King's dominance of the national organization, it also created problems, including persistent jockeying among SCLC officials for King's favor. The organization was decentralized, with local groups sending delegates to an annual convention. But, in local organizations too, governance was firmly top-down and unable, Ella Baker would complain, to generate the multiple layers of leadership that were needed.[28]

It would have been hard to argue with ministers' talents in mobilizing their congregations, however. And pacifists might well have jeopardized their consultative role by pressing for a less hierarchical organization. In addition, alongside their firm commitments to equality, pacifists were comfortable with much stronger notions of leadership than their activist successors in the 1960s would be. This too was partly a function of their political marginality. The cooperative ethos that pacifists embraced, their insistence on collectivized tasks and consensus-based decisionmaking, and their reluctance to centralize or bureaucratize all reflected their opposition to a mass society in which the lust for power had eclipsed the possibilities of human connection. But there were additional, quite practical reasons why pacifists were drawn to collectivist organizational forms. Pacifists had long seen their organizations as sources of support for those whose total opposition even to popular wars subjected them to public opprobrium and sometimes government harassment. A localist organizational structure and an orientation toward the internal life of the group helped sustain pacifists in their lonely cause and preserve a pacifist impulse until a time when it was possible to build a much broader movement. "There were intimate conferences where we walked, talked and ate together, and business sessions . . . where 'the sense of the meeting' took the place of resolutions and votes," Jessie Wallace Hughan wrote later of the early days of the FOR, founded in 1914 in England and in 1915 in the United States to support war resisters. "When our offices were raided by the Department of Justice, when friends were taken to jail and we wondered who would be the next, we felt ourselves drawn together like men in a besieged city."[29]

After the war, with a wave of popular antiwar sentiment buoying their hopes for broad social reconstruction, pacifists were able to act on their Social Gospel commitments to social reform, taking on civil liberties and labor organizing, poverty relief, and education reform. They managed a dual mission of supporting individual war resisters and speaking to a broad audience with the help of a bifurcated movement. While local groups operated autonomously, sponsoring discussion groups and lobbying campaigns and supporting conscientious objectors, a small national FOR staff brought the organization into liberal coalitions to press for legislation and education.

The arrangement worked until the possibility of war loomed again and, with it, pacifists feared, a repeat of their experiences in World War I. When a national poll in February 1937 asked, "If another war like the World War develops in Europe, should America take part again?" 95 percent of respondents answered no. Well before that, however, pacifists had abandoned advocacy in favor of support for war resisters, and they were unwilling now to try to capitalize on public opinion. Instead, they hunkered down, concentrating on sustaining members' commitment—this, their "crisis strategy." Participants in a peace conference held a few weeks before the 1937 poll agreed: "We can endure imprisonment and the obloquy of ninety-nine per cent of our countrymen if we can maintain contact, or even comradeship of spirit, with our intimate circle." Strengthening that comradeship organizationally became paramount.[30]

An orientation to the internal life of the group helped sustain the movement. The problem, however—and this was as true after the Second World War as it had been before it—was that it was sometimes unclear just how unyielding was the opposition that pacifists faced. Pacifists' focus on developing cooperative and egalitarian relationships among themselves might enable them to survive—or might detract from building a broader constituency. Pacifists often divided on the issue. Some might argue, as did members of the CNVR in 1946, that it was "far too early to be primarily concerned with the masses" and that the group should concentrate on "sowing the seeds" of a future order through experimental organizational forms and intellectual discussion—rather than "this grim and ludicrous, though ever so dedicated, procession of picket signs, this trembling of the fist on the street-corner." Others countered that pacifists' own political marginality made it difficult for them to gauge just what the "masses" were open to. In some instances, the tension between ministering to pacifist organizations' memberships and building a broader antiwar constituency resulted in favoring the former over the later, as was the case in the FOR before the Second World War. In others, it led to organizational dissolution as members found themselves unable to resolve their differences.[31]

Either way, few pacifists saw their organizations as the basis for a mass movement. Even those committed to direct action more than community building saw themselves as a tiny band of committed radicals and their organizations as cadres. Again, their distance from the American public as well as their view of the masses as besotted by patriotic fervor and vulnerable to the blandishments of charismatic leaders may have made them comfortable with conventional notions of leadership—this in spite of their radical egalitarianism. To be sure, such views of leadership had firm support in the Gandhian philosophy of nonviolence that they adopted. Gandhi himself envisioned an India governed by autonomous local units. But he believed that the organizational vehicle for bringing about such a society had to be centralized and hierarchical. And for those interpreting Gandhi in the 1930s and 1940s—Richard Gregg's 1934 *The Power of Nonviolence* and Krishnalal Shridharani's 1939 *War without Violence* were enormously influential—leaders' role was clear, conventional, and indispensable.

Pacifists' views of leadership "were very influenced by Gandhi," George Lakey remembers. "Gandhi would go to the Indian National Congress and say, 'I want you to appoint me commander in chief. And if I am killed, this person will be my second in command.' Because Gandhi was such a believer in democracy, he said: '*After* the campaign, I'm just one of [the people].' But nonviolent action was combat, all the metaphors of war. And I believed that too."[32]

Without a "counterpart to the Satyagrahis"—Gandhi's elite corps of experts in nonviolence—a movement of the masses was "inconceivable," the Peacemakers declared in their founding statement. When pacifists talked about democracy within their organizations, they meant among people with similar ideological commitments, formal education, and political expertise. Democratic organizations were important because they would lay the groundwork for a more egalitarian society, pacifists believed. They did not talk about democracy's capacity to train people with little experience of politics. There were exceptions, of course, people whose egalitarianism was combined with a repudiation of conventional understandings of leadership. In a CNVR discussion, David Dellinger complained about pacifist and socialist organizations' "habit of working for equality by exalting a 'leader' or 'leaders' above the rank and file." But, in the ensuing discussion, speakers turned instead to the legitimacy of substantial differentials in pay among staff in pacifist organizations, differentials that were then justified on the grounds that, as one speaker put it, "there is also involved a certain lack of competence and initiative in the memberships affected." "Most positions of leadership in an industrial society require a degree of technical knowledge that the mass of men neither understand nor have the time, nor interest, to follow closely," another speaker concluded. "Education leading to the assumption of responsibility by the rank-and-file is the only ultimate solution to the problem of runaway leadership," a third put in. But "this type of education is impossible today." The possibility that democratic participation could be a *means* of leadership education was not broached.[33]

If pacifists' political marginality helps explain their reluctance to impress on those with whom they worked their participatory democratic organizational forms, it also points to key differences between their understandings of democracy and leadership and those of their activist successors in the 1960s. Pacifists never faced the prospect of turning their participatory democracies into mass organizations. And they never saw participatory democracy as the basis for overcoming differences of status within the movement. For 1960s activists, by contrast, overcoming such differences was central. Truly involving those without prior experience in

The Reverend James Lawson being arrested during the Nashville sit-in movement,
5 March 1960. (Photo © Bettmann/CORBIS; used with permission)

politics would equip them to contend politically. And it would do so through
the developmental possibilities of participatory decisionmaking—this the
linchpin of the union education efforts described earlier. There was another important difference between radical pacifists and the activists who
came of political age a decade later. The sit-ins that swept the South in
1960 showed students that decentralized and participatory organizational
forms could *work*, powerfully, creatively, and with immediate impact. A
confidence born of their historical circumstances would allow student activists to reject the organizational forms that they had known and set out
to invent new ones.

STUDENTS TAKE THE HELM, 1960

On 1 February 1960, four black students from Greensboro Agricultural
and Technical College in North Carolina purchased a few items in the
downtown Woolworth and then sat down at the store's whites-only lunch
counter. Told that they would not be served, they remained seated and
did not leave until the store closed. They resumed the sit-in the next

day and the next, joined by other students from the college and then by students from surrounding colleges. Greensboro touched off a wave of demonstrations around the South: from Durham and Winston-Salem, they spread to South Carolina and Virginia. By the end of February, thirty cities in seven states had experienced sit-ins; by the end of March, fifty-four cities in nine states. By mid-April, fifty thousand people had taken part in sit-ins.[34]

Students in Nashville, Tennessee, had been planning sit-ins for months before the Greensboro Four beat them to the punch. They launched their own citywide campaign a week later, and it won kudos for its scale and, eventually, success. Nashville is the best example of a direct connection between radical pacifism and the organizational forms of the student movement. The sit-inners were mentored by James Lawson, a conscientious objector, former missionary, and FOR field secretary who was deeply versed in Gandhian philosophy. Lawson set up a workshop on nonviolence when he arrived in Nashville in 1958, and he soon attracted a dedicated band of college students—Diane Nash, John Lewis, Marion Barry, and Bernard Lafayette among them. As they parsed Gandhian ideas about nonviolence and discussed their own experiences of radical discrimination, group members developed a faith in the capacity of direct action to effect radical change at the same time as they developed deep bonds of trust with each other. In the workshop format that they used, participants learned as much from each other's insights as from the texts that they read and the expertise of their teacher. They encouraged each other to share their hurts and fears, to boldly envision the society that they wanted to create, and to probe the meanings of faith and reconciliation. Discussions combined patient learning with practical planning—since members had decided from early on that they would put their ideas about nonviolent revolution into action. When the sit-ins began, the relationships that the students had forged in the workshops enabled them to act with confidence and coordination.[35]

During the sit-ins, thirty members of a Central Committee (with a rotating chair) made decisions by consensus. For Lawson, collectivist decisionmaking was essential. Not only did it make it harder for authorities to shut down the movement by arresting its leaders, but it also gave participants a sense that their strength came from themselves rather than from their leaders, thus reinforcing their commitment. Yet another benefit: by requiring that decisions be made by all those involved, "we would not have clergy dominate," Lawson said later. Lawson's remark suggests a virtue of participatory democracy that had not been made much of by pacifists outside the South—and for good reason. In small groups of direct actionists with similar backgrounds and levels of commitment, there was little danger that moderate leaders would take over from people deemed less conventionally qualified for leadership. But, when a direct action campaign promised to involve an entire community, the danger that traditional leaders would take the reins was real. Participatory democracy was, for Lawson, a way to keep students in control.[36]

The Nashville sit-ins were atypical, however, in the training that preceded them and in the rigor of their deliberative forms. "On most, if not all, campuses," a Raleigh, North Carolina, sit-in leader wrote, "a particular group of students generally gathers to discuss the problem and to offer solutions and plans. This group is usually the intellectual power behind the movements and exists cohesively by the high degree of interest among its members. The group usually emerges as the leadership force and is accepted unequivocally by the student body on the basis of merit." Many student groups acknowledged the help of adult leaders, pacifists among them, in learning direct action techniques. But their organizational forms were largely their own. And they were a mixed bag. Sociologist James Laue was struck by the students' ignorance of "orderly procedure" and scant leadership skills. In Portsmouth, Virginia, a sit-inner wrote, "Our group was a loosely-knit collection . . . each with the same ideal: 'Equality for All.' Frankly speaking, that is all we had in common. We were lacking organization, leadership, and planning. . . . We had no leaders." Raleigh sit-inners relied on an "Intelligence Committee" that "planned all the strategy." After spirited meetings, where sit-in leaders "delivered scintillating orations and students left the meetings clapping and singing until they got to their dormitories, . . . Intelligence would convene to make all the necessary preparations of the following day." In Atlanta, two cochairs and an executive officer referred to as "Le Commandante" were assisted by a "Senior Intelligence Officer" and "field commanders."[37]

In most cases, students knew sit-in leaders: they were student council members or active in campus political groups or star athletes. Their leadership during the protests was legitimated by their prior leadership role, their willingness to serve on the front lines of the struggle, and the collective acclamation of a mass meeting. This was not consensus, says Connie Curry, who had worked with the American Friends Service Committee, a Quaker group, and served as an observer for many of the sit-ins. "It was more trickle down—or trickle up." "If everyone kind of went along with the decision," that was consensus. For a centralized high command to have planned the sit-ins would have been unthinkable, as the students saw it, would have jeopardized their extraordinary momentum. Students were wary of what they referred to as "adult" organizations, whose careful calculus of the pros and cons of any action made for a glacial pace and the predominance of officials over activists. Nor, on the other hand, was students' repudiation of formal structure an unthinking expressivism indifferent to the demands of effective politics. Informal organization enabled them to make fast decisions, to tailor their actions to the settings in which they worked, to build solidarity and commitment among people who had no other way to enforce collective decisions.[38]

When sit-in leaders met to take stock of their movement and to plan next steps, they were adamant that the movement not be absorbed or controlled by adult organizations. And they were just as clear that any entity that they created do nothing to jeopardize the movement's momentum. At an April meeting of sit-in leaders called by the SCLC's Ella Baker, students rejected bids by CORE and the SCLC to affiliate them as a student branch. Atlanta sit-in leader Julian Bond recalls, "Here were students like Ed King who had been beaten and still had his bloody shirt in his suitcase ... and now these older people were very obviously wanting to capitalize on what we were doing. So there was this general feeling that students had done a certain amount already, alone, and we didn't need these older people telling us what to do. We didn't have to wait for leadership figures." In this and a second meeting in November, sit-in leaders created an organization complete with officers, criteria for affiliation, and formal deliberative procedures. Campus groups named representatives to the Coordinating Committee, which also included SNCC's chief officers and adult advisers. But SNCC's founders were insistent on preserving the autonomy of local groups. "In relation to local protest areas, SNCC's role is suggestive rather than directive," they agreed. "In relation to those national and regional groups where some form of negotiating is necessary, SNCC may serve as a spokesman, but in a cautious manner in which it is made quite clear that SNCC does not control local groups." The Coordinating Committee agreed that it would not initiate action without a two-thirds majority. In a bow to Atlanta students, who were sophisticated and articulate, SNCC was headquartered in that city. And, in a bow to Nashville students, whose sit-ins were recognized as the best organized, SNCC's first chair was the Fisk University student Marion Barry.[39]

At SNCC's founding conference, James Lawson says now, "if there was a vote, we tried to get a vote that everyone would agree with. That was consensus." Consensus is usually seen as quite distinct from majority vote. Here, it was more an ethos, a determination to involve all participants and to respect their opinions. Students joining the movement had had little experience in protest or politics, Lawson and Baker recognized. Many were unused to framing positions in public debate and easily intimidated or manipulated by students who were more sophisticated. Lawson and Baker encouraged conference participants to be patient during the decisionmaking process, to allow everyone the time to formulate their opinions, and to solicit the input of the timid among them. The process emphasized respect for the opinions and skills of others and efforts to make one's reasoning understandable to others. The point of participatory decisionmaking, in other words, was to overcome differences among members of the group by developing the leadership skills inherent in each of them.[40]

The use of participatory decisionmaking to create new leaders was something that would be much more fully exploited as SNCC workers moved into the organizing that is the subject of the next chapter. Here, I want to underscore the novelty of this rationale. As a tiny minority of longtime activists with largely similar backgrounds and education levels, pacifists had not had to deal with dramatically varying levels of expertise among those participating in their strategic decisionmaking. As a group indigenous to no geographic community and marginalized by all, they did not face the difficult task of circumventing traditional community leaders without alienating them. If participatory democracy's developmental virtues were not learned from pacifists, neither were they being promoted by the mainstream civil rights organizations or by the left. At different points in labor's history, as I argued earlier, labor organizers had seen internal democracy as a way to develop workers' ability to contend for their interests. But, by the time newly active students looked around for organizational models, the organized left did not seem to offer much in the way of guidance. The deliberative forms developed by Southern black activists were thus invented as much as inherited.

DISCIPLINED DECISIONMAKING

The sit-ins changed direct action. They took a protest strategy that was disciplined, solemn, and linked with an ascetic repudiation of bourgeois life and made it youthful and expressive, appealing to students for whom bourgeois aspirations were only newly imaginable and often fiercely held. For college students in the North as well as in the South, the message was that moral action need not be restricted to otherworldly utopian sects or the quixotic efforts of true believers. Protest in the service of high ideals, and enacted with love and mutual respect, could be militant, radical—and effective. Students were astounded by their capacity to act collectively, and their excitement alone surely helped generate common resolve. But would such a process work over the longer haul—and in an organization where decisionmakers could not draw on prior warrants for their leadership?

Or where the task was as much to thrash out common purposes as to act on them? When building an organization rather than a campaign, how would students avoid the action-stymieing bureaucratic paraphernalia of the groups that they criticized? SNCC largely avoided the problem of coordinating action on the part of autonomous groups by metamorphosing the next year into a small cadre of full-time organizers. But activists planning direct actions in the civil rights movement as well as in the new left and the anti–Vietnam War movement would wrestle continually with tensions between full democracy and concerted action. Their efforts could too easily be derailed by participants unwilling to adhere to any prior plan, many concluded. If they had embraced participatory democratic decisionmaking in part for the individual freedom it promised, they now recognized their powerlessness before the tyranny of individual whim that came with it.

Years earlier, however, pacifists *had* developed ways to negotiate such conflicts. Had they schooled those practicing direct action in the 1960s in their deliberative etiquette, they might have helped them avoid sometimes debilitating tensions between the absolutism of personal conscience and the demands of concerted group action. For liberal Christian pacifists before World War II, a deliberative etiquette came naturally. Many were Quakers and found it easy to combine the apparatus of voting and motions with Quaker practices: appeals to the "sense of the meeting" with pauses for reflection, issues "laid aside" for future discussion, and decisions made by consensus were common. They relied also on Quaker decisionmaking's distinctive combination of collective and individual authority, with certain people seen as legitimately "weightier" than others on account of their expertise on an issue. Minutes of FOR National Council meetings show that speakers frequently invoked the behavioral requirements of "fellowship" to soften criticisms, wheedle compromises, chasten hardliners, and ease tensions. For example, when members of the council argued over the framing of a motion in one discussion, the chair urged, "We should settle these things in a spirit of fellowship." Another member insisted that they "try in the interest of fellowship to eliminate personalities." "Fellowship" referred both to the group's political commitment to moral reconciliation through nonviolence and to a set of behavioral norms for making decisions.[41]

This interactional framework seemed to serve the FOR well, and the kinds of complaints about usurpations of power that would plague new left and feminist organizations are nowhere evident in the records of its discussions. But how norms of fellowship would guide those who did not subscribe to the framework's religious underpinnings was left unclear. Moreover, the very familiarity of the concept and its higher-order legitimation made it easy to confuse substantive dissent with a lack of fellowship. Fellowship as a political goal was obviously connected to fellowship as a behavioral etiquette, but the connection could become elision, with challenges to the political stance dismissed for the manner in which they were raised.

This seems to have occurred in the course of at least one decision: the forced resignation in 1933 of FOR's executive secretary, J. B. Matthews. Matthews was an avowedly revolutionary Marxist, and FOR leaders were uncomfortable with his atheism. When, in a prolonged debate, several discussants argued that a non-Christian could represent the organization, those arguing for Matthews's resignation protested that their objection was to Matthews's failure to act in the "fellowship spirit," not to his "principles or basic philosophy." But there was slippage between the two, with speakers invoking the norms of fellowship to argue against Matthews's proclivities for dissent. "It seems to me that J. B. Matthews does not represent at all the spirit of conciliation," one speaker averred. "He brings out the worst that is in me. It seems to me that this group has to be somewhat of a unit . . . I have no doubt that if J. B. is retained, the name [Fellowship of Reconciliation] will have to be changed." Another: "J. B.'s continuance as secretary is splitting the Fellowship. . . . I feel in a great many ways he lacks the spirit of fellowship and reconciliation, which as I view it is the heart of the Fellowship of Reconciliation movement. This, as you well understand, is not personal." Others expressed similar sentiments, used similar formulations, and eventually won the day. This was only one part of what was going on in the protracted debate over Matthews's tenure. But it does illustrate the danger that the behavioral demands of fellowship could be invoked as much to discourage the expression of substantive disagreement as to sustain a mutually respectful discussion. By defining J. B. Matthews's challenge as one of etiquette rather than one of politics, FOR members reinforced their unity but at the expense of more seriously confronting the issues that Matthews had raised. What I have called the *deferential* character of pacifist decisionmaking offered little warrant for negotiating the terms of democratic authority.[42]

The radical pacifists who came of age during World War II were anxious to distance themselves from the religiosity of liberal pacifists as well, perhaps, as from the pressures to conformity that sometimes accompanied that religiosity. They refused to ground either their rationales for protest or the arguments they made in deliberations in their faith commitments. This meant that they had to invent a new deliberative etiquette, a new set of procedures and criteria for evaluating options. They began to develop a novel conception of discipline to do that. Action was motivated by "individual conscience or spirit," Peacemakers explained in the late 1940s, but given form by the discipline of participation in a pacifist cell. "We recognize as the two poles around which life is built, the individual conscience or spirit and the concept of community or fellowship which brings people together in cells." Peacemakers decided against requiring new member groups to submit a written account of their discipline, provided that it was consonant with commitments to civil disobedience, conscientious objection, and personal self-transformation. Like other pacifist groups, they were careful to emphasize the voluntary character of a discipline and its benefits to individuals. "Discipline is based on acceptance of a common purpose, discussion, the leading of the spirit," they wrote, "and aims at enhancing, not submerging, the personalities of members, being based on the concept of ultimate respect for the consciences of human beings." It was through their collectively produced discipline that "personal conscience could be joined with group strategy." The concept of pacifist discipline thus crafted a unique relationship between individual and group. Members would individually and voluntarily agree to submit to the discipline of the group, to the "terms of one's follower-ship," as a member of the CNVA put it in 1961. But, unlike the notion of fellowship, whose authority rested not with the group itself but with God, the terms of a group's discipline were open to scrutiny and redefinition. The result was an evolving framework for cooperation.[43]

This emphasis on group discipline and on self-discipline in service to the cause was responsible for whatever successes pacifists had, one concluded in 1961. But it was new and unfamiliar. An idiom of personal conscience was much more familiar as the basis of action and easy to invoke as a basis for internal dissent. When a shift in the political climate in the 1950s made Americans newly receptive to peace initiatives, pacifists began to secure unprecedented attention for daring acts of civil disobedience. However, they struggled internally with some members' penchant for what others saw as strategically ill-advised actions justified on the grounds of personal conscience. Such actions risked alienating the public support that pacifists were on the verge of building, critics said, and they disparaged a "holier than thou" attitude, a tendency, as one put it, for protesters to see their "purity of witness" as adequate rationale and measure of success. The problem with pacifists' notion of discipline, then, was simply that it could too easily cede to a more familiar idiom of conscience, in which individual purposes were justified by a higher authority and removed entirely from group scrutiny.[44]

It was the absolutism of personal conscience rather than the more variegated concept of discipline that would be absorbed by the 1960s activists who inherited pacifists' techniques of nonviolent direct action. In the teaching guides on nonviolence that pacifists made available when they visited campuses in the 1940s and 1950s, they did not elaborate on the discipline required of direct action. Their stock statement ran: "Discipline is very important at this point, but it must never be discipline for its own sake. Discipline comes as the situation demands." At least one trainer in nonviolence was unhappy with a tendency to neglect internal relations in the group. In an evaluation of a 1959 workshop on nonviolence held in Atlanta, FOR field secretary James Lawson called for "adding a major dimension on training and preparation of leadership. This could include the working out [of] a common discipline for those of us who participate in the struggle for a new society. Such a common discipline should help to more clearly unite us in spirit and mind." Lawson called for "an entire day given to what might be called *group therapy*. This would mean the analysis of emotional conflicts, and role playing as a method of such therapy." In his own work with students, as I showed, Lawson put a premium on that kind of discipline. The Nashville students whom he trained in nonviolent direct action and collectivist decisionmaking would be committed to those things when they became the first leadership cadre of SNCC. However, the deliberative form that Lawson introduced to the Nashville activists competed with many others when student protest broke the bounds of Southern apartheid in 1960.[45]

DEMOCRACY AND EFFICACY

Activists have made of their organizations radical democracies to express their egalitarian convictions and to experience relationships that are free of competitiveness and manipulation. But they have also done so for practical reasons. True, the pacifists who created intentional communities and cooperatives, who appealed to the "sense of the meeting" and strove for consensus, were motivated by more than instrumental concerns. For many, a commitment to consensus reflected a firm belief that there was one true way, God's way, discoverable through joint contemplation. But pacifists also saw their organizations at times as refuges in a militaristic world. Collectivist decisionmaking strengthened the fellowship that war resisters found in pacifist organizations, and it preserved democratic possibilities for a reinvigorated pacifist movement in the future. That this purpose conflicted with the demands of appealing to a broader constituency of potential war opponents cannot be reduced to a tension between ideological consistency and instrumental effectiveness. The draws on both sides were instrumental.

When maverick union leaders or rank-and-file unionists fought for more democracy, they had something different in mind than pacifists did: not consensus and group leadership, but open voting and regular elections. Such reforms offered the best hope for keeping union leaders accountable to the rank and file, they believed. Research indicates that, contrary to the still-prevailing common sense, internal democracy did translate into concrete gains for workers. Similarly, when educators in labor colleges and summer schools promoted democratic methods in teaching and in the administration of programs, they did so in order to build an "effective" labor movement, as one put it, a labor movement that was farsighted in its aspirations and militant in its methods. What militated against internal democracy in workers' education and organizations was less the objective demands of instrumental effectiveness than a complicated mix of labor officials' investment in controlling their turf, the sectarian disputes that sometimes gave nondemocratic movements a stake in democratic unions and more democratic ones a stake in democracy's suppression, and workers' familiarity with hierarchical organizational forms.[46]

The power of familiar forms is a second theme that I have pursued in the chapter. If democracy requires relationships as well as procedures, the best models may not come from the relationships with which we are most familiar: family, for example, friendship, or religious fellowship. Activists have often tried to build internal democracies on such relationships or tried to build democracies among people for whom those relationships were paramount, and they have found it difficult to do so. Labor organizers in the 1930s, for example, were ill equipped to deal with the ethnic, religious, and neighborhood loyalties that made workers uncomfortable with unionism's antiauthoritarianism. FOR members extended their belief in fellowship to a set of norms for mutually respectful and cooperative decisionmaking, but they sometimes mistook substantive dissent for incivility. Radical pacifists found themselves unable to rein in protesters whose actions were undermining their chances of building broader support because to do so would have required abrogating the dictates of individual conscience. In each case, democracy stopped working at the limits of the relationship underpinning it.

But evident in the movements I have discussed in this chapter are also alternatives. Activists have built movement democracies on novel modes of association. Rose Pesotta did so by making the union a setting for workers' political self-development and for forging the egalitarian relationships that would compete with the hierarchical ones of church and family. In the notion of a group discipline, pacifists negotiated the tension between individual and group purposes by asking members to subscribe voluntarily to a set of behavioral norms—but norms that were subjected to reevaluation and change. Finally, James Lawson's workshops on nonviolence provided a setting for reflecting on the aims and means of activism and the relationships that would guide it. Like the others, this associational form provided the normative framework for deliberations that were mutually respectful but also open to dissent and mutually solicitous but also inclusive.

3

A BAND OF BROTHERS STANDING IN A
CIRCLE OF TRUST: SOUTHERN CIVIL RIGHTS
ORGANIZING, 1961–64

Local people have really begun to find a way they can use a meeting as a tool for running their own lives. For having something to say about it. That's very slow, but it's happening.

BOB MOSES, SPEAKING AT A CONFERENCE IN THE FALL OF 1964

Genealogies of participatory democracy have been generous in the credit they give the young civil rights organizers who worked on the knife's edge of racial oppression in early-1960s Mississippi. Martin Luther King Jr. had long talked about the "beloved community," passionately and powerfully. He had made it possible for people to fight without violence and to see the possibilities for reconciliation in moments of severest strife. But, in a daily way, the young staffers of the Student Nonviolent Coordinating Committee (SNCC; pronounced "Snick") *lived* the beloved community. They lived it in the seriousness with which they sang the "Black and White Together" verse of "We Shall Overcome," arms linked and hands clasped. They lived it in their refusal to name leaders—since everyone in the "band of brothers" was a leader—and in their insistence on making decisions by consensus. And they lived it in their belief that, if the nation could be made witness to the injustices perpetrated against Southern black people, it would act to end those injustices. Before it was turned into a slogan, say chroniclers, participatory democracy flourished in SNCC's beloved community.[1]

This picture of SNCC is compelling. But closer analysis of SNCC's actual deliberative style and its broader activist strategy yields a different one. Some former staffers remember with pride their efforts to create in their own operation the seeds of a profoundly different society. Others do not. "I really don't remember ever being at a meeting where somebody would say, 'Well, now, the job at hand is to create the beloved community,'"

Mississippi organizer Martha Prescod Norman recalls. Indeed, by the time Prescod Norman came south in 1963, SNCC's first leadership of Nashville sit-inners had been largely eclipsed by political organizers, many native Mississippians, who were untrained in Gandhian nonresistance and largely uninterested in modeling a radical democracy. What they called the "band of brothers" was not the beloved community. It was self-consciously black, if with a few valued whites, and its members were dispatched places and delegated tasks on the orders of state, district, and project directors.[2]

Yet SNCC workers continued to rely on deliberative practices that we would call participatory democratic—but for practical reasons as much as principled ones. Decentralized, participatory decisionmaking helped sustain the commitment of overworked and underpaid organizers and provided them the flexibility that they needed to respond to local conditions. It enabled them to accommodate a range of individual positions with respect to a group decision while maintaining organizational unity. Most important, participatory decisionmaking was a valuable tool in organizing. Former Mississippi project head Bob Moses outlines the organizer's task: "How are you going to, as early as possible, move in the direction of [local] people taking ownership? One of the first areas is the meeting—that's your tool for building. So how do people take ownership of meetings? And there you get into what has come to be called *participatory democracy* . . . in which the people who are meeting really get more and more of a feeling that this is [their] meeting."[3]

SNCC workers rarely used the term "participatory democracy." But evident in Moses's remarks is what I have called a *developmental* rationale for the form. Involving political novices in decisionmaking developed their confidence in their own leadership abilities. It trained them to weigh strategic options and negotiate common interests. In addition, it fostered mechanisms of challenge and accountability that might discourage co-optation once the movement began to gain recognition. The rationale for participatory deliberations was thus quite explicitly political: the point of involving people in decisionmaking was to train them to mobilize against existing political structures. Characterizing participatory democracy as principled rather than practical or as aimed solely at personal self-transformation rather than at institutional change thus misses the mark here as it did in the pacifist and labor movements that I described in the last chapter. Nor was collectivist decisionmaking antagonistic to leadership. Its purpose was precisely to create leaders—and to create the mechanisms that would hold leaders responsible to their constituents.

When I asked former SNCC organizer Charlie Cobb what published accounts of SNCC have missed, his response was immediate and emphatic:

"Grassroots organizing as the driving force and primary characteristic of the movement." SNCC workers' ideas and commitments developed in response to the demands of local political organizing, Cobb argued. It was the learning process of "figuring out what worked and what didn't" that made ideas like participatory democracy more than "intellectual teacups on your coffee table." Indeed, he believed that SNCC began to collapse when its abandonment of organizing for speechmaking and international tours "short-circuited" that process. Of course, even the most pragmatic, nonideological grassroots organizing is shot through with ideas: about the scope of the state, the boundaries of the community, the relationship between leaders and led. But one cannot understand SNCC workers' conception of participatory decisionmaking—and both its strengths and its limitations—outside the organizing context in which that conception was developed. My aim in this chapter is to provide that context.[4]

FROM THE BELOVED COMMUNITY TO THE BAND OF BROTHERS, 1960–63

By April 1960, more than fifty thousand students had sat in at segregated lunch counters around the South. They had done so with adult assistance—probably more assistance than they acknowledged—but also with a powerful sense that their protest represented something generationally and politically new. The organization that they formed was determinedly decentralized and nonhierarchical because the sit-ins had shown that locally autonomous and informally organized movements worked. The "spontaneity" of the movement was its strength. Students' commitment to group decisionmaking reflected the Gandhian training that some had received and a desire on the part of others to preserve this new unity. For James Lawson and Ella Baker, older advisers who had helped structure SNCC's founding conferences, consensus-based decisionmaking was also a way to compensate for the fact that some lacked the skills in parliamentary maneuver and verbal sophistication that others had in spades.

SNCC's position as the organizational spearhead of the student sit-ins was short-lived. The movement began to lose momentum halfway through 1960, and SNCC struggled to find new purpose. At the same time, however, a small cadre of activists distinguished by their willingness to confront segregation at its most repressive was developing within the group. In January 1961, sit-inners in Rock Hill, South Carolina, decided to go to jail rather than accept bail, and four SNCC representatives joined them. They acted again that spring during the freedom rides, integrated bus trips organized by the Congress of Racial Equality (CORE) and designed to test a Supreme Court ruling against segregated bus facilities. After passengers were brutalized and drivers refused to take them any further, SNCC volunteers traveled to Birmingham to resume the rides. They gained a national profile when they were assaulted by a mob in Montgomery, and, by the time federal marshals were dispatched to escort the riders to Jackson, hundreds of supporters had joined the protest. The rides would continue through the summer, with over three hundred people eventually jailed in Jackson and prominent liberals joining the protest. Behind the scenes, Justice Department officials lobbied for an Interstate Commerce Commission ruling prohibiting segregated facilities in bus and train terminals. It was issued on 22 September.[5]

While these negotiations were unfolding, the Kennedy administration was pitching a different course of action to SNCC: a Southern voter-registration drive. SNCC representatives, and especially the Nashville group, were wary. The proposal came with the promise of foundation support and, some said, of draft deferments for student organizers and federal protection for registration efforts. But the freedom rides had provoked a federal crisis. Why give up that power now? Because voter registration had the potential to gain black Southerners lasting power, said the proposal's proponents. Later, they would adduce another argument: voter registration provoked the same level of white retaliation that direct action had. The internal debate was not easily resolved, however, and the two sides reluctantly agreed to form separate wings of the organization. Soon after, SNCC hired its first executive secretary, an older Chicagoan named James Forman.[6]

Bob Moses would be SNCC's point man in Mississippi. A New York City schoolteacher, he had come south to work for the Southern Christian Leadership Conference (SCLC) in the summer of 1960 and soon moved to the SNCC corner of the office. In July, he toured Mississippi in search of student delegates for SNCC's upcoming inaugural conference. There he met Amzie Moore, a local official of the National Association for the Advancement of Colored People (NAACP), who quickly made it clear that he had other things in mind for Moses than recruiting student delegates. Along with other longtime black activists in the state—Medgar Evers, Aaron Henry, E. W. Steptoe, Vernon Dahmer, and Hartman Turnbow, among them—Moore was convinced that gains for black Mississippians would come through political organizing. "I had to go after the vote!" he said later. "And you say, 'Well, what the vote going to do?' It's going to put people in there who are primarily concerned, yes, about their [own] welfare, but also about the progress in the given community." Moore saw in the student sit-ins the beginning of a potent voter-registration force.

Moses too was soon convinced. "The most promising thing we've been able to cook up is a voter registration program to start this fall and go full blast next spring," he wrote SNCC's administrative secretary Jane Stembridge in late August. "Amzie thinks, and I concur, that the adults here will back the young folks but will never initiate a program strong enough to do what needs to be done. . . . The project will be SNCC's with whoever wants to give QUIET help welcome!" Moses's enthusiasm was contagious. "Bob is doing miracles. I cannot believe your letters . . . absolutely cannot and I got so excited that things almost happened to my kidneys," Stembridge wrote back. "This VOTER REGISTRATION project is IT!"[7]

Moses returned south the following summer. Moore had not been able to secure the voter-education facilities that they needed, and he encouraged Moses to accept an invitation from the Pike County NAACP head C. C. Bryant to go instead to McComb. Located in the southwestern corner of the state, McComb had a population of thirteen thousand; in the entire county, two hundred blacks were registered to vote. SNCC volunteers Reginald Robinson and John Hardy joined Moses soon after his arrival, and together they opened a voter-registration school to train residents for the literacy test. Events unfolded quickly. Although few of the residents whom they convinced to attempt to register actually succeeded in doing so, SNCC's efforts drew the attention of people in Amite and Walthall Counties, who requested their own voter-registration schools. Moses was arrested shortly after he accompanied three black residents to the registrar in Liberty. A week later he was beaten by Billy Jack Gaston, a cousin of the local sheriff. When Moses pressed charges, Gaston was tried and acquitted, and the SNCC workers were urged to leave the county. They refused and brought in more of their SNCC comrades.

McComb high school students were eager to get involved. Trained in nonviolent tactics by SNCC workers Marion Barry and Charles Sherrod, they attempted to desegregate a Woolworth's and a Greyhound station. Five teenagers were arrested and jailed until October. When the high school principal refused to readmit two of them, students once again took to the streets. Meanwhile, on the voter-registration front, threats and violence continued. When the Justice Department attorney John Doar arrived to investigate the beatings of SNCC workers Travis Britt and John Hardy, voter-registration leader E. W. Steptoe reported that he was receiving threats from E. H. Hurst, a white neighbor and state representative. Other farmers who were active in the voter-registration effort had received similar threats, Steptoe said. The day after Doar left, one of those farmers, Herbert Lee, was shot to death by Hurst. Claiming that the unarmed Lee had attacked him with a tire iron, Hurst was acquitted by a coroner's jury that afternoon. In the climate of terror that followed Lee's death, voter-registration efforts ground to a halt.

If, in that sense, McComb had proved a failure, it had nevertheless sealed SNCC workers' determination to continue such efforts elsewhere. With a small amount of money provided by a group of liberal foundations, SNCC workers launched more voter-registration projects. In 1962, SNCC was running projects in fourteen counties in Mississippi and southwest Georgia and, by mid-1963, had added projects in Selma, Alabama; Danville, Virginia; and Pine Bluff, Arkansas. Federal officials had urged SNCC to concentrate its voter-registration work in the cities, SNCC executive secretary James Forman later recounted, but SNCC workers reasoned that "the Deep South contained 137 rural counties with a black majority." Their plan, accordingly, was "Negro control of the . . . rural counties in the Deep South in which there is a Negro majority." The goal was "political power."[8]

Not coincidentally, majority-black counties were also those characterized by the most stringent efforts to keep blacks off the voting rolls. Prospective voters in Mississippi were required to interpret a near-incomprehensible section of the state constitution, those in Georgia to submit character vouchers signed by several registered voters (in counties where no blacks were registered). Applicants were rejected for having participated in civil rights demonstrations or turned away for such trivia as having underlined rather than circled *Mr.* on the registration card. Or else the registrar might, without warning, just close the office on registration day. The names of those who registered were published in the local paper (to give others an opportunity to challenge their "good character"), and residents thus knew that, once they made the trip to the courthouse, they were fair game for reprisals. Measured in terms of their capacity to keep people disenfranchised, the strategies were effective. In Worth, Marion, and Baker Counties in Georgia, 8, 3, and 0.5 percent, respectively, of the black population, and 110, 111, and 145 percent of the white population, was registered to vote. The figures would be laughable if they did not bespeak such a level of repression. The people whom SNCC organizers canvassed worried about losing their jobs, homes, and credit. And they worried for others close to them, as did the teacher who feared harm to her pupils and the elderly woman who worried that the men in her family would be fired. "It seemed like a good afternoon," one southwest Georgia organizer reported cautiously in 1962. "But it was like any afternoon, with the same tired phrases, the same appalling nebulous fear. What's holding you back? you ask. 'Well now, I jest ain't got up there yet. I jest ain't got up there.' You cannot come around and break a world in two. You cannot forget the force of two hundred years."[9]

Yet breaking a world in two was what they needed to do. SNCC projects had different priorities and methods. The massiveness of the task that they faced made for openness to anything that seemed to have a chance of getting people "moving." Charles Sherrod, the director of SNCC's southwest Georgia project and an ordained minister, insisted on a racially integrated project and believed firmly that garnering Southern blacks their "psychological freedom" was more important than expanding the voter-registration rolls. Ask former SNCC staffers now about the "beloved community" ideal, and they talk about Charles Sherrod. "This is one of Sherrod's arguments," southwest Georgia staffer John O'Neal observes, "that whatever you seek to achieve as an end must be evidenced in the process by which you seek to accomplish it." Mississippi organizers were steeped in the traditions and culture of the black church and saw their work in profoundly moral terms. But they were less concerned with its exemplary nature. Indeed, by 1963, minutes of a staff discussion show that Sherrod's view of SNCC's purpose was a minority one: "It appeared that most of the participants wanted to deal with political questions, and wanted to deal exclusively with the political orientation." Myles Horton, the head of the Highlander School, who was leading the discussion, observed at one point, "SNCC has continually had debates of whether the emphasize [sic] should be political or religious, spontaneous or rigidly political," but the rest of the discussion focused on the political organizing that had become the core of SNCC's activism. The famed brutality of Mississippi's brand of apartheid and the fact that most SNCC organizers there were native born led many to see SNCC's organizing in that state as the cutting edge of radical protest.[10]

Much of SNCC workers' organizing was by the seat of their pants, in Mississippi as elsewhere. "We didn't know what we were doing," laughs Hollis Watkins, one of SNCC's first Mississippi organizers. "It was hit and miss; it was trial and error. We didn't have no idea of what all was involved in actually organizing. But we had faith, we had confidence, we had courage, and willpower—and blessings from the Almighty." They also had valuable training. From veteran Mississippi activists like Amzie Moore, Aaron Henry, and E. W. Steptoe, they secured places to stay, funding, strategic advice, and protection. "We were on Amzie's page," Bob Moses says now. At the time, Curtis Hayes wrote gratefully that he "had been informed by Amzie Moore before arrival that my best bet would be to work with the cafe owners, for the professional people were brain-washed by the whites." His most useful contact proved to be a wealthy owner of a house of prostitution, bisexual and a grandmaster of the Masons. "Compliments to Mr. Moore for he warned me that this is the kind of man I will have to work with."[11]

Other organizing lessons came from activists based outside Mississippi such as Anne and Carl Braden, who headed the Southern Conference Educational Fund, and Spelman College historian Howard Zinn. Long-time organizer Ella Baker and staffers associated with the Highlander School for Folk Education, among them Bernice Robinson, Septima Clark, and Myles Horton, proved influential. For Baker, Horton, Clark, and Robinson, collective decisionmaking was essential to effective organizing, and it would become an important part of SNCC workers' tactical repertoire.[12]

ELLA BAKER, MYLES HORTON, AND THE HIGHLANDER CENTER

Ella Baker came to SNCC after stints in the NAACP and the SCLC. In both organizations, she had set out to use the radical pedagogy she had imbibed at Brookwood to build local leadership—and had been stymied in the task. Promoted from NAACP field secretary to national director of branches in 1943, she established a training program for local leaders and encouraged field secretaries to focus on local issues. She had found, she said, that getting people involved in the NAACP often meant starting "with some simple thing like the fact that they had no streetlights, or the fact that in the given area somebody had been arrested or had been jailed in a manner that was considered illegal and unfair, and the like. You would deal with whatever the local problem was, and on the basis of the needs of the people you would try to organize them in the NAACP." But she was powerless before the national NAACP's view of chapters as mainly sources of revenue—and a tendency on the part of some branch officers to accept that role. Unable to make good on her commitment to expanding the policymaking role of local delegates in the organization, she resigned in 1946. As executive director of the SCLC, she again struggled to promote local leadership, this time in the face, not of top-heavy bureaucracy, but of what she later called the "cult of personality" that was developing around Martin Luther King Jr. She recalled a meeting in Montgomery to celebrate the anniversary of the bus boycott, "and there was nothing, nothing, but nothing in the call to the meeting that dealt with people or involving people. The basis of the call was the honoring of our great leader....I spoke to [King] about that.... [H]e said, 'Well, I can't help what people do.'" But Baker believed that he could and that he was missing strategic opportunities. Neither male nor a minister, and older than her colleagues, Baker was bound to encounter hostility from King's lieutenants. But she was also unstinting, if tactful, in her criticism of the SCLC's failure to expand its leadership base.[13]

In SNCC's founding, Baker saw new possibilities. It was a student group, it was uninterested in the prerogatives of individual status, and it was born of hundreds of local, autonomous movements. And it was effective precisely insofar as it was free of the organizational apparatus that delayed action in favor of waiting for national directives or the word of a charismatic leader. "I have always thought what is needed is the development of people who are interested not in being leaders as much as in developing leadership among other people," she said. In SNCC she believed that she had found just that. The students at Raleigh were impressed by Baker's encouragement of their autonomy, and she remained for many years a trusted SNCC adviser. Baker's preference for what she called "group-centered leadership" has led several analysts to attribute to her SNCC's participatory democratic ethos. But by no means did Baker abjure either organization or leadership. She felt, says her biographer, "that an organization should have regular procedures, a clear idea of who was responsible for what and to whom: in other words, a chain of command." Indeed, she was later critical of those in SNCC who came to believe, in her words, that "the right of people to participate in the decisions that affect their lives" meant "that each person working had a right to decide what ought to be done . . . to do your own thing." In SNCC meetings, always impeccably dressed and articulate in her interventions, she prodded staffers to clarify their positions, raised questions that they had not addressed, drew into the conversation people who seemed excluded, and proposed compromises when meetings reached an impasse. Curtis Hayes Muhammad, a Pike County teenager when he came to work for SNCC, remembers Baker in protracted staff meetings "going from person to person quietly asking them, how do you feel about this? Do you want to say something?" On the other hand, says Muhammad, "if the conversation started getting circular, she would get up and say, 'You all are saying the same things!'" But she gave her young colleagues a powerful sense that all their opinions were legitimate.[14]

Baker also taught SNCC workers to see building indigenous leadership as the primary goal of the struggle, to privilege organizing over mobilizing, to approach divisions within black communities carefully—neither challenging older leaders unnecessarily nor being afraid to circumvent them—and to see asking questions as a way of arriving at good decisions. Many of these lessons would be reaffirmed in SNCC workers' encounters with Myles Horton and other staffers from the Highlander Folk School. A working-class Tennessean, Horton had become convinced of the radical potential of adult education while at Union Theological Seminary in New York, and he returned to Tennessee to found Highlander in 1932. For the next thirty years, Highlander ran workers' education programs and union organizing drives. It took on school desegregation in the late 1950s. Violating Tennessee's Jim Crow laws, it was racially integrated.[15]

A number of sit-inners, including Marion Barry, John Lewis, Diane Nash, Jim Bevel, and Julian Bond, attended Highlander's annual college workshop in 1959. Lewis credits Myles Horton with the Nashville group's commitment to rotating leadership, for he had warned them about the "dangers of passing power into the hands of individual 'leaders,'" Lewis recalls. But it was as SNCC shifted to voter registration that Highlander's role became pivotal. The debate over SNCC's priorities took place at Highlander, and, shortly after, Horton offered to run a voter-registration workshop for SNCC staffers. The workshop proved so successful that Highlander staffer Bernice Robinson was asked to repeat it in Mississippi. When she did, she found that SNCC workers were already using Highlander "techniques." Robinson repeated the exercise the following summer, and, the time after that, the workshop was run entirely by Mississippi organizers themselves.

What were Highlander's "techniques"? Horton wrote later that he saw the school as "a place where people could learn how to make decisions by actually making real decisions." Schools and universities privileged expertise; they did not "make poor people feel comfortable. . . . They had never been able to make decisions on anything of importance in their own lives. In a factory you make decisions within the limits set by the boss. But here, at this new education center I dreamed of creating with other people, they were going to make decisions, the biggest decisions possible in that setup." Highlander's resources prohibited it from doing more than training small groups of potential leaders, but workshop participants were expected to continue the education process when they returned to their communities. "We debunk the leadership role of going back and telling people and providing the thinking for them," Horton emphasized. "We aren't into that. We're into people who can help other people develop and provide educational leadership and ideas, but at the same time, bring people along."[16]

I want to underscore several features of Horton's view of decision-making. First, it was deliberately educational. The point was to give people the tools to articulate their grievances and goals and to organize to realize them. The process of decisionmaking was as important as its end point. Just providing the time that people unschooled in political strategizing needed to think through unfamiliar issues was important. "Horton soon learned that poor people were usually quiet around strangers, or people they considered 'well-spoken,' meaning educated," his wife, Aimee Horton, said later. "When asked a question, some might take half an hour before answering. They'd be puzzling what the question meant, what words to use in reply, even why the other person had asked that question." Collective decisionmaking succeeded when it trained people to weigh options and articulate positions, not necessarily when it demonstrated the possibility of unanimity. This view of decisionmaking was not hostile to expertise. Rather, people should learn to identify what kind of expertise they needed rather than have their agendas determined by experts. "There's a time when people's experience runs out," Horton explained. The danger was in letting experts run the show, not in relying on their skills. Finally, Horton saw formal organization as a two-edged sword. When he founded Highlander, he said later, he "didn't believe in hierarchical structures." But his position changed: "I'm not critical of organizations.... [T]o separate Highlander's thinking from organizations is a mistake, because we think organizations have to be the first step toward a social movement.... [W]e wouldn't take anybody at Highlander who wasn't a product of an organization, who wasn't involved in an organization, who didn't come from an organization."[17]

Horton's commitments were exemplified in Highlander's citizenship schools, which he developed jointly with Esau Jenkins, Septima Clark, and Bernice Robinson. Jenkins was a farmer and bus driver on St. John's Island in South Carolina who came to Highlander hoping to secure for his fellow islanders the literacy training that they needed in order to register to vote. Clark was a Charleston schoolteacher who had been fired for her work with the NAACP. With Horton, she began to develop an educational program for St. John's residents. The first teacher whom Jenkins and Clark hired was Bernice Robinson, Clark's cousin, a former St. John's resident and a beautician. Robinson was chosen precisely because she was not a trained teacher—she would be more likely to experiment, Horton and Clark believed, and to treat her adult students with respect. Like Horton and Clark, Robinson was determined to teach students what they wanted to know. They wanted to make out money orders, to write to their sons in the military, to read their Bibles. Letting people shape the instructional process and anchoring its content in their daily lives sustained their commitment. But students in Robinson's class also read the UN Declaration of Human Rights. They learned by engaging "big ideas," "adult ideas," by seeing themselves as "world citizens and adults."[18]

The program was a success, with most of the first class taking the voting test and the next one doubled in size. As the schools proliferated beyond Highlander's capacity to manage them, the program was transferred to the SCLC. By 1963, twenty-six thousand black residents in twelve Southern states had learned to read well enough to apply to register to vote, and volunteer teachers ran four hundred schools for over sixty-five hundred adults. For Clark, who headed teacher training in the expanded program, the schools' potential reached beyond voter registration. "The basic purpose of the Citizenship Schools is discovering local community leaders," she wrote. "It is my belief that creative leadership is present in any community and only awaits discovery and development." Like Baker, however, Clark found that the SCLC was less than fully committed to that goal. At one point, struck by the number of requests that King received to march in Southern towns, "I sent a letter to Dr. King asking him not to lead all the marches himself, but instead to develop leaders who could lead their own marches. Dr. King read that letter before the staff. It just tickled them; they just laughed." The incident reveals the very different understandings of leadership that coexisted within the movement. Impressed by King's courage and intelligence, the students who formed SNCC and who would put the organization out front in political organizing were nevertheless more influenced by the populist views of Baker, Horton, and Clark.[19]

That influence is evident in SNCC's evolving strategy. In a SNCC workshop in 1963, Horton gave a rich portrait of black communities in the Deep South. Long-standing black organizations like the NAACP, churches, and social fraternities now coexisted with unions, cooperatives, and

Highlander Workshop, Monteagle, Tennessee. Myles Horton is on the far left; Ella Baker is in the center right, without glasses. (Photo courtesy of Wisconsin Historical Society, Braden Collection, negative WHi-36576)

voter-registration organizations. "SNCC's primary purpose is to blend into the community organizations and to organize as many people from each of these organizations as possible," Horton urged. The task was a tricky one: even those few members of the older organizations who were willing to work with SNCC were usually "more influenced by their institutional connections than by the goals and projects of SNCC." The key to organizing in these circumstances was "personal contact" with leaders of the established organizations and a willingness to accommodate "the established mode of thought within the community." Canvassing and mass meetings would turn up people outside existing organizations who had the potential to become leaders in their own right; they should be encouraged and, as soon as possible, made responsible for canvassing in their neighborhoods.[20]

WORKING WITH AND AROUND LOCAL LEADERS

Critical to SNCC's organizing efforts, as their guidelines for new organizers put it, was identifying "people who are looked up to and who are already recognized as leaders ... [who] can bring many of their people along with them." SNCC workers targeted ministers, heads of voters' leagues, people prominent in social clubs, and school principals. Getting traditional leaders involved meant more than gaining their permission to hold a mass meeting in a church or school assembly hall. Organizers pitching voter registration as God's will were desperately handicapped if the local minister was saying otherwise. "If you're ever going to be effective, that's one thing you've got to do—get in the church, get with those people there, the ones in high standing—the deacons, the church officials," Mississippi organizer John Buffington said in 1965. But he went on to describe the authoritarian tone of some clergy. "You're not allowed in the church to question anybody. [The minister might] say, 'Keep still, and I'll fight your battle.' Things like that. It's a hindrance, it's a help. It's...it's really confusing," he concluded.[21]

Strategic movement decisions—whether to hold a march in response to an arrest, how to organize voter canvassing—simply had to be made with local leaders rather than for them. But organizers' field reports also make clear that in many rural communities it was a struggle to get traditional leaders on board the freedom train—even with the support of an E. W. Steptoe or an Amzie Moore. "My immediate opposition comes from the ministers of the local churches who won't consider letting me use their churches for mass meetings," a Batesville, Mississippi, organizer complained. "This is not just one preacher in Batesville—All. This means that I have to conduct my mass meetings in pool rooms, taverns and wherever else I can get an audience." While, in cities, ministers' livelihoods came from their parishioners, in rural areas many were forced to work part-time for whites. The small size of rural communities made clergy, heads of political and social organizations, and other members of the black elite easy targets of white repression, and their geographic isolation distanced them from people in their profession who were more militant. Prepared for this by veteran activists, SNCC workers were nonetheless frustrated by the timidity of those whom they took to calling "leaders" with ironic quotation marks.[22]

Sometimes organizers were able to persuade, cajole, or challenge traditional leaders into a more militant stance. "I frankly don't have too much faith in Mr. Stubbs, and am skeptical about the other prominent people," Charlie Cobb wrote of his first contacts in Leland, Mississippi, "but I have to begin somewhere. Mr. Stubbs may surprise me." The Mr. Stubbses did sometimes surprise SNCC organizers. Other prominent black residents also assisted them anonymously, on occasion so anonymously that organizers did not realize until years later that individuals they had denounced as "Uncle Toms" had, in fact, provided the food or bond money on which they depended. SNCC organizers were also discovering, however, that those most willing to bear the costs of repression for joining the movement—"strong people"—were often not traditional leaders. Hollis Watkins: "We were in a little community trying to find a church to have a mass meeting. And we had talked to all of the quote unquote leaders, ministers, the head people in the church." They were having no luck. "Then we bumped into this little old lady on the porch and we stopped to tell her what we were doing. And she said, 'oh you should have the meeting at my church.' . . . 'Can you do that for us?' 'Oh yes.'" Watkins explains: "We bumped into a strong person. . . . She was just a member. But she was a strong person who was willing to take action. In many cases, without having that kind of understanding, you went and looked for the heads of organizations, the ministers of various churches, who in many cases were the weakest."[23]

Strong people were sometimes sharecroppers and domestic workers, and they were often women, who worked through their everyday networks of kin, congregation, work, and neighborhood to draw people into the struggle. They were poorly schooled, sometimes illiterate. "I think the kind of people we were bringing to register to vote was embarrassing to their Negro Voters' League, which we were supposed to be working with," Charlie Cobb wrote in 1963. When SNCC workers met Fannie Lou Hamer, she was a plantation worker who did not know that blacks had the right to vote. But, as an organizer pointed out, "she knew all the people on the

San Padeo Workshop, 1964. Bob Moses is second from the right and Lawrence Guyot is on the far right. (Photo courtesy of Wisconsin Historical Society, Highlander Folk School Collection, negative WHi-44678)

place and they all respect her and we feel that she will play a big part in getting people from the plantation to register." Hamer would become a key movement activist and cochair of the Mississippi Freedom Democratic Party (MFDP). She was just one of the many ordinary people who were transforming organizers' views of what counted as leadership as much as they were transforming their own.[24]

DECISIONMAKING IN ORGANIZING

Deferring to residents in decisionmaking was a way to prove organizers' trustworthiness and to show that they had no desire to press residents into service on behalf of their personal agendas. SNCC workers discovered that joint decisionmaking was also a way to counter some residents' acute sensitivity about their lack of political sophistication. It helped them define common interests and craft an agenda, identify opportunities and assess costs, and, at the same time, convince them that this was their movement as much as anyone's. "People learned how to stand up and speak," Bob Moses says now. "The meeting itself, or the meetings, became the tools." He continues: "Folks were feeling themselves out, learning how to use words to articulate what they wanted and needed. In these meetings, they were taking the first step toward gaining control over their lives, by making demands on themselves. . . . They were not credentialed people; they did not have high school diplomas for the most part. They were not members of labor unions, or national church associations. Yet through the process, they became leaders."[25]

The sense of ownership that people developed through joint decisionmaking helped them court the risks that participation demanded. Participatory decisionmaking strengthened the movement, but, more than that, it *was* the movement. It tendered new political possibilities, new bases and criteria for leadership, and new mechanisms of participation. "Now nobody sat down and theorized all this," Moses said in 1964. "It's just that you went down there and started to try to do something. You didn't know what there was to do. You started working and you learned what couldn't be done. That helped to define what could be done." The movement organizations that SNCC workers helped build often had formal positions of chair, secretary, and treasurer. Some relied on parliamentary procedure; others tried to dispense with it. But the important thing was that members felt that they were making the decisions that counted. SNCC workers were coming to believe that this was a crucial step in building power. They had not had much luck in registering voters, SNCC's executive committee concluded in late 1963. The climate of repression was just too severe. But "voting has always been in our minds as a vehicle for organizing. . . . We haven't registered people but we have found leadership and have begun to build community organizations."[26]

If that was the optimistic conclusion to be drawn from SNCC's only minimal gains in voter registration, however, the more pessimistic one was that the organization's only hope for breaking Mississippi whites' stranglehold on the state lay in the kind of high-profile and well-coordinated action that would compel federal intervention. SNCC became known to much of the world in 1964 for its role in the Mississippi Summer Project, a campaign that put that hope into action. The project was sponsored by the Council of Federated Organizations, a coalition of the groups working in Mississippi for which SNCC supplied most of the field secretaries. The project brought south almost a thousand young volunteers, mainly white, to work on voter registration and community education. Volunteers also helped organize the MFDP, an alternative to the segregated state Democratic Party. In August, the MFDP demanded recognition at the Democratic Party's national convention. By that time, the Summer Project had hardly been out of the headlines. It began with a crisis right at the beginning of the summer when three project workers were kidnapped and presumed murdered by white segregationists. While the FBI launched a massive search for the three young men, Northern liberals were vocal in supporting both the Summer Project and the MFDP's cause.[27]

In helping organize the MFDP, SNCC workers were also pursuing their commitment to building the leadership of those conventionally dubbed unqualified for political participation. The MFDP was dominated not by traditional black leaders but by sharecroppers, farmers, and domestic workers. And it began to experiment with forms of political association that were familiar neither to white politics nor to black protest. Staughton Lynd, a longtime pacifist who directed the freedom schools, contrasted the typical Southern mass meeting to the MFDP precinct meetings held to elect delegates to the Democratic National Convention. "The [M]FDP precinct meeting appeared to offer a setting in which members of the rank and file could be drawn into the expression of their ideas...in which the distinction between rank and file and leaders could be broken down." Records of precinct meetings show that delegates were nominated by formal parliamentary procedure and were usually approved "by acclamation." That is, when nominees could be found—for all their commitment to the cause, people were understandably worried about making themselves such visible targets for retaliation. But the meeting minutes also show participants sharing their reasons for participating in the struggle, creating a vocabulary of motives for participation in activities whose payoff was by no means clear. Just as important, participants were redefining traditional criteria of leadership. "If he had to, he'd die for his rights," one meeting's minutes paraphrased a Mr. Giles of Indianola. "'I'm here,' he stated, 'because I'm not satisfied—I won't be until I see justice for all.'" That was the best qualification for leadership, he concluded. "Education doesn't mean anything." After a long discussion of candidates and resolutions, the meeting concluded with resounding cheers of "Freedom!"[28]

Over the next months, MFDP branches launched boycotts and cooperatives, organized around welfare benefits, and ran candidates for agricultural stabilization boards as well as for the U.S. Congress. Collective decisionmaking continued to be a critical tool. "The basic tool of political education and decision-making in the [M]FDP at the local level is the workshop," SNCC San Francisco head Mike Miller wrote. "Workshops are designed to do two things: 1) to share information; 2) to open discussion and begin to break through the feeling of being unqualified that still exists among many Negroes in the state. In most places, workshops are now led by members of the FDP." Participants in meetings were encouraged to question what counted as authority, leadership, and especially "qualifications." "Show them that qualification has a different meaning, that you don't have to be a college graduate to be qualified," a Mississippi organizer explained. "Maybe in some cases you don't even have to read and write to be qualified." In a precinct meeting in Oktibbeha County in early 1965, twenty-five people discussed "What is politics? What are political parties?" In McComb, after the MFDP decided to run candidates in an election to replace two selectmen, organizers reported: "We spent about two months talking about this election, running candidates, and issues people felt should be raised in this campaign. A great deal of time was spent discussing 'what does it mean to be qualified?' When we first started discussing this, names mentioned as possible candidates were those of ministers and prominent businessmen. Then people started saying 'but those people don't come to meetings—they don't represent us.'" The candidates that the MFDP ended up running predictably lost: of 3,410 registered voters in McComb, only 200 were black, and many refused to vote for a candidate "who isn't 'qualified,'" organizers reported. "All in all, though, this campaign was very good because a great many people were involved in making decisions that affected their lives."[29]

The notion that the unqualified could take control of their political destinies tendered radical possibilities, ones that would be eagerly appropriated by Northern activists. If ordinary black Mississippians could expose the arbitrary character of the voting rules that kept them oppressed, then presumably students could do the same for curricular standards, poor people for welfare rules, and potential draftees for foreign policy. "What will happen to America if the people who least 'qualify' for leadership begin to demand control over the decisions affecting their lives?" Tom Hayden of Students for a Democratic Society (SDS) wrote in 1965. "What would happen to Congress with all those sharecroppers in it? What would happen to bureaucracies if they had to be understood by the people they are supposed to serve? . . . These questions are among the most upsetting ones that this country can be asked to face, because probably the most thoroughly embedded, if subtle, quality of American life is its elitism—economic, political, social, and psychological." By 1965, SDS activists had been talking about people "making the decisions that affect their lives" for some time; three years earlier they had coined the term "participatory democracy." But what they saw of and heard about the Mississippi movement infused their understandings and practice of participatory democracy with a powerful populist impulse and with the conviction that differences of skills and status were no barrier to egalitarian decisionmaking.[30]

Yet another set of long-term political possibilities animated Mississippi activists' distinctive approach to deliberations. Collective decisionmaking would help develop the mechanisms of political accountability that would keep future black leaders directly responsible to their constituents. These were Horton and Baker's long-standing concerns. SNCC staffer Casey Hayden recalls, "Ella's notion of raising up new leadership came directly from her experience of organizing blacks in a segregated system. In such a system, as soon as you had a leader, the leader was co-opted by the whites, unavoidably. The leaders' power came from whites rather than their constituents, and they retained power by delivering those constituents. So you had to keep creating new leaders who were responsible to their base." A movement politics that developed leaders—many leaders—was the way to prevent the co-optation to which all movements were vulnerable. By actively remaking criteria and conventions of representation, participatory practices would ensure that a future black politics remained truly collective, responsive to its most disenfranchised participants.[31]

Bob Moses later reflected on what might have developed in Mississippi. "If we had thought of the [M]FDP as a political party ... training, say, thousands of people, black people, to take elected offices," it could have provided political education for grassroots politicians. "We don't have any mechanism in the country for doing that. I mean if you think about it, in this country there's no mechanism for educating people who go into office. I mean the Kennedy School [of Government at Harvard] is the first step in that direction, and it's a drop in the bucket, and geared to the elite." Some MFDP projects were beginning to develop along those lines. Yet, within a year of its challenge to the National Democratic Party, the MFDP had become the prize in a battle between militants and moderates, and Bob Moses, along with many of SNCC's Mississippi staff, had left the state. I trace those developments in the next chapter.[32]

DEVELOPMENTAL DEMOCRACY

What I have described can be characterized as a developmental rationale for participatory decisionmaking. Involving novices in decisionmaking and sharing leadership tasks helped nurture movement leaders. From veteran activists like Ella Baker and Myles Horton, SNCC workers learned an organizing strategy that emphasized indigenous local leadership. Firm in their dislike of utopian communities, Baker and Horton also saw group decisionmaking as prime ground for radical education. Continuing in that tradition, SNCC workers treated decentralized and participatory practices not as at odds with effective political action but as essential preparation for it.[33]

As I noted in chapter 1, some analysts have recognized participatory democracy's capacity to nurture activists' solidarity and commitment and to contribute to later rounds of activism. The difference here is that the emphasis is on political engagement now. One can also contrast this developmental rationale for participatory democratic decisionmaking with the prefigurative commitment that commentators have attributed to SNCC and the new left. Where a prefigurative commitment envisions change through personal self-transformation and moral suasion rather than through institutional political change, a developmental commitment is not in conflict with an explicitly political one. To the contrary, its very purpose is to produce activists and organizations capable of taking on powerful officials and agencies. From early on, Horton said, he had been "more concerned with structural changes than I have with changing the hearts of people." A prefigurative commitment tends toward absolutism since the object is both to "oppose" a current regime and to be truly "opposite"; a developmental commitment tends more toward an acceptance of the conventional. The two projects have very different views of organization. A prefigurative project is suspicious of organization, concerned that it molds people in its own image, valorizing efficiency and conformity over the purposes for which the organization was created, raising means to the level of ends. Enacting the ends *in* the means, committing to the "here-and-now revolution," favoring community over organization—all these counter the oligarchical tendencies of organizations. By contrast, the broader organizing strategy of which a developmental project is a part sees organizations as one of the key arenas for developing political efficacy, leadership, and accountability and, not least, for securing power. An organization is doomed to failure unless people have a stake in its preservation, however. Participation in decisionmaking provides the sense of ownership and the pleasures of learning that sustain people's participation.[34]

The relationship underpinning a developmental democratic project is a pedagogical one. People learn to articulate concerns and evaluate options by doing so. At the same time, they learn from each other, and they may also learn from a facilitator or teacher, someone who encourages, guides, questions, and challenges them. This accounts for the *guided* character of participatory democratic decisionmaking. Of course, there is much more to the organizer's role than tutelage. Organizers also publicize, research, chauffeur, and coordinate—but developing leadership is one of their most important tasks. This raises an important question, however. Can one even talk of real participatory democracy in an organization when members relate to each other as teacher and student? Even if the teacher is eager to see the student excel, she influences what information the student has access to, what opinions he can freely express, and how he shall be judged. If student and teacher make a decision together, the student is vulnerable to subtle pressure on the part of the teacher to follow her preferences.

However, a pedagogical relationship—especially one between adults—rests on certain assumptions that minimize the disparities in authority: that the student has expertise and authority in areas outside the curriculum; that the relationship should move toward one of fuller equality as the student gains the knowledge and skills that the teacher has; and that the teacher's status is based on how well the student performs. In other words, the inequality in the relationship is domain specific, limited in duration, and mitigated by the parties' mutual dependence. In an organizing context, the teacher-student relationship is further equalized. In SNCC, organizers themselves depended on the tutelage of longtime activists like Amzie Moore, Aaron Henry, and Ella Baker. They depended also on residents' cooperation, on their food, shelter, and, often, physical protection, and on their willingness to take even greater risks than the organizers themselves were. Organizers knew, moreover, that, if they were expert in matters tested by voting registrars, the people with whom they worked knew the layout of their communities, the habits of their neighbors, and the ways of white folks better than outside organizers ever could. So the tutelary relationship was close to an equal or mutual one. More generally, one can see the inequalities in a tutelary relationship mitigated by a commitment on the part of those more skilled in some areas to validating the experiential knowledge of others, to making transparent the components of their own skills, and to ceding as much power as possible.[35]

This is not to say that such a relationship, and a developmental project of democracy more broadly, is not without intrinsic problems. Authority in one area does threaten to spill into other areas. SNCC workers often struggled mightily to avoid being deferred to as leaders. For all Bob Moses's efforts to transfer power to adult Mississippians and young SNCC workers, he was increasingly made into a figure of veneration. Taking a backseat role in discussions did not diminish his charismatic authority. In organizing generally, what makes the issue complicated is that organizers' charisma, skills, and status are in some ways useful to them. In explaining later why he and Septima Clark had chosen Bernice Robinson to teach in the St. Johns citizenship school, Myles Horton noted that, as well as being known and trusted by island residents and not being a professional teacher, she had been a beautician. "A black beautician, unlike a white beautician, was at that time a person of some status in the community. They were entrepreneurs, they were small businesswomen, you know, respected, they were usually better educated than other people, and most of all they were independent." Robinson's status gained her respect; the fact that she was black and a former resident gained her trust. Horton and Clark were clear that whites simply could not secure that trust. But this raises tricky questions. When is some difference too much difference? When does respect cede to intimidation? What is the line between influence and manipulation?[36]

The literature on organizing is rife with injunctions against leading: organizers should rather help residents articulate their own agendas and build their leadership. Yet, in the process, organizers are often expected to help identify goals, push people to question their preferences, and rally them to act. How can they do that without thereby undermining the leadership capacities of those whom they are organizing? Myles Horton's answer was to ask questions. "I use questions more than I do anything else. They don't think of a question as intervening because they don't realize that the reason you asked that question is because you know something. . . . Instead of you getting on a pinnacle you put them on a pinnacle." Horton described a Highlander director in a workshop who "asks one question, and that one question turned that workshop around and completely moved it in a different direction." Was the Highlander workshop leader leading? Should one ask questions that open the whole enterprise up for scrutiny? That purposely move a discussion in a new direction? In SNCC, asking questions later became a way for organizers to hold onto their radicalism without feeling that they were imposing it on the people whom they organized. The tactic ended up alienating people more than involving them. What comes across in the stories that Horton tells, in SNCC workers' tales of the best organizers, and in the broader literature on organizing is good organizers' creativity: their ability to respond to local conditions, to capitalize on sudden opportunities, to turn to advantage a seeming setback, to know when to exploit teachable moments and when to concentrate on winning an immediate objective. Sometimes you insist on fully participatory decisionmaking; sometimes you do not. Albany SNCC project head Charles Sherrod urged fellow organizers not to "let the project go to the dogs because you feel you must be democratic to the letter." Horton recounted on numerous occasions an experience that he had had in a union organizing effort. At the time, the highway patrol was escorting scabs through the picket line, and the strike committee was at its wit's end about how to counter this threat to strikers' solidarity. After considering and rejecting numerous proposals, exhausted committee members demanded advice from Horton. When he refused, one of them pulled a gun. "I was tempted then to become an instant expert, right on the spot!" Horton confessed. "But I knew that if I did that, all would be lost and then all the rest of them would start asking me what to do. So I said: 'No. Go ahead and shoot if you want to, but I'm not going to tell you.' And the others calmed him down."[37]

Giving in would have defeated the purpose of persuading the strikers that they had the knowledge to make the decision themselves. But Horton sometimes told another story. When he was once asked to speak to a group of Tennessee farmers about organizing a cooperative, he knew, he said, that since "their expectation was that I would speak as an expert...if I didn't speak, and said, 'let's have a discussion about this,' they'd say, that guy doesn't know anything." So Horton "made a speech, the best speech I could. Then after it was over, while we were still there, I said, let's discuss this speech. Let's discuss what I have said. Well now, that was just one step removed, but close enough to their expectation that I was able to carry them along.... You do have to make concessions like that." What better time to make a concession than when you're looking down the barrel of a gun? Horton presumably knew that he could get away with refusing to be an expert in the first situation and not in the second. Perhaps the difference was that he was unknown to the farmers and was known to the strikers. But one could argue that a relationship with a history could tolerate aberrant exercises of leadership while first impressions die harder. In other words, extracting rules from the stories that Horton tells is difficult. When to lead and when to defer, when to ask leading questions and when to remain silent, when to focus on the limited objective and when to encourage people to see the circumscribed character of that objective—the answers depend on the situation and are not always readily evident.[38]

Another source of tension concerns what happens when local people *do* become leaders. Why should we think that once people develop the competencies to judge political opportunities they will evaluate them in the same way? Actually, the problem is there from the beginning. No group of people is ever truly unified; there are always divisions of aspirations and interests. To whom should the organizer defer? To what extent is her task to work with existing leaders and to what extent to support those who are challenging the established leadership? And how does one choose without a clear sense of the best course for a community? With respect to a developmental project of democracy, the question is who should be included in decisionmaking and who can be excluded from it.[39]

These difficulties are intrinsic to a tutelary relationship and are common in a participatory democracy modeled on such a relationship. In other words, the participatory democratic dilemma lays not in the very idea of egalitarian decisionmaking but in the relationships that have supplied such decisionmaking its deliberative norms. As I showed in chapter 2 and will again in chapter 7, when participatory democrats have been joined mainly by their common religious commitment, the authority that they give those with access to God's will, whether clergy or members acting

Student Nonviolent Coordinating Committee staff, Atlanta office, 1963. *From left*: Mike Sayer, MacArthur Cotton, James Forman, two unidentified men, Marion Barry, Lester MacKinney, Mike Thelwell, Lawrence Guyot, Judy Richardson, unidentified man, John Lewis, Jean Wheeler, and Julian Bond. (Photo by Danny Lyon, *Memories of the Southern Civil Rights Movements* [Chapel Hill: University of North Carolina Press, 1992]/Magnum Photos; used with permission)

on their personal conscience, has made it difficult for them to challenge individuals claiming such access. When participatory democrats have been joined mainly by friendship, as I will show in chapters 5 and 6, the chief source of conflict has been between those in the group who are friends and those who are not. The latter have been likely to feel excluded from and distrustful of what they see as a powerful friendship clique. In each case, to respond to the conflict requires drawing norms from outside the framework on which the group's relations have been based. Thus, for example, just extending friendship to newcomers in the group would likely not work since it would risk denuding friendship of its intimacy. Friendship, by definition, is exclusive, just as religious fellowship, by definition, privileges religious conviction over the demands of the group. When participatory democrats are joined primarily by relations of tutelage, the potential for conflict lies in the question of how much tutelage is necessary for people to gain access to, and act on, their interests. Conflicts around the question may be between organizer and residents, among organizers, or among residents. Such conflicts stem less from people's different interests than from their different opinions about what people's interests are. What makes them so difficult to resolve is that tutelary relations provide no means for evaluating the ends to which education is directed.

DECISIONMAKING IN THE BAND OF BROTHERS

By 1962, SNCC had become a staff-led cadre organization. Although it was still formally governed by a coordinating committee of campus representatives, in practice decisions were made by staff, by an executive committee composed of staff, campus representatives, and older advisers, and by local and state project directors. Records of discussions show that Robert's Rules were sometimes used and adopted formally in the spring of 1964: "It was the consensus that parliamentary procedure should be followed in future meetings." But SNCC workers continued to try to secure consensus. "The dangers that we all faced were too great to risk the possibility of someone not implementing a decision made by the group because he personally disagreed with it," Executive Secretary James Forman explained later. "We had to talk things out until we all agreed on all decisions." Forman confessed that when he first encountered it he found SNCC's decisionmaking disconcerting: "There seemed to be no order to the discussion—no going from this point to the next point on to the next one—but instead a constant introduction of new matters for discussion, forgetting what the other speakers had said." Only later did he realize that the style reflected organizers' need to talk through the dangers and fears that they faced. "Through this process the individual no doubt was reinforced by the group and was thus able to sustain himself for a while in his hazardous work."[40]

"People were making a decision about how they were going to use their lives," staffer Muriel Tillinghast observes. "And that's not something that you could vote on. That was something that everybody was going to have to grope for." Group decisionmaking gave staffers a stake in the organization for which they were daily putting their bodies on the line. SNCC meetings went on for days sometimes, yet people went to great lengths not to miss them. Meetings, of course, serve functions other than making decisions. In a Durkheimian sense, they are the collective rituals that re-create group solidarity. SNCC meetings included freedom songs, long testimonials about the group's purpose, and epic-comic stories in which narrators mocked their own fears in organizing. Whereas in the field, organizers tried to downplay their own opinions, to listen more than speak, in staff meetings they could voice their anxieties and complaints, could themselves take center stage.[41]

There was another rationale for collectivist decisionmaking. Most project staff were young and inexperienced. SNCC workers knew that they were training activists on staff as much as they were training residents. Hollis Watkins was a recent high school graduate when he joined SNCC. "To me," he later recalled, "understanding was the most important part. Through the participatory process, all of the things that we were dealing with would be brought out, explained, and talked about." Unanimity was often reached by collectively deferring to the judgment of the organizer most involved in the question. "A basic principal in decisionmaking is that people who do the work make the decisions," staffers at a 1964 meeting affirmed. Then why even deliberate? It was a way of trading information, solving problems, and highlighting issues that might come up elsewhere. "There were many cases where we would be discussing issues in reference to Mississippi in the SNCC staff meetings, where you got people from all of the different states trying to resolve how we're going to deal with this [issue]," Watkins remembers. "And there would be some times when we wouldn't resolve that, and we would simply say, now that we all understand what's involved, who's involved, the implications of all this, and since we can't come to any general agreement, we who will be most directly involved will make that decision. And the same kind of thing would take place, for example, if we're having a statewide meeting." Staffer Casey Hayden describes discussions going on "until some level of understanding was reached, at which point we could act. Once this broad consensus was reached, I didn't argue with people about what they should do. There was more than enough to do, and plenty of room for experimentation."[42]

Records of a SNCC meeting held in June 1964 corroborate these recollections. The issue was a thorny one: the group's position on nonviolence. Staffers had long debated whether nonviolence should be embraced as a philosophy or as a tactic and what their stance should be toward the many local people they worked with who carried guns. Now, on the eve of the Summer Project and the arrival of hundreds of volunteers, the issue came up again. "Whites in the state are organizing," Charlie Cobb opened the discussion. "Violence would be aimed at Negro staff people, i.e. Greenwood staff." The Greenwood project had been given two guns, and they were keeping them, Cobb declared. "Local people say the white man thinks it's war; [they] will defend [their] homes," Willie Peacock pointed out. He had been shot at in front of the SNCC office, and witnesses had described the getaway car to the FBI. Yet "they haven't found them yet; they're not going to find them." The man who had killed Medgar Evers—Jackson's intrepid NAACP head—was out of jail, Peacock continued. "Whites more convinced than ever before that they can kill a Negro and get away with it."[43]

There had always been a "gen[era]l agreement that people would defend homes," Hollis Watkins put in. "Seems that things have changed now." But Frank Smith took a different angle, "You should decide, if you go to Miss[issippi], to get ass whipped, go to jail, get shot.... You'll be functionally useless if can't decide this. If [we] get hung up with personal safety, we're not going to get anything done." Courtland Cox agreed: "To extent we think about self-defense of ourselves, to that extent we are immobilized." Cobb put his concern bluntly: "If he's in house when locals defend house," would SNCC back him up if he were arrested? "No one can be rational about facing death," Prathia Hall observed. "What is hap[pening] now is that for 1st time we are coming to grips with fact." It was a "question of constituency," Mike Sayer suggested. "If you're working with people who believe in defending honor, how to gear program to that. Not necessarily true that nonviolence breeds white violence. Can't assume what response will be to self-defense." But longtime Mississippi organizer Charles McLaurin was irritated. Everyone was talking about the need for black people to remain nonviolent. Why was no one proposing "to hold up nonviolent banner before whites?" The minutes of the meeting read that his comment met with "applause—Cobb, Greenwood staff."

"Think best to discuss controllable things," Bob Moses argued. They would keep up pressure on the FBI to investigate assaults. And he did not "know of anyone in this org[anization] who preached to local N[egro] that he shouldn't defend himself. Closest is when I asked [the local activist E. W.] Steptoe not to carry gun when we go out together at night. And so he hides it and I find out later. So deep[ly] engrained in rural southern America that we can't possibly affect that at all. Not contradictory for farmer to say he is nonv[iolent] and promise to shoot marauder's head off. Diff[erence] is we on staff have committed ourselves not to carry guns." Moses was becoming angry at the Greenwood staff's hard line: "Did Greenwood office think it was worthy of talking about[, or was it] something unilateral [that they had decided]? Maybe if [they] did, [they had to make] a choice between whether [to] stay with group or leave group."

"We all know we can leave SNCC," John Love responded. The more important point was to come up with a "gen[era]l rule this summer." "I'm not going to carry a gun," Sam Block asserted. "But if [local people are] going to protect them[selves], let them protect me." Cobb posed another hypothetical situation. "Where does SNCC stand when Mr. S. is killed when defending his home, rifle lying on floor, 2 daughters there, where does SNCC stand when I pick up the gun as I will, [and then] police arrest me?" Ella Baker could not "conceive of SNCC [that] I thought [I] was associated with not defending Cobb." She continued: "What are the bases on which it is now necessary to raise this question? In my book, Cobb would not be operating outside SNCC if he did what he said." "Lot has to be determined by person in situation and own confidence in nonviolence," Forman observed. Mike Sayer wanted something firmer, a "stance that we will stand completely behind any SNCC who defends his life; that Cobb has a right to carry weapon. Can say people in SNCC have individual right to carry weapon [without] saying [that] carrying arms is programmatic solution." Cobb demurred: "I won't carry a gun but I foresee situation like being in house or farmer's truck when faced with decision. What makes this different is man's daughter. If I were alone, I'd head out back door. Question is purely protection." Matthew Jones: "If I picked up the gun that would be the day I'd be leaving SNCC. I'm in SNCC bec[ause] I believe in non[violence]." Personally, Lawrence Guyot said, "if I decide to take up arms, I'll leave Miss[issippi]." But "the only reason I ask others to work in v[oter] r[egistration without] arms is because there's protection in it. They'll shoot quicker at us if we're armed." At this point, Cox put "up for consensus: No guns permitted in F[reedom] Houses or offices; no one on staff to carry guns or weapons." Robert Weil added: "Policy for volunteers in summer project: those who carry weapons to be asked to leave." Staffers agreed. One version of the handwritten minutes records a final caveat: "Discussion shall be left open for discussion of specific"—"specific situations," one presumes.

The impression one gets from the discussion is by no means that Guyot's argument—the last one made—was trumping. Nor is it that everyone had agreed on a single encompassing position on nonviolence. Rather, SNCC workers had had an opportunity to flesh out a series of arguments for and against nonviolence, to clarify their own positions on the issue, and to identify a range of individual stances that were consistent with the group decision. They had also gained group recognition for the incredible obstacles they faced and reinforced their willingness to stand up for each other. What was the upshot of the decision? Throughout the summer, SNCC staffers and volunteers were subjected to threats, arrests, beatings, and bombings. There were no incidents of organizers retaliating against whites or of using firearms to defend themselves. Nor were there any conflicts with locals around their use of guns for self-protection.

When it worked, SNCC workers' internal deliberative style maximized what I have described as participatory democracy's developmental, innovatory, and solidary benefits. What made it work? The Nashville sit-inners trained by James Lawson, recall, had learned not only techniques of nonviolent direct action but also consensus-based decisionmaking and a habit of collective planning and reflection. They brought that to SNCC. From Ella Baker, too, SNCC workers learned to listen to each other and to solicit the views of the diffident among them. Their respect for the demands of organizing made for flexibility and pragmatism, they say now. Staffer Judy Richardson remembers feeling intimidated in some meetings by especially articulate Howard students. "But when we got out of that room and went back to the field, we're going back to communities who don't care about Kant; they don't care about Marxism; they just care about whether we're going to organize them and gonna be there with them." Staff meetings were typically structured around group reports on projects, a format that encouraged group problem solving.[44]

SNCC's deliberative style and the behavioral expectations that under-pinned it had additional sources. The culture of the black church perme-ated SNCC workers' interactions, a source both of insight and of solidarity. Observers of SNCC meetings were struck by the fluidity with which they moved from a sophisticated discussion of voting litigation, to a participant's wrenching description of what it meant to face one's own death, to group singing, hands clasped and eyes closed. SNCC workers' deliberations were also shaped by tutelary relationships. James Forman and Bob Moses, older than many SNCC workers, responsible for the organization's relations with outsiders, and skilled in defining long-term strategy, had disproportionate authority in the group. Yet, by all accounts, both men were careful to combine unilateral exercises of power with efforts to involve others in the process. Moses was famous for sitting silently in the back of a meeting to avoid influencing the flow of discussion. Forman, who was always more comfortable with directive leadership than Moses was, nevertheless often sent less experienced staffers to high-level meetings for a crash course in political negotiation. "This is Forman's theory," staffer John O'Neal explains. "'We're all leaders ... you're developing leadership, brother.'" "Forman always wanted to know, What do you think about this? What do you think?" Atlanta staffer Betty Garman Robinson recalls. "So that was a mode that you just operated on."[45]

Beyond a common commitment to securing black people the right to vote, SNCC workers held diverse political views. But they were friends, and that also facilitated their deliberations. Most SNCC workers knew only one or two other staffers when they were hired or volunteered. But the total commitment required of them and the political isolation in which they worked created deep bonds of mutual trust and affection. "When we gathered for staff meetings," staffer Mary King wrote years later, "we always greeted one another with emphatic rocking embraces, wrapping our arms around each other in bear hugs." As friends, SNCC workers knew each other's priorities and preferences and had a stake in each other's concerns. Their mutual respect led them to defer to each other's expertise. When someone made a unilateral decision, his or her friends were likely to interpret it as a function of the issue's complexity or trivial character rather than as an illegitimate exercise of power. "A band of brothers, standing in a circle of trust"—this self-description captured even better the intensity of SNCC workers' bonds and the life-and-death necessity of mutual trust. It also expressed their sense that what they were creating was both powerful and powerfully *new*. "We thought we were something special," Casey Hayden says now. "Some of us had nonviolent ideas around that, some had ethnic ideas around that, some had Marxist ideas. But the trust and community were core for everyone." Martha Prescod Norman, the SNCC activist quoted at the beginning of this chapter as saying that SNCC workers never talked about the beloved community, added, "There's this active support of each other, I think, and solicitation, of thinking through, that made it politically like a beloved community."[46]

If SNCC's workers' bonds of friendship and their respect for each other as organizers transcended ideological differences, what of racial ones? Whites were members of SNCC's Coordinating Committee from the beginning, and the group's first administrative secretary, Jane Stembridge, was white. Bob Zellner was hired by the Southern Conference Educational Fund in 1961 to do organizing work on white campuses but soon joined black SNCC demonstrators in McComb. After that, white students came to work for SNCC by way of the YWCA, the National Student Association, and Northern campus support groups. Still, SNCC was seen by those drawn to it, black and white, as a black group. White SNCC staffers seemed to have had a complex understanding of their role. Feeling a full and equal participant in the organization did not mean to white SNCC workers that their organizational roles and prerogatives should be identical to those of black workers. "I didn't particularly crave to be the project director," says Penny Patch, who worked in southwest Georgia and then Mississippi. "It's a huge responsibility. And I didn't really think it was my place." Both because of the danger that they posed black residents and because of their intuition that it should remain a black movement, many early white staffers felt that their roles should be supportive ones. Of course, early white SNCC staffers were also young and often inexperienced; they floundered on the terrain of race relations as much as they navigated it. "I was terribly naive and ignorant," says Patch. Dorothy Miller Zellner, who was recruited by Forman to work in the Atlanta office, says that she was seen as that "bossy white woman" and recognizes in retrospect that she *was* bossy. My point is not that white activists in SNCC's early days were more sensitive than those who came to the organization later. Rather, it is that equality in movement membership was defined differently than it would be later, defined in ways that tolerated more variation in roles.[47]

If SNCC workers' deliberative interactions were modeled on a combination of friendship and tutelage, this also points to likely areas of conflict in their practice of participatory democracy. In fact, as I will show in the next chapter, the intensity of staffers' friendships made it easy for disagreement to be experienced as betrayal and easy to fight over things like decisionmaking rather than say or hear things that friends would find hurtful. It also made it difficult to integrate newcomers into the group. With respect to tutelage as a basis for participatory democracy, SNCC workers were increasingly sensitive to the tensions inherent in that model. Firmly renouncing any desire to impose their visions on the people with whom they worked, they were just as anxious to avoid manipulation within their own ranks. Activists' uncertainty about where to go next was translated into battles over what people's real aspirations were. I turn to these developments in the next chapter.

CONCLUSION

Forty years after the Highlander Folk School's founding, Myles Horton reflected on its ability to avoid debilitating friction: "Struggling with the real problems growing out of conflict situations and our participation in community life kept the school from becoming a detached colony." Similarly, in 1964, Bob Moses contrasted SNCC organizers with the beatniks whose rejection of social convention had gained them critics and admirers. Whereas the latter were "closed in on themselves," "what happens with students in our movement is that they are identifying with these people— people who come off the land—they're unsophisticated, and they simply voice, time and time again, the simple truths you can't ignore because they speak from their own lives. . . . As long as the students are tied in with these, their revolt is well-based. Not like the Beatnik revolt."[48]

SNCC workers' approach to decisionmaking cannot be understood outside the organizing context within which it was developed. In this chapter, I have shown how SNCC workers built on techniques they learned from Ella Baker and from people associated with Highlander. Movement decisionmaking was a key venue for training people how to confront authorities, define movement agendas, negotiate alliances, and recognize the interests on behalf of which people would be willing to stake their lives. Especially for people with little experience in political organizations and sensitive about their lack of qualifications, SNCC workers found that participatory decisionmaking was a way to develop political capacities.

Far from its image as unwieldy, if principled, participatory decisionmaking may be eminently practical in social movements for several reasons. First, since the rules of the game in political contention are often fuzzy—options are unclear, costs and benefits unknown, and criteria for evaluation ambiguous—wide participation helps decisionmakers gather and evaluate information. It provides political novices skills in negotiating common agendas and engaging with political authorities. In conditions of uncertainty, then, participatory deliberation serves a valuable informational and pedagogical function. But the developmental functions of participatory decisionmaking go beyond education narrowly conceived. Since people's preferences are not fixed, participatory deliberation helps clarify and shape them. This is especially the case in social movements, where breaking with the conventions of routine politics unsettles one's preexisting preferences: how does one weigh a preference for safety against a preference for freedom? In conditions like these, participatory deliberation helps clarify, modify, and supplement preferences. Third, collective decisionmaking often aims not to secure agreement on a particular action but to specify a range of positions that individuals can take with regard to that action. This is especially important in social movements because people who feel marginalized may not stay and because visible unity helps legitimate the movement's claims to authorities, third parties, and potential supporters. Finally, participatory deliberation can foster conventions of scrutiny and challenge that endure past the movement phase of contention to battles waged in electoral institutions. In the mid-1960s, with black electoral power in the South still an elusive dream, SNCC organizers could only begin to outline such a possibility. By the time black candidates began to win offices, SNCC had repudiated electoral politics altogether. But recovering a vision of electoral officials made accountable to the less powerful among their constituents through something like permanent movement organizations is important simply because it has figured so rarely in assessments of participatory democracy.

Recuperating the organizing strategy of which SNCC's participatory democratic decisionmaking was a part also points to sources of tension, however. If participatory democracy is intended to train leaders, one can imagine that, when the *ends* of action become either contentious or unclear, tutelary relations supply no way of adjudicating among them. In SNCC's case, as I will show in the next chapter, such tensions were exacerbated by complex and often unspoken but nonetheless influential racial dynamics.

That that was the case is hardly surprising. Indeed, that the group managed alternately to confront, ignore, turn into a source of insight, and sometimes transcend racial divisions is more worthy of note. Nor should it be surprising that activists' assessments of organizational forms and deliberative styles were also shaped by racial associations, given the ways in which race is, like gender and class, subtly worked into most institutions and practices. Yet the topic remains largely unexamined, both by historians of the movement and by analysts of participatory democracy. I turn to it now.

4

LETTING WHICH PEOPLE DECIDE WHAT?
SNCC'S CRISIS OF DEMOCRACY, 1964–65

In the fall of 1964, fresh from its success in coordinating the high-profile Mississippi Summer Project, with financial contributions surging, a staff doubled in size since the previous year, and its place among the "Big Five" civil rights organizations secure, the Student Nonviolent Coordinating Committee (SNCC) seemed well positioned to build on its record of political organizing. Instead, the group plunged into months of rancorous disputes about the correct procedures and prerogatives of decisionmaking. Some saw the battle as one between Forman and Moses, others as one between two philosophies of organization. Defenders of centralized organization and top-down control—"hardliners"—called SNCC's participatory democrats "freedom high." They charged them with overintellectualizing instead of organizing, leaving hard-won bases to "float" around the country on a whim, pushing to excess an antipathy to organization and regimentation, and squandering resources as they pursued their own liberation. The hardliners won the battle in the spring of 1965 and began to replace SNCC's decentralized and consensus-based structure with a more centralized administration and majority voting. But the debates had taken their toll. By the fall of 1965, SNCC's Mississippi staff had shrunk by two-thirds, and SNCC had forgone its place on the cutting edge of the state's black politics.

On first reading, SNCC's saga seems to be just what theorists of participatory democracy worry about. A commitment to democracy become absolutism, a belief in the dictates of individual conscience become self-indulgence, consensus made impossible by disagreements that are only deepened through their endless discussion. And, indeed, SNCC's battle over decisionmaking has been rehearsed in numerous chronicles of the 1960s. Analysts have tended to see it as reflecting the opposition between utopian and pragmatic orientations that had been there from SNCC's beginning. Participatory democracy was too unwieldy for a group grown in size and pressed to respond quickly to new national opportunities, they have argued. SNCC workers who resisted the trend to tighter structure were closer to the group's earlier utopian aspirations but were simply out of touch with the demands of organizational effectiveness. On a different but complementary explanation for the group's organizational crisis, some SNCC workers' continued belief in the power of moral witness put them at odds with the group's new Black Power agenda. After years of brutal repression and a practically nonexistent federal response, SNCC workers after 1964 were more intent on gaining power than on appealing to a liberal establishment now perceived as corrupt. Both developments—a Black Power ideology and the new size and stature of the group—exerted strong pressures for a centralized and hierarchical organization. On these scenarios, freedom highs were powerless before the demands of environmental adaptation and ideological consistency.[1]

However, closer examination of what SNCC workers were actually talking and arguing about during this period casts doubt on both scenarios. SNCC did indeed expand during and after the summer of 1964, although not as much or as haphazardly as most accounts have suggested. SNCC staffers did wrestle with the dilemmas of size. But the staff had nearly doubled between 1962 and 1963 (from 40 to 70) and again by early 1964 (to 130), without suffering debilitating consequences. Moreover, in the fall of 1964, deliberative practices came under attack on local projects as well as in state- and regionwide staff meetings, projects whose members rarely exceeded a dozen. Characterizing proponents of decentralized and nonhierarchical structure—"loose structure"—as insisting on principle over pragmatism misses the fact that, in the fall of 1964, their arguments were primarily instrumental ones. As I showed in the last chapter, organizers viewed participatory decisionmaking as essential to their work. Tight structure would jeopardize the flexibility essential to effective organizing, they believed. By the spring of 1965, a preference for loose structure *would* be seen by many in the organization as impractical, as ideological, and, not coincidentally, as white, but, in the fall, that was not yet the case. The argument that a Black Power agenda mandated a more centralized and hierarchical structure misses the fact that SNCC workers adopted such a structure *before* they embraced a Black Power agenda.[2]

Why did a deliberative form that earlier had been extraordinarily effective come to be seen as the height of inefficiency? The story that I tell in this chapter is a complicated one, with ambiguous positions and surprising reversals. One way to summarize it is to say that SNCC workers came up against the limits of tutelage and friendship as bases for participatory democratic decisionmaking. SNCC workers had for some time relied on collectivist decisionmaking to build residents' capacities for political leadership. Tutelary norms were combined with the deference appropriate on the part of young people toward their elders. But the notion of teaching democratic leadership came with problems. How much teaching should organizers do? How far should they press the questioning that might lead residents to identify new interests? What was the line between organizing and leading? Such questions could divide residents against organizers, but they could also divide the organizers themselves as they debated what people's real interests were. This was the case in the fall of 1964. In desperate need of a program capable of sustaining the energies of weary organizers and residents, SNCC workers were also determined not to reproduce the manipulation that they had experienced in their dealings with the federal government and mainstream movement leaders. They insisted ever more strongly that "the people" should chart their own course, but they worried that local residents would be taken in by merely symbolic gains. Unclear about what the alternative course was, they attacked each other for trying to manipulate residents into supporting their personal agendas. The wrangling reflected the group's programmatic uncertainty more than it caused it. But, increasingly, participatory democracy was held responsible for the group's programmatic morass.

Participatory democracy was also held responsible for the erosion of the tight-knit bonds that had joined SNCC workers. Again, the connection was not straightforward. As black staffers struggled to find a way to give voice to new feelings of racial identity, they grew frustrated with a deliberative style on which whites seemed to be insisting as a way to hang onto their positions in the organization. Participatory democracy came to be seen *as* white, and, in contrast, a centralized and top-down organizational structure came to symbolize not only programmatic certainty but also a black orientation. I say *symbolize* because the connections between organizational structures, on the one hand, and programmatic purpose and the role of whites, on the other, were not explicitly drawn. Implementing centralized and hierarchical decisionmaking reflected a hope for programmatic direction and an inchoate antipathy to whites rather than an explicit claim that tight structure would supply compelling programs or curb the role of whites.

The real liability of such associations, however, was their effect on SNCC workers' deliberations after the debates were over. Once top-down organizational structure was associated with programmatic clarity, it was easy to substitute organizational reform for the more difficult task of thrashing out programs. And, once time-consuming and agonizing debates about the appropriate relationship between organizer and organized were labeled ideological, impractical, and white, it made sense to stop having

Voter registration meeting, Mississippi, summer 1964. (Photo by Herbert Randall, used with permission, and by courtesy of McCain Library and Archives, Hattiesburg, Miss.)

them. The racial bonds that joined organizers and residents would make it unnecessary for organizers to second-guess their own purposes. But that stance had costs. Under the mantle of radicalism, it tended to a more traditional conception of leadership, in which a single leader could speak on behalf of an allegedly unitary constituency.[3]

AFTER ATLANTIC CITY, FALL 1964

In August 1964, Council of Federated Organizations (COFO) workers accompanied sixty-eight Mississippi Freedom Democratic Party (MFDP) delegates to the Democratic National Convention in Atlantic City. Barred from regular party meetings in the state, the MFDP had held open precinct and county meetings and a state convention to elect convention delegates. They were the legitimate state representatives, they maintained, and they called on the National Democratic Party to unseat the all-white Mississippi regulars. In Atlantic City, MFDP delegates and their young allies alternated silent protests on the boardwalk with behind-the-scenes efforts to gain the support of convention delegates. It was clear that they would not secure a majority vote of the Party Credentials Committee, the organizers of the Challenge recognized, but they anticipated enough votes to be able to bring the issue to the convention floor, where they already had pledges of support from state delegations. Represented by the labor attorney Joe Rauh, they were pushing for a compromise that would seat both delegations.[4]

Presidential-nominee-to-be Lyndon Johnson had other ideas. Fearing a white Southern walkout, and determined that his nomination proceed without any embarrassing dissension, he ordered that the Challenge be quashed. The FBI set up wiretaps in SNCC and CORE headquarters and in Martin Luther King Jr.'s hotel room in order to keep Johnson apprised of the MFDP's plans, and Johnson reportedly made it clear to vice-presidential hopeful Hubert Humphrey that his place on the ticket hinged on how he handled the Challenge. When eloquent televised testimony by MFDP Vice Chair Fannie Lou Hamer and round-the-clock lobbying of delegates began to build support for the MFDP, Johnson threatened to retract the jobs and appointments that he had already promised to individual Credentials Committee members. Support for the MFDP began to erode. After a series of compromise proposals fell through, the administration made its final offer of two at-large delegate seats and a promise to bar an all-white delegation from the next convention. Johnson reportedly was insistent that "that illiterate woman," Fannie Lou Hamer, not be permitted on the convention floor. In a marathon meeting, moderate black leaders as well as King, Rauh, and SNCC mentor Bayard Rustin urged the MFDP to accept the compromise. After hours of discussion, MFDP members voted to reject it. Unita Blackwell, a delegate from rural Mayersville, remembers being taken aside during the meeting by a black Meridian businessman: "He had on a silk suit and he called us off and told us we've got to get this thing together. . . . Them people had not even been talking to us poor folks. . . . They had decided they was going to take that compromise, but the little folks told them no, they wasn't going to take it."[5]

The failure of the Challenge was deeply disappointing to MFDP members, who nevertheless went on to support the Johnson-Humphrey ticket. Their endorsement was criticized by some SNCC workers, who were convinced now of the perfidy of the Democratic Party. For SNCC, the defeat of the Challenge "was an absolute blow," staffer Stanley Wise said later. It was less the defeat itself than the underhanded maneuvering of Democratic Party operatives that so angered SNCC workers—that and being castigated as naïfs for their unwillingness to accept a paltry compromise. And it was the *way* they had treated Hamer and the other Mississippians—civil rights luminaries telling MFDP delegates that they had "put their point over" and should "pack up and return to Miss[issippi]," that they should "follow leadership." As MFDP leaders wrote in response to those who criticized them for not accepting the party's compromise: "This kind of dictation is what Negroes in Mississippi face and have always faced, and it is precisely this that they are learning to stand up against." SNCC workers did not talk much about Atlantic City in its immediate wake. They were too demoralized. "We were kind of at loose ends," SNCC communications director Julian Bond recalls. "There was no plan, no operational plan, absent any kind of theory or anything, there was just no plan to go beyond that. It was sort of, What do we do now? What comes next?...By the time the Atlantic City convention was over, you're just whipped, dead, beat, drained. Everything had been built up toward that, and no one looked beyond."[6]

James Forman, SNCC's executive secretary, believed that he did know what needed to be done. Anxious to build on the momentum of the Summer Project, he wanted to begin work immediately on a "Black Belt Project" that would replicate the Summer Project on a larger scale. The proposal received preliminary approval from SNCC's Executive Committee in September—it had been discussed even before the Summer Project began—and it was slated for approval at SNCC's October staff meeting. There, however, it became the target of angry attack by meeting participants, criticized not for its substance but for how it had been decided on. As Forman later described it, after one staffer questioned "who had decided on the Black Belt Summer Project," others joined in, "raising the cry, 'Who made that decision?' as if somebody had tried to sneak something over on them." When the discussion returned to the project itself, one of its drafters refused to present his report since the staff "really wanted to discuss decisionmaking. This threw the meeting back into the morass we had just escaped. The debate over decisionmaking went on and on....As a result of these developments, the Black Belt Summer Project of 1965 was tabled—never again to hit the floor of SNCC for discussion." SNCC's anti-elitism and individualism had once been sources of political creativity, Forman concluded, but the opposition to all authority now surfacing was debilitating. "No one, including myself, foresaw the crippling effect of certain habits and values common among middle-class students: a fear of one's own power, egoistic individualism, lack of discipline, generalized rebellion against authority, and self-indulgence." This, Forman said later, was the first indication of the freedom-high tendency that would eventually threaten the organization's very survival.[7]

However, records of the meeting that Forman describes show that there was more going on than staffers' general suspicion of authority. Even to consider launching a massive new regionwide project when Mississippi projects were struggling to scrape by seemed, to many, premature. Rumors of a million-dollar budget, New York fundraisers living in luxurious apartments, and Forman purchasing a wall-to-wall-carpeted building for Atlanta's headquarters were galling to Mississippi field workers who lacked supplies, transportation, even food. When projects were surveyed on their needs the next month, the picture was one of severe austerity. "How can we let local people stay in jail for months on end because there's no money for bail and then turn around and buy a building for $160,000?" one field worker wrote. If, in the wake of the high-profile Summer Project, donations to SNCC were surging, the money coming in was still inadequate to support SNCC's many field projects. This made for wariness of likely expensive initiatives. Staffers' attack on decisionmaking also reflected their concern that the Black Belt Project was a bid to centralize power in Atlanta and that it would curtail the project autonomy that they saw as critical to SNCC's effectiveness. In fact, Forman wrote later that he *had* envisaged SNCC becoming a mass organization with a "more centralized structure"—and admitted that his view was a minority one. Most staffers believed that SNCC's strength was in its capacity to nurture indigenous movements. As one put it in a meeting that fall, "Are we interested in building a political empire for SNCC, or in building local leadership?" No one bothered to answer a question that was perceived as rhetorical.[8]

A commitment to nurturing indigenous leaders and movements was radical in its confidence that ordinary people could guide the movement. Still, SNCC workers faced pressing programmatic questions. What role should SNCC play in the challenge to the seating of the soon-to-be-elected Mississippi congressmen that the MFDP was planning? What was the future of COFO, the coalition of civil rights organizations that had coordinated the Summer Project? Should SNCC keep up the community centers and freedom schools that it had launched over the summer? Should it continue to focus on Mississippi, even at the expense of other state projects? And who should make these decisions? Everyone agreed that SNCC's formal decisionmaking structure, which still vested power in campus representatives, was obsolete. In practice, no one paid it much attention. While many staffers were skeptical of Forman's proposal for tighter structure, they did want some alternative. It was with questions like these, as well as a sense that the anger expressed by group members at the October meeting boded ill for the group's unity, that SNCC workers convened a week-long retreat in Waveland, Mississippi, in November.

Staffers were posed a series of questions in advance of the retreat: "Where is SNCC going—what are its goals? What programs do we need to achieve those goals? What structure should we have in order to carry out those programs?" They prepared position papers on topics ranging from union organizing, to relations with Northern support groups, to sexism within the organization. Several called for SNCC to map out an agenda.

"It is admirable to talk of democracy and giving the staff full participation but at the moment this is not what needs full attention," one wrote. "We as an organization have never sat down and decided what needed to be done as a long-term drive, why it needed to be done, whether or not we were going to do it and if we were, how were we going to do it." But this and the other position papers were largely ignored as participants battled over organizational structure. Early on in the meeting, they decided to break into small groups to discuss "program" explicitly. But minutes show that the groups did little more than restate their commitment to building local leadership. A later report summarized the meeting: "From Waveland, the general feeling is that we are here to help organize people." The rest of the time staffers spent arguing over organizational structure.[9]

Contrary to a view of practical centralizers confronting utopian decentralists, most people argued in terms of practicality. "Tight-structure" proponents held a "more traditional view of organization," a Waveland participant wrote, one in which an executive secretary hired by an executive committee would be responsible for an administrative staff. "Loose-structure" proponents argued that centralized and hierarchical decisionmaking would hamper organizers and undermine SNCC's efforts to empower local people. They countered complaints about a lack of accountability with proposals for a structure that would maximize local autonomy in fundraising and decisionmaking. Programmatic work groups would meet periodically to solve problems and coordinate common efforts. Loose-structure proponents cited not the requirements of ideological consistency—of enacting a participatory democracy in the here and now—but Mississippi field organizers' need for organizational flexibility.[10]

However, many of those field organizers had already left the retreat, frustrated by days of rambling discussion. There were moments of the old camaraderie at the retreat, but there were sharp animosities as well. Mary King, a veteran white staffer, remembers: "Racial tensions surfaced openly in a blunt and assaultive way, with cutting acidity. Some of it was too much for me. For the first time in my life, I walked out of a meeting because of the brutally aggressive hostility being expressed. Many staff members were bitter, accusatory, and confrontational." With that level of antagonism, King goes on, "the process of achieving consensus—our standard method for conducting business—was impossible. Passionately concerned for SNCC's future, I felt uncertain and confused. The whole retreat seemed catastrophic." Others do not remember racial animosities expressed directly. But there was a palpable sense that the group was no longer what it was. And not simply because it was larger (in fact, only staffers had been invited to Waveland, and participants numbered about

Student Nonviolent Coordinating Committee staff retreat, Waveland, Miss., November 1964. (Photo by Danny Lyon, *Memories of the Southern Civil Rights Movement* [Chapel Hill: University of North Carolina Press, 1992]/Magnum Photos; used with permission)

forty). Rather, SNCC had become "big" in its reputation, in its fundraising and publicity operations, and in the celebrity of some of its staffers. It was no longer a politically isolated and tight-knit band of brothers. The fact that the structure question was still unresolved at the end of the Waveland meeting was a sign that things had changed. SNCC meetings, often long, sometimes tortuous, had been a place to work through to common purposes, not to erode them. "This structure discussion has led to something of a paralysis in the organization," SNCC's San Francisco office head reported. "The structure discussion will be continued at a full staff meeting to be held sometime in February."[11]

LETTING THE PEOPLE DECIDE, WINTER 1964–65

In the meantime, SNCC workers returned to local projects. "They had gotten kicked in the teeth," staffer Ed Brown said later of the Atlantic City debacle. "They said, 'we have the people. I don't care what else we have, we have the people and we are going to go around and organize, do some concrete, hard organizing.'" In some counties, the Challenge's defeat only renewed workers' determination. Organizers in Panola County worked with a group of independent farmers on a vigorous voting-registration program and began to organize plantation workers and plan a challenge to the local agricultural board. Elsewhere, projects launched cooperatives and welfare organizing. But many projects were floundering. The unending threat of white violence strained the nerves of exhausted staffers. There were reports of drinking and fights on projects and persistent complaints about administrative bungling.[12]

There was also some acknowledgment, although usually in asides at meetings or at the close of field reports, that "letting the people decide" was not generating the radical initiatives that it was supposed to. "So far I've been using the SNCC technique of prying and prodding with questions until the idea comes out," wrote one organizer, "but it is slow. . . . [P]eople really have no ideas for programs." "Have some of our programs turned out to be, frankly, a burden on the time and energy of the staff, with no real compensation?" another worried. The author of a field report from Monroe County, Mississippi, noted, "There has been a stopping of all projects, with an attempt to let the local people say what they want," confessing, however, that "the programs have been very slow. In fact I can't think of one program that is progressing." In Hattiesburg: "Apathy stems from problems of program. . . . [V]oter registration has worn off as a 'novelty.'" In Meridian: "What we've had so far is discussion and workshops, but no programs." In Neshoba: "The extent to which decisionmaking can become a community-wide activity is less clear than that it must become one." In Holly Springs: "There is no plan. There is no procedure either."[13]

One of the virtues of SNCC's earlier voter-registration campaign had been its capacity to rally groups as different as radical organizers, Northern white liberals, and moderate local black leaders around an agenda with short- and longer-term potential. Depending on how one saw it, voter registration would increase black electoral participation, help elect less racist white officials, get the streets paved, secure Black Power, or bring about large-scale economic redistribution by freeing Congress of the power of Southern Democrats. Its potential ranged from local reform to the creation of a welfare state. SNCC workers devised the MFDP Challenge when they realized that political change in Mississippi required the massive federal intervention that was unlikely in response to voting-rights violations but that might come through pressure from the Democratic Party. But the Challenge too had wide-ranging potential. It would lay the groundwork for a statewide black political organization and more challenges to other state Democratic parties, and it promised a realignment of the national party. Its defeat threw those possibilities into question.[14]

SNCC workers' answer to the obsolescence of their previous agenda was to "let the people decide." Hollis Watkins, one of SNCC's earliest

Mississippi organizers and still organizing poor people there today, says that SNCC workers could have truly committed to letting the people decide. They could have developed procedures for hammering out common agendas among diverse interests within black communities and moved only slowly from local agendas to regional ones. But SNCC's orientation toward building local movements had always coexisted with the organization's role as cutting edge and conscience of the national movement. For much of SNCC's career, that meant forcing the federal government to intervene in the Deep South. SNCC workers saw themselves as a "vanguard, pushing ahead," said a volunteer in 1965. "Other people follow . . . sort of keeping things intact." So far, SNCC had succeeded in joining roles of local-movement catalyst and radical vanguard: the organization's radicalism lay in its deference to the aspirations and agendas of the disenfranchised. But could nineteen- and twenty-year-old radicals be expected to commit to an agenda of local incremental change for the long-term?[15]

A pervasive anxiety ran through SNCC discussions in the winter of 1964–65 that, without a radical program, SNCC organizers would become little more than "social workers," content merely to help black Mississippians salve the pain of their oppression. "Too damn many nursery schools, and milk programs," one organizer phrased a not infrequent complaint. Community centers "are hung up on superficial programs like day care and games," reported another. "Many of us do not see the relationship between community centers, sewing classes and political and economic freedom." "Question of whether we are a social service agency or a band of revolutionaries. . . . It was decided we were the latter." "Social service" merely tinkered with existing social problems, a view common among SNCC workers. They were after something more fundamental, lasting, radical: "militant civil rights work," not "social work." They worried about becoming a "social welfare organization," "a service organization," "a do-gooders club," "a social gathering." "How do we deal with poor people whose aspirations are justifiably middle class?" an organizer agonized.[16]

In their efforts to develop an agenda that was both local and radical, project workers confessed that they sometimes vacillated between exercising leadership and renouncing it. More commonly, however, to expose local residents to programmatic possibilities without imposing a course of action, they asked questions. Hundreds and hundreds of questions. Agendas for and, indeed, records of project meetings during this period often consisted simply of lists of questions. Posing questions was a version of the organizing strategy that Myles Horton and Ella Baker had taught SNCC workers and that Bob Moses had turned into a much admired personal style. Questions were a way to elicit the discussion that would flesh out options and give people a sense of the larger issues at stake. But now SNCC workers sometimes relied on such questions to elicit an agenda that would validate their own radicalism. The results were often unproductive. Minutes of a Mississippi meeting record: "Two local people followed: local people have never been asked what *they* want, they need. They need more *information*." A local man in another meeting complained that "he doesn't know where he stands. No one knows who we are responsible to. Everything is too confusing—questions are always asked but no answers are given." The discussion ended soon after, the minutes recording,

Again it was asked—What are we going to do? Nothing has been said.
Again it was asked—What are we going to do? Nothing has been said.[17]

"You talk about we gotta have a program," a project worker satirized her colleagues. "Baby, just talking to people is a program." But SNCC workers had always had programs: voter registration, the 1963 Freedom Vote, the MFDP. Now, with no obvious program capable of connecting local claims with national ones and winnable issues with radical possibilities, SNCC workers became increasingly aggressive in their efforts to push local people to articulate their "real" interests and increasingly critical of each other for failing to draw out in black communities the radical interests that they knew were there.[18]

In the process, they began to define the people and their interests narrowly. Some organizers were critical of any but purely local efforts, seeing appeals like the Challenge as doomed to failure. When MFDP leaders decided to launch another challenge, this time to the seating of the Mississippi congressmen elected in November, some organizers in SNCC and COFO dissented. "All we've talked about is Washington," one organizer complained. "Well and good. But right here is more important.... [T]his is where the local people have contact with government, right here. Washington can't solve this problem. These people are elected by local people. The foot is on our necks here. We have got to start helping these people here regardless of what Jackson or Washington says." Organizers complained about an oligarchic decisionmaking process in the MFDP, charging elitism not only in the efforts of Washington attorneys pitching the MFDP's case to Congress but in the MFDP Executive Committee as well. "Has the principle upon which the [M]FDP was founded, the right of all individuals to have a voice in making decisions which affect their lives, been forgotten?" they asked. "It seems to us that many of the decisions of the [M]FDP are not made on the 'grass-roots' level but are imposed on communities by the [M]FDP 'power structure.'"[19]

The charges missed the mark in several ways. The best organizers had always known that organizing benefited from symbolic confrontations. In order to prove discrimination in voting registration for the Congressional Challenge, six hundred witnesses were deposed around the state in public hearings. Witnesses included black residents denied their voting rights as well as voting registrars, the former governor of Mississippi, the state attorney general, a state senator, and an official from the notorious Citizens Council. Organizers found the hearings a valuable organizing tool. An organizer in Bolivar County reported, "People from all over the county came to hear the depositions.... [T]here were never less than 100 in the room, and at some times, more than 180 (absolute capacity)." After the hearing, the organizer went on, "everyone piled into each other's cars and traveled 20 miles to Rosedale for a rally attended by 200-plus people, outdoors and in the rain, the first such meeting held there." The prospects looked good for a "Bolivar County–wide organization." The charge that a national, symbolic, and elite-driven legal protest was expensive, futile, and at odds with SNCC's commitment to building the leadership of black Mississippians misled in other ways. The major contributor to the cost of the Challenge, $60,000 in total, was the Southern Christian Leadership Conference (SCLC). The charge of elitism was made against MFDP chair Lawrence Guyot and the party's candidates Victoria Gray and Annie Devine. These were Mississippi natives who had become leaders in and through the movement—exactly the kind of leadership development that SNCC championed. To be sure, local project workers and residents were hampered by sometimes confused and vacillating MFDP directives. The educational purpose of the freedom vote was undermined by the sheer rush of getting it done. Too, critics did note that the Challenge served a demystifying function of exposing the futility of such appeals—since the Challenge was, indeed, defeated. Evident in some of SNCC workers' complaints, however, were newly rigid understandings of the relations between symbolic protest and grassroots organizing and between leaders and the rank and file.[20]

The transcript of a COFO project meeting during this period shows an organizer charging that "the idea of the Congressional Challenge is something too far disconnected from the people's lives." In response, another participant turned for confirmation to a local resident, one of the people who had traveled to Washington to lobby for the Challenge and make contacts with federal officials: "Somebody who went to Washington—

Mrs. Hudson—Did the trip to Washington tie in with local problems here?" When Mrs. Hudson said that it had and described the group's visits to the Departments of Agriculture, Justice, and Health, Education, and Welfare, a third staffer—Phil—put in, "Let's not kid ourselves about going to various departments in Washington. That's essentially a gimmick." The exchange continued, Dick asking, "Who do we believe? Mrs. Hudson says it's connected at home and you say it isn't." "Mrs. Hudson has been *told* that there's a connection," said "Phil and others." Dick turned again to Mrs. Hudson, asking, "is there any tie in your mind at all between [Mississippi Congressman] Prentiss Walker holding office and Mississippi citizens visiting Washington?" When she answered in the affirmative, he probed, "Is she parroting words?"[21]

In the last chapter, I described several sources of tension in a participatory democratic project based on relations of tutelage. Differences over who knew best what the people's authentic interests were could as well be fought out among organizers as between organizers and residents, and this seems to have been the case in SNCC. Organizers increasingly funneled their own disagreements over the movement's long-term goals into attacks on each other for insufficient dedication to letting the people decide. One meeting's notes record that, when Jim Forman "stood up and said we have significant political program in the Congressional Challenge," a white project worker "challenged this as 'our' program." This prompted Forman, who was probably less daunted than anyone by this kind of attack, to make a "speech about his identification with Miss[issippi, and] his right to speak." Accusations and counteraccusations that organizers were "manipulating" the people were now common.[22]

"Tight structure" increasingly seemed to be the solution. Forman's proposal for a centralized structure had had few supporters in the fall. Southern black organizers, especially, had been wary of an arrangement that would shift power from the field to Atlanta headquarters. By early winter, however, many organizers were beginning to rally around proposals for a more centralized structure as a way to get past the group's programmatic paralysis. "Southern staff workers favor strong leadership and structure," a staffer reported in February. Hardliners' "guarantee," as staffer Cleve Sellers put it, that they could move SNCC beyond its current crisis was more hope than claim. Just as the endless injunctions to "let the people decide" were as much a product of SNCC's programmatic vacuum as they were responsible for it, so the centralized structure that hardliners proposed was appealing more for its association with programmatic certainty than for any evidence of how it would actually provide direction. Such a structure probably could keep better track of personnel and resources and shorten meetings. But its capacity to generate the programmatic initiatives that were desperately needed was by no means clear.[23]

Some staffers recognized that. Stokely Carmichael complained that "people here are incapable of dealing with the real problem, which is lack of programs." But drawing attention to the group's avoidance of the topic did not seem to remedy the problem. Minutes of meetings during this period show that when issues of agenda were introduced the discussion often shifted, sometimes abruptly, to organizational structure. Why? "Sometimes it's more comfortable to talk about structure because it's so concrete," staffer Judy Richardson explains now. "And goals were so much more difficult to talk about." Casey Hayden agrees. "For most of the time I was with SNCC, I felt we knew, as SNCC staff, what we were doing and how each person's work fit into that." When that was no longer true, after the summer of 1964, "the structure discussion reflected that confusion. Structure was a secondary problem." In other words, SNCC workers battled over how decisions were made and resources allocated because the real problem—generating the sense of radical purpose that would re-energize organizers and appeal to residents—was difficult to get a handle on. For all contenders, then, the preoccupation with structure, whether tight or loose, radically democratic or hierarchical, both substituted for and deferred a discussion of goals. "If you're locked in this structural struggle," says staffer and hardliner Dorothy Zellner now, "then you're not thinking what are we going to do next."[24]

RACE AND DEMOCRACY IN THE BAND OF BROTHERS

"Tight structure" also seemed to be a solution to deepening divisions among staff. As I noted in the last chapter, SNCC's deliberative style had been based on respect for the requirements of local organizing and on the bonds uniting a group of friends. Now those bonds were eroding, and conflicts that had their source elsewhere were fought out through disputes over decisionmaking and structure. Provisional decisions were attacked for being imposed on staff, and strategy sessions were halted to discuss "why people don't speak." "Who decided that?" became a familiar, dreaded, rebuttal. A staffer described a statewide Mississippi staff meeting: "After about 11 hours involving the combined cerebral processes of more than 75 people, one minor administrative decision was made." Another recounted: "In Jackson I asked someone to deal with the two personnel problems. . . . [W]e sat there and nobody talked, and Stokely said he was the only one there who was willing to make decisions. He said people were afraid someone would ask them who gave them the right to make a decision." "I don't know" had become a "refrain." Former staffers emphasize in retrospect the pervasive anxiety and distrust that lay behind charges and countercharges of manipulation. Comments made privately by staffers at the time suggest the same thing. "I've given up hope that the problems we're talking about can be solved," one veteran staffer complained. "I strike out at the nearest target. When I hear a rumor about someone I don't like, I eat it up." Another described twelve-hour meetings that were "as ritualistic as any Japanese tea ceremony. People attack positions, and everyone knows what they are doing is attacking the people who hold them because they know of no other way of dealing with them.... [Y]ou talk for twelve hours and then leave wishing you could talk to somebody."[25]

The lines of conflict were numerous: between Northerners and Southerners, field staff and Atlanta office staff, Mississippi project workers and those in other states, staff and volunteers, newcomers and veterans. Some people were most concerned with Atlanta's control of resources and others with the relations between SNCC, the MFDP, and COFO, some with disciplinary problems in local projects and others with decisionmaking in them. Over time, however, the multiple lines of dispute were channeled into the conflict over structure. An array of organizational problems was attributed to each side, ideological motives pinned to one side and practical ones to the other, and the contending positions seen in terms of two opposed groups. As I noted, native Mississippian field secretaries had been staunch advocates of the decentralized structure that would maintain their independence in organizing. Over the fall, as the organization's problems came to be identified with Northern intellectuals more interested in arcane ideological discussion than in making tangible change, Mississippi organizers' allegiances began to shift. They shifted more decisively when the cleavage became a racial one.

By the late fall of 1964, some staffers were describing others as "freedom high." Freedom highs were "against all forms of organization and regimentation," Cleve Sellers wrote later. "If a confrontation developed in Jackson, Mississippi, and a group of freedom high floaters was working in Southwest Georgia, they would pile into cars and head for Jackson. They might return to Georgia when the Jackson confrontation was over—and they might not." It was their demeanor within the organization as much as their lack of discipline that annoyed their critics. "They loved to bring meetings to a screeching halt with open-ended, theoretical questions. In the midst of a crucial strategy session on the problems of community leaders in rural areas, one of them might get the floor and begin to hold forth on the true meaning of the word 'leader.'"[26]

Who were the freedom highs? Bourgeois sentimentalists, said Washington staffer Mike Thelwell in a widely circulated satire that fall. "The children of the middle class with the middle class intellectual penchant for nuance, metaphor and symbol, impelled, one suspects, by middle class neurosis and guilt." James Forman too later described their antiauthoritarianism as "middle class"—as well as an import from the white new left. New York SNCC staffer Elizabeth (Sutherland) Martinez says now, "I remember a long discussion, there must have been three hundred people there, and after a whole day, no agreement on the program could be reached. And I remember some people attributing it to the fact that with the influx of white people had come an influx of ideas about participatory democracy that required consensus before you could agree on anything. How could you have three hundred people reaching consensus on a program in all its details? And [people felt] that it was a northern white import, from SDS. . . . Now it wasn't as though the white people were the only people arguing for consensus at this meeting. But a lot of people felt that the black people who were arguing for it had been influenced by these ideas through white participation." Staffer Muriel Tillinghast remembers: "'Freedom high' meant people who were more cerebral and theoretical and, I would say, people who didn't do any work . . . there were a lot of whites." The proclivity for endless talk and the commitment to personal liberation were seen as indulgences that Southern black SNCC workers could ill afford.[27]

Those labeled freedom highs did tend to be more interested in the philosophical underpinnings of their work than were other SNCC workers, more willing to make bold statements in meetings about the virtues of a leaderless movement, and more sensitive to breaches of a radically democratic ethos. But they were now being held responsible for a variety of problems: the exhaustion and burnout that were leading some of the most effective organizers to abandon their projects, the confusion about just what "letting the people decide" should mean, and, most important, the fact that no one knew what to do next. They were also, increasingly, seen as white. "The 'freedom highs' are essentially white intellectuals, hung up in various ways," a staffer wrote in the spring of 1965. "Maybe these whites are trying to break free of the need to be like the strong people (which they can't ever be like 'cause they're not black) and their role as supplements to the work of the 'strong people.'" Conflicts between Northerners and Southerners, veterans and newcomers, and blacks and whites were gradually displaced by a black-white cleavage—but fought out through positions on organizational structure.[28]

There were reasons for the sharpening racial tensions. Black staffers skeptical of the Summer Project to begin with had seen their fears materialize. White volunteers' inexperience and unfamiliarity with the intricacies of Southern race relations created awkward and occasionally dangerous situations. They sometimes offended black Southerners by flouting norms of dress and demeanor, and their command of formal political skills was intimidating. Black workers had worried not only that whites would inadvertently reproduce patterns of racial deference but also that their own roles in the movement would be overshadowed, and these concerns too seemed to materialize. SNCC workers had milked the publicity that the volunteers generated, recognizing that it brought funding, Northern political support, and some modicum of protection. But there were costs. SNCC communications director Julian Bond recalled, "We had this traveling guy who went from project to project in the summer of '64 sending home reports on the white kids because we knew [that] a neighborhood paper in a suburb in Columbus, Ohio, would print a story about what little Johnny Jones, the son of Mr. and Mrs. Jones, who live in that $50,000 house on Oak Street, was doing this summer in Mississippi. So we, I think consciously, contributed to that feeling, to the feeling of the press that the white kids were the important ones. But we resented it, nevertheless, resented very deeply that they were interested in what Susie Smith from Vassar was doing and whether she had stubbed her toe in the middle of a demonstration in which fifty Negroes had been beaten."[29]

After the summer, more volunteers stayed on than expected, and eighty-five of them were added to the staff in a decision that many longtime staffers perceived as simply handed down. No matter the benefits of more manpower, staffers lamented the erosion of what had been a tight-knit group of friends. "They didn't know who the hell you were; you didn't know who they were," said staffer Donald Harris of the newcomers. "It used to be a band of brothers, a circle of trust, but that's not true anymore," another SNCC worker complained in a meeting. White organizer Elaine (DeLott) Baker wrote in her diary in December: "The movement talks a lot of the 'good old days.' The kids worked together, went to jail together, suffered together, at times starved together. They were, for the most part, black."[30]

White newcomers, for their part, came south awed by SNCC organizers and were taken aback by the barely concealed animosity they encountered. They were bombarded with rules—about not leaving the project, not appropriating project cars for their personal use, not socializing with local young people—that veteran SNCC workers ignored. They wanted guidance from project directors whose authority had been impressed on them but received little. "How many times did you try to get your project director to talk to you?" a project director from another county asked a complaining worker. "You've got to press people to talk to you." Some white newcomers asserted the dictates of the model community against the antagonism that they were encountering: "What qualifications should a project director have? Some are chosen just because they are Negro and from the South. Who chooses them?" Another white worker: "We should all have some say.... COFO has degenerated into a clique of people who have been here.... [A]uthority lies in some vague place, decisions come from some mysterious oligarch. Maybe we should define big brother." And a third: "I was told by a person of some authority that the role of the project director is left totally vague to keep new people in check.... This sounds pretty undemocratic." Elaine Baker wrote to herself: "Many of the white [volunteers], isolated, distrusted, faced with programs that are in a lull, get nervous, bicker, and begin to quarrel with the project director over their lack of power in the course of the movement.... The project directors, on the other hand, are guilty of not communicating with the volunteers."[31]

Records show that in project meetings an enormous amount of time was spent discussing the roles, responsibilities, and prerogatives of project directors, with newcomers calling simultaneously for more guidance and more democracy. "Problem is that people can't trust project director," a worker complained in Gulfport. "Who decides who goes where and what to do if people don't work out?" Another questioned the "whole concept of a project director as a feudal lord." And a third, plaintively: "There are people who are in positions of power and they are interested in retaining this power and then there are the have-nots." Comments like these, accusatory and often framed in an idiom of democracy and illegitimate power, were understandably annoying to veteran organizers who had long ago proved their commitment to the struggle. But, in a long paper about relations on the Gulfport project written the next fall for a sociology class, veteran white staffer Cathy Cade described white volunteers pleading with the black project director for guidance. The project director, an experienced organizer, had been opposed to the Summer Project and had been uninterested in managing the Gulfport volunteers. He had, nevertheless, worked hard to secure housing for them and had taken on the job of project director when asked. But he found that the managerial responsibilities it entailed hampered his ability to organize effectively. Used to working solo, he was unprepared to deal with volunteers' desire for constant guidance. The result was that volunteers questioned his leadership, he withdrew from much interaction with them, and they complained about his failure to consult with them.[32]

In some cases, black project directors were new to Mississippi themselves and were struggling to learn the lay of the land at the same time
as they were expected to guide volunteers. In others, they were simply
burned out, exhausted by the grueling work and constant danger and in
need of some time to regroup. Even for those in the best of physical and
moral strength, the presence of the volunteers transformed their work,
making it more difficult to meet informally with local people and putting
them in the position of mediating between locals and volunteers.

Volunteers often challenged project directors, not on the basis of an
individualist ethos of "doing your own thing," but rather in terms of
ideals that they had imbibed from SNCC itself. With radical democracy
within the movement seen as essential to popular empowerment outside it,
volunteers asserted their own prerogative to leadership in the name of the
people. One project's long and contentious battle with its project director
prompted MFDP leader Annie Devine to intervene. "Unless you forget
yourself and relate to the people, you'll go away without doing anything,"
she warned. A white project worker protested: "All here agree that our
commitment is to the people ... discussions of this sort are perfectly in
order; they help us function better and work better for the people of
Mississippi." Another put in: "How can I hope to get rid of authoritarianism
in Miss[issippi] if I leave it in the Canton staff? ... [I]t's like the bossman
telling his sharecropper to get off the land just because the sharecropper
thinks differently from the owner." A white volunteer comparing her
situation to that of a sharecropper sounds downright embarrassing. On the
other hand, these statements were made after the black project director
had announced that whites would have to leave Mississippi to go home
and fundraise. Whites often invoked the requirements of democracy when
faced with the prospect of their own exclusion.[33]

In a staff meting in late 1964, Stokely Carmichael reported that the
most serious internal problem faced by the projects in his district was "old
vs. new staff." It was "seen as black-white, but is different," he cautioned.
But other district directors at the same meeting disagreed; the problem
was "the 'black-white' issue." It was probably both. The band of brothers
had been a small group, and it had been a mainly black one. In early
1964, Bob Moses told the writer Robert Penn Warren that they had "just
had a tirade—one staff person a few days ago just, you know, for about
fifteen minutes, just getting—letting out what really was a whole series
of really racial statements of hatred. And we sort of all just sat there."
Moses explained the outburst: "Negro students, you know, actually feel
this is their own movement. This is the strongest feeling among the Negro
students—that this is the one thing that belongs to them in the whole

country; and I think this causes the emotional reaction toward the white people coming in and participating." Moses himself had always been deft in mediating between Northern and Southern students and between white and black ones as well as between students and local residents. By the fall of 1964, however, he was rarely in the state. Burned out, and disturbed by his own authority, he was withdrawing from the leadership role about which he had always been ambivalent. People increasingly spoke in his name—for many, the battle over structure was a Moses-Forman conflict—but they did so without his skill in negotiating oppositions between local and national protest and between democracy and leadership.[34]

"If a white man were project director I wouldn't be in the movement," a black project worker declared in an interracial discussion in late 1964. "We have to organize something for ourselves." By late 1964, black activists were becoming increasingly interested in issues of racial identity and consciousness, and some wondered whether these issues could truly be addressed in integrated gatherings. "Although it had always been an issue in the organization," Cleve Sellers wrote later, "the role of whites had never really been openly discussed"—and was not, he says, until 1966. Other former staffers say that there *was* open discussion about the role of whites in the movement in the fall of 1964. But it tended to be about the liabilities of white organizers in black communities, not about people's worry that an essentially black movement might eventually become a majority-white one. Bob Moses observes now, "There's a real need for black people to close the door and meet in their own group, and people were threatened by this. It was a need in the SNCC meetings. The SNCC meetings dragged on interminably partly because they could never do this. So people could never say what they felt. A lot of people, particularly the staff, the black people from Mississippi, who had really deep feelings that they were ready to voice—I don't think they could say them. They might say them in an all black setting but they weren't ready to say them out in the whole meeting." In one such rare, all-black meeting, a local Mississippian admitted: "Before the summer volunteers, we didn't have these kind of hang-ups. Now I sit back because I don't understand what's going on." On another project, after a long debate about the nature of legitimate authority—just the kind of discussion that hardliners criticized—an older minister who was participating remarked, "The thing that bothers me is that there really is a basic black-white problem here which you don't say but which is at the bottom of a lot of what you're saying. Why don't you deal with your black-white problem?"[35]

The "black-white problem" was tough for an interracial group to confront, let alone resolve. And, indeed, field reports during this period make occasional, but never more than passing, reference to it. With decisionmaking the central organizational concern and racial antagonisms difficult to talk about, debates over organizational structure and decision-making both engaged and stood in for those thornier antagonisms. Earlier tensions between Northerners and Southerners, newcomers and veterans, and field staff and office staff had been supplanted by a new tension, one between proponents of tight structure and those of loose structure and, less overtly, between blacks and whites. By the spring, a form of organiza-tion that black Southerners had pioneered was becoming unappealing by its association with whites. "Whites tended to be for loose structure and southern Negroes were the ones most resentful of whites," Julian Bond put it a few years later.[36]

The new formulation of the problem absorbed other organizational problems. "Floaters," for many people, referred to organizers whose ex-haustion and burnout had led them to abandon their assigned projects. But, along with other disciplinary infractions—people taking cars for their personal use, drinking, flouting community mores—floating was now subsumed under the epithets "anarchist" and "obstructionist" and attached to the loose structure position. "Look at the people at Waveland who supported loose structure," one staffer paraphrased the complaints cir-culating. "Look what they've been doing since Waveland; don't you think it's strange that the very people who don't want structure are off doing whatever they like without anyone in a position to ask them for an account of their actions?" By February, whites had come to be seen as insisting on participatory democratic practices to retain control of the organization. A white staffer reported that the drive for "looser structure" was being framed in terms of "conspiracy theories about white intellectuals."[37]

The increasing resonance of the tight structure position was evident in its incorporation into SNCC workers' organizing lexicon. "Strong" had always described people who were willing to risk reprisals to participate politically. That the word now described centralized hierarchical organiza-tion ("the executive committee should be strong"; "Southern staff workers favor strong leadership and structure") and people willing to take unilat-eral action ("the strong people . . . are the ones who go off to do work"; "when a crisis arose 15 strong people came in and took over") suggests that a new set of associations had become attached to a term denoting political efficacy. Similarly, "revolutionary" had once described an orga-nization committed to effecting radical social change by building local movements. By the spring of 1965, however, it described centralized and hierarchical structure—both to proponents and to detractors. Loose struc-ture's proponents, meanwhile, found themselves battling unsuccessfully the perception that their preference for decentralized and egalitarian decisionmaking reflected a politically careless anarchism. Thus, a participant in a February meeting was thankful, she recorded, that "for the first time anyone spoke [about] loose structure as not being 'no structure' but different structure."[38]

Those promoting centralized and more hierarchical structure were not an organizational faction bent on gaining acceptance for a particular agenda or ridding the organization of whites. The appeal of top-down structure lay rather in its relation to inchoate preferences and problems. A self-consciously strategic orientation and preference for centralized authority stood in for programmatic certainty and an organization not dominated by whites. But it did not offer any methods for achieving programmatic coherence or reducing whites' role. Indeed, since a decentralized structure would have vested personnel decisions in project directors, it would have enabled them to curb the role of whites on their projects, if they so chose. Moreover, SNCC's most successful projects in the past had been launched by individual organizers. Decentralized and informal structure here, as in other movements, had facilitated individual initiative and tactical innovation. The source of top-down structure's appeal was not its capacity to yield more efficient outcomes or its consistency with an existing ideology but its symbolic resonance.

ORGANIZATIONAL REFORM, SPRING 1965

Planners of SNCC's February 1965 staff meeting took pains to avoid the endless debate that had characterized previous meetings. They asked staff members to sign in advance a statement that "I will be willing to follow the plans as outlined here of the planning committee at the staff meeting." The hardliners had already organized to gain control, however. Halfway through the meeting, one staffer admitted that a group had "lobbied before the staff meeting, wanted to see structure, made sure that's what happened, [took a] hard line, anyone who opposed us was made to feel it. There was united front before [meeting] done in such a way that it prevented people from talking." Hardliners were accused of intimidating local people and silencing opposition. But, by the meeting's close, they had gained the upper hand, winning a reformed Executive Committee and plans for firmer administrative structure. Of the nineteen members of the new Executive Committee, eleven were Mississippi field workers, most native Mississippians.[39]

Since loose structurists had originally sought more power for field organizers, this might have been construed as a victory for them. But, by the February meeting, Mississippi organizers were firmly on the side

of tight structure. Shortly after the staff meeting, a new personnel committee conducted a systematic review of every SNCC staffer in order to root
out those who were insufficiently productive. Reports of "self-appointed
troikas" traveling to projects to fire workers began to circulate. Speakers at
subsequent meetings continued to call for discipline and a "revolutionary"
attitude toward resources. The hardliners' victory would not be complete
for another year, but the tone of discussions did become more stringent,
disciplined, and aggressive. Talk of "tightening up," of "tightening the
organization," of the staff "becoming tougher and leaner," of "mov[ing]
from morality to reality," of not letting people "stand in our way," was
increasingly pervasive. Organizational hierarchy, not its absence, was now
associated with political militancy. "Anyone who doesn't like things . . . can
go home," read a memo announcing that staffers' checks would be sus-
pended if they failed to file timely reports. "If a person refuses to abide
by the decisions about program, then he will be given a leave of absence
to pursue his program or he will be dropped from staff," read another
memo. A disgruntled staffer responded, "I wish all of you, whoever 'you'
are, would stop treating me like a financial item. What's happening in
Snick? The letter I just received sounds like something from a lousy
loan company." SNCC's efforts at "tightening up" were being guided by
an image of "how a tough militant organization is supposed to work," San
Francisco office head Mike Miller complained. But the tide had turned.
"We're not individuals anymore—just 'screwed up' or 'freedom high,'" a
white staffer wrote to Jim Forman.[40]

What was the relation between SNCC workers' bid for a more centralized structure and the organization's new Black Power agenda? As I noted
earlier, analysts have argued that when SNCC workers abandoned efforts
at moral suasion in favor of gaining independent black political power
they also adopted the kind of top-down organization that could efficiently
mobilize people for power. I have argued, to the contrary, that SNCC's
adoption of a more centralized and hierarchical organizational structure
preceded rather than followed its espousal of Black Power. During the
period of organizational reform that I have just described, staffers voiced
in informal conversations some of the components of Black Power: skepticism of liberal alliances; an attraction to political organizing outside the
Democratic Party; frustration with nonviolence; and a growing belief that
the movement should be all black. But these ideas were still tentative and
difficult to express in an interracial group. In a sense, the progressive association of participatory democracy with whites made it easier for SNCC
workers to move toward an all-black organization. This explains self-
described hardliner Cleve Sellers's later observation that the hardliners

"were primarily black. We were moving in a Black Nationalist direction." There was actually no reason that top-down organizational structure would further a nationalist agenda, except that ideological positions and racial allegiances had been mapped onto organizational preferences. While a number of whites labeled freedom high drifted away from the group after the February meeting, most black staffers so labeled remained. By November, SNCC's staff meeting included only one of the whites who had advocated loose structure. The few other remaining whites were hardliners.[41]

If the hardliners' victory began to address the racial problem, it did not solve the programmatic questions that the debate had also reflected. Clear lines of command and strict cost-benefit analysis of strategic options could not by themselves supply the programmatic direction that was so desperately needed. One staffer criticized the organization's preoccupation with reforming itself, saying that "it was work that needed to be discussed. . . . [Y]ou (SNCC) believed all that shit they told you that you are a great revolutionary organization, and when you believed you were great and revolutionary, you had to weed out people who weren't." Another organizer reported: "People really have no ideas for programs. . . . This is a reason that a lot of SNCC people have gone off to the frontiers of Alabama— that's exciting and you don't have to consider the real future." SNCC's Alabama head confirmed in April that dozens of Mississippi staffers were leaving their projects to come to Alabama, this in spite of efforts to dissuade them: "People came because of frustration on their projects."[42]

By November, SNCC's Mississippi staff had dropped to one-third of what it had been the previous fall. "We had jolted the country," MFDP organizer Lawrence Guyot remembered regretfully. "The state of Mississippi was on the defensive." SNCC's inability to forward programs opened the way for more moderate black leaders to claim the helm of the movement. To be sure, there were other reasons for SNCC's failure to build on its hard-won gains in Mississippi, chief among them continuing white repression, co-optive efforts on the part of white political moderates, and staffers' burnout. And many organizers did press on, combining voter registration with economic cooperatives, welfare organizing and other issues. However, by the time SNCC found in Black Power a new programmatic "lever," as Cleve Sellers put it, and turned its attention to organizing in Lowndes County, Alabama, it had all but abandoned Mississippi.[43]

LEADERS AND COMMUNITIES

Other costs of the prolonged debate over structure were less obvious. The symbolic associations established by the debate became part of SNCC workers' tactical repertoire, ruling in and ruling out particular options. The process is evident in the records of SNCC's May 1966 annual conference, held in Kingston Springs, Tennessee, over a year after the loose structure position had been rejected. The conference was a critical one. Staffers began to articulate a Black Power agenda, confronted explicitly the role of whites in the organization, made clear their antagonism toward the Johnson administration, and voiced open skepticism about nonviolence. They also elected Stokely Carmichael SNCC chair after a bitter election contest with John Lewis. Carmichael represented a new SNCC, less wed to nonviolence, willing to organize outside the Democratic Party, and committed to the idea that real change required cultural transformation— "black consciousness" as well as black power. In wide-ranging discussions during the meeting, SNCC workers assessed their work in the previous few years as a way to chart new directions. Speakers criticized what they saw as the organization's period of self-indulgent individualism: "[in] 1964–1965 people tried to be individuals. But they were beginning to realize there is no room for individual black people in the movement. The essential question is: How do we as technicians and organizers develop the black community?" Their mistake, they agreed, was that they had "assumed that when we went into a community, we did not assume leadership." They referred to this as their misguided "Camus period." They were determined not to make the same mistake again.[44]

The discussions ratified two developments. "Leadership" had come to be a good thing, distinguished from the "local-people-itis" that had prevented organizers from taking any action at all. "Individualism" had come to be a bad thing, associated with an organization-sapping preoccupation with personal freedom. The new associations are understandable, but they also narrowed SNCC's range of tactical options and made it harder to organize effectively. I caution, however, that appraising their effects is difficult given the fact that SNCC workers were simply up against so *many* obstacles after 1966: continued violence by local white Southerners; new competition on the part of moderate groups and, in the North, militant ones; and unremitting government surveillance and harassment. Add to that what seemed a single-minded media focus on the separatist implications of the slogan "Black Power." Shortly after the Kingston Springs conference just described, Stokely Carmichael used the slogan on the Mississippi Meredith march, and it provoked a firestorm of publicity and attack. SNCC workers found themselves absorbed in trying to interpret a phrase that, they say now, they had not fully defined, defend themselves against vituperative attacks by press, pundits, and former liberal allies, and reassure their supporters that they were not plotting a race war. "It just freezes up your whole motion," a weary Ivanhoe Donaldson complained to New York City supporters.[45]

The media attention given Black Power and Carmichael as its spokesperson also made it difficult to organize by undermining the collective leadership on which SNCC had relied. For Carmichael's new profile as a media-savvy militant encouraged other SNCC workers to bid for a media role. SNCC had traded "leadership by sweat" for "leadership by rhetoric," staffer Stanley Wise observed later. At the time, Wise warned, "It seems there is a new mood in the org[anization] that a Stokely and a Rap Brown get created ... then ... I am waiting to be discovered too." Again, these obstacles had little to do with SNCC workers' conceptions of individualism, participation, and democracy. But SNCC's conceptual repertoire of organizing had changed. For one thing, a nondirective organizing style had become associated with white freedom highs' supposed penchant for endless, unproductive talk. SNCC workers were now willing to abandon time-consuming discussions about the proper relationship between organizer and community. Instead, a shared racial identity would make the relationship one of common interests. Carmichael, who had not been clearly aligned with either side in the structure debate, did reject what was seen now as a romantic refusal to exercise leadership. When he launched the organizing project in Lowndes County, Alabama, that would be the incubus for Black Power, he "got out of that bag of manipulation," he said shortly after. "I went in there with certain ideas. One idea was to organize people to get power. And if that is manipulation, so be it."[46]

In fact, the drive to establish the Lowndes County Freedom Organization (nicknamed the Black Panther Party on account of its logo) proved to be a remarkable exercise in community-wide organizing, and the group's local leaders proved fully capable of running their own show. However, in SNCC workers' public statements about Black Power, giving voice to the voiceless sometimes shifted to speaking in the people's putative voice. "An organization which claims to speak for the needs of a community—as does the Student Nonviolent Coordinating Committee—must speak in the tone of that community," Carmichael said in a typical formulation. "This is the significance of Black Power as a slogan." Speaking in the "tone" of the community was a way to radicalize it, to "break open the chains in the minds of people in black communities," "awaken ... the black community," "educate the black people who have in the past been brainwashed." SNCC workers were speaking to a national and international audience in statements like these, and, of course, all organizations speak in the name of their constituencies. Broad consciousness-raising efforts can have real mobilizing effects. But internal SNCC discussions also suggest worries among some that the role of ideological vanguard was becoming popular—and destructive. "The whole generalizing about 'the black community feels this' and 'the black community feels that' has to stop," Jim Forman insisted. "It is presumptuous of us to feel that we know what all the black community is saying and doing."[47]

The danger of claiming radical spokesmanship for the black community—and of abandoning efforts to wrestle with the relations between organizers, leaders, and communities—was that it represented black people as a passive mass awaiting direction by leaders. Whether leaders were thought to lead on the basis of their mainstream political credentials or their racial authenticity, the model remained one in which leaders' accountability was a function of their individual characteristics rather than a result of institutionalized mechanisms for citizen input, scrutiny, and challenge. SNCC workers had begun to envision and experiment with just such mechanisms in their Mississippi projects. Under the mantle of radicalism, SNCC risked reverting to a more traditional notion of leadership.[48]

SNCC had not abandoned its commitment to local organizing, in principle at least. In 1967, staffer Donald Stone described SNCC's arrival on the scene in Dixie Hills, Atlanta. "We went in there with our rhetoric and nobody had done organizing previously in that community." SNCC staffers were there "rah rahing," Stone recounted. "This was completely unnecessary. The press played that up, that we were the ones who did not express the sentiments of that community . . . even though we were there rhetorically, we weren't in there telling people about programs that we had, etc." SNCC workers were agreed that the solution was to come up with the programs that would gain them publicity for their concrete organizing rather than their public pronouncements. But they were hampered in the effort to develop such programs by a second conception of organizational functioning that had gained ground as a result of the debates over structure. Once individualism had been defined as antithetical to programmatic coherence, it was difficult to exploit the individual initiative that had always been the source of SNCC's most effective campaigns.[49]

This was evident in SNCC workers' discussion in January 1967 of a series of planned workshops devoted exclusively to crafting a new program for the organization. When Stokely Carmichael questioned the merit of centralized program planning—"My own feeling is that you don't tell SNCC people anything. You just go out in the field and do it"—staffer Courtland Cox argued that that was just the problem: "We proceed on individual initiative. That is, Sam gets an idea and he goes out and he does it and it's his thing and his way and in his area. . . . I just think we need to end that and begin moving in a way that is comprehensive." In

March, however, Cox was forced to concede that nothing much had been accomplished in the February meetings. The problem was still that the group was "proceeding under the concept of individual initiative instead of an organizational approach." Members were not "speak[ing] out of a collective thing," someone else concluded. Carmichael was dismissive of those kinds of arguments, insisting that programs would grow from people's organizing efforts, not the reverse. Another staffer observed that, while the fact that "everybody sort of goes for himself" was "a legacy of SNCC's history," there was more to the group's lack of concerted effort than that. "Part of it is probably rooted in the fact that people inside the org[anization], for various reasons, don't like facing one another and therefore refuse to communicate with each other."[50]

The speaker captured a critical problem. The same individual initiative that was seen as responsible for Stokely Carmichael's freelance career as a movement celebrity and the group's inability to craft a coherent program was also what had yielded creative programmatic initiatives in the past. SNCC's Mississippi project began when Bob Moses arranged with Amzie Moore to start a voter-registration campaign and a full year later got SNCC support for it. Organizing in southwest Georgia proceeded against near-insuperable obstacles on account of the initiative and tenacity of Charles Sherrod and Cordell Reagon. Carmichael was frustrated by the internal conflicts that were paralyzing the Mississippi movement and went to Lowndes County, Alabama, to organize on his own; the result was SNCC's Lowndes County project. Julian Bond, Ivanhoe Donaldson, and Charlie Cobb believed that SNCC should take advantage of the opening of a new Georgia congressional seat in the spring of 1965 and successfully ran Bond for the post. What was responsible for all these efforts was just the individualism that staffers were now deploring. Why had it worked then and not now? In part because, as the staffer just quoted pointed out, SNCC had once been a group of friends. Among friends, individual initiative is rarely seen as threatening group interests. But individual initiative had also stopped working because it had gotten a bad name. The earlier debates over structure had permanently recast individual initiative as self-involved, undisciplined, counterrevolutionary, and white.

SNCC never managed to revive its organizing efforts. The organization's internal life came to be dominated by disputes between pan-Africanists, Marxists, and cultural nationalists. "SNCC had begun to fall apart on precisely the lines that it had always found so abhorrent, that is, ideological lines," Stanley Wise observed later. "Our work became what we said as opposed to what we did." The splits were not repaired when SNCC pursued and then abandoned an affiliation with the Black Panther Party amid mutual accusations and threats of violence, threats that were most likely amplified by the FBI. SNCC's downhill slide continued rapidly after that. As cohort replaced cohort in controlling the organization, SNCC veterans found themselves with little standing. By 1968, some FBI agents had longer SNCC histories than many staffers did. Financial support for the organization was virtually nil. In June 1968 program secretary Phil Hutchings announced that SNCC's goal was the creation of a national black party, but the idea garnered little interest inside or outside the organization, and, in any case, SNCC did not have the resources to bring such a party into being. By then, SNCC existed in name only, and, shortly after, not even in name: in July 1969, H. Rap Brown announced that SNCC was now the Student National Coordinating Committee.[51]

STRATEGY AND IDENTITY

Chroniclers of the movements of the 1960s have traced a striking metamorphosis mid-decade. As SNCC and Students for a Democratic Society (SDS) slid into an apocalyptic rhetoric of revolution, they say, bearers of the utopian impulse found refuge in self-liberatory efforts that were entirely disengaged from effective politics. Behind the shift in SNCC, on most accounts, lay the group's growth in size and status, which made its earlier exemplary commitment unsustainable, and the ascendance of a Black Power ideology, which made unappealing a strategy of moral witness to a corrupt establishment. SDS's trajectory was similar. Its own battles between purists and pragmatists were followed by the rise of sectarian ideologues with little interest either in exemplifying a moral politics or in practicing an effective politics.

Contrary to these explanations, I have argued that a decentralized and participatory organizational form was initially viewed by SNCC workers as strategic. It came to be seen by many of them as at odds with a strategic orientation when it came to be held responsible for the group's programmatic impasse and when it was connected to what seemed the excessive role of whites in the organization. The Atlantic City convention had demonstrated the recalcitrance of the system to change, and, in its wake, goals were simply unclear. SNCC workers' preoccupation with organizational structure and decisionmaking reflected and at the same time deferred the agenda setting that was desperately needed. Like the champions of radical democracy, proponents of top-down structure were responding to programmatic and racial tensions. But, in gaining acceptance for that structure, they ended the organizational battle without solving the programmatic and racial problems that it engaged.

SNCC staffer Courtland Cox later described the difference between those who favored a centralized, mass organization and those who believed that SNCC should remain a cadre organization working with local movements but not absorbing them as akin to the difference between giving people fish and teaching them how to fish. I like this description because it recognizes the instrumental and explicitly political purposes behind the arguments for loose structure. Many of those who made such arguments were, initially at least, by no means hostile to power, strategy, organizational structure, or staff discipline. Loose structure's association with a strictly moral approach—and with programmatic limbo, a breakdown in discipline, and the dominance of whites—occurred during the debate rather than causing it. Both sides contributed to that association. Both sides made participatory democracy into an *identity*—assessing it exclusively by virtue of the groups with which it was associated. For its champions, participatory democracy *was* SNCC. For its detractors, it was *not* SNCC, or, at least, participatory democracy was not consistent with the predominately Southern black organization that SNCC had once been. One consequence of those symbolic associations, however, was that, precisely at the time when SNCC workers' commitment to developing criteria and mechanisms of accountable leadership was most needed, that is, when new political opportunities were encouraging moderate black and white leaders to bid for control of the movement, many SNCC workers renounced the idea of leadership altogether. And then, in repudiating that stance, others renounced the idea of accountability, except as guaranteed by a developed black consciousness.[52]

SNCC's struggle with participatory democracy reveals dynamics that reach wider. Where pacifists tended to build their participatory democracies on the interactional norms of Christian fellowship, SNCC workers built theirs on the tutelary relations between organizer and community and on the relations among friends. Like organizers before and after, they believed that residents should plot their own political course since they would bear the heaviest burdens of activism and its consequences. However, for all their denigration of "leading" rather than "organizing," the best organizers, then and now, have challenged residents on their provisional choices. When to challenge and when to defer is a question that enters even routine deliberative processes. Another is who "the people" are, in other words, whether organizers should try to develop leadership outside existing leadership circles and how they should mediate conflicts between new and old leaders. Yet another issue has to do with organizers' own relationship to a broader movement. Each of these tensions can affect the deliberative process. Participatory decisionmaking can be manipulative or ineffectual, narrow in its range of participants and topics and so focused on issues of immediate concern as to preclude any connection to a broader agenda. Or, handled well, and under the right conditions, it can build accountable leadership, a coherent agenda, and wide participation. SNCC's experience with participatory democracy demonstrates both the extraordinary potential of participatory decisionmaking in movements of the powerless and the pressure points along which such efforts are likely to fragment.

5

PARTICIPATORY DEMOCRACY IN THE NEW LEFT, 1960–67

We regard men as infinitely precious and possessed of unfulfilled capacities for reason, freedom and love.... [W]e seek the establishment of a democracy of individual participation governed by two central aims: that the individual share in those social decisions determining the quality and direction of his life; that society be organized to encourage independence in men and provide the media for their common participation.

THE PORT HURON STATEMENT (1962)

In 1965, twenty-eight-year-old *Studies on the Left* editor Norm Fruchter returned from a trip to Mississippi to herald profound changes in the civil rights movement. Student Nonviolent Coordinating Committee (SNCC) activists and the black residents with whom they worked had "abandoned the goal of eventual integration into existing Mississippi society as both unrealistic and undesirable," he wrote. Rejecting the "totemic demands" of the left for federal housing and employment programs, they were instead experimenting with alternative political and economic institutions. But, probably even more "disconcerting" to "orthodox left-wingers," Fruchter speculated, they were challenging what counted as radical organization. "Primarily a movement... only incidentally an organization," SNCC should not be condemned for its bureaucratic inefficiency since one of its chief purposes was "to raise the question of just how well all the organizations operating on bureaucratic assumptions within the majority society have served human freedom."[1]

Fruchter's piece provoked an indignant response from old left stalwart Victor Rabinowitz. "For many of the young of our nation, including, of course, many in the Movement, freedom may mean the right to smoke pot, to drive a car while drunk and to goof off when the spirit so moves," Rabinowitz wrote. "To a Negro farmer in Mississippi, it means the opportunity to organize to achieve the right to vote, the right to be treated like a human being, the right to be integrated into the human brotherhood.

These rights come along with the right to eat a square meal and to live in a house with flush toilets." To gain those rights required a political program and a "disciplined, efficient organization," precisely what SNCC was attempting to remake itself as—with a Coordinating Committee, Executive Committee, and a Secretariat, a policy statement, and formal rules for personnel decisions. Such a "bureaucracy" would be anathema to Fruchter and his friends, but to suggest that program, organization, and "totemic" political demands were of no interest to Mississippi blacks was at best romantic, at worst "both condescending and insulting." Against the prefigurative vision that Fruchter saw animating SNCC's organizational form and decisionmaking style—organization aimed at effecting a cultural revolution rather than mere political reform—Rabinowitz countered that institutional change demanded bureaucratic organization and a clearheaded instrumentalism, something the old left had long recognized.[2]

The Fruchter/Rabinowitz debate is interesting in part for what it missed. SNCC staffer Mike Miller wrote but did not publish a response to the two pieces. Both Fruchter's and Rabinowitz's renderings bore "so little resemblance to the day-to-day realities" of SNCC "as to be almost frightening," Miller observed. SNCC's goal was not to develop new assumptions "about identity, personality, work, meaning, and aspirations not accepted in the majority society,'" as Fruchter claimed, but to gain "power to break into the society and get a share of its resources." "Believe it or not," Miller pointed out, there was an administration in SNCC. "It has offices in Atlanta. Checks are made out there by an honest to goodness book-keeper, there are files, forms, duplicate copies, secretaries, machines and all the rest of the paraphernalia of bureaucracy." But Rabinowitz was equally off the mark in reducing SNCC to its policy statements and organizational charts. SNCC workers were experimenting with "decentralized forms of administration"—but forms "designed to effectively service the staff and field without controlling all activity at the local level." Their purpose was practical. SNCC's day-to-day operations were driven above all—and this apparently eluded both commentators—by staffers' commitment to "being 'an organizer' and being in the field." To Fruchter and Rabinowitz's characterizations—SNCC as a utopian community and SNCC as a "disciplined army"—Miller countered, "many of us in SNCC prefer a different formulation. We are a band of organizers seeking to open the tremendous potential of human resources that has been locked up in the racism of the South. That potential cannot be opened by anyone but the Negro people who live in Southern bondage." SNCC organizers eschewed neither political power nor the "totemic demands" of old leftists. "It is the additions to the old demands, not their dismissal, that is important. It is the new

demands of participation, local control in decision making, leadership from
below rather than from above that distinguish SNCC from the old left."[3]

This is the SNCC I described in chapter 3. By the time the Fruchter/
Rabinowitz debate appeared, however, the group was floundering. Hardliners in SNCC were just as dismissive of those who wanted to experiment with
new forms of democracy as Rabinowitz was, and some of their opponents
were just as convinced as Fruchter that SNCC's chief purpose lay in such
experimentation. Miller's critique overshot the mark: many in the new left
saw the merits of organizing, and some of them were very good organizers.
Still, it is not hard to imagine that, in defining themselves against the old
left, new leftists would sometimes assimilate SNCC's purposes to their
own. That is the other interesting thing about the Fruchter/Rabinowitz
debate. As it had before and would again, the new left staked its claim to
political authority on its capacity to celebrate and, not least, interpret the
purposes of its civil rights heroes. Challenges to the old left's misplaced
faith in bureaucracy, its myopic focus on securing federal programs that
were no more realistic than a revolution from the bottom up, its obsequious
allegiance to the Democratic Party, its stodginess, all would be made in
the name of the alternatives forwarded by activists in the Deep South.

Chroniclers of the new left's experiments with participatory democracy have recognized SNCC's influence, but they have tended to interpret
it narrowly. On most accounts, SNCC workers' enactment of a "beloved
community," in which a band of young idealists transcended not only
race but also the impersonality and alienation of modern American life,
inspired new leftists to do the same. In their own participatory democracies, new leftists would live the community they sought to bring into
being. They would join a passion for radically democratic forms with a
commitment to effecting structural change. Yet the "dilemma inherited
from SNCC," chroniclers agree, was that building the better society
demanded different skills than did living it. The new left foundered, on
most accounts, because it was unwilling to create the kind of centralized,
bureaucratic organization that might have endured but was antithetical
to its antihierarchical values. It could not reconcile a prefigurative commitment with a strategic one, could not, in the end, reconcile community
with politics.[4]

This account misses critical elements of what new leftists admired
in SNCC—and why their own participatory democracy proved so difficult to sustain. SNCC showed that creating a moral community within
the movement was essential to making political change. Mutual trust,
respect, equality, solicitousness, and a commitment to group leadership
enabled organizers to build the leadership of the politically inexperienced

and reinforced their own commitment to organizing. Against the backdrop of old left organizations whose political paranoia and internecine squabbling seemed to be matched only by their ineffectuality, a movement characterized by radical democracy made good sense.

However, few of the founders of Students for a Democratic Society (SDS) had had experience in directly democratic organizations. To make decisions—to frame issues, identify and adjudicate options, and negotiate compromises—they instead took behavioral norms and expectations from a relational style with which they were familiar: friendship. Treating their fellow SDS members as friends made it easy to delegate tasks and to resolve differences of opinion and interest. By infusing friendship with political commitments, moreover, activists countered the traditional division between public and private spheres. By extending friendship to a wide circle, they countered its usual exclusivity.

However, new leftists modified friendship's behavioral mandates only so far. When a new cohort joined the organization, SDS veterans sought self-consciously to cede power. They were far from Michelsian bureaucrats,

Students for a Democratic Society National Council meeting, Bloomington, Ind., September 1963. *From left*: Tom Hayden, Don McKelvey, Jon Seldin, Nada Chandler, Nanci Hollander, Steve Max, Danny Millstone, Vernon Grizzard, Paul Booth, Carl Wittman, Mary McGroaty, Steve Johnson, Sarah Murphy, Lee Webb, Todd Gitlin, Dick Flacks, Mickey Flacks, Robb Burlage, Gennie Davis. (Photo by C. Clark Kissinger; used with permission)

committed to democracy but even more so to maintaining their own power. Their much stronger bonds with other veterans than with newcomers led them to continue to rely on each other for information and counsel, however. Newcomers, for their part, interpreted their own marginality in political terms, charging the old guard with autocratic control. To be sure, when newcomers demanded democratic reforms, veterans acceded willingly. But the fact that such reforms were made in the context of a generational battle had lasting effects. With representative structure come to be seen as synonymous with elitism, campaigns for internal reform concentrated on limiting the power of executive officers rather than on better conveying chapters' needs and concerns to the national office. Even as successive regimes pressed for more democracy, national SDS became increasingly remote from the campuses. The denouement was by no means inevitable. There had been a real will on the part of SDS members new and old to develop a national organization that was both radically democratic and accountable. In part as a result of dynamics of friendship and exclusion, SDS lost the chance to do so.

SDS, PORT HURON, AND "PARTICIPATORY DEMOCRACY"

SDS's fate was self-consciously intertwined with that of the black student movement from the beginning. In 1959, University of Michigan graduate student Robert Alan Haber took over the campus chapter of the Student League for Industrial Democracy and renamed it Students for a Democratic Society. Haber's prodigious organizational skills notwithstanding, the group would probably have limped along on the left political fringe indefinitely had not the southern sit-ins exploded. In the North, sympathy pickets and demonstrations caught on immediately, and Haber found the demonstrations in Ann Arbor prime recruiting grounds. Sharon Jeffrey and Bob Ross were both first-year students when Haber tapped them. Jeffrey was a student council member and the daughter of a prominent union official. Ross, new to protest, had just joined the Ann Arbor group formed to coordinate pickets.[5]

Haber had been planning an April conference on civil rights even before the sit-ins began, and the conference turned into a high-profile encounter between Northern white students and sit-in representatives. Shortly after, Haber and Jeffrey attended SNCC's inaugural conference and pledged SDS's assistance in fundraising and political lobbying. They scored a coup back in Ann Arbor when they recruited the *Michigan Daily* editor Tom Hayden, whose articles on campus politics had been stirring student interest. That summer, Hayden hitchhiked to California and took a crash course in student politics, meeting with Berkeley activists, picketing the Democratic National Convention for civil rights, and talking with Southern sit-inners at the National Student Association (NSA) meeting. Sandra "Casey" Cason's speech calling on white students to act in support of the sit-ins held rapt an NSA audience, including Hayden. He pursued his courtship of her after she returned to Austin, and they married in the fall of 1961.[6]

Meanwhile, Haber and Hayden toured college campuses looking for new members. They found Paul Booth at Swarthmore, Paul Potter and Rennie Davis at Oberlin, Robb Burlage and Dorothy Dawson at the University of Texas, and Steve Max in New York and active with the left there. All became part of the SDS core. "They would go find people they . . . connected with on a gut level," Barbara Haber (then Jacobs) said later of Haber and Hayden's organizing efforts. "It wasn't, 'Do you believe in the principles of unity?' It was, 'You feel good to me. I have a feeling you're very bright and you're very spirited and we see things basically the same way.' So this was a hand-recruited bunch of people who really wanted to use their lives to change the world, and who loved finding each other." Long conversations in college dorms in Ann Arbor and Chicago, meetings that went on for days with considerable revelry, romantic relationships— all these made for strong ties.[7]

SDS leaders still had not decided what the organization should be *doing*, however. Tom Hayden had been dispatched to cover the Southern movement, and he sent back riveting accounts of SNCC organizing in southwest Georgia and Mississippi. For Sarah Lawrence student Betty Garman Robinson, like others, Hayden's briefs from the front were "the reason I went into SDS." Hayden himself was unabashed in his admiration for SNCC. "The Southern movement has turned itself into that revolution we hoped for. . . . We had better be there," he wrote excitedly. But he was also convinced that Southern racial apartheid was only one piece of the picture, along with militarism, limits on academic freedom, and middle-class alienation. SDS's task was to provide the larger picture, to show how—in a phrase becoming popular among the SDS core—the issues were related.[8]

In December 1961, after frustrating forays into campaigning for local peace candidates and organizing around campus issues, SDS leaders decided that they needed a working paper to chart a course. They had more in mind than a dry statement of organizational principles. They saw themselves as a *new* left, and they wanted a manifesto to match, one that dispensed with exotic Marxist phraseology and tortuous ideological disputes in favor of a uniquely American language of radical change. Hayden was instructed to write a draft, and, for the next several months, he read everything he could get his hands on: Marx, Dewey, Dostoyevsky, Daniel Bell, C. Wright Mills, Paul Goodman, issues of A. J. Muste's *Liberation* and David Riesman's left-liberal *Committees of Correspondence Newsletter*. In June, fifty-nine students and a few adult advisers met in a union work camp on Lake Michigan to discuss and revise Hayden's draft. The meeting began with the League for Industrial Democracy's Michael Harrington and Hayden duking it out over the necessity of taking a strong anti-Communist stand—again the battle between old and new lefts. The battle escalated when the group refused to eject an observer from a Communist group. Students were determined not to fall prey to the paranoia they believed had sapped the energies of the American left. But the next three days of the conference were different. In small groups, convention members went over the major sections of Hayden's manifesto, identifying issues that demanded substantial discussion ("bones," allotted an hour of debate) and those that could be dealt with more expeditiously ("widgets" and "gizmos"). On the last day, the entire group hammered out the substance of revisions that would be fine-tuned by a writing committee.[9]

What the students at Port Huron came up with covered a range of reforms important to a budding new left, including party realignment, disarmament, and foreign aid. But the statement's most exciting part was the section on "values," which participants had insisted Hayden move to the front of the document. It was here that SDS introduced its vision of participatory democracy: "In a participatory democracy, the political life would be based in several root principles: that decision-making of basic social consequence be carried on by public groupings; that politics be seen positively, as the art of collectively creating an acceptable pattern of social relations; that politics has the function of bringing people out of isolation and into community.... [C]hannels should be commonly available to relate men to knowledge and to power so that private problems— from bad recreation facilities to personal alienation—are formulated as general issues." The economic sphere, the statement went on, should also be characterized by democratic participation, and work should be "educative, not stultifying; creative, not mechanical; [and] self-directed, not manipulated."[10]

Participatory democracy would become one of the most powerful ideas of the era. By decade's end, thousands of groups, from bookstores, food cooperatives, and health collectives to newspapers and law firms, would dub themselves participatory democracies. But what did "participatory democracy" mean? Its framers in SDS are clear that it did *not* mean consensus-based and leaderless decisionmaking. Bob Ross wrote later that "the phrase was interpreted, by some mass media and even friendly observers, to imply 'consensus in group decision-making.' To this author's knowledge that meaning was not used at all at the Port Huron meeting in 1962, and rarely until 1965–66." "Participatory democracy" did not refer to organizational procedures at all. Dick Flacks, a University of Chicago graduate student new to SDS at Port Huron, later wrote: "Participatory democracy did not mean abandoning organizational structures of the usual sort, like elected officers and parliamentary procedure. We were thinking of participatory democracy at that time as a concept of social change, not as a set of principles for guiding the internal organizational life of SDS."[11]

What the term did mean is not entirely clear. In his draft notes for the statement, Hayden had followed his University of Michigan philosophy professor Arnold Kaufman in conceptualizing participatory institutions as distinct from but complementary to representative ones, providing citizens the education to participate wisely—the impulse Deweyan. Drawing on C. Wright Mills, however, Hayden went on to define the key political task as piercing the state of robotic, "acquiescent dread" that made Americans' participation rote and meaningless. In his account of the writing of the Port Huron Statement, James Miller argues that Hayden and his colleagues "took their central political ideas not from the civil rights movement, but rather from the tradition of civic republicanism that links Aristotle to John Dewey." According to Miller, when Hayden wrote that the Southern movement's "moral clarity" had not been accompanied by a "real political consciousness," he was "complaining that the civil rights movement lacked an adequate understanding of participatory democracy." Indeed, says Miller, Hayden's "almost patronizing call for a 'precise political vision' to guide the civil rights movement should help lay to rest the misconception that the idea of participatory democracy was a product of this movement."[12]

Participatory democracy's origins were, as Miller claims, bookish. However, by Hayden's own account, he was mining the literature for a framework in which to place his experiences in the South. In SNCC projects in McComb and Albany, Hayden later recounted, he had experienced the core components of what would become participatory democracy. One was a Camus-flavored willingness to lay one's body on the line for justice: this was the existential commitment to action that, as Miller points out, was joined somewhat uneasily with a Rousseauian vision of civic republicanism. But Hayden's experience of black Southerners sacrificing jobs, homes, and safety to secure rights of political participation that whites took for granted was also influential. Participatory democracy came from the gap between the grassroots activism that Hayden observed in Mississippi and the sterility of mainstream politics. It voiced the possibility that political institutions could be made deserving of constituents' participation. In the South, Hayden said later, he began to see "proof... that ordinary people can change conditions." "If everything could be restructured starting from the SNCC project in McComb, Mississippi," Paul Booth, also at Port Huron, reflected later, "then we would have participatory democracy."[13]

So participatory democracy as a macropolitical agenda, a "concept of social change," as Flacks described it, was influenced by SNCC's activism. Its deliberative style was too. Indeed, if "participatory democracy" did not originally refer to a set of organizational procedures, the subsequent confusion is understandable. On one hand, SDS before and after Port Huron was conventionally structured, with a National Council, executive officers, regular elections, majority voting, and Robert's Rules of Order. These forms were familiar to people whose political experience for the most part had been in student councils, college political clubs, and the NSA. Some among SDS's leaders had had exposure to consensus-based decisionmaking: the contingent from Swarthmore College, students who had been involved with the Congress of Racial Equality (CORE) and Women Strike for Peace, and some others. Still, the main organizational templates for students who had had experience in political organizations—many students, like seventeen-year-old Ross, had had none—was a bureaucratic one. Yet, when I ask Tom Hayden about SDS meetings, he remembers them as being long and consensus based. He is surprised when I remark that the SDS minutes actually record the use of motions and voting. But the ethos was one of inclusion, Hayden explains. People were leaders before the meeting, and they were leaders after the meeting. But during the meeting they were not. "Much care was expended to encourage reticent members to express their views," Barbara Haber wrote later of the Port Huron discussions. "Ideas and questions were responded to without condescension or acrimony."[14]

This was participatory democracy as a commitment to surmount the usual barriers of status, a commitment on the part of participants to treat each other as equals, not by dividing power up equally, but by fostering each person's self-development. And it came, Hayden says, directly from SNCC. What Hayden and other SDS leaders saw in SNCC was that the mutual trust and respect that bound participants were not ancillary to their political activism but preconditions for it. In the isolated and dangerous conditions in which they operated, organizers' confidence that they could draw on the advice and input of people facing similar circumstances and their knowledge that no decision would be made over their heads helped sustain them. And, in a movement that depended on mobilizing people deemed unqualified for political participation, an organization that treated participants as fundamentally equal and as already leaders was a matter of necessity. If the message of the sit-ins was that moral action could be politically effective, the message of SNCC's work now was that building affectively rich and cooperative relations across boundaries of class and education was truly radical.[15]

There were other threads in SDS members' deliberative ethos: a suspicion of bureaucracies; a negative vision of life as an "organization man," whether of the middle manager or Leninist variety; a very practical concern with how to keep people's loyalty in a voluntary organization. Together, these threads made for a determination to do things very differently than the organizations they knew. SDS was a "hybrid," Norm Fruchter wrote later, "an organization proclaiming a set of new values as its goals, yet attempting to achieve those new values through a traditional set of structures and forms." As Fruchter's observation suggests, to do so should not have been easy. Adversarial structures and procedures should have promoted distrust, competition, and efforts to win converts rather than reassess one's own position. That doing so *was* initially easy— so easy that Tom Hayden, for one, forgot that they had even used adversarial procedures at all—demands explanation. Participatory democracy just "came naturally," former SDS national secretary Jim Monsonis remembers—another tantalizing clue. Records of meetings tell us more. When the National Council met between conventions, discussion among its members was sometimes heated but always cooperative and downright affectionate. People were easily drafted into tasks: "McEldowney: 'Paul, Rennie, and Clark should set up a system with the LID [League for Industrial Democracy] for deciding who gets what' "; "Webb—will Paul develop a fund-raising program? Paul—yes." Participants were vocally supportive of the interests of others, arguing for a programmatic focus because someone in the group was interested in it or for a division of labor that would put a particular person in charge. For example: "[Doug] Ireland: [Steve] Max wants project to exist. He is interested in doing this kind of work. If such a proj[ect] is established, Max should be director."[16]

Bob Ross remembers supporting projects with which he disagreed because others saw them as important. He also remembers not being able to attend a meeting and giving his vote to the majority. In a National Council discussion of whether some correspondence with the national office should be kept confidential, Ken McEldowney took issue with a proposal that they "should lay down specific reasons why things are kept confidential." "Important thing is our trust in Clark [Kissinger, the national secretary,] and Paul [Potter, the national president,] and their ability to decide," he asserted to what seemed like general agreement—the conversation ended soon after. Trust thus substituted for formal rules. "During a brief recess," minutes recorded, "Clark Kissinger did 15 pushups; Bob Ross did 28½ pushups; Don McKelvey (hero of socialist labor) did 30 pushups." There was a playfulness about adversarial procedures. Minutes of another meeting record that "NC censures R. Davis for unproletarian activities (he was seen having his shoes shined by a child of a minority group). (Passed unanimously)." Discussions were peppered with humorous asides and teasing. They suggest nothing so much as a group of friends.[17]

Note that, in the excerpts just quoted, the friends were all men. Women's experiences were more complicated. They included both the excitement of connecting with people who shared their political passions and the niggling sense that their contributions were not as valued—or as valuable. Yet women too felt part of the group of friends, and it was the group's basis in friendship that made participatory democracy come so "naturally." Early SDSer Helen Garvy explains that, as a "community of friends," they wanted to persuade each other of their views—and wanted to be persuaded. "We were open to having our minds changed." "We were in love with each other," Dick Flacks says simply. Where pacifists in their internal deliberations relied on an associational model of Christian fellowship, then, new leftists relied on friendship. Friendship was an especially salient model for young people, and it supplied the trust, affection, and intimacy that were so palpably missing from mainstream politics. Friendship made for an easy tolerance of differences amid the excitement of consensus, and it fostered an experimentalism with respect to means.[18]

The network of friends was wider than the ones most of us are used to, extending into SNCC and other student groups. "Any friend of yours is a friend of mine," Garvy characterizes SDSers' thinking. "That means I go to your house. I sleep on your floor. I totally trust what you say. I trust your friends. Maybe I've heard you talk about your friend, maybe I haven't—I make assumptions." In this sense, new leftists were building on relations of friendship but also extending their behavioral mandates, making friendship into something more politically oriented and more inclusive than usual. National SDS correspondents concluded letters with a variety of salutations ("Peace," "Luck," "Peace and Friendship") but frequently used "Fraternally"—and this to people whom they did not know. Veterans solicited new members' opinions—"Would be interested in your thoughts on the debate which has been going on in the SDS *Bulletin* about campus/community organizing," Assistant National Secretary Don McKelvey wrote to one—and urged them to attend national conventions and National Council meetings. "That sort of face-to-face contact is, I think, optimal and highly important," McKelvey wrote to another student, more important than whether people took out formal membership in the group, he was convinced, and more important even than politics. At the last convention, McKelvey wrote, "the political discussing never got done"— but the convention had "played the important function of (re)establishing a community of people who are SDS people."[19]

If, in its early years, SDS was conventionally structured, it was nevertheless imbued with a powerful commitment to participatory deliberations. This was "participatory democracy as a spirit not a mechanism," as Bob Ross puts it. It depended on an ethos of care and mutual regard that had been made radical by its enactment in the most repressive areas of the Deep South. And it depended on the bonds of affection, trust, and openness that linked a far-flung group of friends. There were already hints of recognition that this might not be enough to sustain a democratic organization, however. In December 1962, Barbara Jacobs warned of an "arrogant resistance to the 'new people.' . . . I think that incest is beginning to lead to inbreeding." In the same vein, Tom Hayden wrote to a Harvard student in 1963 that SDS needed to forge more of a "counter community," where activists could "create new forms of action and life." By that time, some SDS members were already feeling excluded by a leadership elite that treated them like "little people," as one put it in retrospect. These tensions would become sharper.[20]

Finally, if national SDS remained conventionally structured, by 1963 some SDS chapters were already beginning to experiment with formal modes of participatory democratic decisionmaking. For example, in VOICE, the Ann Arbor SDS chapter, leaders were rotated, and members strove for consensus. However, it was in SDS's community-organizing projects, explicitly modeled on SNCC's, that participatory democracy evolved from a macropolitical vision to an internal movement practice.[21]

LETTING THE PEOPLE DECIDE: PARTICIPATORY DEMOCRACY IN ERAP

Al Haber had been eager to cast SDS as SNCC's Northern counterpart, and he applauded SNCC's shift from direct action to political organizing in 1961. But SDS, to his mind, was a *campus* organization, its job to influence national policy and train a cadre of student activists who would go on to radicalize their professions. Tom Hayden, by contrast, was growing frustrated with the life of the campus radical. "Should everyone be living and organizing outside of institutions?" he wondered in 1962 during a winter he later called "depressing." "Can the methods of SNCC be applied to the North?" he queried SDSers.[22]

Students for a Democratic Society National Council meeting, New York City, December 1963. Discussion of Wittman and Hayden's "An Interracial Movement of the Poor?" *From left*: Unidentified man, Tom Hayden, Carl Wittman, Nanci Hollander, Steve Max, Paul Potter, unidentified woman. (Photo by C. Clark Kisssinger; used with permission)

The answer, Hayden proposed, was yes on both counts. SDS's Economic and Research Action Project (ERAP) was launched with a $5,000 grant from the United Auto Workers in September 1963. Its purpose was to organize poor whites in a class-based alliance with blacks. Poor people's "alienation and a discouragement with existing economic policies" made them prime candidates for organizing, SDS leaders theorized. Under pressure from ERAP projects and other "new insurgencies," and in the face of an automation-induced economic crisis, the liberal-labor coalition would be forced to push for a transfer of national resources from the arms race to the creation of a welfare state. In addition, and perhaps more important, organizing the white side of what SDS leaders called an "interracial movement of the poor" would enable white students to move beyond their role as cheerleaders for the Southern movement. Todd Gitlin, who was SDS president at the time, explained later: "There was a strong feeling on the part of black organizers in both SNCC and NSM [Northern Student Movement] that SDS was this bullshit talk organization that put out a lot of smart working papers and talked a lot, but didn't do anything." SDSers hoped that ERAP would change that. In late spring 1964, over one hundred student activists were dispatched to projects in Cleveland; Chicago; Newark and Trenton, New Jersey; Hazard and Louisville, Kentucky; Philadelphia and Chester, Pennsylvania; and Boston.[23]

Launching an interracial movement of the poor was hard work. Residents were naturally suspicious of college students knocking on their doors, and some local authorities spread rumors that they were Communists. ERAP organizers lacked the entrée to communities that had been provided SNCC workers by people like Amzie Moore. The communities in which ERAP worked were rarely unified by strong churches, and residents often did not know their neighbors. Add to that the fact that the theory underpinning the ERAP project was flawed. "We were not met by armies of white unemployed," Paul Potter wrote ruefully later. "When the ERAP projects began, unemployment was actually decreasing in most of the cities we worked in." In fact, an economic upswing was beginning, one that would be hastened by war expenditures. In response, most ERAP projects gave up trying to organize around employment and turned instead to issues that residents themselves raised: welfare cases, housing conditions, local services. In Cleveland, ERAP organizers resuscitated a moribund welfare organization and began to organize women to demand a school lunch program and higher welfare benefits. In Newark, they challenged the urban-renewal program and launched rent strikes for better housing. In Chester, they organized a school boycott. Chicago's Jobs or Income Now (JOIN) retained a commitment to organizing around jobs but branched out into other issues as well.[24]

From the beginning, participatory democracy was central to ERAP organizers' efforts. "We got enthralled by ourselves and our group process," Cleveland organizer Sharon Jeffrey reflected later. "That became more important than any other issue." Staff on the Cleveland project made decisions by consensus and referred to positions as "research keeper" and "broom keeper" to equalize their status. On other projects, too, staff lived in group households and experimented with egalitarian relations. But they also saw participatory decisionmaking as a critical tool in organizing. Creating committees of residents to run projects, rotating leadership, making decisions by consensus, bringing residents onto staff, and keeping organizers in the background as much as possible—these would build the community leadership that would endure after organizers left. "We are a transient force in the community, and must leave indigenous leadership and organization there permanently," Tom Hayden wrote from Newark, where he had set up shop.[25]

By 1965, some ERAPers and supporters were envisioning an "anti-Establishment network" of alternative political, economic, and educational institutions run on participatory democratic principles. But, for most ERAPers, formulating a macropolitical agenda was less important than building the capacities of local people to make decisions about their lives independent of authorities or organizers. Success was a Dovie Thurman, a working-class Chicagoan who described her first JOIN meeting: "I stood up and made a couple of statements" in response to an organizer who asked how she felt about welfare. "'I'm sick and tired of this welfare system. I don't know what to do about it, but I want to fight, too. It's doing the same to all of us.' It was my first encounter speaking to a group of people, and I got a big hand. . . . At the next meeting I was nominated to be chairperson. Just that quick. What was most exciting was somebody wanted me. I didn't even know what a chairperson was."[26]

If organizers were agreed that their job was to build indigenous leadership, it did not make the task either easy or free of ambiguities. How much should organizers plan, push, and speak for the group? Initially, some SDS leaders were clear about organizers' tutelary role. "Of course organizers are learners, but they must be educators as well," Gitlin wrote in 1964. Organizers would teach residents the skills that they needed to mount a campaign and confront city hall. They would help people see beyond their personal misfortunes to the structural forces responsible for them and move from local agendas to broader ones. Over time, however, ERAPers began to consider that view counterproductive and downright arrogant. Residents knew better than they did the needs of their communities. Organizers' job was simply to help them put their demands to those in power. And even then they worried about the power of their influence. "At what stage in the growth of a movement of poor people, or of an organization, do ERAP staff withdraw from decision-making, if at all?" an ERAPer put up for discussion, adding parenthetically, "Maybe it's relevant here to deal with the concept of 'manipulation.'" "Manipulation" was becoming, as it had in SNCC, a dread word.[27]

In fact, it was the SNCC organizer's seeming capacity to avoid manipulation—the organizer "who never organized, who by his simple presence was the mystical medium for the spontaneous expression of the 'people'"—that made him such a venerated model. "ERAP was heavily influenced by the SNCC legend," Chicago JOIN's Richard Rothstein wrote a year later. "'Manipulation' was an oft-heard term. . . . [T]he thought that the students, too, might be making decisions for the poor in the guise of helping them was enough to turn the hardiest stomach. To many, the very existence of the organizer had paternalistic implications. Why would an organizer be there if he didn't assume that he was better than the ghetto residents, had some superior knowledge about a movement which he was imposing (by fact of superior articulateness) on the innocent, unknowing residents?" The syndrome, said Rothstein, was puzzling—and paralyzing. "Why this inability to resolve the definition of an organizer? Why this cropping up of the word 'manipulation' whenever we might otherwise have been on the verge of action or decision?"[28]

Rothstein was sharply critical of his fellow ERAPers' experiments in democracy. The lack of organizational structure put almost complete power in the hands of organizers, who began "to pretend (at the time even to themselves) that 'the people' were deciding issues that only organizers knew about, let alone understood." In some cases, organizers' claim to be letting the people decide was disingenuous, in others, naive. As part of a drive to democratize, ERAP head Rennie Davis had abolished the national ERAP office on the grounds that strategic decisions depended too much on local conditions to benefit from input from anyone outside the project. As a result, project staffs stopped meeting to compare and evaluate their work: "Not feeling itself part of an experimental, tactically variegated movement, each project acted as though it bore the burden of history on its shoulders alone. . . . How could a project experiment with factory organizing, or even with leadership training in such a context?" Decentralization actually discouraged innovation.[29]

Rothstein's critique obscured some problems and overstated others. As had been true in SNCC, the problem was often less that organizers were imposing their own vision or abdicating their role altogether than that they simply did not know what to do. At the same time, many organizers managed to avoid both a stance of behind-the-scenes control and passivity, instead experimenting with new ways to build residents' capacities without scaring them off. In Cleveland, for example, organizers tried out a system of residential "clusters" in which active residents met regularly in their homes, thus avoiding the inconvenience and formality of a public meeting. Some ERAPers today also dispute Rothstein's conclusion that the dismantling of the national ERAP office spelled an end to information sharing among the projects. To the contrary, many ERAP projects were in regular contact with others nearby.[30]

However, organizers' efforts to "merge their lives with poor people," as Dick Flacks wrote in 1965, may have had other unrecognized costs. As in SNCC, periodically reaffirming the tight bonds among a far-flung group had helped sustain organizers' energy and commitment in hostile circumstances. Organizers' sense of acting on a national stage made it easier to tolerate setbacks and gave them a sense of accomplishing radical change even as they fought for incremental gains. In this respect, the ERAP summer institutes had been valuable, their organizers agreed, not only or even mainly in trading information but in fostering a sense of collective identity, creating a "welded group." Now, they worried that such efforts were self-indulgent. "We say we want to immerse ourselves in a community," Cleveland ERAPers wrote. "On the one hand, you have to stay in the community and work and that's the way to build a movement. On the other hand, you have this national thing going and you want people to really be able to travel and talk and be with each other."[31]

Giving up the chance to relate to other student activists had costs. Once people realized that "the role of the organizer . . . turns out to have manipulative content and places young people in quite artificial relations with the people in the neighborhood . . . what we then observe is that some people on ERAP projects stop organizing, or become moody, disaffected, inarticulate or 'crazy,'" Flacks wrote. ERAP organizers simply had to "replace themselves in the community with indigenous organization." And SDS would "have to develop the idea that what we are trying to do in these communities is education more than anything else." That Flacks was proposing an educational role as a novel one suggests that participatory democracy's pedagogical purposes had been abandoned. ERAPers' earlier claims to pedagogical authority had been misplaced, "arrogant" Gitlin calls them now. But their shift to the other extreme illustrates the tension between deferring and leading at the heart of organizing—and at the heart of participatory democracy as an organizing strategy.[32]

ERAPers increasingly defined radicalism in terms of a denial of their own agency. And that denial was exceedingly difficult to sustain. The resulting situation was curious. On the one hand, ERAP proved remarkably useful to SDS as a recruiting device. When students wrote to SDS requesting information about the organization, the letter they received emphasized SDS's work with poor people in Northern cities, work that was "roughly comparable to what SNCC is doing in the rural South—building a radical movement of the dispossessed in order to give the people voice." "Symbolically it was great," says Carl Oglesby, who would become SDS president in 1965, "because it gave SDS a dimension, a sense of presence in the real world that it could never have had if it was seen as operating exclusively in a campus context. It projected our image beyond the campus, past campus sandlot politics, to the real world of poverty, racism, police brutality." When students heard about SDS and wanted to "do something," SDS put them to work in ERAP projects. On the other hand, the spurt was short-lived. Lacking the missionary zeal of ERAP's founders, new cohorts of organizers were less willing to subordinate their radical aspirations to endless meetings with poor people, and they were easily lured back to campuses, where, in the wake of the Gulf of Tonkin bombing, antiwar activism was beginning to heat up. Of the thirteen ERAP projects under way at the start of the summer of 1965, only five were left by late fall. By the following year, only Chicago and Newark were still functioning.[33]

Was participatory democracy responsible for ERAP projects' inability to rack up much in the way of tangible successes? No. By 1965, ERAP was competing with poverty programs for residents' allegiance and with anti–Vietnam War activism for student organizers' interest. The people they were trying to organize lacked the social infrastructure that might have generated solidary incentives to participate. Probably the long philosophical discussions on ERAP projects alienated people whose jobs and families gave them little time for such luxuries. And ERAPers' vision of an ideal democracy was not always appealing to those with whom they worked. But these problems paled before the other ones that organizers were up against. Moreover, ERAP's commitment to building residents' leadership can be credited with some of the project's accomplishments. In Newark, residents won rent strikes and took over the local War on Poverty board. In Chicago, they gained concessions from the welfare office. Cleveland became one of the organizing centers for the National Welfare Rights Organization (NWRO) in 1966, and, according to a scholar of that organization, those residents who had had experience in ERAP were the least likely to fall prey to a permanent dependence on NWRO organizers.[34]

If participatory democracy was not responsible for ERAP's travails, was it responsible for SDS's? By 1965, ERAP counted some of SDS's top leaders on its staff. Did those leaders bring their passion for grassroots democracy into the national organization—trying to run a chapter-based organization with thousands of members like a community meeting? No. ERAPers tended to be more concerned with sustaining their own projects than with reforming the national organization. Indeed, some in national SDS found them downright dismissive of movement work outside community organizing. "'We ERAPers, the authentic ones here, are over there trying to do this quiet, difficult but serious and significant work, while you all are back there at the campus, maybe once a month kicking over the tables about Vietnam,'" Carl Oglesby later caricatured them. In fact, staff on some ERAP projects seemed to be able to shift from campus protest to community organizing and back again. Others had no gripe with campus organizing; given the fact that they were no longer students, however, they saw less of a role for themselves in it. The important effect of ERAP on SDS's internal functioning was rather that so many of SDS's major figures were ensconced in local projects and had little contact with newcomers to the organization. Yet they continued to be consulted by SDS's formal leaders. This combination of remoteness and influence would sharpen the divide between newcomers and what newcomers perceived as an elite "old guard." The strongest calls for participatory democracy emerged in the context of this divide.[35]

DECISIONMAKING IN SDS, 1965–66

In September 1964, Berkeley students raising money for SNCC and CORE protested a university ban on campus solicitation, and the protest quickly escalated into a full-scale confrontation with the university administration. The Berkeley Free Speech Movement ignited a round of campus activism. Some SDS leaders were quick to see the possibilities for radicalizing students around their own grievances and, not least, for moving SDS's emphasis from the ghetto back to the campus. After the Gulf of Tonkin bombing, campus demonstrations around the war in Vietnam began to pick up tempo, and, at a December meeting, SDS leaders decided by a narrow margin to sponsor a march on Washington against the war. About three thousand participants were anticipated. The three thousand turned into twenty thousand, and the event thrust SDS into the media spotlight. SDS mushroomed: from 29 chapters and one thousand members in June 1964, to 80 chapters and more than two thousand members in June 1965, to 124 chapters and forty-three hundred members by the end of 1965. The "community of friends" suddenly had an opportunity to become the leading organization of a burgeoning antiwar movement. The situation was in some ways similar to SNCC's eight months earlier: a newly high profile, a surge in membership, demands by the press for "leaders" as spokespeople, and confusion about the place of community organizing in a broader agenda. In both organizations, lines were drawn between those pushing for full internal democracy—whatever the cost, as those antagonistic to such a move saw it—and those willing to temper their democratic principles in the interests of political efficacy. Whereas in SNCC the battle ended with the defeat of the decentralists and the moralistic commitments that had become associated with them, in SDS the decentralists triumphed. Formal offices were progressively eliminated, voting criteria abandoned, and major decisions made by referenda.[36]

For SDS's leaders, the June 1965 national convention held on Lake Kewadin hinted at what was to come. Discussions went off on tangents, position papers were ignored, people stood up and made outrageous statements and then wandered out of the room. Some participants seemed more interested in drugs than in discussion and more interested in action for its own sake than in political effectiveness. They seemed different than old SDS members—more rebellious, uninterested in retaining liberal alliances, with an antiauthoritarian bent that seemed in keeping with their Western and Southwestern origins. They called for eliminating the offices of president and vice president and were stopped only by the promise of a member referendum on the issue; they showed no interest in finding a national secretary. Veteran SDSer Steve Max was furious about Kewadin. In a paper circulated among SDS's membership, he mocked the prevailing mood: "Structural democracy is an obvious fraud; out with it! Representative government doesn't really represent anyone; out with it!" It was not democracy, he continued, when chairs for the plenary sessions, often with more than 250 participants, were selected at random and votes were not counted. Or when "several hundred delegates assembled for a national conference or convention see an officer of the organization get up and ask, 'Well what would you like to talk about?'" Max feared for the future of SDS. He described the last night of the convention: "A handful of 'old-timers' watched the sunrise and recalled a similar morning four years ago at Port Huron. We have come a long way together since then, and four years is a long time in the lives of young people, long enough to make me realize how much farther we have to go. The difficulties we have faced are no doubt trivial compared to what the future holds for us; but we emerged from the convention determined to face these new trials as friends united. Perhaps after all is said and written, it is this fact which differentiates us from other organizations, past and present."[37]

Left unclear in Max's conclusion, however, was whether the "friends united" who were charged with the future of the organization included more than a "handful of old-timers." And that was precisely what newcomers were reacting to when they charged "elitism." Max's picture of SDS betrayed the problem. For many of those at Kewadin, the main experience was neither one of democracy run amok, nor one of a group of friends united, but rather one of exclusion from the group of friends running the show. Robert Pardun, representing the Austin SDS chapter at his second national convention, later described the meeting as dominated by "a few articulate men who spoke often and seemed to enjoy political bantering." They showed little interest in newcomers: "Except for Helen Garvy and Clark Kissinger, people I already knew, I don't remember having a conversation with more than one or two old guard people during the entire convention. . . . We wondered why the old guard seemed so stand-offish. . . . The personal conversations and friendship that would have helped break down the boundaries between 'us' and 'them' never occurred at Kewadin." This was not participatory democracy, Pardun observed. "Less articulate or less experienced members" felt "excluded or irrelevant." SDS leaders earlier had prided themselves on their solicitousness toward the shy and inexperienced among them. This was part of how they understood participatory democracy. That newcomers experienced precisely the opposite suggests that there were limits to how far that solicitousness extended.[38]

Pardun and his Austin colleagues had come to SDS's national convention the year before and had been impressed by SDSers' political sophistication. "Smartest people I'd met," Austin activist Jeff Nightbyrd (then Shero) said later. "They were all-stars. It's like if you're a baseball player and you've been playing in Class A leagues and all of a sudden you go up to the Bigs and, you say, '*Jesus!* Look at those guys hit.'" Nightbyrd was elected to the National Council. But, in letters to Helen Garvy that fall, he expressed a combination of excitement and frustration. "I'm writing to you because we folk in the boondock seem to get forgotten by the vast N[ational] O[ffice] except by the old worker girl and *Bulletin* editor," he wrote in November. He was "burbling over with ideas and thoughts and other various insanities," and he was eager to reconnect with the SDS heavies he had met earlier. But he was sensitive to their indifference. Nightbyrd was not alone. Letters sent by chapter members to the national office in 1964 and 1965 referred repeatedly to the founding generation of SDS as a group of "friends" and complained about their exclusion from the clique. "The main problem seems to be to reach new people," Helen Garvy wrote to a chapter member who complained of being shut out of "the mysterious inner workings of SDS." "You weren't alone in feeling lost at the convention." She wrote to another chapter member, "I'm really concerned with the lack of communication between chapters and the national organization," and proposed "to have more retreats ... where people can just go off and talk for a few days—both old and new people, local and national SDS." To SDS's leadership, she wondered, "How do we permeate an informal leadership that grew from the days when SDS was a small group of friends?"[39]

Consider the problem in more general terms. If friendship supplies the trust, mutual affection, and respect that facilitate fast and fair decisions, it also makes it difficult to expand the deliberative group beyond the original circle. Newcomers lack an understanding of the history of the issues at stake as well as the idiosyncratic practices of *this* organization. Veterans may fail to inform and consult them. But newcomers' lack is affective as well as informational. Since newcomers by definition threaten existing friendships, they may find it difficult to secure the trust, respect, and solicitude that veterans enjoy. Newcomers' social marginality may translate into political marginality, or they may fear that it is doing so. What veterans see as a friend's momentary lapse in a participatory democratic ethos, newcomers may see as yet one more instance of elitism. And veterans may realize that they have been exclusive only when newcomers attack them for their insufficient commitment to participatory democracy.[40]

Wanting to be part of a group they perceived as exciting and charismatic, some people at Kewadin, especially young men like Nightbyrd, alternated between competing with, challenging, and appealing to those whom they perceived as running things. "It was common knowledge that the only way to insert yourself into the elite, as a newcomer, was to take on members of the leadership in political debate and argumentation, in order to prove credentials," Norm Fruchter wrote later. Nightbyrd won the SDS vice presidency after he challenged Hayden to a public debate on the merits of community versus campus-based organizing. Hayden ended up ceding the debate entirely. But, if the old guard interpreted this as a win for the young Turks, Nightbyrd and the Austin activists experienced Hayden's unwillingness to engage with them as a sign of dismissiveness. Their bid to reconfigure the offices of president and vice president was motivated, Pardun says now, by the sense that current national officers had little accountability to SDS's membership: "If you were friends with the National Secretary, then you could have an influence, but not if you weren't." But Pardun also admits that those who challenged the existing structure had not worked out much of an alternative. Helen Garvy agrees: "I thought it didn't make any sense, and it wasn't articulated very well. The solution got argued about, not the problem." The problem, Garvy says, was newcomers' continuing sense of exclusion. And only this solution got argued about, not the other proposals that members had made for reforming SDS's organizational structure. For, in fact, a number of people, both veterans and newcomers, had prepared thoughtful memos drawing attention to the challenges of SDS's new size and proposing organizational reforms that would allow it to maintain a decentralized but coordinated structure. But the papers were largely ignored. The challenge to SDS's national offices was deferred to a membership referendum (with only six hundred people casting votes, retaining the offices was favored three to one). In the contest for president, the old guard's candidate, Dickie Magidoff, was defeated by Carl Oglesby, new to the organization and sympathetic to the emerging counterculture and the antiwar movement. No programmatic agenda was hammered out.[41]

In the wake of the Kewadin meeting, SDS struggled to juggle the complexities of its position in the antiwar movement, its suddenly high media profile, the hordes of chapters petitioning for membership, and the tense relations between old and new guards. The newcomers *were* different. Their antiauthoritarianism was upfront. They held little truck with the long intellectual analyses or with the thrust and parry that had been the old SDS style. They wanted action now and were indifferent to maintaining the sympathies of liberal allies. The term *prairie power* captured their Western origins and outlaw image. Certainly, they came from different places than the old guard: Texas, Iowa, Kansas, southern California. The "outlaw" image was probably overstated. As historian

Doug Rossinow points out, the University of Texas SDS activists who were most strongly identified with the prairie power label had not grown up in vehemently antiradical households, nor were they the working-class hillbillies that some pictured. Their ideological commitments were diverse; their antiauthoritarianism was neither uniform nor fully worked out. People like Nightbyrd and Pardun may have been clearer than others about what a thoroughgoing cultural radicalism would look like, but such clarity was rare. In the Austin SDS, wrote Nightbyrd in 1964, "we have Leninists, Humanists, social democrats, liberal democrats, and a couple of beatniks." The wider stream of newcomers similarly espoused everything "from counterculture utopianism to a budding Marxism," says Bob Ross.[42]

Newcomers banded, not around shared ideological commitment, or even tactical styles, as much as around their sense of exclusion from the group of friends. Again, the problem was not entirely new: as early as 1962 SDS leaders had raised the dangers of an in-group. It had been easier to integrate newcomers when veterans knew them, however. Friends brought friends into the group. They were likely to tap people who were like themselves—an obstacle to diversity but a way to sustain the integrity of preexisting friendships. Now, however, there were hundreds of new people. "The friendship group just reached the saturation point," Hayden recalls. And Gitlin: "The Old Guard, preoccupied with ERAP and the we-happy-few mystique of the early years of face-to-face organizing, failed to take these 'prairie people' into our old-boy networks."[43]

Ignored by the old guard, newcomers responded by challenging them on the hypocrisy of an elitist clique of participatory democrats. Old-guard members were vulnerable to the critique. They too believed that SDS's task was to forge a radically democratic alternative, and they acquiesced readily to the elimination of organizational arrangements that hinted of oligarchy. But it was more ceding ground to the newcomers than a joint effort to develop an alternative structure. Austin activists had been invited to run the national office that summer, and they chose to do so as a collective, sharing tasks and decisionmaking. But they had not anticipated the flood of requests for information that came into the office, the scarcity of funding (they took jobs in the middle of the summer to bring in funds), and the failure of anyone to orient them to the system. Nor had they anticipated the hostility that they encountered from SDS veterans. Robert Pardun recalls, "The first thing we did was to send out this mailing, and we got these letters from old guard people saying, 'I don't mean to be hostile, but . . . ,' and then just tearing into us, saying how we had done everything wrong.'"[44]

The office *was* chaotically run—but it continued to be so after Paul Booth took the position of national secretary in response to the crisis. He reported that office functioning "hit an all-time low" in the fall of 1965. In any case, the episode pointed to deepening splits between new and old guard. Booth himself was soon widely attacked within the organization for presuming to articulate to the press an SDS position on the draft when none had yet been decided ("PARTICIPATORY DEMOCRACY BEGINS AT HOME," wired one angry SDS member). But the June convention had not established national program directives: there had been talk of a draft-resistance program, but nothing had come of it, and, when Paul Booth spoke, it was in the absence of an organizational position. Helen Garvy remembers that Booth's friends saw his move as "misguided, not evil, and trusted that he wouldn't do it again once soundly reprimanded." But those outside the friendship core had no reason to think that. In a memo to the SDS membership late that fall, Jeff Nightbyrd complained, "The old leaders are those that have been in SDS since its early days (two to three years), and have a rather developed sense of friendship and mutual respect." When the organization had had to decide whether Carl Oglesby should accept an invitation to visit Hanoi, Nightbyrd went on, "The National Secretary [Paul Booth] did the phone consultations and naturally tended to call people he knew and respected. Thus members of the older leadership shared in another decision, while members of vigorous chapters like Buffalo, Iowa, Sacramento State, Texas and Indiana were not asked to formulate opinions."[45]

Friendship operated in subtle ways. Old friends sat in on the National Council meetings and enjoyed an easy camaraderie and shorthand knowledge of issues. They probably spoke more than newcomers. When they held office, they called their friends for advice, and they sought each other out at meetings. These were all natural behaviors for friends, but they had the potential to alienate newcomers. SDS leaders *were* highly conscious of the need to give newcomers a sense of belonging and generous in their desire to turn over the reins of power. "We weren't saints," Bob Ross says now. "Maybe at a conference we'd be having a conversation and wouldn't be as welcoming to a new person as we should have been. But we were really very conscious of trying to integrate them." But something as innocuous as not being welcoming at a meeting may have been enough to confirm newcomers' anxieties. "Absolutely," says Helen Garvy now when I ask her about that dynamic. "You wanted to see your old friends. You probably hadn't seen each other since the last national meeting, and so you would gravitate toward your friends. I'm struck now by the number of people I didn't even know at meetings. They say now, 'I was at Clear Lake too,' and I have no memory of them."[46]

Before Kewadin, Robb Burlage had called for "more 'free time' and 'play periods'" at SDS's June convention, "untitled and unstructured discussion, small group get-togethers, etc., to allow people to become better acquainted with each other as people as well as 'representatives' or 'programmers' or 'partisans.' This might mean more parties, more access to liquor at or near the convention site, etc." Burlage was recognizing, however awkward his solutions, the importance of forging affective bonds among members of a group that could no longer rely on the natural dynamics of friendship. That kind of recognition was rare, however. "We were unsophisticated about human resources issues," Bob Ross says now, using a term more familiar in relation to for-profit organizations than to movement ones. "I would have focused much more on the personal stuff," Helen Garvy says, also groping for language. "We didn't know anything about small groups." She notes that, at the first SDS reunion, participants broke down into small groups to get reacquainted, recognizing, years later, the importance of intimate connections to forging larger group bonds. In the 1960s, however, Garvy goes on, "we would have dismissed that as touchy-feely. We were suspicious of that stuff."[47]

In the absence of attention to the "personal stuff," and with the bonds of friendship no longer serving to unite the group, tendencies toward just the kind of ideological battling that SDSers had found so repugnant in the old left became more pronounced. "Looking back," Hayden said later, "what I really think is that you had an organization with a lot of very strong male egos. And leadership tendencies and ambition. And having a one-year check on leadership and automatic rotation prevented certain kinds of rivalries. . . . [Consensus] was the perfect organizational formula for the suppression of middle-class ambition . . . [b]ecause it made you harness your own conditioning." But Kewadin, said Robert Pardun, reminded him of nothing more than his "high school debate team." SDS's next major meeting, a "Rethinking Conference" held in December, was even worse. People had written papers proposing new programmatic directions and organizational reforms. Again, they were ignored as the meeting dissolved into factionalism and speechmaking. People talked about "'the Texas guys,' 'those New York coalitionists,' 'the Chicago bunch,'" Todd Gitlin wrote in *New Left Notes* shortly after. Speechmaking had become the "premium style. If you make a good speech, you're in; otherwise, you're out."[48]

The convention failed to stem the tide of antiorganizational, anti–old leadership animus. At the National Council meeting that followed, members tried and failed to agree about a draft plan. To deal with SDS's organizational turmoil, they endorsed the regional organizations that had been springing up and made plans for the *Bulletin* to be produced weekly in order to inform chapters of developments elsewhere. These were fairly small solutions to the sharp divisions that were evident at the conference. Old-guard members began to drift away from the organization.[49]

GROWTH AND DISCONTINUITY

Steve Max had warned after the Kewadin convention that a "failure to begin working out a common political position will increasingly turn SDS into an arena for propaganda and recruitment by all manner of left-sectarian organizations." His prediction eventually would prove accurate. At SDS's 1969 convention, sectarian factions battled for control of the organization, each one elaborating its own vision of revolution in Marxian jargon. By the convention's end, SDS had ceased to exist.[50]

But this was a full four years after Kewadin and three and a half after the December Rethinking Conference. And, for at least several of those years, SDS was both growing dramatically—it counted 100,000 members by 1968—and active in a variety of reform efforts, from antiwar organizing and draft resistance to university curricular change. One cannot draw a line from Kewadin to SDS's collapse—unless, that is, one sees centralized organization as the sine qua non of organizational survival. If that is the case, then the point at which SDS members determined to do away with conventional representative structures was the beginning of the end. Likewise, if one sees "success in the world of Democratic party politics" as the yardstick of movement impact—this, says Wini Breines, is what SDS's historians have tended to do—then the indifference to liberal alliances and revolutionary millenarianism that marked the late 1960s was already there by the time of Kewadin in the antiauthoritarianism of the prairie people. Finally, if one believes that SDS could have kept sectarians out by better policing its borders, then eliminating membership criteria in the name of participatory democracy gave Progressive Labor cadres intent on taking over just the entry ticket they needed.[51]

These are the assumptions that have underpinned the standard analyses of SDS's downfall, and they miss the mark in several ways. A "disciplined, centralized organization could neither have 'saved' the movement," Breines writes in her perceptive critique, "nor was it congruent with the New Left's suspicion of hierarchy, leadership, and the concentration of power." It could not have saved the movement because, by 1965, the real action was taking place on campuses largely outside the auspices of any formal organization. Alongside the agonies of national SDS, local chapters were forming, expanding, and experimenting with a variety of actions and targets. It is silly to think that national SDS could have controlled the upsurge. Infused by countercultural notions of freedom and personhood, participatory democracy now had multiple incarnations. SDS leaders could not have stepped in at that point to take charge of its meaning. If protesters' radicalism eventually became hard-edged and polarizing, it is hard to imagine that unrelenting exposure to liberal betrayals on civil rights, state-perpetrated violence in Vietnam and in the American South, and televised images of urban racial riots and war zones could have produced something different. To chastise new leftists for their language of apocalypse forgets that they were living in apocalyptic times.[52]

So the eclipse of SDS's old guard cannot be held responsible for the eventual collapse of the organization. However, there were lasting consequences of the way the succession took place. Programmatic, strategic, and organizational issues were conflated in the debates: when people argued that chapters should have more power, sometimes they meant that SDS should focus on campuses rather than communities, sometimes that SDS should not try to lead a national antiwar movement, and sometimes that discussing the appropriate structure of the national organization was a waste of time since SDS's real heart was in its chapters. With structure so much on the table and goals so difficult to talk about, discussions about programs shifted to discussions of structure, and structural reforms substituted for hashing out programmatic plans.

Organizational reforms in some ways took the place of substantive policies, but those reforms were not developed very carefully or implemented effectively. Despite the real will on the part of its members to do so, SDS failed in its attempt to create a functioning participatory democracy. The failure was not to create a structureless national organization—no one wanted that. But, in position papers, memos, and letters, people had sketched routes to an organizational structure that was democratic and accountable, participatory and effective. In one such piece, Paul Potter suggested that chapters could supply two people as full-time staff to the national office for six months per year. The arrangement, he said, would provide intensive exposure to SDS functioning and would keep the organization controlled by its constituents—but by giving them responsibility for it. There were many other proposals of this ilk, some hardly viable, but others sensible and creative. In the history of American movements, this was the first time that such experimentation had been proposed in a national mass movement organization. Liberal pacifists, remember, even with their ideals of personal conscience and community building, had been comfortable with strong individual leadership. Radical pacifists' organizations were small, homogeneous, and restricted to direct action. SNCC was a staff organization, not a membership one. SDS was a national membership organization, was active on numerous fronts, and targeted national authorities as well as local ones. Those who proposed to make it a participatory democratic organization were trying something truly new. Had they succeeded in getting people to talk about the issues seriously and cooperatively, they might have reaped a benefit that I have seen as being among participatory democracy's most important, namely, its orientation toward experimenting with new criteria of authority.[53]

However, the memos and position papers were ignored. And efforts to talk about how to make the national office more representative were met with calls to restrict the power of national officers. Little attention was paid to how members would have input into the positions taken and policies made by the national office. This made for a national office that was increasingly remote from the chapters. Some officers did make a point of traveling frequently to chapters to tap members' concerns. But this was not a lasting mechanism. Chapter members, for their part, could with good reason feel that "where the action was"—autonomous, exciting, near spontaneous action—was on their own campuses. But what happened in the national office was not irrelevant to them. They did take the trouble to take out memberships, after all. And their letters to the national office and to *New Left Notes* suggest that they identified with SDS as a national organization. They wanted help and recognition and representation from national SDS—not programs handed down ready-made, but information about other projects, ideas for gaining support, and evidence that their efforts were contributing to a national movement. Chapters with less and less input into the national office and a national office that was itself becoming the prize in battles over an ideologically correct line—these developments set the stage for the "center's" collapse even as the organization around it was, in terms of size and scope, exploding. Could those developments have been prevented? Clearly not by implementing centralized organization and top-down command. But they might have been, had SDS leaders better socialized newcomers, had some veterans not become indifferent to the problems of a national organization just when it was exploding in size, and had veterans made a firmer effort to replace friendship with more open and accountable associational models.

FRIENDSHIP AND COMMUNITY

Where pacifists modeled their internal democracies on fellowship, new leftists modeled theirs on the kind of radical pedagogy they had seen operating in SNCC and on friendship. By "modeled," I mean they relied on the interactional norms characteristic of those relationships in order to deliberate in ways that seemed to conform to an ethos of participation and equality. Those relationships shaped how they framed questions and answers, considered options, dealt with conflict, distinguished insiders and outsiders, and sought participants' compliance in enacting decisions. Each relationship also tendered broader political possibilities. The pedagogy characteristic of community organizing assumed that everyone was "qualified" to make decisions about the issues that affected them, and opened the way to challenges to welfare offices and university curricular committees, draft boards and the State Department. Modeling democracy on friendship brought into political deliberations the trust, openness, and affection that were as absent from left organizations as from mainstream politics.

This is not to say that either friendship or an organizing pedagogy offered an entirely clear set of behavioral mandates. To the contrary, I have emphasized ambiguities as well as constraints. Increasingly uncomfortable with what they perceived as their own capacities for manipulation, ERAP organizers became convinced that real equality was at odds with pedagogy of any kind. Committed to building the leadership of local people, they sometimes so denied their own independent interests and opinions as to weaken their investment in the democracies they had helped create. Friendship also generated behavioral ambiguities and constraints. Newcomers were mainly responsible for the challenge to SDS's organizational structure in 1965, and they were motivated at least in part by their exclusion from the tight bonds among SDS's founders. Their interests and ideological commitments were not palpably different from those they challenged; more important, their ideologies were internally diverse and undeveloped. Newcomers came together, rather, around their shared experience of marginalization from a founding group of friends. Veterans had never compensated for friendship's intrinsic exclusiveness by implementing formal mechanisms to give authority to those outside the group of friends. Now they reaped the consequences. The participatory democratic dilemma that new leftists faced lay neither in the tension between democracy and efficacy nor in that between unity and difference. Rather, it was in the intrinsic limits of pedagogy and friendship as models for democratic relationships.

6

FRIENDSHIP AND EQUALITY IN THE WOMEN'S
LIBERATION MOVEMENT, 1967–77

Friendship among women has been the cement . . . of the various historical waves of the
feminist movement.

MARILYN FRIEDMAN, "FEMINISM AND MODERN FRIENDSHIP"

This particular characteristic—friendship as the primary basis for unity—is one that
pervaded the CWLU from start to finish. . . . *It was a mistake to follow blindly based simply
on ties of friendship.*

MEMBER OF THE CHICAGO WOMEN'S LIBERATION UNION COMMENTING ON THE ORGANIZATION'S
DISSOLUTION IN 1976–77

The women who launched a movement for liberation in the late 1960s
were determined to do better than the new left in creating a radical
democracy. New left men's monopoly on discussion and their condescending dismissal of women's interventions had marginalized women just as
effectively as formal barriers would have done. In their own movement,
women's liberationists would eradicate competitive posturing and macho
self-promotion. Seeing in the slogan "the personal is political" the man-
date not only to recognize the dailiness of their oppression but also to
focus on their relationships with each other, they discovered in women's
friendships new sources of insight and bases of political solidarity. And
something more: they talked about "sisterhood" to capture both the intense character of their bonds and the potential of those bonds to reach
across differences of race and class. That activists in many movements
today refer to consensus-based decisionmaking as "feminist process" attests to the centrality of the women's liberation movement to a genealogy
of participatory democracy. More than any of the movement groups that I
have treated thus far, feminists in the late 1960s and early 1970s made the
internal life of the movement the stuff of political experimentation and
innovation. Refusing to bow to the conventional separation of "private"

and "public" realms, they determined to transform both. What resulted was extraordinary creativity in charting new sites of political contention and new kinds of political relationship. Women's liberationists insisted on a democratic practice that was egalitarian in a deep and encompassing sense.

Yet such advances were hard-won. When former activists talk today about their lives in the movement, pride mingles with hurt, nostalgia with bitterness. Activists remember the joy of newfound political agency and solidarity with women too long viewed as competitors. But they also remember being denounced by fellow activists for exercising initiative or leadership and being "trashed" for trying to take a feminist message to the wider public. With some puzzlement, they describe what had seemed a worthy antiauthoritarianism coming to require a leveling of all talents and what had seemed an admirable collectivism producing a censoriousness that discouraged anyone from voicing a dissenting opinion. They describe feminist collectives imploding in anger and mutual recriminations that left some members traumatized for years.[1]

By all accounts, the one place where participatory democracy is supposed to work is in a small collective of like-minded and demographically homogeneous people. While participatory democrats in the pacifist and civil rights movements and in the new left could blame their failures at least in part on external pressures such as government repression, demands for nationally coordinated action, and the requirements of funding a mass organization, those pressures were less salient in the radical wing of the women's movement. The movement was intentionally localist and its organizations small. Those organizations depended mostly on the volunteered time and resources of mainly middle- and upper-middle-class women. The movement was subjected to government harassment, but that was not by itself debilitating. When Naomi Weisstein and Heather Booth wrote in 1975 that feminist organizations "die from internal bleeding long before they succumb to external pressure," their conclusion was not much disputed. Why did women's liberationists sometimes end up creating organizations that stifled dissent and undercut rather than enhanced women's leadership? Had they set the bar too high? Were their expectations of creating radically egalitarian settings capable of maximizing both individual freedom and a collective agenda such that any shortcoming was perceived as failure? Ellen Willis, who helped found the group Redstockings, attributes the animosity to leadership to the "rage of those who find themselves at the bottom of yet another hierarchy." Sociologist Verta Taylor argues that the emotional pain that women brought into the movement led them to turn on each other. Others have argued that the notion of sisterhood was simply inadequate to gloss over the very real differences of interest among women. Despite their common aspirations for radical equality, their views of how to achieve equality were too diverse for consensus.[2]

There were indeed strong ideological disputes among women's liberationists from the beginning. "Politicos" who viewed sexism as inextricably connected to capitalism and who were unwilling to sever ties with the left vied with "feminists" who were convinced that men (or institutionalized masculinity) were the problem and an autonomous women's movement the solution. Some activists believed that the insights generated in consciousness raising were the radical frontier of the movement, others that women should be in the streets. Sometimes differences like these split groups into competing factions, and sometimes they were simply exciting, the stuff of debate and learning. "The movement changed everything," Seattle activist Barbara Winslow recalls, "how we lived and worked, and thought, and had sex. Every question became intense." While recognizing the importance of disputes over ideology in accounting for strains in participatory democratic decisionmaking, I focus in this chapter on a different source of conflict: the friendships that structured many feminist organizations. Friendships among women were a novel basis for political solidarity, and they supplied the intimacy and trust that allowed women both to probe the limits that they had previously accepted and to take risky and creative collective action. The problem was for women who were excluded from the friendship circles that constituted groups' leadership. For these women, newcomers or somehow "different," the excitement of new political possibilities contended with the frustration of being marginalized. Friendship in practice rather than as a political ideal did not extend far enough to include the numbers of women petitioning for membership.[3]

The situation was even more complicated, however. When women's liberationists did try to establish formal mechanisms to mitigate the power of friendship cliques, they found that such mechanisms undermined one of the most important benefits of their deliberative styles. "Lot" systems to randomize the allocation of tasks and "disc" systems to prevent people from monopolizing discussions effectively equalized women's power. But they made it difficult for women to learn from the deliberative process except in a purely individualized way. In other words, if friendship militates against expanding the group, it does foster the complex equality within which joint learning can take place. Friends can recognize each other's different but equally valuable skills and can learn from each other without sacrificing respect. They are patient with each other and know how to make criticisms constructive and unalienating. When women's liberationists tried to counteract the unequal aspects of friendship with more formal provisions for ensuring equality, they eroded the complex equality that made political self-development possible. This was not the reason that disc and lot systems so rarely lasted. Rather, women experienced them as "artificial" and "unnatural"—probably in part because they seemed at odds with friendship's voluntary and informal character. Nevertheless, the problem for women's liberationists was one facing all participatory democrats: how to counteract the inequalities characteristic of informal intimate relations without sacrificing the bonds of trust and mutual respect that so often accompany them.

In offering a decidedly mixed view of friendship as a model for political cooperation, I break with a number of feminist theorists who have seen in friendship the basis for political relationships marked by autonomy, equality, and care. Before I turn to the women's liberation movement, let me briefly rehearse these arguments.

FRIENDSHIP AND DEMOCRATIC DECISIONMAKING

Feminists have been sharply critical of a traditional liberal view of people as essentially independent, self-interested, and utilitarian. From the perspective of someone who has given birth, philosopher Virginia Held writes, "it is absurd to assume that we are born free. We are born helpless infants, and will remain unfree for many years. We are only relatively free if those who have cared for us have empowered us to be so." Like liberal views of liberty, say Held and others, liberal views of equality and of justice omit entirely the experiences of interdependency, cooperation, trust, and concern that are so much a part of women's lives—and of men's lives, should they choose to recognize it. These experiences need to be taken into account in theories of a just society. Indeed, they point to a wholly different conception of such a society, one based on a feminist "ethic of care." Such an ethic assumes that self and other are interdependent but that that interdependence need not be ignored or bemoaned. Rather, women's relationships both yield insight into what social relations actually look like—in contrast to the false picture painted by liberals—and provide normative ideals for more just norms of political cooperation.[4]

The question, however, is whether women's relations today, in a still profoundly patriarchal society, can serve as real alternatives. Where some writers have championed the relationship between mother and child as one characterized by the kind of trust and care that should inform political relations more generally, others have seen this relationship as inherently unequal. Feminist writers have been much more enthusiastic about friendship as a normative ideal. "When caretaking and responsibility are connected to the more equal and reciprocal relations of friendship, rather than to the inequality of the parent-child relation," Kathy Ferguson writes, "the connection of the caretaking values to a reconstituted public life becomes more clear." Friendship provides both a model for political relationships in a reconstituted polity and a means of getting there, since friends support each other in their efforts to challenge the status quo. Indeed, say some theorists, "sisterhood" was a misnomer for the politics of the women's movement: what women were after was friendship.[5]

What is it about friendship that makes it attractive as a model for political cooperation? In the last chapter, I drew attention to the mutual knowledge and trust that friendship requires and reinforces. These features make it easy to reach joint decisions expeditiously. Friends are unlikely to suspect each other of cutting corners or cutting deals, and their affection for each other makes the deliberative process tolerable, even pleasurable. Two other features of friendship bear note. Unlike kin and coworkers, friends usually see themselves as equal. Not as identical—friends, rather, recognize each other's different competencies. Difference makes for a richer relationship, not for an unequal one. Feminist philosopher Marilyn Friedman writes, "One friend's superiority in one area, for example, in breadth of life experience, need not give that friend a privileged place in the relationship if it is balanced by the other friend's superiority in some other area, for example, in vitality of imagination." Indeed, since we know each other intimately, our equality may be based on talents of which most outsiders are unaware, on our inner attributes or potential strengths. This combination of equality and difference facilitates the interactive learning that is, I have argued, one of participatory decisionmaking's most important benefits. A second key feature of friendship is its voluntary, chosen character. One does not record or contract for or negotiate in advance the prerogatives and responsibilities of friendship. Unlike marriage or kinship, there are few rules of friendship. The relationship is a self-governing and dynamic one; friends shape their mutual obligations over time. This too can facilitate personal development. "Families seem to demand one's fitting into prescribed roles," political scientist Martha Ackelsberg observes. "By contrast, friends seem to support us to 'become the person I am.'" The informal and voluntary character of the relationship also means that friends are used to working out the rules as they go along, in ways that best meet their individual and joint needs. This facilitates an experimentalism with respect to their interactions.[6]

Each of these features of friendship also comes with risks, however. In the last chapter, I focused on friendship's exclusivity. Friendship can by definition be extended only to so many people; past that point, the intensity and trust of all one's friendships suffer. When a movement old guard is made up of friends, its efforts to incorporate newcomers may be compromised by the subtle ways in which members reaffirm their bonds with each other, inadvertently excluding newcomers. In addition, friends tend to choose friends who are like them, in terms of both their values and beliefs and their demographic characteristics. They probably do this both to minimize their own discomfort with difference and to avoid threatening the existing network of friends. The result, however, may be much less diversity than members wanted. Another danger: if friends are generally likely to agree on major issues, profound disagreements may be experienced as emotional betrayal. For that reason, intimacy may come with pressures to conformity. Finally, taking friendship as a model of deliberative interaction may make activists unwilling to formalize any aspect of decisionmaking. To do so would seem at odds with the determinedly informal, voluntary, and private character of friendship. Activists may reject efforts to formalize any of their procedures, not because they necessarily contravene democratic principles, but because they seem so "unnatural" or "inauthentic."[7]

The empirical question, then, is whether friendships in social movements have indeed supplied trust, intimacy, and complex equality for some members of the group at the expense of others. And two more questions: What has happened when groups have tried to counteract the inequalities and exclusivities characteristic of friendship-based organizations? And have activists had any success in developing new associational models, analogues to friendship in the affection and trust that they provide but without friendship's exclusivity and hostility to formality?

SNCC, SDS, AND WOMEN'S LIBERATION

Chroniclers of the women's liberation movement have tended to highlight its animosity to the new left, treating that animosity as the movement's very inspiration. But, as historian Alice Echols points out, that picture minimizes the ideological continuities between the two movements—and between them both and the student wing of the civil rights movement. Most feminists shared new left men's indignation at a liberalism devoid of feeling, a war without justification, and a public life in which pulling a voting lever passed as participation. Most of all, they shared a commitment to a politics that was radically democratic. The new left women who went on to launch the women's liberation movement found repugnant their male counterparts' manipulation of democracy for their own aggrandizement, but they did not therefore reject the form. Participatory democracy was a flawed reality, but it remained a powerful ideal.[8]

This is evident in what is widely seen as the first feminist salvo of the 1960s: an anonymous position paper presented at SNCC's Waveland retreat in November 1964. "It needs to be made know[n] that many women in the movement are not 'happy and contented' with their status," the paper read. "It needs to be known that just as Negroes were the crucial factor in the economy of the cotton South, so too in SNCC, women are the crucial factor that keeps the movement running on a day-to-day basis. Yet they are not given equal say-so when it comes to day-to-day decisionmaking." The paper listed a series of indignities: women excluded from important SNCC meetings or made minute taker, never chair; experienced female organizers relegated to clerical duties; women consistently referred to as "girls" and forced to defer to male decisionmakers. Conceding that "this list will seem strange to some, petty to others, laughable to most," the paper's anonymous authors called for "discussion—amidst the laughter—but still discussion."[9]

The paper, along with Stokely Carmichael's ribald response that "the proper position of women in SNCC is prone," came to occupy an important place in the story women's liberationists would tell and retell about the origins of their movement. It was initially attributed to Ruby Doris Smith Robinson, black and a SNCC veteran—wrongly attributed, historian Sara Evans asserted in her 1979 history of the episode. In fact, two white women, longtime SNCC workers Casey Hayden and Mary King, wrote it. Like hundreds of other white women involved in SNCC's community-organizing projects, Evans went on, King and Hayden had experienced in the movement a freedom, responsibility, and self-respect normally unavailable to middle-class white women. It was their newfound sense of power, along with the language of radical equality that they imbibed in the South, that made the minute taking, freedom house–cleaning, and sexual exploitation that they experienced insufferable. And it was this contradiction that generated an incipient feminist consciousness. Met with the ridicule in SNCC that they had anticipated, Hayden and King directed their next missive in November 1965 to forty women in the new left. Their "A Kind of Memo" was passed from friend to friend in a widening circle, and, a month later, women staged a walkout from SDS's Rethinking Conference.[10]

However, in their own accounts of the Waveland episode, Hayden and King deny that they were the victims of sexual exploitation and, indeed, of sexist treatment within SNCC. "I didn't feel exploited," Hayden says firmly. "None of this stuff that's written about sexual exploitation applied to my experience. None of it." For Mary King, "Our status in the movement was never the issue." Instead, King says, she saw the paper as a way to "reassert...the basic values of the early sit-ins and SNCC's original concept of leadership"—leadership that was participatory and decentralized. Indeed, most of the eleven examples of discriminatory treatment detailed in the first section of the paper center explicitly on decisionmaking: women never asked to chair meetings, excluded from a committee charged with constitutional revisions, and so on. Whatever the sources of their dissatisfaction—and they were surely multiple and complex—women turned to an idiom of democratic decisionmaking to express them.[11]

They would continue to do so. In the white new left, as in SNCC, women's attacks on the movement's sexism came first as bids for greater democracy. I noted earlier that, for most of SDS's founders, "participatory democracy" referred not to a set of organizational procedures but to political institutions run by their constituents. SDS founder Sharon Jeffrey, by contrast, remembers participatory democracy in terms of her own desire to participate. "'Participatory' means 'involved in decisions.' And I definitely wanted to be involved in decisions that were going to affect *me!* How could I let anyone make a decision about me that I wasn't involved in?" This was a retrospective view; perhaps Jeffrey was at the time as focused on a national political vision as were her male counterparts at Port Huron. But other statements made by SDS women to the group at large suggest that, in SDS, as in SNCC, participatory democracy provided a justificatory idiom for women's claims *as* women.[12]

This was the case, for example, in the women's workshop that was held at the December 1965 SDS conference. Later the night of the workshop, Carol McEldowney listed the questions that women had grappled with: "If SDS is the organization that envisions itself as a small-scale model of the new society, as a living example of participatory democracy, why has it been unable to deal creatively with the role of women? Why does most of the intellectual leadership in SDS consist of men? Why do women so rarely participate in large discussions? Why do many women feel inhibited from participating in the decision-making and discussion processes of SDS?" Several of the groups that met to discuss those questions decided that they would be all-women "because they felt that the presence of men might be inhibiting," McEldowney reported. A few men formed their own workshop, however, and McEldowney was heartened by what seemed the "serious interest that many SDS people have in the problem, including a substantial number of men." *New Left Notes* published a respectful synopsis of the workshop, and former campus traveler Jane Adams was elected national secretary six months later, only the second woman to hold a national office (the first was Assistant National Secretary Helen Garvy).[13]

Yet women's issues were not widely discussed in SDS in the next year and a half. Members' growing preoccupation with antiwar organizing made the dissatisfactions of women seem beside the point. Chude Pamela Allen (then Pamela Allen), who eventually launched one of the first women's liberation groups, was shocked at the level of opposition that she encountered to the idea of organizing around women's issues—from radical men *and* women. Other budding feminists had the same experience. When Heather Booth, a former SNCC volunteer and SDS activist who was married to SDS's Paul Booth, organized a women's workshop at a December 1966 antidraft conference, the few women who turned up agreed that "our duty [is] to support our men." For many women, the war dwarfed their "personal" issues, especially since they saw themselves as much less constrained than women outside the movement.[14]

The SDS women who called for a participatory democracy that was truly open to women probably expected that the organization's progressive decentralization would help. But the opposite occurred. With formal positions increasingly demeaned, women had to compete informally for attention and often found themselves dismissed or ignored. The exclusiveness of old-guard friendship circles had made it difficult for newcomers to break in except by dramatically challenging a "heavy," and that kind of competitive intellectual bluster was rarely tolerated in women. But SDS women had always had some voice through their relationships with old-guard men. At about the time of the eclipse of the old guard, new versions of masculinity were in the ascendant that were not especially sensitive to women's desires for political recognition. Writer Marge Piercy described the new left's "men of steel": tough, sexually posturing, and eager to imitate their black nationalist heroes.[15]

What opened ideological space for feminist arguments was not, then, a greater commitment to participatory democracy on the part of the new left. Rather, it was a consequence of the black movement's claim that people could fight only their own oppression. For some women in the white new left, this meant that they should focus on their own interests rather than putting their hopes and energies into some other revolutionary agent, whether poor blacks, poor whites, or draft resisters. They should organize as women. Still, moving from that recognition to an autonomous women's movement was not an easy step. For one thing, by late 1967, the new left had a new line: urban blacks really were the revolutionary vanguard, and whites' duty was to support them, only not in the simpering, violence-renouncing way of the early movement. According to Greg Calvert, SDS national secretary in 1966–67, it became increasingly fashionable "to denounce something called personal liberation. If you talk about what you feel or what's meaningful to you in a political forum, you're suddenly one of those personal liberation people." Women's liberationists refused to give in to that kind of silencing, but they were not unsusceptible to worries that their protest was somehow self-indulgent. Although relatively few minority or working-class women joined women's liberation groups, "there was an unspoken assumption that 'their' approval was necessary to our legitimation," activist Jo Freeman recalls, even though "the message white women got from black activists was to stay away; our presence, our ideas, our whiteness, were oppressive."[16]

For another thing, many women's liberationists were also unwilling to sever their ties with the new left. They shared with new left men a view that the "issues were connected" and were initially reluctant to make men the enemy. A series of episodes of condescension and outright contempt by men toward the women who were raising issues of sexism changed all that. Recounted in widening circles, these episodes convinced many women of the need for autonomous organization. After participants in a "Women's Liberation Workshop" at SDS's spring 1966 national convention secured passage of a resolution calling for child-care centers, abortion, birth control, shared housework, and an SDS program of education on women's liberation, *New Left Notes* printed the programmatic section of the resolution, accompanied by a cartoon of a girl with polka-dot minidress and panties holding a sign reading "We Want Our Rights and We Want Them Now." At the National Conference for a New Politics two months later, Jo Freeman and Shulamith Firestone tried to present a minority report after they were told that Women Strike for Peace had already submitted a resolution on women. Prepared to read their alternative resolution, they were ignored. When they rushed the podium, the chair, William Pepper, patted Firestone on the head, saying, "Cool down, little girl. We have more important things to do here than talk about women's problems."[17]

Episodes like these simply added to women's anger at their routine marginalization in decisionmaking, their relegation to "shit work" like mimeographing and minute taking, and the sexual etiquette that expected them to give up intimacy for sexual liberation. But women also began to talk and to turn their conversations into groups and then organizations. In Chicago, Heather Booth and psychologist Naomi Weisstein taught a course on women. Jane Adams organized a women's meeting at SDS's Chicago headquarters. Political science graduate student Jo Freeman began holding discussions in her Chicago apartment. Booth, Weisstein, community organizer Amy Kesselman, former civil rights activists Sue Munaker and Shulamith Firestone, and a dozen other women attended.

Demonstrators from the National Women's Liberation Party picket the Miss America Pageant, Atlantic City, N.J., 7 September 1968. (Photo from AP/Wide World Photos; used with permission)

Booth knew Marilyn Webb from SDS, and, after they talked, Webb founded a group in Washington, D.C. Chude Pamela Allen was with Staughton Lynd at a meeting in Chicago when Sue Munaker came up to tell him about the women's meeting that she had just attended. Munaker mentioned to Allen that someone named Shulamith Firestone was about to move to New York, and Firestone and Allen started New York Radical Women (NYRW). NYRW's Kathie Sarachild (then Amatniek) visited her friend Nancy Hawley in Boston, and Hawley then organized a group there. Meredith Tax read Cell 16's *No More Fun and Games* and "fell in love with the voice of women's liberation." Put off by Cell 16's anti-man line, Tax and Linda Gordon launched Bread and Roses. "All of us traveled," Jo Freeman remembered. "Airfare was cheap. Conferences were plentiful. People moved."[18]

RATIONALES FOR DEMOCRATIC DECISIONMAKING

The first women's liberation groups were formed in 1967 in New York and Chicago, and they spread rapidly. By 1970, there were at least fifty consciousness-raising groups in New York, thirty in Chicago, twenty-five in Boston, and smaller numbers in over three dozen cities. Whether they focused on consciousness raising or action, women's liberation groups were small, informal, and determinedly egalitarian. Founders had diverse rationales for rejecting hierarchical and adversarial organizational forms. "Because we wanted equality!" San Francisco feminist Cathy Cade bursts out when I ask why making decisions collectively was important, as if the answer was obvious. And for many women it was. But former activists cite additional rationales. For Chude Pamela Allen, more participation produced more diversity in views and perspectives. And that was necessary to creating a movement that represented *women* rather than just some women. Heather Booth cites that benefit too as well as the fact that equal respect demanded equal participation. But the rationale that Booth offers first is that "women had been so blocked from positions of authority that they needed to learn those skills." Making decisions jointly, rotating leadership, and taking turns articulating the group's position to the public—all these were means of gaining leadership skills. In a similar vein, Chicago activist Vivian Rothstein wrote later that, "in order to be politically potent, women must have opportunities to develop skills and leadership." For some early women's liberationists, then, the developmental purposes of participatory decisionmaking were central.[19]

Maren Carden found four components of a feminist ethos voiced by the women's liberationists she interviewed in 1969 and 1970. A commitment to "self-realization"—that participants should be "encouraged to develop or realize their full human potential, both intellectually and emotionally"—was combined with a belief in the "authority of personal experience." "One's own experience, rather than the abstract formulation of some 'expert,'" was the appropriate source of new ideas. Along with commitments to women's individual growth, Carden found that women's liberationists put a premium on "sisterhood—the genuine attempt to understand and to establish common bonds with other women" and "equality": "No person or persons shall dominate over the other group members after the fashion of the 'male chauvinist' outside world."[20]

What did this ethos mean in practice? How did early feminist organizations actually make decisions? "We parceled out tasks," says Ann Sutherland Harris of Columbia Women's Liberation: You're good at this, you do this; I'll do this." When chapters of the Chicago Women's Liberation Union were asked to report on how they structured meetings, a few of the thirteen said that they "had an agenda" beforehand; the rest just gathered and began talking. Most women's liberation groups had some minimal structure. Larger ones often had "work groups," a steering committee, and sometimes speakers' bureaus with rules on how speaking engagements would be assigned. Even in larger groups, decisionmaking was informal.

The activists with whom I talked remember more an ethos and a quality of relationship than the organizational procedures that accompanied them.[21]

Making decisions collectively and informally reflected activists' commitment to equality, sisterhood, and mutual respect. But it was bolstered by at least two other features of many women's liberation groups. One was their practice of consciousness raising. The term "consciousness raising" was popularized by former SNCC summer volunteer and NYRW member Kathie Sarachild to describe the organizing technique that she had seen in SNCC. Others likened it to the process of "speaking bitterness" that anthropologist William Hinton had described in a Chinese village in his influential *Fanshen*. Initially viewing consciousness raising as a way to elicit women's experiences before moving on to an action plan, Sarachild and her colleagues soon came to see it as a strategy in its own right, a way of reaching the insights that would enable women to change their own relationships. It is important to note that consciousness raising was not aimed at building movement solidarity; that was not its purpose. However, it did help create bonds of trust and intimacy among activists, and these facilitated collective decisionmaking about other issues.[22]

A second feature of many women's liberation groups also facilitated democratic decisionmaking, at least in the short run. Decisionmakers were often friends. Freeman's characterization of the younger wing of the movement as more "social system" than political movement is apt. It was a set of overlapping friendship circles bound by shared experiences and commitments, travel to demonstrations and conferences, and conversations that were picked up and broken off and continued elsewhere. Sometimes, women joined liberation groups in clusters of two and three friends. Or they knew no one when they came but were absorbed into the circle. When discussions that had begun in someone's living room spilled over into a bar or continued late into the evening, women strengthened relationships that carried over into their meetings the next week.[23]

For movement women, friendships with other women were exciting, provocative, *new*. "As girls we usually had had one or two close friends and maybe a small friendship grouping, but by the time we were in puberty, [we] ... related to boys, not to each other," Chude Pamela Allen explains. "We were to wait, to be chosen." And that "socially enforced passivity meant we didn't have the social tools for interacting with one another." Women had had roles in the new left, as independent participants as well as people's wives or girlfriends, but their interactions with each other had always ranked second to their relationships with men. To meet deliberately, separately, as women, was a heady experience. For some women, the intensity of a friendship deepened into a romantic relationship. In the small circle of a feminist group, women came out as lesbians.[24]

New left historian James Miller argues that at the heart of participatory democracy was a fundamental tension between a civic republican ideal of democracy, "a face-to-face community of friends sharing interests in common," and an existentialist vision "of an experimental collective embarked on a high-risk effort to test the limits of democracy in modern life." But when one thinks of friendship as a model of democracy, the tension dissolves. Friends encourage and help each other take risky actions. The affection, respect, trust, and confidence that women experienced with each other in their new groups made it possible for them to do everything from shouting down a legislator, to leaving an abusive husband, to acknowledging to themselves their fears of independence.[25]

As some black feminists pointed out at the time, when white women used the term "sisterhood," they were imitating Black Power activists' practice of calling each other "brother" and "sister." By implicitly claiming connection with that movement to legitimate their own efforts, white women were presuming bonds between themselves and black women that by and large did not at that time exist. But white feminists also talked about sisterhood to convey the depth and intensity of their relationships. What men had were "friendships." What women were experiencing in the early years of the women's movement was something more, and they used the term sisterhood in part to capture this difference.[26]

The recollections of five women who participated in Chicago's Westside group illustrate some of the appeal of friendships in the movement—and begin to get at some of their liabilities. Amy Kesselman titled her 1998 autobiographical essay, jointly written with Heather Booth, Vivian Rothstein, and Naomi Weisstein, "Our Gang of Four: Friendship and Women's Liberation." In it, she captures the joy of friendships in a nascent movement. "Formerly, women's close friendships had been seen as secondary to the main business of life: finding a man," she writes. In the early years of the women's movement, by contrast, "they reinforced our strengths, not our weaknesses, and provided the matrix within which many of the ideas of women's liberation developed." She remembers meeting Heather Booth: "I felt I had been awakened from a deep sleep: her observations were brilliant; she listened appreciatively to my ideas; together we figured things out." Naomi Weisstein was similarly excited by her meeting with Kesselman. "I wanted to talk to Amy forever," she recalls. And Booth, Weisstein, and Kesselman were "immediately drawn to Vivian [Rothstein's] sense of moral purpose, her intelligence, and her unshakable commitment to organizing. The four of us began to spend time together, always talking about women's condition and how to change it." The Westside group, with about fifteen members at its height, was made up of several of these friendship circles. Kesselman, Booth, Rothstein, and Weisstein recall the excitement of discovering shared perspectives and passions. "I can hardly describe the joy!" Weisstein writes. "Unbeliev-able! The sound system had just been turned on. We couldn't wait to go to meetings, where we talked ecstatically about everything." Kesselman: "Suddenly and jubilantly, I was released from the need for the approval of the male establishment."[27]

What comes across in these accounts is the sense, not only of newly revealed commonality, but also of respect for each other's distinctive skills. When the Westside group talked about how women's behavior was shaped by social expectations, "our friendship was a crucible for this idea," Kesselman writes. "We had created a countervailing force to the sexism around us, and the transformative effects clarified in a graphic and im-mediate way the power of social context." Then Weisstein, an experimen-tal psychologist, developed the group's idea into an influential article, "Psychology Constructs the Female." The friendship group also sup-ported each other's different interests. The Chicago movement at the time was surging, with new groups proliferating. Rothstein worked with several women on the Women's Liberation Center, Booth with others to launch the Action Committee for Decent Childcare. Weisstein founded and toured with the Women's Liberation Rock Band, and Kesselman organized teenagers. "While we worked with lots of other women, we always looked to each other for political support and guidance, consulting each other about almost everything we did," Kesselman remembers. Together, they launched the Chicago Women's Liberation Union, a citywide federated structure of women's activist groups.[28]

Jo Freeman was also in the Westside group; in fact, it met in her apartment. But her experience was very different from that of the "Gang of Four." For reasons that were unclear to her at the time, she began to be excluded from social gatherings outside the group. Members were increasingly cool, and she was given "a couple of dark hints about my 'male' ambitions—such as going to graduate school—and told no one responded because I didn't have anything valuable to say." "It was like coming into a room with the lights out," Freeman says now. "I kept bumping into things." When she asked someone who seemed sympathetic what was happening, she was told that she was being "trashed." She soon dropped out of the group and began to write for and speak to a broader audience of those interested in women's liberation around the country.[29]

THE TYRANNY OF FRIENDSHIP

Freeman's experience in the Westside group formed the basis for her 1970 paper "The Tyranny of Structurelessness." After circulating widely among feminists, the piece was published in the *Berkeley Journal of Sociology* in 1972. For many activists, it struck an uncomfortable chord. Freeman wrote that the idea of "structureless" groups characterized by looseness, informality, and intimacy had been attractive as a counter to the "over-structured" character of mainstream society as well as of many left-wing groups. For that reason structurelessness had become the dominant organizational form for the women's movement. Since many radical women's groups began as "rap groups" devoted to consciousness raising, a lack of formal structure initially was no liability. To the contrary, it promoted an intimate and supportive environment that made it easy for women to reach personal insights. But, when rap groups turned from talk to action, Freeman observed, they rarely changed their organizational structure. And, faced with the demands of coordinating large numbers of people, they ended up relying on the knowledge of a small group of self-selected friends. Control of the many by the few was not eliminated; it simply operated covertly, through the friendship cliques that actually ran women's groups. "Sisterhood"—Freeman did not put it this way, but she might have—was extended to only some among the group.[30]

That the informal structures operating in the absence of formal ones were unfair is easy to see, but Freeman also argued that they were ineffective. Her argument is less clear here but seems to be that failing to make responsibilities explicit undermined efforts to coordinate regional and national actions and organizations. In addition, the fact that small cliques of friends made all the key decisions limited strategic input to whatever those particular women happened to know. With respect to the first point however, it is not at all obvious that national or regional organizations would have best served the movement. Women's liberationists' localism was ideological, but it may also have made good strategic sense. With respect to the second point, if friendship cliques were as cohesive and powerful in their control of women's liberation groups as Freeman suggests they were, then the strategic disadvantages of a narrow base of expertise may well have coexisted with some strategic advantages in decisionmaking by a small, cohesive group. In other words, part of the appeal of formal structurelessness, and, in particular, the friendship relations that stood in for formal structure, was surely the fact that in some ways it *worked*.[31]

Structurelessness was probably appealing for another reason. The intimate bonds forged in consciousness raising and in friendships fostered

Meeting of Columbia Women's Liberation and Barnard Women's Liberation, 1971. (Photo by Jonathan D. Kandel; used with permission of Columbia Yearbook)

trust, respect, and an acceptance of each other's differences. They made possible the kind of complex equality that is a precondition for joint learning. By contrast, the simple equality enacted in disc and lot systems—the "structure" that some women's liberationists would adopt in response to charges of egocentrism and autocracy—discouraged such learning. To anticipate the punch line of this chapter, in the absence of some functional substitute for friendship, formal rules may not create fair and functioning democracies.

INSIDERS AND OUTSIDERS

Anthropologist Joan Cassell attended meetings of a New York City women's liberation action group for a year and a half beginning in October 1971. Unnamed in the study that Cassell eventually published, the group was Columbia Women's Liberation. Cassell's observations are fascinating. She found that a "core group" of participants sat together at meetings and was able to mobilize other women to participate in projects that they proposed. People were eager to help out a friend on a project she had conceived or at least were willing to be pressed into service if the friend was hard up for volunteers. Members of the core group were likely to support each other's positions enthusiastically in group discussions if they agreed with them—and to disagree openly if they did not.[32]

Cassell asked one member to keep a diary of her contacts. Over the course of one week, the informant "had thirty-seven contacts with group participants during the week—an average of five a day (plus the participants she saw at the weekly action-group meeting and at the meeting of her consciousness-raising group)." These contacts included telephone conversations, and many were primarily social, Cassell reported, "although action-group news may have been discussed." Counting informal dinners with group members, "the informant spent all or part of five evenings that week with other action-group members. During that time group activities were discussed, ideas and information exchanged, and personal help offered and accepted."[33]

For women not in the core group, the experience was different. The non–core group member was likely to be "excluded from the informal conversational groupings that clustered before the weekly meetings began. The places near her might remain empty during a meeting. Participants might converse while she gave an opinion, or listen politely and then ignore what she said. When a group of women went to eat at a restaurant after the weekly meeting they might not invite her." "It is hard for all but the most dedicated, insensitive, or aggressive woman to survive such treatment," Cassell concluded. "A woman who did not fit in and make personal friends would be frozen out." Today, Cassell describes her own frustration when she discovered in her second year that she had been excluded from the core group, whose composition had changed from older, mainly heterosexual students to mainly undergraduate, bisexual and lesbian students. A graduate student, married and with children, she no longer fit in. The meetings became "cold," she says now. "They just weren't fun anymore."[34]

Group members did try to welcome newcomers. Indeed, they set aside special time periods for doing so. However, Cassell points out, "one could hardly order active participants to make friends with all recruits. This was seen as a private, personal activity." Cassell's observations illustrate the liabilities of relying on friendships to create a movement democracy. The frequent informal contact enjoyed by members of the core group provided them information that was unavailable to those outside it. Without affective ties to other women in the group, moreover, it was difficult for non–core group members to mobilize people to sign on to projects that they

proposed and to support ideas that they advanced. Worried that challenging any argument made by a member of the core group would marginalize
them further, they kept silent. In this way, the ostensible openness of the
group was combined with a self-censoriousness that made effectively for
a party line. The core group was not entirely impenetrable to newcomers.
But, with friendship its basis, those invited in were likely to be similar
in values, tastes, and demographic characteristics. It was not so explicit
as women being overtly rejected for not matching set criteria. Rather, as
Cassell put it, as a married woman with children, she was not friends
with members of the group outside the meeting setting. And with that a
requirement for influence in deliberations, those who felt uncomfortable
tended to withdraw rather than bid for power.[35]

All movement groups face tensions between insiders and outsiders.
Newcomers vary in their political backgrounds and often come with different political outlooks. Even if that is not the case, they lack the organizational know-how that veterans have, the knowledge of how *this*
organization operates. Participatory democratic organizations should be
better at incorporating newcomers, however, because they encourage them
to participate in group deliberations from the beginning. People should
feel immediately that they are full members. However, allowing people a
formal voice in decisionmaking is not necessarily enough to give them a
sense of belonging. In the Columbus, Ohio, feminist collectives that Nancy
Whittier studied, older members were determined not to seem patronizing
to newcomers, but newcomers still experienced "this vague invitation to
provide input . . . you never really got the impression that that input was
going to be taken seriously or acted upon in any way." Older members
acknowledged worrying that their bonds would be attenuated by an influx of new members. Said a member of an anti-rape group, "When we
put together our training, we were very careful. It was like, we had this
little group of seven, and we all knew each other, and now we're going
to open it up to the group of sixty and we don't know what's going to
happen now. . . . How we feel about things might get diluted, or altered,
or misinterpreted."[36]

The challenge, more generally, is to create the affective connections
between newcomers and existing members of the group that give the
latter reason to spend time with, trust, teach, and learn from novices. Joan
Cassell found that, in her group, the mechanisms established to welcome
and orient new members were in practice ignored. They were thought
of as "mak[ing] friends" with new recruits, and making friends was considered a "private, personal activity." It was difficult to turn a relationship perceived as personal, voluntary, and informal into an organizational

obligation. The same tension between equality and friendship undermined New York Radical Women's effort to deal with an influx of new members. One of the first women's liberation groups, NYRW gained wide publicity for its picket of the Miss America Pageant in Atlantic City in 1968. After that, meetings that had counted ten to fifteen members swelled to a hundred or more. Round-robin consciousness raising no longer worked in such a large group, and veterans complained about people who would come once and not return. Newcomers, for their part, charged that a small clique was in control. Determined to act on its egalitarian commitments, the group decided to split randomly into three new groups. Although they agreed to the plan for reorganization, however, veterans were not happy with it. "Nobody had the nerve to say that they didn't want to do it by lot, that they wanted to be with their friends," founder Anne Foror recalls. Rather than question the procedure, many women simply ignored their lot assignments. They continued to meet with their friends and then left the organization altogether. Newer NYRW members, for their part, did not have the internal integration or movement experience to sustain the group, and NYRW collapsed six months later.[37]

EQUALIZING DELIBERATIVE POWER

As I noted, Columbia Women's Liberation did make an explicit effort to socialize newcomers. And NYRW tried to respond to organizational growth in a way that preserved the egalitarian character of its decisionmaking. Other women's liberation groups also devised mechanisms to combat inequalities in decisionmaking. On a "lot" system, organizational tasks were divided into "creative" and "routine" categories and assigned randomly rather than on the basis of members' expertise. On the "disc" system, women were allotted equal numbers of discs, one of which had to be surrendered each time they spoke. Former NYRW member Robin Morgan wrote enthusiastically in 1970: "The first time this system was tried, the apocryphal story goes, no one in the room had any discs left after fifteen minutes. The second meeting was slow almost to silence because everyone was hoarding her discs. Gradually, the device worked its way into everyone's consciousness as a symbol of the need to listen to each other, and not interrupt or monopolize the conversation."[38]

   In fact, such measures rarely lasted long. They were too "mechanical," says Chude Pamela Allen. They seemed artificial, irritating. Activists' discomfort was not based on a simple reverence for "spontaneity" and animosity to anything that threatened it. For they had committed to implementing such measures in the first place, viewing them as necessary to democratic decisionmaking. One source of activists' displeasure with disc and lot systems may have been that they were so incongruous with what one expects of friendship. Insofar as activists' relations were modeled on the informality and intimacy characteristic of friendship, relations governed by the formal rules of lot and disc systems may have seemed unnatural.[39]

But it was even more complicated than that. Friendship among activists had also allowed them to learn from each other while feeling equal. Disc systems may have counteracted persistent inequalities but at the expense of women's experience of learning. Women's liberationists wanted all women to be leaders, an aspiration that required commitments both to individual self-development and to radical egalitarianism. The two were in some tension, however. If the first emphasized women's developing their talents and interests beyond the strictures of a feminine role, the second viewed people's capacities as equal but stymied by their socialization. If those socializing forces were removed, the argument ran, women would have equal skills. Accordingly, the task for feminist organizations was to remove those forces—and scrupulously to avoid doing anything that would reproduce them. *Equality* in this sense meant a strict division of authority within the group and caution on the part of members not to betray any sense of superiority. Not only, however, did this mean a ban on the exercise of leadership. It could also be interpreted as prohibiting efforts to help, coach, or support other members. In Cassell's group, novices were often given immediate responsibilities, but tutelage was viewed with suspicion. "For women to develop their talents—since everyone supposedly had the same capacities—some women had to mute theirs," Cassell says now. But could not women skilled in some areas teach others less experienced in that realm? "If you could teach without standing out," Cassell remembers. "Women should be spokespeople and teachers. But not be so good that others would be envious." When one woman in the group was attacked for being "too verbal, too rational, of putting across her viewpoint with such power and brilliance that she 'oppressed other women,'" she responded by offering to teach her skills to other members of the group. But she was told that she had to "'learn to be part of the group, just a member like all the others.'"[40]

A different understanding of equality would have allowed women to excel in different areas, provided that their authority in one area did not translate into other areas, and provided that they helped train others in the skills they already had. It would have made it less likely that tensions between aspirations for equality and self-development were fought out on the grounds of decisionmaking. Such an understanding—what I have called a *complex* notion of equality—is characteristic of friendship, and it makes it possible for people to learn from each other without dominating or feeling dominated. Recall Amy Kesselman of the Chicago Westside group describing her and her friends' desire to nurture new skills in each other. One can see that mechanisms like lot and disc systems designed to equalize participation might forfeit not only the appealingly casual character of decisionmaking by friends but also the developmental benefits of participatory decisionmaking.

This was true, for example, in the Feminists, a group started in October 1968 by former National Organization for Women (NOW) New York chapter head Ti-Grace Atkinson. Atkinson had left NOW in frustration at its undemocratic character and resolved to create a different kind of organization. The Feminists' goal was "a just society, all of whose members are equal," the group's manifesto read. "Therefore, we aim to develop knowledge and skills in all members and prevent any one member or small group from hoarding information or abilities. . . . [G]roups with leaders are hierarchical, and hierarchy necessarily suppresses the initiative of at least the majority of the membership." The group used a lot system to allocate tasks, arguing that "one's growth develops in proportion to one's contributions." Equalizing power was thus seen as important to participants' political development, rather than only as a symbolic expression of their mutual respect. But what is interesting is that the Feminists so minimized processes of learning and teaching. A member "may call on the knowledge of other members," their manifesto specified, "but her own input and development are of primary importance." The developmental benefits of participatory democracy would be arrived at only individually rather than jointly, on this view of equality. NYRW veteran Carol Hanisch was invited to a Feminists' meeting and was put off by their disc system. "I could not see how one could develop one's speaking abilities in such tightly controlled conditions," she wrote later. "Debate, judgment and even comments on what someone said—all critical to political development— were not allowed. There was little of the to and fro of debate, which gives people a chance to build on their knowledge by truly investigating an idea." There was thus a curious irony: women's liberationists' efforts to combat the inequalities produced by basing democracy on friendship sacrificed some of the democratic benefits of friendship.[41]

DEMOCRATIC ALTERNATIVES

Were there other ways to integrate developmental aspirations with egalitarian ones? In the Seattle movement, says Barbara Winslow, "we did not discourage the development of spokeswomen. Our policy was to make each member a spokeswoman. We always sent two members to a speaking engagement, one more experienced than the other. That way, newer members would learn in a supportive, mentoring environment." The pedagogical function of joint appearances was perceived neither as restraining some women's desires for leadership nor as at odds with the demands of equality. Winslow explains that she and others had imbibed notions of "cadre development" from the old left activists who helped found Seattle Radical Women, the precursor to Women's Liberation–Seattle. "Lenin said that under socialism, every cook would become a statesman. That's the old left idea, that everyone had to become cadre. Radical women pushed women forward." Although she learned that idiom later in the 1970s, she says that it was familiar to her from her earlier involvement in Seattle Radical Women. Seattle feminists' old left ties may have given them access to the egalitarianism that had always existed in peculiar combination with authoritarianism in old left political practice.[42]

Women's liberationists also experimented with entirely new associational forms: consciousness-raising groups, cooperative households, and "free spaces," among others. Not only did such forms tender a vision of an alternative mode of social life. They also provided workable models of political interaction that were accompanied neither by the selfishness of liberal contractualism, nor by the dependency and constraint characteristic of familial relationships, *nor* by the exclusivity characteristic of friendship. "The group processes as described here are impersonal," Chude Pamela Allen wrote in a 1970 handbook outlining a four-stage consciousness-raising program for small groups. But the impersonality, she went on, was necessary to push participants beyond their familiar ways of interacting. In emergent groups like these, feminists were developing new foundations for political trust—foundations that would be as useful in a feminist action group as in an ideal society. The pity, perhaps, is that the perceived divide between consciousness raising and action, and then between cultural feminists and political ones, discouraged activists from doing as much of this kind of work in their action-oriented political organizations as they might have done.[43]

That said, since the heyday of the women's liberation movement, feminists have engaged in a good deal of organizational experimentation. Some groups put more structure in place to counteract demonstrably inegalitarian and inefficient features of collectivist organizations. In the Chicago Women's Liberation Union, for example, members agreed to give the group's Steering Committee the power to make decisions rather than relying on meetings of the entire membership when it became clear that the earlier process was cumbersome and unrepresentative of most members. In addition, cochairs were elected and a Planning Committee established to handle the group's longer-term financial security.[44]

In feminist organizations generally, however, the most significant impetus to implementing more bureaucratic and adversarial-democratic arrangements proved to be the demands of securing external funding. As one wing of the women's movement began to set up battered women's shelters, rape crisis centers, and women's service organizations, activists found that government and foundation funders required strict financial reporting and, often, hierarchical chains of command. This did not necessarily lead them to abandon their feminist agenda or their commitments to what has come to be known as feminist process. But it did force them to modify how they enacted that commitment. Pressed to implement formal structures of accountability, groups that began as collectives created standing committees, then steering committees, then boards of directors. They were determined to retain the broad input that informal and collectivist structures had allowed them, however. The result was "modified collectives" or "modified bureaucracies," combining elements of both forms. For example, in the women's health center that Kathleen Iannello studied, staff had always valued the specifically developmental benefits of joint decisionmaking and rotated responsibilities, but they were frustrated by the costs of constant retraining. The solution was to distinguish between decisions that were "critical" to the organization as a whole and therefore should be made by all members and those that were "routine" and could be made by "coordinators" in charge variously of personnel, medical affairs, business, and outreach. Coordinators were also expected to educate staff members in their areas of expertise.[45]

This kind of evolution has not been uncommon. Indeed, observers have suggested that modified collectives are now the norm among feminist organizations. This is what sociologist Rebecca Bordt found in her analysis of ninety-five women's nonprofit organizations in New York City. Few of the organizations approximated either bureaucratic or collectivist forms; the vast majority were hybrids. For example, in what Bordt calls *professional organizations*, made up of health-care professionals, legal professionals, party politicians, or mental-health professionals, people in formal positions of authority informally but almost always consulted with other members of the group. In *pragmatic collectives*, by contrast, women were committed to the mutual care characteristic of collectives but relied on formal decisionmaking criteria to speed up decisionmaking. Another recent study of feminist organizations, these ones national, found that all of them combined bureaucratic and collectivist elements. One shifted from a management model to a team model; another made the executive directorship a shared position; a third required consensus among board members but reduced the size of the board when it became clear that it was impossible to reach consensus with sixty-seven people participating. What was critical to the success of the organizations was less the particular form of decisionmaking that each used than the substantial consultation among board, staff, and members that took place and the fact that the deliberative form evolved through a continual process of negotiation. Where participatory democracy has worked, it has involved a similar recognition that conventional criteria of deliberative authority may not serve the group and an effort to construct and legitimate new criteria. This is the experimentalism that I have seen as so important to participatory democracy's political contributions.[46]

Interestingly, as feminist activists have been moving toward more formalized organizational structures, in part because of the dangers of rule by friendship clique, some feminist theorists have been promoting the virtues of friendship as a model for political interaction. "Sisterhood," the rallying cry of 1970s feminism, was the wrong model for feminist solidarity, they say. It presumed commonalities across race and class that simply were not there and took solidarity as given rather than as something to be struggled for. By contrast, a "pluralist" friendship in which each person is committed to understanding the other's difference, rather than erasing it, offers a better model of feminist solidarity. For these writers, friendship depends on a chosen mutuality and cooperation lacking both in conventional liberalism and in traditional conceptions of family and community. Friendship defies the superficiality of standard political interactions while promoting the experimentalism and openness lacking in families.[47]

Can we square these arguments for basing political relations *more* on friendship with contemporary feminist activists' increasing embrace of forms that seem at odds with friendship's values of intimacy and informality? Proponents of feminist friendship, I believe, rightly recognize the importance of relationships as well as rules in creating organizations that are effective and egalitarian. Formal procedures for making decisions depend on members' trust in the procedures themselves, in the outcomes, and in each other. Especially in social movements, where so much is uncertain, suspicions that decisionmakers are ill intentioned or uninformed are likely to compromise the process. A shared ideological commitment to the group's goals is important, but it is not enough since goals can be interpreted and achieved in so many ways, all of which can be subject to dispute. Democratic organizations (and democratic societies) require relationships characterized by trust and what I have referred to as *complex equality*, in which differences in skills in one area are not seen as compromising equal status.

What I have argued in this chapter, however, is that friendship is not the best model for these kinds of relationships. Like all forms of long-standing social associations, friendship carries implicit exclusions, hierarchies, and inequalities. In particular, its tendency to exclusivity militates against expanding the group and diversifying its membership. And its resistance to formality makes it difficult to implement mechanisms designed to equalize power. So what is the alternative? Feminist theorist Maria Lugones points out that, among Latina activists, the term *sister* (*hermana*) is not used politically. One uses it rather in "times of crisis when one wants to offer a deep sort of empathy, sympathy and practical support. At such times one embraces a woman and says, meaningfully, 'hermana.' This can be done only by siblings and by solid, responsible, close friends. It is a litmus test of the trueness of a close relation. It feels fake otherwise." But the term Latinas use "for the sort of relation that consists of joining forces and efforts and imagination in common political struggles" is not *amiga* (friend) either. It is *compañera*. *Compañera* does not require the depth of emotional attachment and sympathetic communication that *hermana* and *amiga* require. "Compañera connotes egalitarianism, but the egalitarianism is one of companionship and participation in common political struggle. . . . [T]he term does not connote unconditional bonding. The struggle is that about which the parties to the relationship are companions. So, if someone ceases to be involved or interested in or betrays the struggle, the relationship is at an end with respect to that person."[48]

Lugones invites us to think about the affective relations on which democratic polities inside and outside movements can be built. We need to better understand how associational metaphors such as *sister*, *comrade*, *colleague*, or *friend* shape actual deliberative relations. For example, the norms of professional "collegiality" that structured many of the women's nonprofits that Rebecca Bordt studied enabled directors to make decisions in consultation with those recognized as expert on an issue, without members feeling passed over. One might ask, however, whether women without professional backgrounds were comfortable with those norms— or whether such norms were even extended to them. The task may be to frame alternative relationships in which trust and affection are not accompanied by inequalities and exclusions. Practically speaking, one of movements' most important resources may be the new associational forms they create.[49]

In this chapter, I have argued that decisionmaking's developmental benefits are put at risk both by hierarchical structures and by what I have called a simple equality in which differences of skill, interest, and opinion are neither recognized nor permitted. The solution seems to be to institute rules *and* relationships. A formal division of labor, specified areas of authority and responsibility, protocols for decisionmaking: all these are important to organizational efficiency and accountability. Without rules, people risk being pressured into decisions with which they do not agree or held hostage to the minority preferences of those with informal clout. However, absent relationships of mutual trust, respect, and concern, not only are formal deliberative systems likely to become rigid, but the learning that is one of the most important products of joint decisionmaking is also likely to suffer. The challenge—and it is one to which I return in the next two chapters—is to develop deliberative relationships that are trusting *and* open, caring *and* inclusive.

7

DEMOCRACY IN RELATIONSHIP: COMMUNITY ORGANIZING AND DIRECT ACTION TODAY

We've got to get past the dominant ideology that says that we're clients and consumers and that politics is about electronic plebiscites. . . . We've got to develop a civic culture of conversation and house meetings and public actions and negotiations and reciprocity.

TEXAS ORGANIZER ERNESTO CORTES JR. SPEAKING AT A 1995 TRAINING WORKSHOP

Virginia Ramirez, a full-time homemaker and mother in San Antonio, Texas, in the early 1980s, was angry about the condition of her neighborhood's housing. Someone at her church told her that Communities Organized for Public Service (COPS) was agitating city officials to do something about it. Against her father's wishes—"Don't make waves," he said—Virginia joined COPS. As she tackled first housing, then community development and health care, she began to rise through the ranks, becoming vice president, then cochair of her COPS organization. Miriam Bearse, now a graduate student in her twenties, began her activism in the antinuclear movement in the early 1980s. At Smith College, she was active on feminist and lesbian issues and in demonstrations against the Gulf War. Many of the groups in which she participated were committed to "direct democracy," and this was for Miriam part of their appeal. She discovered, however, that they were often less than serious about it. A small clique usually made decisions. In the Direct Action Network (DAN), a spin-off from the 1999 Seattle World Trade Organization demonstrations, Miriam found a group that had formalized its commitment to radical democracy and relied on two facilitators, a formal queue of participants, and a variety of mechanisms for registering agreement and dissent. Indeed, Miriam would prefer even more structure. Frustrated by the fact that women were talking much less at DAN meetings than men did, she won approval for a third facilitator, a "vibes watcher," in charge of monitoring the participation of underrepresented groups.[1]

Virginia Ramirez and Miriam Bearse represent two strands of contemporary activism. Community organizing goes back to the settlement house movement of the late nineteenth century and to Communist Party organizing in the 1930s and had its first major strategist in Saul Alinsky. COPS is part of the Industrial Areas Foundation (IAF) network that Alinsky founded. Today, community organizing of the IAF variety involves thousands of local churches in campaigns to improve schools, secure affordable housing, and pass living-wage laws. The contemporary direct action movement traces its roots variously to Spanish anarchists, the early civil rights movement, and the antinuclear movement of the late 1970s, and it gained high public visibility in Seattle. New York DAN has working groups tackling labor conditions, police brutality, and corporate globalization and has members active in demonstrations at the national party conventions and meetings of the World Trade Organization.[2]

COPS and DAN alone do not capture the range of contemporary activist styles. Evidence suggests that social movements have increasingly moved in the direction of the single-issue advocacy organization, with a board chosen for its financial connections more than its relation to its constituency and policy made by a professional staff. Commentators worry that the trend is skewing Americans' political participation toward small volunteer groups and away from the professionalized organizations that shape policy in such diverse areas as health, education, and employment. On their own, DAN and community-organizing groups are not reversing the trend. DAN is, after all, tiny, and community organizing has just begun to move beyond local issues to statewide ones, barely addressing national issues at all. But, in 2000, somewhere on the order of thirty thousand people participated in direct action demonstrations coordinated through a directly democratic model of affinity groups and spokescouncils. Faith-based community organizing, by last count, involves three million Americans, and it is growing rapidly.[3]

What is striking about both groups is the emphasis that they put on democratic participation. Both want more popular control of political and economic institutions, from public housing and schools to transnational financial institutions like the International Monetary Fund. And both groups see democracy within the group as vital to building democracy outside it. How they understand and practice that commitment differs substantially, as I will show in this chapter. A DAN activist would be dismayed by COPS leaders' practice of securing agreement on an issue before even bringing it to a meeting. She would likely see the pro forma ratification of positions that takes place at delegates' assemblies as a masquerade of popular control. A COPS leader, for her part, might be put off by the time that DAN activists put into meetings with no clear outcome. A debating society she might call it, armchair activism for the middle class.

As experimenters in democracy, however, both COPS and DAN have traveled some distance from the 1960s. They view consensus differently, equality differently, and what goes into effective decisionmaking differently. If 1960s activists were casual about the social relationships on which they based their participatory democracies, COPS activists call their organizing strategy *relational*. They capitalize on the affection, trust, and respect shared by active church members, but they also try to counteract the deference built into those relations by affirming the importance of acting on one's "self-interest"—even against one's leaders. DAN activists, for their part, put a great deal of emphasis on a deliberative process that is not just formally equal but that begins to overturn the hierarchies built into conventional definitions of equality. But they also rely on a distinctively process-oriented and personalistic culture of activism and on the bonds that come from shared participation in that culture.

Together, these strategies have enabled contemporary participatory democrats to avoid some of the problems that beset their predecessors. The difficulties that remain point to the importance of forging models of democratic interaction that have enough of the familiar in them to be accessible but also avoid the inequalities embedded in familiar relations. The challenges for faith-based organizations, I will suggest, are to make fuller use of the *diverse* relational styles that are familiar to their members and to admit more of the "big-picture" questions into their very practical deliberative process. DAN activists, meanwhile, must struggle to prevent their deliberative style from becoming so distinctive as to be offputting to those unfamiliar with it and so preoccupying as to discourage activists from developing agendas and planning actions.

COMMUNITY ORGANIZING

If community organizing has developed in ways that Saul Alinsky never envisaged, nevertheless he remains the Freud of community organizing, says Heather Booth of the Midwest Academy, an organization that trains community organizers. Booth, recall, was a key figure in the Chicago women's liberation movement. Contemporary community organizing counts other 1960s veterans in its ranks, notably Steve Max of Students for a Democratic Society (SDS) and Mike Miller of the Student Nonviolent Coordinating Committee (SNCC) among those who have appeared in previous chapters.[4]

Alinsky himself was critical of the late 1960s movements, seeing their revolutionary fervor as grandiose and unconnected to a people's politics. Grassroots organizing, he insisted, had to be pragmatic and grounded in people's self-interest. Trained as a criminologist, and with connections to the Congress of Industrial Organizations, Alinsky began to organize in the 1930s in Chicago's notorious Back of the Yards neighborhood, immortalized in Upton Sinclair's *The Jungle*. Alinsky cajoled Catholic priests into a surprising alliance with radical labor organizers and then drew in an array of neighborhood civic, youth, and ethnic organizations. The new Back of the Yards Neighborhood Council succeeded in short order in raising stockyard wages, getting a hot-lunch program in schools, and winning jobs for residents in the Works Progress Administration. Alinsky's technique, outlined in his best-selling 1946 *Reveille for Radicals*, came to define a new style of organizing: building alliances among churches, union locals, and other neighborhood organizations, using confrontational tactics against officials and employers, and insisting that residents rather than the organizer dictate the group's agenda. Alinsky envisioned a national network of radical "people's organizations," but his work toward that goal was interrupted first by World War II, then by the loss of organized labor as an ally. His efforts revived in the 1960s, and projects in Chicago, Rochester, and Buffalo won plaudits for their pragmatic organizing style and concrete gains. By the mid-1970s, however, some of the highest-profile IAF projects had shifted from confronting city hall to administering federal housing and vocational training grants. Alinsky died in 1972, but, already, some of the attractions and dangers of co-optation were becoming clear.[5]

Alinsky-style organizing's more agitational side was reinvigorated, along with the IAF's fortunes, when Ernesto Cortes Jr. began organizing in San Antonio, Texas, in the mid-1970s. Cortes organized Mexican American residents to demand $100 million worth of neighborhood improvements. Confrontational in style, COPS backed up its challenge with an extensive organization built on pastoral and lay networks within the Catholic church. COPS won its improvements, and, in the process, it also helped topple Anglos' control of the City Council and elect the country's first Hispanic mayor, Henry Cisneros. Cortes's success convinced IAF leaders of the value of a brand of organizing that engaged residents' faith traditions. Since then, with IAF affiliates proliferating, Cortes has helped launch statewide education reform efforts and built bases in neighboring states. The national IAF network, meanwhile, now boasts over sixty local affiliates, many in the Southwest, but also in New York, Baltimore, Philadelphia, Washington, D.C., the Bay Area, Seattle, Atlanta, and Chicago. Three other congregation-based organizing networks have joined IAF: the Pacific

Institute for Community Organizations (PICO), the Gamaliel Foundation, and the Direct Action Research and Training Center. Together, the four networks work today with 133 projects across the country, involving over four thousand member institutions, mainly churches, but also some labor unions, schools, and ethnic organizations.[6]

The organizing scenario in the four networks is similar. An organizer's services and those of her network are contracted by a group of community leaders—usually pastors who have raised money from their congregations and denominations as well as from foundations. The organizer, who is rarely from the community herself, begins her work by meeting with congregation leaders in as many churches as possible to put together a working group. Then, with the help of pastors and lay leaders, she conducts hundreds of "one-on-one" interviews and "house meetings" with active church members to identify areas of concern and potential leaders. In the house meetings, residents have an opportunity to begin to voice their worries and concerns in a semipublic setting. The organizer is there to learn, she makes clear. Such interviews and meetings go on for some time: the task is to build the infrastructure of relationships that will sustain an organization and to move from broad discussion of people's concerns and values to actionable issues. Once an issue of real concern to the community has been identified, the group begins to craft a solution in the form of a set of demands to be put to selected targets: municipal officials, housing developers, the city council, or state legislators. Closed-door negotiations conducted by representatives of the group are combined with "accountability nights," in which the group's entire membership turns out to challenge invited officials on their commitment to the issues in question. Such meetings—"public dramas," Cortes calls them—are scripted, rehearsed, and evaluated by leaders afterward. Community organizations' political leverage comes in part from the numbers of people that they can turn out, regularly one thousand and often more. (The meeting of the Greater Boston Interfaith Organization that I attended in the spring of 2000 drew thirty-five hundred people to demand commitments from the mayor and State Assembly leader to securing affordable housing.) Such shows of numerical strength hint at power in the voting booth and are combined with the legitimacy that comes from the group's interdenominational religious basis.[7]

The victories won by such groups have been significant, including increases in the minimum wage, school funding, an end to banks' redlining of minority residents, crime-control reforms, and public housing. Aside from their policy wins, organizers see the empowerment of people with few credentials and little prior experience of politics—twenty-four thousand

Founding convention of the Texas Industrial Areas Foundation network, San Antonio, 1990. Ernesto Cortes Jr. is in the foreground, standing alone. (Photo by Alan Pogue; used with permission)

such individuals now are "core leaders" in community projects—as a radical end in itself.[8]

LEADERSHIP AND DEMOCRACY

Faith-based organizing puts great emphasis on the developmental prerequisites to enduring change. People have the capacity to act collectively on their interests and to win concessions from those in power. But their ability to frame their interests as viable objectives and to build effective organizations must be nurtured. This means more than learning new skills. It also means building the self-confidence necessary to contend with authorities. Organizing, say its practitioners, *is* teaching. "The organizer's job is like a tutor's," the IAF's Ed Chambers writes: "to share insights, to teach methods of analysis and to provide tools of research, to challenge citizens to sharpen their public skills, to develop their ability to reflect and to act." After staff salaries, training is often the largest budget item in organizing projects. Training takes place in one-on-one meetings between organizers and leaders, in larger meetings to plan and evaluate group actions, and in the national training sessions that are sponsored by the networks.[9]

For community organizers, decisionmaking affords opportunities for developing leadership capacities—within limits. Endless meetings sap people's energy, and, for middle- and low-income people with jobs and families, they are an unnecessary luxury. The routine meetings that make up the work of a community organization accordingly follow a standard format. They begin on time with a prayer, move systematically through a set agenda, conclude with an evaluation, and end on time. Speakers are expected to be brief, but the meetings are also expected to be participatory.

The chair, usually a lay leader rather than the organizer, often goes around the table to solicit people's input. When tasks are agreed to, those responsible for them are asked to report back to the group on their progress.[10]

An observer of routine project meetings, as well as of the larger membership meetings held to determine issue priorities, agree on action plans, and elect formal organization leaders, might be surprised by the absence of contention in them. There are differences of opinion but rarely fundamental disagreements on program objectives or the best means of reaching them. This is no coincidence. Much of the work of collective decisionmaking goes on before the meeting. This is the case in the Texas IAF organizations that sociologist Mark Warren studied. Formally, decisions on new campaigns, on the allocation of resources, and on hiring new organizers are made by delegates' assemblies, which meet quarterly and are composed of the organization's active members ("leaders" in IAF parlance). Informally, the lead organizer and several members of the group's executive committee develop an action plan and consult with other leaders to secure their agreement in advance of a delegates' assembly. In the assembly itself, the plan is ratified, usually by acclamation, with votes taken only on minor provisions. If a plan looks likely to generate serious opposition, leaders shelve it. The same informal consensus process is used to choose leaders, with delegates' assemblies ratifying nominations for offices that have been forwarded by current members of the executive committee. Until the mid-1980s, COPS elected a president, a vice president, and other top positions through contested elections. The group switched to a system of cochairs, however, after deciding that contested elections ended up losing it the leadership of people who had served their terms or been defeated.[11]

Organizers and leaders justify this style of decisionmaking and leadership selection in several ways. Delegates' assemblies *can* refuse to ratify an action plan or a slate of nominees. Leaders are prevented from monopolizing power by a set of clear rules: they cannot run for political office, administer public funds, or take administrative positions in programs spun off from their organizations. Organizers, for their part, cannot make decisions or speak publicly for IAF organizations, and they are moved from community to community every three to five years to prevent them from developing a stake in a particular agenda. Most important—and this is true of congregation-based organizing generally—the pro forma character of deliberation is justified by participants' commitment to building consensus. Organizers and leaders spend a great deal of time talking to their organizations' members: sounding them out on issues and choices, negotiating alternatives, assuring them that their concerns will be respected. Indeed, pastors are told during training sessions that the one-on-one interviews in which they solicit members' concerns should be the biggest part of their job. All these interactions are intended to forge areas of common resolve and the compromises that are necessary to effective decisionmaking.[12]

Organizers say that what makes the consensus authentic—what prevents people from kowtowing to their pastors or to organizers—is the emphasis organizers place on *self-interest*. Self-interest rather than altruism or ideological principle is what motivates people to effective action, organizers maintain. But self-interest is distinguished from selfishness. Organizers often point out that the Latin root of the word *interest* is *interesse*, which means "to be among or between." Interests are seen as developing in and through relationships with others. Self-interest is also seen as encompassing more than material concerns. "A person's self-interest incorporates all of their concerns, values and desires, including the need for self-preservation, creativity, self-definition, power, money, love, and meaning in life," Cortes writes. Organizers often say that one's fundamental self-interest is what one hopes will be one's epitaph. On the other hand, the emphasis on self-interest does imply that differences are normal. Common interests and agendas are not assumed; rather, they are arrived at through a process of negotiation.[13]

Another way organizers try to maximize solidarity without quashing disagreement is by making a firm distinction between the behaviors that are legitimate in private settings and those that are legitimate in public ones. In an exercise that has been used since the 1970s, an IAF trainer lists a set of contrasting terms on a blackboard, each one corresponding to "appropriate behavior" in the public or private realm. "Sameness/commonality" in the private sphere is contrasted to "diversity" in the public, "fidelity/loyalty" to "accountability," "the need to be liked" to "the need to be respected," and "self-giving" to "quid pro quo/self-interest." The exercise encourages participants to think about confronting public officials in ways that might otherwise be seen as impolite and to hold firm when officials offer only token concessions. "You learn what's appropriate and inappropriate for politicians. They shouldn't try to get us to love them, for instance," said a San Antonio COPS leader. Within the organization too, this kind of training raises awareness of the dangers of importing familial modes into activism. The same COPS leader—she had become president of the group by the early 1980s—went on, "We would never have been able to challenge the priest to stop acting like our 'father' without this sort of training." IAF supervisor Christine Stephens observes, "In the world as it should be, we should all be one big happy

family. But in the real world, we're not. There is nothing wrong with
tension as long as the relationship endures.... Leaders should be able
to tell each other what they think. The worst thing is for someone to
break the tension, that is, to paper over difference and make everyone feel
better."[14]

In a Gamaliel training session that sociologist Stephen Hart attended,
trainers were critical of the church for promoting humility and meekness.
Women, especially, "are encouraged to be powerless people," one trainer
said. After sitting through dozens of similar statements, a pastor among the
trainees walked out, accusing trainers of "church-bashing." The session
leader assured the group that he loved the church but that he had to "speak
the truth" about the passivity of many churches. Organizers thus try to
build on existing relationships while counteracting their demobilizing
tendencies. They want the organization's internal relations to be marked
by trust and mutual respect but are alert to the dangers of modeling those
relations on family, friendship, or church. As Cortes insists: "We are not a
substitute family. While we can never do for each other in our organizations
what a family ought to do for its members, we can teach each other how
to develop trust in a relationship with people who are not part of our
families."[15]

In the evaluative work that goes on in community organizations, participants are encouraged to "challenge" each other on how much they
think they can and should do. Lay leaders are challenged by organizers
to take more of a public role than they think they can handle. Pastors are
prodded to pick up the pace on an issue, and organizers encourage leaders to question organizers' own tactical choices. This support for internal
challenge reflects community organizing's desire to balance authority with
accountability. There is nothing wrong with authority, faith-based organizers believe, and it is perfectly legitimate for skilled organizers to tap leaders, for pastors to veto lines of action likely to divide their congregations,
and for those who have dedicated time and energy to an organization to
represent its members before authorities. Likewise, as sociologist Richard
Wood points out, participants respect the authority of elected officials, provided that it is not used illegitimately. Indeed, organizers do not see their
confrontations with public officials as ruling out the possibility of later
collaboration. But legitimate authority, as they see it, requires a continual
process of consultation with a widening circle of community members,
accountability, and a commitment to making leadership skills available to
others.

Is this participatory democracy? It is in its vision of public decisionmaking freed of the power of economic and political elites. It is in its embrace

of a political strategy of making elected officials accountable to their otherwise less powerful constituencies by developing constituents' abilities to act jointly and effectively. And it is in its enactment of a deliberative procedure that puts a premium on developing leaders and on developing solidarity among people with diverse interests.[16]

THE LIMITS OF DEMOCRATIC LEARNING

When the deliberative approach used by community projects works, pastors are accountable to their congregations, organizers are accountable to their organizations, and leaders are accountable to each other. Of course, it does not always work. When pastors are less than committed to a campaign, it is almost impossible to get it off the ground. Organizers may expedite tasks by doing them themselves rather than training others. Some leaders may become overly comfortable in the collaborative relations they have established with officials.[17]

Good organizers can work around these problems. Other hurdles are steeper. Avoiding campaigns' dependence on a single organizer has gotten more difficult as organizing networks have shifted from an exclusively local focus to address problems originating outside community borders. There are now a number of statewide campaigns around issues such as health care, housing, employment, commercial development, and education. When organizers try to build coalitions beyond the locality—and beyond the range of regular, face-to-face interaction—securing informal consensus becomes more difficult. Texas IAF's initial efforts to develop state and regional networks have depended enormously on the personal authority and charisma of regional director Ernie Cortes. Cortes has worked hard to get to know key leaders in each locality and bring them together periodically for meetings, trying thereby to reproduce the consensus-building process that is used at the local level. But, as Mark Warren points out, Cortes's personal stature among local leaders cannot substitute for more institutionalized mechanisms of deliberation and accountability.[18]

Another set of problems, trickier because less obvious, stems from faith-based organizing's conception of self-interest. Again, by *self-interest* organizers do not mean wants that are narrowly selfish or material. Self-interest is relational rather than individual and encompasses moral concerns as well as material ones. The term's meanings are multiple and complex—and sometimes confusing. Why even use it then? In part because organizers recognize that people are often uncomfortable about acting on their own interests when those in power are telling them not to. Even as organizers have expanded the term from Alinsky's rather narrow usage, they have retained its emphasis on the bottom line: people will fight and should fight only in their own self-interest, whatever else leaders, prophets, or pundits tell them. To talk about self-interest is also to personalize it: *you* know what your interests are, and, if you wonder whether an authority is acting on behalf of your interests, you have a right to challenge him or her. Self-interest is the basis both for common agendas and for accountable authority. My question, however, is whether it is an adequate basis for either.

When organizers and leaders conduct hundreds of one-on-ones, their aim is to listen, as intently and sympathetically as possible. They want to get a full account of people's worries and aspirations and then tease from the many accounts they gather a compelling set of target issues. People will not stay involved unless their issues are being represented, so, to build consensus throughout the organizing process, leaders work to carve out areas of common interest that are both wide-ranging and actionable and to negotiate and renegotiate common agendas. Underpinning this scenario, however, is a view of people's individual interests as clear and fixed and of collective agendas as a kind of Venn diagram of intersecting interests. Group interests are brokered from individual ones. The alternative, however, is that both individual and common interests may emerge from discussion and deliberation—not through a process of negotiation (which assumes that interests are fixed) but through a process of self- and collective discovery. Decisionmaking on this model—a model that I have described throughout this book—is aimed not only at matching means to ends but also at scrutinizing and redefining ends.

Community organizers might object to this decisionmaking model on two grounds. One is that to raise the possibility that people may not know what their own interests are is to start down the slippery slope toward telling people what their interests are. Such a position would violate a commitment to popular empowerment. However, the slope is perhaps not quite so slippery as that. If people really are capable of knowing their own interests, then they should be well served by questioning them and having them questioned. In the Gamaliel training sessions that Stephen Hart attended, some participants were uncomfortable with trainers' unwillingness to outline aims beyond empowering congregation-based organizations. "Power to do what?" one trainee demanded in a session. The trainer answered that leaders and members would decide that. The trainee continued, "To what end?" The trainer responded, "To whatever end the people decide." That kind of answer may be increasingly unsatisfying as organizations move into statewide campaigns and collaborations requiring enormous outlays of time and money as well as complex alliances. In those circumstances, it behooves organizations to think more broadly about the relations between community economic development and free trade, between health care and campaign finance reform, and between local organizing and various levels of government. Big-picture questions of this kind, as well as even more fundamental ones about the meaning of democracy, equality, and faith, are a part of figuring out what people's interests are. Decisionmaking that treats interests as fixed and requiring only their conversion into a workable consensus misses that.[19]

Organizers might well have a second objection to the kind of exploratory discussions that I am describing, namely, that people with children, jobs, and homes simply do not have the time for them. The challenge, accordingly, is to incorporate processes of joint reflection and learning into a strategy that prides itself on its expeditiousness. In this regard, longtime organizer Mike Miller argues that the common opposition between organizing and educating, and between followers of Saul Alinsky and Myles Horton, misrepresents both Alinsky and Horton and misconceives what makes for good organizing. The most effective organizers are teachers, Miller argues, but the most effective teaching takes place in the middle of the action, not in a classroom. Practical questions—"What is the problem?" "How many other people feel the same way?" "What precisely do we want?"—should be combined with discussions of people's values, alternative political visions, and the power structures that they are up against. Organizers should pose big-picture questions much more than they do, Miller argues. On the other hand, they should not give up "teachable moments" in the midst of struggle in favor of education outside that crucible. Without sacrificing the expeditiousness of their decisionmaking, organizers might identify sites for more collective reflection and joint learning—in committee work, for example—or types of decisions that lend themselves to a wide-ranging discussion of people's interests and the contexts shaping those interests.[20]

There is a second limitation to contemporary organizing's conception of self-interest. Authorities—whether municipal officials or pastors or organizers—must be accountable, and the way to monitor their accountability is to challenge them on the basis of one's self-interest. But self-interest may not always be an adequate basis for internal dissent. Consider a study conducted in a different setting but relevant for this point. Katherine Sciacchitano studied the leadership styles of a group of rank-and-file nursing-home workers during a union organizing campaign. The workers had been paired with professionals to learn from them, but Sciacchitano found that the workers had their own approach. They were relatively uninterested in "challenging" fellow workers on their perceived limitations or "pushing" them into situations where they had to perform a more demanding role than they had anticipated. Instead, they concentrated on teaching people how to ask questions and making them feel safe enough to disagree. The organizing style that nursing-home workers found most congenial put a premium on collective decision-making and on building the confidence necessary to participate fully in decisionmaking.[21]

The idea of making people feel "safe enough" seems quite at odds with the archetypal Alinsky organizer, blunt talking and confrontational. While many community organizers today have moderated the confrontational style, some still believe that the way to develop leaders is to train them in political and organizational skills and to challenge them to take on more tasks than they imagined themselves capable of. A rhetoric of "pushing" people and "shaking them up" is common. But there is evidence that that style does not sit well with all participants—or all organizers. At the national training workshops that Stephen Hart, Mark Warren, and Dennis Shirley attended, some participants complained about trainers' arrogance and rigidity. Women, especially, were uncomfortable with what they experienced as a macho style. Some also objected to being criticized for expressing motivations for participation that were not "self-interested" enough.[22]

Are there alternatives? In her study of nursing-home workers, Sciacchitano noted that the rank-and-file leaders were all women. This jibes with a recent and growing literature on women's organizing. In contexts as varied as the nineteenth-century black women's club movement and 1960s welfare organizing, historians have identified a distinctively female style of organizing, characterized by group leadership, a preference for informal networks over formal organizations, and an emphasis on internal support and consciousness raising. It should be noted that women occupy top leadership positions in faith-based organizing. And it is women who tell the most powerful stories of their transformation in organizing from passive actors to confident leaders. But consider a COPS cochair's observation that it had been the other leaders, not the organizers, who had the most to do with her development. "It's just like growing up," she said. "Our mothers were our role models and teachers." My point is not that contemporary faith-based organizing is not reaching women. Rather, it is that the model may not have kept up with actual practice. There may be valuable associational models—ways of leading, learning, cooperating, and deliberating—in the interactive styles familiar to the people with whom organizers work. Although women's leadership in community organizing is recognized and valued, the dismissal of behaviors appropriate to the "private" sphere may unnecessarily rule out women's traditional ways of interacting as effective political models.[23]

DIRECT ACTION

Members of DAN would not consider what happens in an IAF Executive Committee meeting very democratic. They would see as rife with inequalities the "informal consensus" that IAF leaders champion. Yet, should an IAF or a PICO or a Gamaliel group be interested in joining them in an action, say, a demonstration against sweatshops, they would be more than happy to collaborate. Their ecumenism is partly pragmatic: they know that few groups have the same enthusiasm for egalitarian decisionmaking that they do. But it also comes from a certain humility—who are they to define the one true way?—and a willingness to question their own principles. "I think that where authority lies in the organization may be more important than how decisions are arrived at," DAN member Mac Scott says, this despite his own commitment to consensus-based deliberation.[24]

DAN was formed to coordinate the 1999 protests against the World Trade Organization in Seattle, but members' activist roots go back much further. Some anti–corporate globalization activists today came of political age in the antinuclear movement of the 1970s and 1980s. Others have had experience in radical environmentalist groups, in anarchist-leaning outfits like Food Not Bombs, in feminist collectives, in ACT-UP, and in the groups like Reclaim the Streets and Critical Mass whose members take over public spaces for mass bicycle rides and parties. What links these groups is their commitment to direct action and a deliberative style that, with varying degrees of rigor, is nonhierarchical.[25]

In 2000, between twenty and fifty people generally attended New York DAN's weekly meetings, and probably another fifty were regulars in working groups. In a meeting I attended that summer, shortly after the Republican National Convention in Philadelphia, about thirty people sat in a circle, with two facilitators—an older white man and a young black woman—on one side. DAN members introduced themselves by naming the work group with which they were primarily connected—"Rachel: Legal Collective," "John: Labor." Agenda items were written in marker on a poster taped to the wall; next to each item was a time limit for discussion. One of the first agenda items was a request for reimbursement by members of two work groups who had traveled to Philadelphia on their own dime to work on the trials of those arrested during the Republican convention. The request provoked strong and conflicting views: should DAN meet requests for funding after the fact? When a timekeeper warned that they had almost exceeded the time allotted for discussion, the facilitator asked whether the group would agree to more time. The group assented, the agenda was reshuffled, the facilitator asked whether everyone was comfortable with the new agenda, and discussion returned to the funding issue. Emotions rose; some of those petitioning for funding complained that they were being chastised for not having been frugal enough. Someone suggested that they table the issue for a future meeting. This seemed to secure general assent until it was pointed out that the issue had been tabled once already. A straw vote revealed that a few people would block consensus on a decision to supply the hundred dollars or so of funding. Finally, someone came up with a new solution: DAN would not reimburse expenses, but people could contribute individually. There was consensus, and a hat was passed around and quickly filled.

At an earlier training session for facilitators, I had seen the consensus process mapped out. A working group or an individual brings a proposal to a DAN meeting. After soliciting informational questions, the facilitator asks for participants' "concerns" about the proposal. If the opposition is overwhelming, the proposal may be tabled. If not, some concerns may be resolved through discussion or turned into "friendly amendments." At various points in the process, the facilitator may ask for a show of hands to sample opinion. When consensus seems possible, the facilitator asks if there are any stand-asides—people who do not support the proposal but will not stop it from going forward or who do not want to participate in an action but will not prevent the group from doing so—or blocks. The latter are to be used judiciously and only when a decision threatens the group's fundamental principles. Facilitation is rotated every few meetings, and everyone is expected to serve as a facilitator at some point.

Participants in DAN meetings display real respect for the process. Over and over again in the meeting I observed, when it would have been easy for someone to jump in and impose a solution that people probably would not in the end have been unhappy with, participants instead relied on the established procedure. They apologized when they jumped the queue. They raised issues of process and seemed genuinely interested when others did. A 1960s activist would be surprised by the procedural paraphernalia that accompanies democratic decisionmaking today. There are formal roles in the process—timekeeper, stacker, facilitator, vibes watcher—and sophisticated hand signals. Waving one's fingers as if playing a piano in the air ("twinkling") signals agreement with a point made; forming a triangle in the air with the forefinger and thumb of each hand indicates a concern about whether the deliberative process is proceeding according to form;

a raised fist indicates one's intention to block a decision. There is a whole literature on consensus-based decisionmaking too, available in handbooks and pamphlets, on websites, and in periodicals. Writers debate justifications for the form and specify ways to register dissent and the grounds on which to do so: from "non-support ('I don't see the need for this, but I'll go along')," to "reservations ('I think this may be a mistake but I can live with it')," standing aside, blocking ("I cannot support this or allow the group to support this. It is immoral"), and withdrawing from the group. There are warnings on what to avoid: "Defensiveness," "Speaking in capital letters," "Speaking for others," "Nitpicking," "Restating—especially what a woman has just said perfectly clearly." There are training programs for facilitators and different "schools" of facilitation.[26]

In a conversation with four DAN activists several weeks after the meeting that I attended, what came across strongly was both their appreciation for DAN's deliberative process—they see it as *important*—and their long experience in consensus-based organizations. I sketched Miriam Bearse's movement experiences in the snapshot that opened this chapter. Mac Scott, Lesley Wood, and Isabell Moore have had equally long activist careers, in Earth First! and Food Not Bombs and in native people's sovereignty solidarity, anti–Gulf War, immigrants rights, alternative transportation, antinuclear, antipoverty, and feminist movements. Both Mac and Lesley have been trained in facilitation, and the others are articulate about how the process works. Their experience suggests that models for egalitarian forms and deliberative styles are simply available to activists today in a way that they were not for 1960s activists. In some segments of the movement field, participatory democracy has come close to being institutionalized.[27]

At the same time, Isabell, Lesley, Mac, and Miriam have all had experience in groups that in principle were committed to egalitarian decisionmaking but that in practice depended on a governing clique. They are sensitive to the ways in which informality can allow inequalities and exclusions to persist unchallenged. They *like* DAN's formality. Another contrast with their 1960s predecessors is striking. If they see in formal processes the best protection against inequalities built into informal relations, they also reject conceptions of equality that require people to be treated identically. Such conceptions embed white, masculinist, middle-class norms, they argue: far from neutral standards, they are already intrinsically biased. To begin to overturn such standards and the broader structures that those standards reproduce, DAN activists put groups that have been disadvantaged first. They "stack" people's interventions so that women speak more, and they try to make sure that when the media seek out spokespeople it is someone of color who speaks first. They require that one of each pair of facilitators be a woman, but they also worry that that makes it unlikely that both facilitators will be women.[28]

There are still other ways in which DAN activists' view of democratic process differs from that of 1960s activists. The goal of consensus is not unity, they argue. "Consensus doesn't mean that everyone thinks that the decision made is the best one possible, but that everyone feels that their viewpoint was heard and synthesized into the proposal," reads a handout for demonstrators at the Republican National Convention. The object is rather for people to agree enough in order to be able to work together. "You have to have a certain humbleness," Isabell observes, "a willingness to learn from people who are different from you. You have to recognize that things are relative. There's not just one way to look at things." Miriam agrees: "Trust is important. 'This isn't what I would do—it's not my bag. But I can trust them to do their thing.'" The Quakers' belief in a single truth that all will arrive at through mutual discussion and contemplation is unappealing to these participatory democrats. There is no single best solution, let alone a single truth. Insofar as they seek to prefigure an alternative society, it is one in which difference is prized rather than erased. Similarly, they view the "affinity groups" established in advance of direct actions as sources of emotional support during confusing and often frightening events—but also as an opportunity to "go outside [one's] comfort zone" by joining people with different backgrounds. *Affinity* as a bond is different both from friendship in its explicitly political character and from shared ideological purpose in its recognition that "identities"—vegan, lesbian, Latina—are as much the basis of political commitments as are more traditional political creeds. In New York DAN, affinity groups are not the basis for organizational membership between actions; instead, people participate as individuals. But, by identifying themselves with their work-groups ("Rachel: Legal Collective"), they recognize the importance of local sources of solidarity, and, in having newcomers met by a delegated "greeter" and organizing periodic social events for all members of the group, they recognize the importance of sustaining affective bonds separate from more spontaneous friendships.[29]

Today's direct actionists are also attuned to the practical benefits of consensus-based decisionmaking, and this distinguishes them from their more recent movement forebears in the antinuclear movement of the late 1970s and early 1980s. As Barbara Epstein concludes in her history of that movement, activists' rejection of narrow and short-term measures of political effectiveness made sense. The kind of cultural revolution that they were after simply could not be accomplished in a few demonstrations. But the primacy that activists accorded acts of personal witness made for strong resistance to discussing issues of strategy and organizational sustenance—something that proved organizationally debilitating. For DAN activists today, there is nothing wrong with talking strategy. "The nice thing about consensus . . . ," one participant said several times in the facilitators' meeting that I attended, citing its ability to avoid alienating people in the deliberative process. Another participant pointed out its value in revealing options that people had not seen before. "The whole idea is a repudiation of the 'either/or' binary thinking approach," he went on. "Blocks are important because one person in a group can catch something that the others didn't." "I believe that it is when a group is under high pressure that it is most important to maintain the consensus process," Mac says in our conversation. During a crackdown, activists tend to want to centralize decisionmaking. But that is the worst thing to do, Mac argues, because then leaders can be arrested. It is precisely then that the consensus process, and respect for affinity groups' autonomy, is most important.[30]

At one point in my conversation with Mac, Lesley, Isabell, and Miriam, someone mentions what sounds to me like the developmental benefits of

Flyer for the Direct Action Network, New York, 2000. (Photo of flyer by Dana Schuerholz; used with permission)

participatory decisionmaking, but no one is very enthusiastic about them. People have different backgrounds and different orientations, Miriam says, and trails off. I sense a wariness of presuming to "teach" people things, especially since DAN activists, mainly white, middle class, and highly educated, are eager to work with people who are not those things. Miriam, Isabell, Mac, and Lesley are all unhesitant, however, when it comes to the solidarity-building benefits of direct democratic procedures. "It just feels better," Isabell says with a laugh. "People always complain that it takes longer than voting. But I tell them, maybe it takes longer to make the decision, but it's much quicker to implement." Mac and Lesley twinkle in agreement. Lesley: "Even an action that fails is OK if it was agreed to consensually. Because then discussing what happened becomes part of the group process and builds solidarity."

A CULTURE OF DEMOCRATIC DECISIONMAKING

DAN activists are pioneering new forms of democratic practice, and they are willing to devote real energy to making their deliberative process work fairly and effectively. But, as I have argued throughout this book, formal rules and ideological commitments are not enough to explain how a deliberative process actually operates. How do DAN activists know what kinds of issues can be raised, how to raise them, how to disagree in an appropriate way, how to negotiate but not seem manipulative? What are the sources of their deliberative etiquette? Such etiquettes keep things civil, but that is not a trivial matter. The cost of incivility is losing participants' trust in the system, its participants, and its outcomes.

In a discussion with another group of DAN activists—Jeremy Varon, David Graeber, Brooke Lehman, and José Lugo—I posed the question explicitly. Why do they trust that no one will tie up the discussion in tangential talk and that people will not hold on to selfish and stupid positions, even to the point of blocking a decision? David argues that the process itself, the orientation not to winning but to making the best decision, discourages that kind of obstructionism. Brooke points out that DAN has a set of principles that people are expected to uphold—again, the formality lacking in 1960s groups. Jeremy shrugs: "There's a commitment there. You see the same people week after week, and you think, 'My God, you really *do* care about this.'" A participatory democratic ethos, a set of formal rules, the affective bonds that develop among a group of people who meet frequently—to these factors Brooke adds something else. For the thousands of people who were new to direct action, Seattle provided a "common language," she says. Not just what twinkling meant and when to form an affinity group, but the microinteractional norms that undergird consensus decisionmaking. Many DAN activists already had this common language—from their involvement in the antinuclear movement, feminism, environmental direct action, and other movements. DAN activists are thus able to draw on a culture of democratic decisionmaking that was simply not available to 1960s activists.[31]

New leftists had wanted to operate in ways that reflected the humanistic values of personhood and community that they sought on a grand scale. But they lacked a behavioral idiom for enacting such commitments. Instead, they treated each other like friends, taking from a familiar relationship instruction on how to interact with political associates, but also in the process coming up against the limitations of friendship as the basis of a diverse and growing democratic body. By the late 1960s, many new leftists had abandoned efforts to create an egalitarian microcosm of a future society in favor of centralized, often militaristic organizations modeled on those of their Third World revolutionary heroes. It was among radical feminists, and in a counterculture largely disdained by politicos, that experiments in movement democracy continued. Communes, alternative bookstores, law firms, health collectives, and schools developed egalitarian forms as they self-consciously withdrew from the political sphere.[32]

Many of the activists who launched the direct action movement against nuclear power in the late 1970s had had experience in the antiwar movement and the new left. They were determined not to reproduce the sectarian battling and organizational maneuvering that had overwhelmed those movements. In developing an alternative, they had help from Quakers, who, according to longtime activist George Lakey, had overcome their earlier reticence about promoting their deliberative style. Two American Friends Service Committee activists attended the antinuclear Clamshell Alliance's first meeting in 1976 and, at members' request, taught them how to make decisions by consensus. The concept of affinity groups had also become available to many activists through anarchist Murray Bookchin's writings, and, in short order, the Clamshell Alliance developed a structure of autonomous affinity groups and a spokescouncil. In the alliance's first major action, fourteen hundred people were arrested for a nonviolent occupation of the Seabrook, New Hampshire, nuclear power plant. Held in armories for two weeks, the protesters made all decisions by consensus. The experience was galvanizing, and new chapters mushroomed. Sister organizations did too: the Shad, Roe, and Abalone Alliances, among others. The movement's decentralized and egalitarian structure was as distinctive as its nonviolent strategy, and many neophyte activists were introduced to that structure by groups like Lakey's Movement for a New

Society, which produced handbooks and manuals and traveled around the country, training activists in nonviolent direct action and small-group dynamics.[33]

Activists' mastery of the use of affinity groups and spokescouncils was tentative, however. Shortly after its stunning success, the Clamshell Alliance was riven and eventually destroyed by battles over what properly egalitarian decisionmaking required. Observers attributed the battles to the obstructionist tactics of the anarchists who had joined the group, but it seems that the familiar tension between veterans and newcomers was also at play. In the next several years, activists' ability to cope with differences within egalitarian organizations improved as a distinctive movement culture developed, informed by traditions of Christian witness, anarchism, and feminism. In the protests organized by the Abalone Alliance to shut down the Diablo Canyon nuclear plant, anarcha-feminists taught other participants an array of rituals that they used to build an internal movement culture. Some were informal: the monthly conferences, for example, where activists shared meals, partied together, and spent nights side by side in sleeping bags on the floor. Others were more self-conscious, like frequent demonstrations of physical but nonsexual affection and free-form dancing at the end of meetings intended, activists said, to wash away the disagreements and anxiety that the meeting might have generated. In interactions like these, activists were building the relationships that could reach across ideological differences.[34]

An evolving culture of radical protest was fed by other currents. The popularization of ideas about self-development from psychotherapy and Eastern religions, widespread acceptance of the feminist belief that "the personal is political," a willingness to see culture and everyday life as sites of radical change—all these have contributed to what sociologist Paul Lichterman describes as a political stance of *personalism*: "ways of speaking or acting which highlight a unique, personal self." Lichterman found these styles prevalent among the Green Party activists he studied in the late 1980s. The group was committed to combating the spread of environmental toxins. But it also spent a great deal of time talking about members' personal interactions and feelings. Discussions were studded with references to "what an issue means to me" and assertions of the importance of "personal values" and "personal empowerment." Lichterman cautions us not to see this as self-indulgence. On the contrary, to make the self the arbiter of political choices was a way to bridge differences of political opinion among people who lacked strong traditions of church, community, or a long-standing left. That such a style could be politically effective was attested to by the self-described "left" activist at a national Green conference that Lichterman attended who characterized the conference approvingly as a "convergence of the new left and the 'new age.'" While acknowledging his own wariness of the individualism and transcendentalism characteristic of new age thought, he pointed out that, by the late 1960s, "treating people with respect" had not been "very high on the new left's agenda."[35]

A therapeutically informed language of the self, an orientation to process, a rejection of masculinist styles, and an emotional expressiveness—all these have become part of the interactional repertoire of direct action protest. DAN activists rely on this repertoire. They phrase their objections to proposals in a tentative and a smiling way; they display few signs of irritation when someone monopolizes the floor; they interrupt usually only to suggest a solution to a conflict. They talk about values and respect for process. However, like the new left activist in the Green conference, they are also wary of "new age," expressive, "Californian" politics. They want to get things done, to make change in policies, politics, and the economy. This poses certain problems. DAN activists worry that their interactional style is offputting to people with whom they want to form coalitions. In a recent group discussion, a DAN member said that there was something nice about a DAN "culture" that prevented the fierce sectarian battles characteristic of the late 1960s. One could meet a DAN person somewhere else in the country and expect the same openness and respect that one would from DAN people with whom one worked on a daily basis, he observed. His listeners bristled. Was he saying that there was something exclusive about DAN? They worried that initiation into the arcana of DAN decisionmaking might become its own source of privilege. Some DAN activists and sympathetic critics also fear that the group is making a "fetish of process." They cite long-running debates over the merits of a third facilitator and shifting to a two-thirds vote when consensus is blocked. Such debates have taken time away from crafting an agenda and have cut attendance levels, they say. Similar to what happened to SNCC in 1964, battles over the deliberative procedure may absorb other kinds of disputes. Not only does this make it more difficult to resolve procedural conflicts—since procedure is not what they are really about. It also keeps such disputes center stage at the expense of discussions of goals and actions.[36]

Another source of tension in DAN activists' practice of radical democracy is an ambivalent relation between practical and normative preferences for consensus-based decisionmaking. Emphasizing the practical benefits of the form surely makes it more appealing to those who lack a prior allegiance to it. It probably also discourages conflicts between pragmatists and purists, with each side insisting on the irreducibility of its position.

However, activists' tendency to emphasize practicality while not acknowledging their principled commitments to consensus may also pose problems. Although this seems counterintuitive, it may actually undercut activists' ability to capitalize on practical techniques in consensus decisionmaking. Several times in the facilitators' meeting that I attended, people called "flaky" or "goofy" procedures like hand signals to indicate agreement, blocking, and standing aside. They were actually arguing for the *utility* of such procedures in moving discussion along more efficiently, but their qualifications undermined the point. A very able facilitator apologized to the group for his "Californian" facilitation style. The proposal that a third facilitator monitor the participation of underrepresented groups was met with strong opposition after the position was labeled a "vibes watcher" and "too Californian." Again, "Californian" seems to mean more concerned with self-liberation than with political change and more interested in how things "feel" than in what they can accomplish. In a dynamic that I have described repeatedly in this book, activists' understandings of what is practical are shaped by the groups with which particular strategies, tactics, or deliberative forms are negatively or positively linked. As a result of these associations, however, activists may devalue practices that actually contribute to practical, externally focused political change.

Contemporary activists' nonchalance about the ideological underpinnings of their preference for participatory democracy may also discourage them from wrestling with some of its sharpest contradictions. For example, several DAN members with whom I spoke justified the provision for shifting from consensus to supermajority vote by citing the potential for infiltrators or sectarians or emotionally disturbed people to derail the decisionmaking process. They did not talk much, however, about the possibility that people might sometimes have fundamentally different opinions or preferences and that the deliberative process would have to allow for that. Sympathetic critics of contemporary direct action have likewise drawn attention to activists' proud respect for individuals' and groups' autonomy—and their unwillingness to confront the costs of such autonomy for joint action. As one commentator observed of direct action protests against the World Bank in Washington, D.C., when some affinity groups wanted to blockade delegates' departure routes, the council coordinating the protest came up with a plan: if groups wanted to blockade, they could do so. In the absence of a plan coordinated across groups, the delegates easily circumvented the few blockades that were established. Longtime direct action trainer Bill Moyer is critical of a stance among direct actionists in which "no one can tell anyone else what to do." If Moyer is right, then the challenge for contemporary activists may be one with which 1960s activists only began to wrestle: to forge new bases of legitimate authority rather than to renounce authority altogether.[37]

DEMOCRACY TODAY: RULES AND RELATIONSHIPS

In the early 1960s, two streams of oppositional politics converged, first in the Southern civil rights movement, then in the new left. One was an organizing tradition reaching back to the settlement house movement of the mid-nineteenth century and to labor education experiments early in the twentieth. The other was a tradition of nonviolent direct action, Gandhian by the 1950s, but with deep roots in traditions of Quaker witness. Through people like Myles Horton and Ella Baker, the two strands came together, inspiring a movement strategy that combined practical organizing with a vision of radical social change, sought local gains while exposing to the nation the injustices of Southern apartheid, and treated participatory decisionmaking both as a strategy and as an end in itself. Today, in some ways, the two strands have diverged. Community organizers are adamant that they are not a movement, something that they associate with charismatic leaders and temporary bursts of fervor without the follow-up necessary actually to secure concessions. They take pride in their disdain for grandiose political visions and their willingness to work within the constraints of the existing political system. Activists in the direct action wing of the anti–corporate globalization movement, like those in environmental, anti–Gulf War, antiapartheid, and gay and lesbian rights movements, have scoffed at community organizers' acceptance of "piece-of-the-pie" politics. Activists say that community organizing is undemocratic; organizers say that contemporary activism is white and middle class.

Of course, a closer look shows that there is more overlap in how proponents of each strand think that social change actually happens. Most community organizers recognize the potency of moral arguments in leveraging concessions from the powerful. Many direct action activists recognize that few movements have achieved gains without grassroots involvement. Community organizing is trying to overcome its localism, direct action its lack of diversity. When it comes to how adherents of the two approaches make decisions, both have moved away from their 1960s forebears—say, Alinsky organizing and SDS, respectively—and have done so in several ways that make them more alike than different. For one thing, both faith-based community organizers and direct action activists of the DAN variety see participatory democratic decisionmaking as at once means and end. For organizers, the development of politically engaged and capable citizens—"leaders"—has benefits that extend beyond the strength of the organization, contributing to the kind of civic infrastructure that can protect low-income residents from the depredations of job insecurity, drugs, and crime. DAN activists, for their part, emphasize the effectiveness of consensus decisionmaking in sustaining group solidarity.

Decisionmaking for both groups is much more formalized than was that of 1960s activists. Both rely on agendas, rules, and routinized procedures. At the same time, neither treats formal procedure as adequate to the task of ensuring democratic decisionmaking. Faith-based organizers rely on relationships that they have nurtured, sometimes for years, to ensure the trust and mutual respect that is necessary for effective decisionmaking. Bonds of church and neighborhood are vital sources of solidarity, and pastors of authority, organizers believe. But people may sometimes have to assert their self-interest by refusing to defer to those relations. DAN activists rely on a distinctive interactional style characterized by open expressions of emotion and visible signs of respect for each other's contributions and for the integrity of the process.

This is not to say that adherents of community organizing and of directly democratic direct action make decisions in similar ways. The former are much more comfortable with traditional sources of authority in decisionmaking—the authority of pastors, of elected officials, of pluralism—provided that they are made responsive. The latter are more comfortable with sacrificing effective coordination in the interests of respecting people's personal commitments. Caricatured, or done badly, community organizing can tend to the authoritarian, directly democratic direct action to the ineffectual. Neither group, obviously, has solved the problems associated with participatory democratic decisionmaking. Besides the perennial question of how to balance wide participation with quick decisionmaking, another thorny issue concerns what counts as consensus. I have argued that faith-based organizers sometimes risk treating consensus as a process of brokering commonalities from fixed interests. They miss the possibility that people's interests may be transformed through collective reflection and deliberation. There may thus be significant benefits to a more exploratory group deliberative process, benefits that should at least be weighed against those of expeditious decisionmaking. DAN activists may make the opposite mistake, underestimating the possibility that people's opinions on an issue may be honestly and fundamentally different. The challenge in such a situation is to make it possible for the group to override dissenters without alliances and conflicts hardening and carrying over into the next discussion.

Finally, the relational character of both groups' decisionmaking style comes with risks. If traditional relationships often leave inequalities and exclusions unchecked because they are so familiar as to go unscrutinized, new associational forms can become just as exclusive by their unfamiliarity. The interactional "expertise" possessed by initiates may become a new form of privilege. This is the quandary that DAN faces. Faith-based organizers are attentive to the demobilizing effects of traditional patterns of deference and exhort people to look to their self-interest to challenge authorities within as well as outside the movement. But they may thereby fail to capitalize on some of the interactional styles familiar to participants that offer alternative leadership styles and bases for internal dissent. This points to a challenge that I have come to see as fundamental to maximizing the developmental benefits of participatory democracy: how to incorporate into decisionmaking the feelings of mutual trust, respect, and concern that are characteristic of relations outside the political sphere without reproducing the hierarchies and exclusions that are also characteristic of those relations. Should groups combine familiar relational models with an emphasis on values of openness and tolerance for difference? Try to forge altogether new relational models? I take up these questions in the next chapter.

8

CONCLUSION: RULES, RITUALS,

AND RELATIONSHIPS

Utopia, like virtue, is a concept shot full of relativity.

H. L. MENCKEN, "WHAT IS THIS TALK ABOUT UTOPIA?" (1928)

Is participatory democracy a relic of an era that gave us bell-bottoms, sit-ins, "Question Authority!" bumper stickers, and an extraordinary belief in the power of ideas—"Freedom," "Democracy," "Love"—to do every-thing from desegregate the South to levitate the Pentagon? The conviction that organizations could be run by their members, without representatives, votes, or a formal chain of command, was certainly admirable. But was it impossible? By the time they collapsed, both the Student Nonviolent Coor-dinating Committee (SNCC) and Students for a Democratic Society (SDS) had been taken over by ideologues hardly concerned with ensuring the participation of those for whom they claimed to speak. Feminist collectives were riven by ideological disputes or paralyzed when they tried to shift from consciousness raising to action. The feminist organizations that did endure, launching rape crisis centers, health clinics, and battered women's shelters, adopted the apparatus of conventional bureaucracies, complete with bylaws, staff positions, and a hierarchy of formal offices. Their re-forms were driven not only by funders' demands for formal accountability but also by activists' own recognition that participatory democracies often ended up governed by small cliques.

Still, the social change efforts that I profiled in the last chapter sug-gest that participatory democracy today is alive and well. It operates in groups on the cutting edge of militant protest and in campaigns involving millions of low-income Americans. It is in some ways a very different version of participatory democracy than that current in the 1960s. No one believes any longer that decisions can always be made by strict consensus. Activists are more comfortable with rules, less hostile to power, and more attuned to the inequalities concealed in informal relations. As a mode of

deliberation, participatory democracy incorporates elements of representative democracy; as an organizational form, it incorporates elements of
bureaucracy.

Yet I have written almost a whole book on movement experiments in
democracy that preceded those current today. I began the book because
I was frustrated by the way SNCC figured in the accepted genealogy of
participatory democracy. The standard image of a beloved community of
young idealists uninterested in practical political gains or instrumental
effectiveness seemed to miss the organizing strategy of which SNCC's
deliberative style was a crucial part. I wanted to recuperate a rationale
for participatory democracy that saw it as essential to building enduring
local movement organizations and leadership. Sociologists have tended
to miss such a strategy by focusing on mass mobilizations aimed at
national political authorities. They have paid little attention to lower-
profile efforts to put mobilizing structures in place and to ensure that
concessions won actually translate into local changes, and they have paid
still less attention to the organizational structures that best serve such
a strategy. By treating participatory democratic organizations as hostile
to considerations of political efficacy, moreover, scholars have sometimes
ruled out in advance the possibility that such organizations can have
political aims and effects. But I also wondered whether the omission
was from activists' strategic repertoires as well as from analysts' conceptual ones. What happened to the belief that participatory democracy
in movements of the powerless would help transform institutional political
structures?[1]

I came to see two more reasons for studying American activists'
experiences with radical democracy. Comparing a number of such efforts
would help us account for the problems that have plagued the form and
the conditions under which only implicit tensions have become organizationally debilitating. And comparing activists' assessments of participatory
democracy over the course of seven movements would tell us something
about strategic choice more broadly, that is, about the processes by which
activists select among the strategies, tactics, targets, organizational forms,
and ideological frames available to them. I suspected that ideological
consistency and instrumental rationality did not sum up the bases for
strategic choice in movements, yet these were the only ones that figured
in sociological models. Let me begin this chapter, then, by briefly recapitu-
lating the story that I have told about participatory democracy in American
social movements. Then, I will try to draw from it some lessons for how we
might think differently about social movements, democracy, and strategic
choice.

INVENTING DEMOCRACY

Much more than I had expected, 1960s activists were making participatory democracy up as they went along. To be sure, the critique of mass parties and bureaucratic politics advanced by pacifists in the 1950s inspired some of the students who would form the new left. From pacifists' avowal that the "the root is man" to the Port Huron Statement's declaration that far from "thing[s] to be manipulated . . . [m]en have unrealized potential for self-cultivation, self-direction, self-understanding and creativity," there is real continuity. In the person of pacifist James Lawson, the connection was even more direct. Lawson instilled in the Nashville sit-inners who would form SNCC's first leadership a preference for consensus-based decision-making as well as for nonviolent direct action. In the North, students had some contact with Quaker activists through campus ministries and with people skilled in nonviolent direct action in the Congress of Racial Equality and in peace groups. But these were rare guides. Student activists' own political backgrounds had been mainly in conventionally structured student councils and liberal campus clubs. The organizational models that they had were largely negative: the old left groups that seemed to combine an enthusiasm for arcane squabbles with minimal political impact, the labor bureaucrats whose narrow self-interest sometimes swung over into corruption, and the civil rights organizations that seemed slow moving and painfully "adult." Student activists did not have much to go on.[2]

This lack of deliberative blueprints left student activists free to draw from other sources, however, and to attach new political aspirations to the organizational structures that they created. One source was a tradition of political organizing that combined radical education with efforts to build leadership among the politically marginalized. From Myles Horton, Septima Clark, Ella Baker, and the maverick longtime activists who would provide entrée into black communities, SNCC workers learned to work with traditional leaders where they could and to quietly circumvent them where they could not. Organizers' deferential stance dispelled the notion that these "outside agitators" wanted to impose their own agendas. More important, participatory decisionmaking in project meetings helped residents who had little prior experience of routine politics take on roles in strategizing and in mobilizing fellow residents. Talking through issues and options enabled people to connect local injustices to national policies, exposed them to diverse rationales for participation, and helped them negotiate short- and long-term goals.

Participatory democracy on movement projects also transformed people's understandings of what counted as leadership—for organizers as much as for residents. Without the involvement of people conventionally deemed unqualified for political participation, black Mississippians had little chance of ending their political disenfranchisement. But this eminently practical strategy also tendered a radical vision. SNCC workers' deliberative style demonstrated to residents themselves and to a national audience—including the white new leftists who were watching the Southern movement—that conventional qualifications were no indicator of people's capacities for political leadership. The notion that ordinary people could make fundamental and far-reaching change was, for many students, a startling and powerful insight. Combined with a tradition of nonviolent direct action that called for morally uncompromising action *now*, it opened up the possibility that local experiments in democracy could have radical effect. The SDS organizer who quoted approvingly a resident's observation that "freedom is an endless meeting" went on to explain that "talk helps people consider the possibilities open for social change." Far from a utopian retreat from the rough-and-tumble of real political contention, participatory democracy within the movement helped powerless people contend politically.[3]

It only made sense that in their own organization, as SNCC staff put it, the "people who do the work make the decisions." There was certainly a prefigurative, utopian dimension to participatory democracy as an organizational process, a sense that building a democratic movement in the here and now would lay the groundwork for a radically egalitarian society. For students who took classes in thousand-seat lecture halls and came of intellectual age reading about gray-faced "organization men" and soulless "other-directed" personalities, collectivist decisionmaking also promised relationships that were emotionally satisfying and refreshingly direct. In addition to these benefits, however, Northern activists saw in SNCC that strong bonds of trust, concern, and respect among members of the group were necessary, not ancillary, to a project of militant activism. Democratic organization made it possible to tap local resources and generate novel strategies, build local leaders, and mobilize constituencies. Activists differed about whether the object of the political development that took place in participatory democratic decisionmaking was to gain concessions from political authorities or to transform the institutions like marriage and the family in which people participated on a daily basis. I have emphasized the explicitly political impulse behind participatory democratic decisionmaking only because it has been neglected in accounts both of the 1960s and of participatory democracy and because it so clearly counters the notion that participatory democracy's yields are expressive, ideological, and personal but *not* political.

By decade's end, this impulse was muted. Activists no longer believed that radical democracy in the movement would help the have-nots gain power. There were several reasons for this. As the prospects for political reform dimmed—the Atlantic City debacle, the escalating Vietnam War, the battles between police and residents in urban ghettos all attested to the sheer imperviousness of the "establishment" to moral pleading—some began to see participatory democratic institutions as permanent alternatives to mainstream political ones. That view was nourished by an emerging counterculture and, later, by a back-to-the-land movement that took thousands to rural communes. Those who stayed behind launched collectivist health-care centers, food co-ops, newspapers, law firms, and high schools. Some envisioned their efforts as building toward an alternative society, others simply as natural, the way one did things. But many retreated from a political world that they now saw as utterly obdurate on the side of authorities and apocalyptic on the side of challengers.

Participatory democracy's developmental purposes were also undermined by activists' growing discomfort with the notion of tutelage. Northern white students who came south to assist in the black freedom struggle discovered the courage and integrity of poor Southern black people at the same time as they discovered their own tendencies to reproduce precisely the relations of deference that they were trying to overcome. They would not lead, they declared, since that was what white people had always done. They talked frequently and agonizingly about the dangers of manipulation. So too did Northern white organizers, who renounced any aspiration to teach or guide those with whom they worked. Equality could not be built on the basis of tutelage, they insisted. If some activists had come to see participatory democracy as an alternative to efforts to effect institutional political change, others stripped it of its developmental aspects. Black activists' disenchantment with a developmental rationale for participatory democracy had different sources. Power still depended on collective self-development, they believed, but participatory democracy was not the way to get there. Unappealingly moralistic, self-indulgent, and white, participatory democracy could hardly be expected to build a sense of ethnic kinship among black people. The example of disciplined revolutionary organizations on a Third World model would better serve as a positive example. In sum, if earlier in the decade participatory democracy had been a resource that was at once political, pedagogical, and instrumental, by the end of the decade it was none of these things.

Aside from these historical shifts in activists' views of internal democracy and external social change, there were also reasons why their participatory democratic organizations could not have lasted. Over and over again, participatory democrats found themselves wracked by battles over decisionmaking, battles that alienated members, halted campaigns, and made some activists despair of the possibility of democratic decision-making. "It turned me into a Leninist," said one. Groups were paralyzed as members charged unrestrained egoism and power mongering in every exercise of initiative, manipulation in every programmatic suggestion, and a betrayal of democracy in every effort to get something done. The joint learning that had been critical to participatory decisionmaking became less important than ensuring that no one intimidate by demonstrating superior skills.[4]

The problems were there from the beginning, I have argued, but they lay not primarily in the perennial tension between individual and collective interests or between instrumental and ideological commitments. Participatory democracy stopped working in the 1960s when its practitioners came up against the normative limits of friendship. Lacking organizational blueprints for creating functioning participatory democracies, activists in the early 1960s retained conventional structures like formal offices, majority votes, and Robert's Rules of Order—but in practice ignored them. To make decisions and allocate resources, they relied instead on a participatory ethos combined with the natural goodwill, trust, and respect that friends have for each other. The groups that I studied did not begin as groups of friends. But the sense of finding allies in what seemed a wilderness of student apathy, combined with the long hours, the hard work, and, in some cases, the danger to which they were subjected as well as the excitement of launching a new movement, created strong bonds. Such bonds, in turn, made for decisionmaking that was relatively expeditious. Participants' knowledge of each others' skills and preferences, along with their mutual trust, discouraged standoffs and stalemates. Friends tended to see one person's strengths as a bonus for the group and another's weaknesses as of only trivial importance. Difference was the source of mutual enrichment, not of inequality.

When new members who were not vouched for by friends joined the group, however, or when veterans' friendships broke down for other reasons, the paucity of alternative interactional frameworks became clear. Newcomers lacked information about the histories of issues, and they lacked affective bonds with veterans. Even when veterans actively tried to cede power to those who came after them, they continued to meet with their friends at conferences, consult with them about decisions, and credit their opinions. Veterans were easily *seen* as monopolizing power, moreover, no matter what they did, by people who were outside their circle. The stage was set for mutiny. That newcomers bid for a place by pressing the group to adhere to its participatory democratic commitments is not surprising, for many had been attracted in part by the group's radically democratic practices. It was not that they brought with them much more exigent standards of democracy. Rather, their interests in democracy crystallized in and through their experience of marginality.

Activists often responded to charges of oligarchy by striving to make decisionmaking truly egalitarian. Everyone would participate; those who had monopolized discussion would be restrained and those who had been silenced speak. But these efforts usually backfired. In SNCC, novice organizers who had so prized the opportunity in staff decisionmaking both to learn from more experienced organizers and to have their own tentative contributions listened to and valued found it harder to speak up when they were the object of disputes among other staffers about "why the quiet people don't speak." In SDS, veterans encouraged newcomers to take over formal offices but left them with the impression that they considered the offices unimportant. If simply encouraging people to participate did not work, perhaps the answer was in more formal mechanisms for ensuring equality. Women's liberationists set up lot systems to rotate tasks and they required people to surrender a disc from their allotted number each time they spoke in order to prevent more verbal members from dominating discussion. Vocal members complained about feeling stifled as a result, while others regretted the loss of the free-form discussions in which they had discovered new possibilities in interaction with each other. This was the irony. Formalizing equality was a way to counter the inequalities between newcomers and veterans common in relations of friendship. But it did so by making equality simpler, measurable in speaking time and veto power. What was lost in the process was the complex equality that had allowed people to learn from each other without feeling patronized or imposed on.

Is there an alternative? Are there ways to promote the mutual trust, respect, and concern that are a precondition for participatory democracy's developmental benefits without relying on familiar norms of friendship—or tutelage or religious fellowship, the other two relationships that have supplied norms of democratic decisionmaking in movement organizations? Yes, and the history of experiments in participatory democracy, both during and since the 1960s, provides evidence of these too. Before I turn to them, let me consider more generally how the experiments that I have discussed in this book modify the balance sheet on participatory democracy.

SOLIDARY, INNOVATORY, AND DEVELOPMENTAL BENEFITS

In the organizations that I studied, decisionmaking was informal, decentralized, and consensus oriented. But it was also deliberative and experimental, and I have emphasized these two features because they have been neglected in most treatments of the form. By talking issues through, people with little experience of political decisionmaking learned to identify the costs and benefits of alternative options and gathered the information needed to make judgments. Reasoning together about options and solutions led to new conceptions of self-interest and new perceptions of strategy. By rejecting conventional criteria of authority and promoting new ones—this was the experimental part—activists helped legitimate new kinds of leadership and developed mechanisms for holding leaders accountable to their constituents. It is important to note that decisionmaking on a deliberative and experimental democratic model was neither dependent on consensus nor wed to the notion of leaderlessness. To the contrary, the point of experimentation was to open up to scrutiny just what did and should count as legitimate authority. And decisionmaking on a deliberative model was aimed, not necessarily at strict consensus, but at participants' mutual recognition of the legitimacy of their different rationales for preferring particular options. One can argue, as activists sometimes did, that solidarity can be better built on that basis than on the pretense that participants' interests are identical.[5]

Analysts have not neglected altogether participatory democracy's value for movement groups seeking institutional change. They have noted the capacity of decentralized, informal, and egalitarian decisionmaking to strengthen group solidarity and spur tactical innovation. But paying attention to the specifically deliberative and experimental features of participatory democratic decisionmaking provides a fuller appreciation of those benefits and points to additional ones. It also sheds light on neglected dilemmas. In the organizations that I studied, deliberative talk did sometimes substitute for action. It sometimes stifled people rather than supporting them, intimidated rather than educating them, and deepened divisions rather than overcoming them. Absent norms of openness and mutual respect, participatory democratic talk did nothing to render people more equal. Likewise, a skepticism of traditional authority at times became a rejection of all authority, an unwillingness to accept any voice as trustworthy, any opinion as meritorious, any interest as other than selfish. But this suggests only that we pay more attention to the conditions in which participatory democracy's benefits are maximized or threatened.

Movement organizations can offer people few selective incentives to participate. Instead, they try to exploit people's preexisting ties—to friends, say, or to the church—in recruiting them, and then rely on the solidarity created within the movement and organization to sustain their participation. Group decisionmaking gives members a stake in the organization and responsibility for its fate. Informality encourages affectively rich relations, and the organization's egalitarian structure makes for mutual respect and, thence, solidarity. The specifically deliberative aspects of participatory democracy add to these benefits. Decisionmakers try to make their reasons for preferring an option transparent and both persuasive and open to challenge. In the groups that I studied, decisionmakers did not aim for a single, inflexible position but sought, rather, to generate a number of positions or orientations consistent with a "collective" one. For example, when SNCC workers reached consensus on whether they could work with people who owned firearms, the discussion leading up to that decision had allowed participants to voice and gain group acceptance for their own positions on the issue. Direct Action Network (DAN) activists too reject the notion of one true answer, looking instead for a solution that people "can live with," and in the process illuminating new possibilities. Unlike strict consensus, the assumption here is that difference is an unavoidable element of solidarity. Group unity comes from recognizing the legitimacy of different opinions as well as shared ones. Decisionmaking that is deliberative may end in a vote, probably one requiring a supermajority. But what distinguishes it from majoritarian voting in an adversary system is its emphasis on having participants make their reasoning accessible and legitimate to each other. Solidarity is re-created through the *process* of decisionmaking, not its endpoint.

In addition to solidary incentives, movement groups depend on their capacity to innovate tactically in conditions of uncertainty. In a decentralized organization, people can respond better to local conditions and can act quickly on decisions. In an organization characterized by informality, input into tactical decisions is not structured along the lines of formal job descriptions and therefore includes different kinds of information. In an organization whose members refuse the notion that political creativity is restricted to those with formal credentials, people can bring diverse skills and insights to bear on determining the best course of action. When I asked activists to describe a good meeting, they usually described one percolating with creative ideas. Open discussion made it possible to solicit numerous proposals and insights; the confidence that all ideas would be taken seriously but also carefully evaluated made people feel that the exercise was worthwhile. An experimental approach to decisionmaking often extended to a more general orientation to tactical choice that made for substantial innovation.

Finally, movements cannot count the battle won when authorities yield some ground. What counts as winning must be a central concern for people whose exclusion from the structure of political bargaining has always been accompanied by efforts on the part of those in power to define their interests for them. Jointly working through options, with an emphasis on articulating and scrutinizing each other's preferences, is a way to build people's capacities for strategizing generally. It encourages decisionmakers to articulate half-formed preferences and concerns, listen to the divergent perspectives of others, make transparent the processes by which they evaluate options and connect means and ends, and introduce alternative ways of conceptualizing problems and solutions. But participatory democracy can also help revise activists' conceptions of political leadership. A group operating on new criteria of political leadership may have better luck winning concessions because it has diminished its dependence on traditional leaders who have a stake in moderation, if not in the status quo. These kinds of benefits animated Rose Pesotta's efforts to build a democratic union of women clothing workers, Brookwood Labor College's democratic pedagogy, and Myles Horton and Ella Baker's civil rights organizing strategy. For these activists, as well as for their heirs in early SNCC and, then, more ambiguously in later SNCC as well as in SDS and in women's liberation collectives, participatory decisionmaking was a way to develop leaders. Today, community organizers are firm in their commitment to leadership development and to creating the mechanisms that will hold elected officials responsible to residents. Processes of collective deliberation are essential to those tasks.

In sum, once we recognize movements' dependence on solidary incentives, tactical innovation, and leadership development and recognize participatory democracy's orientation toward deliberation and experimentation, then we can better appreciate eminently practical benefits of the form. This should also lead us to recognize the variable character of such benefits. Although all movement groups must innovate tactically, some are at greater risk than are others of collapsing when they do not do so. Where a movement is operating in a field of active competitors, countermovements, and authorities, tactical innovation is crucial. But consider a movement organization that occupies a stable position in the structure of political bargaining—say, the Sierra Club or the National Organization for Women. These organizations are regularly consulted by authorities regarding their issue areas, and they have a fairly steady flow of funding. Their survival is probably less dependent on their ability continually to generate new strategies and tactics. For such groups, participatory democracy's innovatory benefits may be less obvious. Participatory democracy's solidary benefits are most evident where the costs of participation are high and the incentives for it weak. In many movements, however, one can participate, not by laying one's body on the line, but by attending a demonstration or sending a check. Neither demands much time or risk, and the sense of jointly "owning" an organization by participating fully in its decision-making is, therefore, probably less important. Similarly with respect to the incentives side of the participation equation, paid staffers may remain loyal to an organization even if ambivalent about its direction. Or other kinds of emotional attachments, for example, members' long-standing allegiance to a leader or to each other, may substitute for a high level of participation in ensuring their compliance.

Finally, participatory democracy's developmental benefits are most obvious in conditions where people have had few prior opportunities for political leadership. This was true of the Mississippi residents with whom SNCC organizers worked, the Northern urban dwellers with whom Economic and Research Action Project (ERAP) organizers worked, the people who made up the women's liberation movement, and the emerging leaders of today's faith-based organizing. Where group members have had opportunities to exercise leadership outside the organization, the opportunity to do so in group deliberations may have less value for training purposes. But it may still aid a group to define enlarged notions of self-interest and collective interests and to craft new notions of political authority.

FOUR DILEMMAS

For groups that want to change laws and policies and political structures, it seems hard to imagine how decisionmaking that is radically decentralized, treats amateurs as experts, and requires a consensus on all decisions could stand a chance. Critics' arguments are compelling. Movement organizations usually strive to increase their memberships—but consensus becomes increasingly difficult with more participants. The time that it takes even in the best of circumstances makes it hard to capitalize on fleeting opportunities. Decentralizing administration and decisionmaking discourages economies of scale as well as making it difficult to coordinate anything wider than local action. A cavalier approach to expertise is dangerous for a group trying to contend in the world of complex policy provisions and alliances. Disdaining the job descriptions and formal accounting procedures often required by funders cuts off vital lines of support. Finally, activists' preoccupation with "living the better society" simply discourages them from working to "build it." Their efforts to perfect a democratic deliberative process within the organization cannot but take time and energy away from their efforts to recruit participants, secure allies and supporters, and sustain campaigns.

Participatory democracy has been faulted for its intrinsic inequity as well as its intrinsic inefficiency. Political theorist Robert Michels called it an "iron law of oligarchy": that, even in democratic organizations, those in positions of authority are likely to resist sharing their power. When groups eliminate all formal positions of power, informal ones substitute, and cliques rule. What Jo Freeman described as the "tyranny of structure-lessness" is no more benign for the fact that people are denied a voice by subtle mechanisms rather than by overt ones. Of course, when members' interests converge, the existence of a small group of influentials is hardly a problem. But, when members' interests diverge, as they are bound to do in all but the most homogeneous groups, the interests of some are inevitably suppressed or ignored in the name of consensus. So, if participatory democracy's inefficiency makes it unrealistic in institutional political terms, its tendency to reproduce the very inequalities that it is trying to eradicate makes it unsuccessful on its own terms.[6]

These criticisms have merit. But reducing the problems that activists have faced in trying to manage participatory democracies to the fundamental inefficiency or the fundamental inequity of the form obscures the fact that such problems have sometimes had their sources elsewhere, in much broader features of movements, politics, and culture. Let me outline four conflicts that operated in the cases treated in this book. One lay in the conflicting demands of making political change. Participatory democracy was not ineffectual, but it served some demands at the expense of others. For example, it strengthened existing participants' solidarity better than it built broader support for the movement. The absolutism in egalitarian decisionmaking that made for solidarity sometimes led outsiders to dismiss the group as unrealistic in its practice of participatory democracy—and, by extension, as unrealistic in its political aims. This was not always a problem. It was not for the pacifists in World War I who were so isolated politically that their main goal was simply to survive until a time when more favorable conditions would make it possible to mobilize broader participation. When political conditions were intractable, concentrating on the group's internal life made eminent sense. But the lines between tractable and intractable, and between isolation and marginality, were sometimes fuzzy. Pacifists, to continue with the example, sometimes missed opportunities to appeal to a broader public, insisting on the purity of moral witness over efforts to communicate the substance of their challenge to an American public that was skeptical but not absolutely opposed. Another trade-off: participatory democracy's refusal to create formal jurisdictions and chains of command has better served to train activists politically than to accommodate the demands of funders. Decentralization has encouraged an orientation toward local actions over regional or national ones. Here, as in the other trade-offs, the pulls on each side have been practical as much as principled. But they have created sharp conflicts.

A second source of conflict for the participatory democratic groups that I studied was between orientations toward goals and toward process. Participatory democratic groups did sometimes become preoccupied with how decisions in the group were made, to the detriment of their efforts to bring about external change. The fact that this was not always the case, however, suggests that the problem had its source outside participatory democracy as a deliberative form. When, then, did groups become preoccupied with process? Often, I found, after a significant setback. In some cases, the group decided that, since the opportunities for securing concessions from authorities or mobilizing anything like a mass movement were virtually nil, it made sense to turn inward—and maximize participatory democracy's solidary benefits. In other cases, activists did not deliberately abandon efforts to effect external change. Rather, in the wake of defeat, the group's goals became unclear. In the fall of 1964, for example, SNCC workers called on each other to "let the people decide" the course of the struggle. That commitment was not inconsistent with their earlier strategy of organizing. Now, however, they were counting on residents to come up with goals that would, by virtue of their radicalism, redeem their *own* claim to occupy the cutting edge of protest. People talked about and argued about decisionmaking rather than thrashing out goals because the latter was so difficult to do.

The latter points to another dynamic, one characteristic of participatory democratic movement organizations and of contemporary politics broadly. Activists, like politicians and policymakers, may champion participatory democracy precisely because it spares them the hard work of having to make choices among possible goals. When urban policymakers were confronted with demands for more democracy in municipal governance in the 1960s, political scientist Theodore Lowi observed, they responded by substituting participatory procedure for program standards. They shifted authority for program design and implementation from government officials to the most organized urban groups, which, government recognition secured, were unwilling to open the process to newer groups. Acceding willingly to the call for more citizen participation thus spared the government the need to make hard decisions about priorities and principles.[7]

Since the period Lowi wrote about, a polity characterized by more participation on the part of its citizens has continued to be a popular ideal, touted by politicians and pundits of the left and right. It resonates with deeply held values of autonomy and equality as well as with a populist antipathy to big government and bureaucratic red tape and seems an alternative to a political world in which campaign advertising and polling has taken the place of reasoned political discourse. But Lowi's concern that an emphasis on process may substitute for discussions of substance remains apposite. If modern Americans have a hard time talking about politics—about what role the state should play in the economy and civil society, about what a fair apportionment of responsibilities among individuals and government would entail—then calling for more participatory democracy may defer those discussions rather than stimulating them. Recall the exchange that I described in the last chapter, where a puzzled participant in a community-organizing training session struggled to get a trainer to say what congregation-based organizations would *do* with the power that they hoped to achieve. Organizers maintain that outlining longer-term political commitments would unnecessarily alienate potential members and would violate community organizing's commitment to a "people's politics" that truly comes from the grass roots. But such a stance does nothing to help link issues, probe the different directions in which a faith commitment might lead, and identify the long-term partnerships and political capabilities that the group wants to develop.[8]

The danger that calls for participatory democracy substitute for efforts to work out goals is not limited to faith-based organizations. One of DAN's credos, a member told me, is that, "as long you're willing to act like an anarchist now, we don't care what your long-term vision is." Such a stance recognizes that, since no one has a lock on the future, it makes sense to be open to multiple visions. DAN activists are determined to avoid the sectarian battling that they associate with the late 1960s. But the danger is that longer-term goals are never discussed for fear that they might create that kind of conflict. Shortly before the 2000 presidential election, one in which Ralph Nader's third-party candidacy divided progressives, a DAN activist complained: "We talk about how close we are as a group, but I don't even know who people in DAN are voting for." Did he not know because DAN believed that people could vote for different candidates while still espousing goals of ending sweatshop labor, police brutality, and unaccountable transnational financial institutions? Or did he not know because the topic of electoral politics could be expected to provoke unpleasant disagreement and so DAN activists shied away from it? To talk about the decisionmaking process, even to argue about it, may make it easier to avoid discussions that are likely to be contentious. But the danger is that ideological differences are displaced to discussions of process.[9]

A third source of frequent conflict for groups striving to operate democratically has been the tension between conventionality and innovation. The pressures to conform to conventional organizational forms may come from supporters and even members as much as from outside agencies. In SDS's ERAP projects, organizers were dismayed to find that residents sometimes wanted precisely the top-down movement structures that organizers had rejected. The same was true for SNCC organizers in Mississippi. Residents with child-care and work responsibilities had less time for long exploratory conversations than did student organizers. Not unsurprisingly, moreover, people who had been so long deprived of formal political standing often wanted formal titles in their own organizations. DAN activists have confronted similar tensions in their work with union workers, who complain about the "touchy-feely" quality of DAN meetings. Insofar as activists see participatory democracy as a means to overcome traditional inequalities, they may be hampered by differences in "tastes" for organizational styles that line up with differences in status.

I want to be clear here. The problem is not that people with less privilege are more comfortable with conventional hierarchical forms. Rather, it has to do with symbolic associations that influence *most* people's preferences for particular deliberative forms. If for many people participatory democracy is associated with high ideals and strong moral commitments, perhaps at the expense of political realism, more hierarchical organizational forms and adversarial deliberative ones tend to symbolize efficiency, conformity, and legitimacy. For example, the middle-class professionals who staffed the alternative health clinic that Sherryl Kleinman studied in the 1980s saw themselves as bearers of the countercultural impulse of the 1960s. They held hands before meetings and had group hugs after them, strove for consensus in all-night meetings, and were critical of conventional markers of professional accomplishment. But they also insisted that each meeting be recorded in "minutes that had a bureaucratic look—lengthy, well-typed, with lots of headings, subheadings and underlinings." One staffer created an uproar when she submitted minutes of a previous meeting in longhand and with illustrations, and staffers carefully rewrote the minutes line by line. Kleinman had never seen anyone actually refer to minutes from earlier meetings, and there was no evidence that staffers believed that imitating mainstream organizational procedures would get them more clients or funding. Rather, it was necessary to their self-conception as a "serious" organization. Minute taking, in as conventional a way as possible, was a sign of legitimacy.[10]

The fact that participatory groups have been more likely to survive when they operate in close contact with similar groups attests to the power of conventional assumptions about democracy, hierarchy, and rationality. What participatory democratic groups offer each other in such settings is less concrete support in sustaining their organizations (after all, they probably have little in the way of resources themselves) than affirmation for their ideological principles and confidence that participatory democracies are viable entities.[11]

So the obstacles to participatory democracy's effectiveness may lie as much in the conflicting demands of social movements, in features of American political discourse, and in even broader cultural conceptions of strategy and democracy as in intrinsic features of the form. What about the argument that participatory democracy generates precisely the inequality that it is supposed to eradicate? When deliberative crises occurred in the organizations that I studied, they did center on perceived inequities in decisionmaking, with some people accused of monopolizing power and manipulating consensus. But to reduce those crises to the difficulty of reconciling individual interests with collective ones misses key features of the organizational trajectories that I have described. In SDS, newcomers' political commitments were in some ways *similar* to those of veterans— the groups on contending sides of the structure divide—and in other ways were *diverse*. In SNCC, people's interests *changed* as a result of the disputes over structure: conflicts between Northerners and Southerners and between Atlanta staff and field organizers were supplanted by conflicts between advocates of tight and loose structure and between blacks and whites. In New York Radical Women, competing interests in a political and feminist line were there from the beginning, during the group's most productive and *least conflictual* phases. In each of these groups, inchoate antagonisms and multisided disputes were turned into conflicting interests in and through the battles over deliberative structure. One could not have identified in advance the interests that would end up in contention.

This does not mean that such crises were entirely unpredictable. Rather, I have argued that they occurred at pressure points in the associational relationships on which participatory democracy was based, chiefly, friendship, tutelage, and religious fellowship. Where friendship's natural exclusivity came up against the demands of expanding the group, where organizers' commitment to respecting residents' own political learning process came up against the need to define political aims, and where religious fellows' commitment to cooperation came up against the absolutism of personal conscience—at these points conflicts occurred. What made these conflicts so hard to overcome was that, to do so, the activists involved in them would have had to go outside the normative framework that governed their interactions. To extend relations of friendship to an ever-widening circle would have threatened the intimacy that distinguishes friendship from other relationships. To implement formal rules would have been to abrogate friendship's voluntary character. To override people's invocation of personal conscience would have been to violate the very basis for their— for all members'—activism. And to define an agenda for residents would have been to defeat the purpose of the learning process altogether. People could, and did, appeal to standards of equality and fairness in deliberative conflicts. But such standards could not supply the complex behavioral expectations and obligations necessary to group decisionmaking. Alongside the three other challenges that I have described, then, a fourth has been the behavioral limits of the social relationships on which activists have modeled their deliberative interactions.

Are there solutions? Can movement groups avoid the inefficiencies characteristic of governance by amateurs and avoid the inequalities built into nonpolitical forms of cooperation? One solution is to establish and enforce rules allowing expertise to coexist with democracy and, at the same time, protecting minorities in decisionmaking. Students of movement organizations have tended to treat organizations' adoption of formal rules as synonymous with an acceptance of hierarchical organizational forms and majoritarian deliberative ones. But rules can also be used to strengthen self-consciously egalitarian decisionmaking. I will describe several decision rules that are intended to do that. Rules are not enough, however. A second solution to the problem of democratic friendship—to give a simple name to a complex problem—is to develop new kinds of democratic relationships, ones that maximize the mutual respect, trust, and concern characteristic of formally nonpolitical relationships but avoid their weaknesses.

RULES, RELATIONSHIPS, AND RITUALS

Viewed as a process of organizational learning, the history of participatory democracy has since the 1960s been marked by the insight that structures, rules, and formal procedures are essential to decisionmaking that is efficient and fair. Activists have worked to incorporate formal mechanisms into participatory democracy as an organizational form and as a deliberative style.[12]

The yields of such adaptation are evident in the women's movement. As feminists began to establish support centers and services in the early 1970s, they came up against demands on the part of government and foundation funders for more conventional structures. Many found that combining aspects of collectivist forms with aspects of more conventionally bureaucratic ones did not mean sacrificing their radical aspirations. Indeed, few feminist organizations today approximate either ideal-typical collectivist or bureaucratic forms. Evidence suggests that successful hybrids have retained the deliberative aspects of participatory democracy in insisting on broad and continual consultation across all levels of an organization even as they have instituted formal job descriptions and jurisdictions. They have also made experimentation with different structures and procedures a central commitment. In other words, while moderating participatory democracy's informal, decentralized, and strictly egalitarian dimensions, successful hybrids have continued to emphasize its deliberative and experimental character.[13]

Participatory democracy as a decisionmaking mode rather than an organizational form has also moved today in the direction of rules. DAN members, for example, have a complex and fairly formal decisionmaking procedure, and, like most participatory democrats today, they have provisions for shifting from consensus to supermajority vote. They have not fully resolved the issue of when such a shift should take place, however. And, indeed, this is a question that continues to preoccupy those, academic and activist alike, who admire the virtues of consensus decisionmaking but recognize its limitations for groups that are not small, homogeneous, and unhurried. When should groups shift from consensus to majoritarian or hierarchical decisionmaking? One answer centers on the characteristics of the group and the kind of protest in which it is engaged. When the group is oriented toward personal change more than institutional change, financially self-sufficient, and united in its goals and values, say some scholars, consensus can probably work. However, when the group is institutionally focused and resource dependent and its members have diverse goals, majority voting should be the rule. But these conditions may be overbroad and may miss the functions of consensus deliberation in *forging* programmatic and tactical agreement as well as in building solidarity and the skills necessary to effecting change in political institutions.

An alternative is to distinguish between "routine" and "critical" *kinds* of decisions or, in a similar formulation, "technical" and "adaptive" ones. Since critical and adaptive decisions require participants to reassess and possibly rescale their priorities, they are better served by a participatory process, in this view. Presumably, however, critical or adaptive decisions will spur sharper differences of opinion than routine or technical ones. In such situations, people are more likely to see their current preferences as fundamental interests. Collectivist processes, then, risk either pressuring people to conform to the majority over and against their own perceived interests or confirming people in their original preferences, thus precipitating stalemate. The challenge is to recognize that collective deliberation *can* change people's interests *and* that it will not always do so.[14]

One solution is to shift to an alternative deliberative mode—whether majority voting or proportional representation—"when conflict remains after good deliberation," as Jane Mansbridge puts it. In other words, the decision rule is procedural rather than categorical. But how do we know how much, and what kind of, deliberation is good enough? Perhaps that point is reached simply when people are making the same points over and over again and there seems little likelihood of movement in any direction. Recent writers on "deliberative democracy" urge that such a situation not be seen as a stalemate. Joshua Cohen and Charles Sabel argue that good-enough deliberation is when all participants have acknowledged that the arguments for and against an option advanced by other participants are reasonable ones. We may not weight our rationales identically, but we acknowledge other rankings as legitimate. I may argue persuasively that not alienating our funders by taking a militant position is our only hope for surviving organizationally, and you may recognize that to be true but believe that organizational survival should not trump what is a moral imperative. Once participants have articulated their reasons for preferring a given option, heard other people's reasons, and possibly modified their own preferences, the outcome may be decided on the basis of a majority vote. Participants see that they are being asked, not simply "to accede to the larger number," Cohen and Sabel maintain, "but to accept what they can see to be a reasonable alternative, supported by others who are prepared to be reasonable."[14]

I have argued that movement democracies have often operated implicitly on that kind of rule. Some of them operated on a variant that has not been much discussed in the literature. A group might agree that some people will have more authority than others on some kinds of decisions. Activists who live in the city where a demonstration is being planned may be given more authority than are those who live elsewhere. A committee charged with researching an issue may be authorized to make a decision if consensus cannot be reached by the larger group. What counts is the effort to generate fairer bases for authority than conventional ones. Social movement organizations may thus see themselves as laboratories for new criteria of authority. If a group takes itself as a kind of baseline for establishing such criteria, then group decisionmaking would involve endorsing certain skills or experiences or passions as legitimately authoritative in certain contexts. This view of decisionmaking is prefigurative in the sense that movement groups enact relations of authority and deference that they hope to see institutionalized outside the movement. But, far from a utopian retreat from the world of politics, democracy in movements is, in this view, a way to fashion new criteria of political authority, leadership, and accountability.[14]

I agree with critics that a consensus-based, nonhierarchical, and radically decentralized form of organization is not optimal for movement groups that are internally diverse, complex, and resource dependent. But I would not leave it at that. The skepticism toward institutional authority inside and outside the organization and the orientation toward collective reasoning that have characterized many participatory democratic groups offer valuable resources for *all* movement organizations. Effective organizational forms are necessarily hybrids. The problem for movement groups is that they have had such an impoverished menu of options from which to assemble such hybrids. The salient issue with respect to participatory democracy, then, is less whether movement organizations should adopt the model wholesale than whether they would benefit from decisionmaking that is more deliberative and experimental than is usually the case. I believe that, in many instances, they would.

Note, however, that instituting procedures for modified consensus, consultation across the levels of an organization, rotation of some, but not all, positions—any number of formal rules—is not enough to guarantee cooperative decisionmaking. Trust among the parties is essential, and trust, in turn, is most often developed in long-standing relationships.[17]

RELATIONSHIPS

Aristotle saw friendship as the foundation of politics. What he had in mind was a "civic friendship," in which the harmony and like-mindedness of friends were extended to all citizens. At the time Aristotle wrote, however, the friendships that did drive politics were forged in political clubs—"hetaeries"—made up of young men of similar age and class. During Athenian democracy's golden age, hetaeries sought to manipulate and control popular assemblies, bribing and intimidating officials, packing assemblies, voting in blocs, and assassinating opponents. Democracy was finally brought down by hetaeries' conspiratorial efforts. In practice, then, friendship was quite at odds with democracy.[18]

This is the participatory democratic dilemma. The very relationships generating the trust and respect that democracy requires may also come with norms that undercut a democratic project. When activists modeled their democracies on friendship, tutelage, and religious fellowship, they brought into politics the values of cooperation and care that characterized these relationships and that posed a real challenge to the competitiveness characteristic of conventional political relations. Friendship, tutelage, and religious fellowship provided the microinteractional norms—the rules behind the rules—that enabled people to make decisions without constant negotiation over the terms of engagement. The problem, I have argued, was that, along with caring, cooperation, and a complex equality that made for mutual learning, those relationships also came with norms that undermined democratic projects: variously, exclusivity, deference, conflict avoidance, and an antipathy to the rules that might have made for more accountability.[19]

If the problem is perennial in the history of American social movements, elements of a solution are also evident in that history. American activists have consistently innovated, not only tactically and organizationally, but also relationally, inventing new "structures of cooperation," as long-time pacifist George Lakey calls them. The affinity group, the workshop, the organizational discipline, the residential cluster, the consciousness-raising group, and the house meeting: each one has fostered new kinds of relationships among movement participants. As I have shown, the formal purposes of these structures and their relationship to other decisionmaking structures within the group have differed. The affinity group, for example, is the basic unit in decisionmaking among many contemporary direct action groups; feminist consciousness raising, by contrast, was seen by women's liberationists as separate from decisionmaking, although conversations often moved from one to the other. What is similar and so important about these otherwise different associational forms, however, is that each one created a setting in which participants were expected to behave in ways that were unlike both conventional political interaction and the interaction expected of people in their churches, workplaces, families, and friendships. They encouraged cooperation that was mutually respectful but tolerant of disagreement, caring but inclusive, and personally enriching but firmly directed toward the public sphere. In doing so, they negotiated the tensions that analysts have seen as perennial to collectivist decisionmaking between individual purposes and group ones, equality and authority, unity and difference, and political and personal change.[20]

For example, when radical pacifists encouraged their members to work out a "discipline" that would guide their activism, they were asking them to subject themselves to the norms of the group voluntarily. Writing the discipline down institutionalized it. But the discipline was to be jointly agreed to, and it remained experimental, subject to scrutiny and modification by the group. Unlike norms of Christian fellowship, its authority was provisional and constrained individual action only for the period between the time that its tenets were last agreed to and the time that they would next be scrutinized. If a pacifist discipline suggests a way to mediate the tensions between individual and group interests, the contemporary affinity group points to resources for mediating the conflicts between unity and difference. Affinity groups in direct action today can be formed around any identity—political, sexual, or cultural. Traditional political creeds are only one among many bases for solidarity, activists recognize. Such groups provide the support that allows people with minority interests or views to stand up to the larger group, making a false consensus less likely. But activists are encouraged to "go outside their comfort zone" in choosing affinity groups, joining people with different backgrounds. There are two insights here. One is that democracy must encompass difference in all settings, from the most intimate to the most public; the other is that joint action can create new and hybrid identities.

With respect to the tension between equality and authority, the "workshops" of the Southern civil rights movement fostered relationships that were intimate but action oriented, firmly supportive but encouraging internal challenge. Inequalities in the relationship between leader and participants were domain specific, limited in duration, and mitigated by the parties' mutual dependence. Finally, novel associational forms have bridged public and private spheres in ways that have engaged people not experienced in public political action. Contrary to a popular stereotype, consciousness raising in the women's liberation movement was not group therapy. It sought political change rather than personal insight alone, and the relationships that it forged among women were political also, different from relationships of friendship and sisterhood. Another example: in Cleveland's ERAP project, organizers formed "clusters" of active residents who would meet in each other's homes in housing projects, forging an association that was somewhere between friendship, neighborliness, and political meeting. And, in the "house meetings" used by faith-based organizers, residents are able to voice their concerns in a semipublic setting, among neighbors and organizers who both support and push them.

Activists participating in groups like these have compared them to more intimate relationships: "We were like family"; "we became incredibly close." But the point is that they are *not* like intimate relationships, at least insofar as the latter are vulnerable to exclusivity and an avoidance of conflict. Why is developing them more effective in producing a successful participatory democracy than simply encouraging members to be respectful, trusting, caring, and open is likely to be? Probably because they provide a space within which participants can experiment with new behaviors knowing that other participants are also committed to the enterprise and will be supportive of their efforts. The resulting relationships can then encompass a variety of behaviors in diverse settings.[21]

There is surely much more experimentation to be done. Industrial Areas Foundation organizer Ernie Cortes talks about the need for Catholic social thought to elaborate a theory and a practice of social relationships. Feminist theorists have called for developing relations of "comradeship" and "pluralist friendship" in which difference is recognized rather than wished away. Others have suggested wholly different models for political cooperation: the "city" as an alternative to the "community" or relationships based on "covenants" rather than "contracts." In each case, the aim is to maximize solidarity without denying differences. Such forms may feel unnatural at first. But they can be learned. The affinity group, for example, was fairly recently known only to students of Spanish anarchism, but it is now a familiar feature of direct action.[22]

Before they are familiar, however, such forms are fragile. Activists under the pressure of time and scarce resources have understandably found it difficult to invest in experiments in interaction that can be seen as taking time away from more important work. But it is precisely during moments of pressure and uncertainty that people are most likely to revert to familiar relationships and to the exclusivist, conformist, and intolerant behaviors that can accompany them. This is what makes novel forms of cooperation so important. There is an opposite danger too, however. New associational forms can become their own source of exclusivity, with those not in the know about how a workshop operates or what twinkling means alienated from the group. One solution may lie in rituals. As Emile Durkheim observed, rituals strengthen group solidarity by taking people out of the routine of daily life and reenacting their essential groupness. Rituals may be used to strengthen new forms of group solidarity as well as older ones, infusing new relationships with a power and appeal that transcend narrow calculations of interest. One can imagine rituals and symbols used to foster norms of solidarity *and* dissent, respect and self-confidence, trust and accountability, all of which are necessary to successful participatory democracies.

Nothing that I have said so far should be taken to mean that people in movement groups should not be friends. The opportunity to make new friends and to spend time with old ones is a good reason for joining and staying in a movement organization. So are the opportunities to enact one's faith commitments in fellowship with others and to learn new skills and discover new political possibilities. My point is simply that activists should guard against the deliberative conflicts and inequalities that often come with friendship, religious fellowship, and tutelage. Formally egalitarian mechanisms to which those who feel marginalized can appeal are

important, but they are not enough. Without a democratic culture and
relationships governed by norms of mutual concern, trust, and respect, a
simple equality manifest in formal standards will not serve a participatory
democratic project. So rules, relationships, and rituals are all necessary to
viable participatory democracies. This means rules that are open to scrutiny
and modification, relationships that routinize norms of openness, mutual
respect, and complex equality, and rituals that celebrate the group's unity
and its internal difference.

STRATEGY AND IDENTITY

Sociologists did well thirty years ago to abandon a view of activists as driven
by uncontrolled impulses and system strain. Granting activists their rationality was a first and essential step to recognizing the strategic obstacles
and opportunities that they confronted. Just as important, treating social
movements as collections of organizations rather than just as individuals
countered a view of protest as unplanned and undirected. Having recognized that organizations are influential actors in protest, however, sociologists have paid surprisingly little attention to the processes that take place
within social movement organizations. Decisionmaking is an obvious one.
We still know little about how movement groups set agendas, how they
select among the tactical options available to them, why they choose particular frames, slogans, narratives, and images with which to represent
themselves, and when and why they modify any of the above. Our failure
to tackle these questions reflects our inclination to see organizations *as*
actors rather than as *made up of* actors and their interactions. But it also
reflects a tendency to substitute a classically rational calculus for empirical
analysis of actual deliberative processes. In other words, scholars have seen
movement leaders choosing among options on the basis of their rational
assessment of the costs and benefits of each for various tasks of mobilization
and contention. Where movement scholars have criticized this rationalist
account, they have sometimes replaced it with an equally narrow ideological one. People choose options that conform to their ideological vision. Or
they juggle strategic concerns with ideological ones.

    I have argued that, even together, instrumental rationality and ideolog-
ical consistency by no means exhaust the bases of strategy choice. An option
may be appealing because it conforms to who we are—not to our formal
beliefs, but to a more fundamental sense of collective identity that super-
sedes ideological assessment. Alternatively, an option may be appealing
because it is familiar or because it is associated with groups that we view
favorably for other reasons. One might argue that choosing options on the

basis of their congruence with our collective identity or that of another group is strategic. If we see a tactic, target, or frame as "us," as resonating with who we are in a deep sense, we are likely to devote real time and energy to it. We may be especially good at it. Likewise, as neoinstitutionalist theorists tell us, to adopt an organizational form because groups perceived as effective have done so is likely to gain the group doing the imitating credibility and the support that flows from that credibility. Similarly, distancing one's group from people viewed as ineffectual or as unappealingly mainstream or radical can garner recruits and supporters. One can thus see these choices in instrumental terms. But such rationales were not very much in evidence in the cases that I studied. In SNCC in late 1964, black activists did not argue that abandoning a participatory democratic structure would gain them new black recruits by disassociating the organization from whites. Rather, they themselves were dismayed by what they perceived as the dominance of a "white" style of decisionmaking. When DAN activists dismiss vibe watchers and group hugs as "Californian," they do not argue that being associated with "touchy-feely" Californian protest will ill serve them in their efforts to recruit people uncomfortable with that style. It is more that their own identity comes in part from whom they define themselves against.

Rationales like these shape what choices a movement group makes and what consequences it reaps. The analytic costs of omitting them from our analyses extend beyond our capacity to explain movement trajectories to our explanations of behavioral choice more generally. My research provides the material only for the barest speculation on what is an obvious question: when the rationales that I have identified are likely to be more or less prominent. Groups that have experienced a significant setback when their competitors have not may make decisions on the basis of identity rather than of strategy or ideology; that is, they may adopt or retain a particular tactic because it is seen as basic and essential to the group and invested with high emotion. In the face of defeat, without evidence of the efficacy of their strategic choices, activists may hold on to what makes them unique to justify their superiority over other groups and to provide rationales for not defecting. Activists are likely to choose options that are familiar rather than ones that are instrumentally effective or ideologically consistent when what is instrumental is by no means clear, and when the strategic entailments of ideological commitments are not clear either. Reproducing what is familiar may impart stability more generally to an unsettled situation.[23]

Finally, if activists' ratings of particular options come in part from the groups with which those options are symbolically associated, which groups will they be? Activists are probably likely to see the practices of the group that was formed before theirs—perhaps with which they are often compared and with which they compete for membership—as a negative model. Thus, strategies, tactics, and styles associated with the Southern Christian Leadership Conference were unappealing to SNCC members; those associated with old left groups were unappealing to SDS; those associated with SDS were unappealing to many women's liberation collectives; those associated with Californian direct action were unappealing to DAN activists. On the other hand, where two groups are unlikely to compete for membership or support, one is more likely to see the other as a positive model and to judge favorably the strategies, tactics, and ideas associated with it. Thus, SNCC was a model for SDS, and Third World revolutionary organizations were a model for SNCC. Again, however, this is just the beginning of an answer to a question that is complex. It invites us to probe much more deeply the sources of the vocabularies of motive, to borrow a term from C. Wright Mills, that shape movement decisionmaking.[24]

PARTICIPATORY DEMOCRACY ON A GRAND SCALE?

This book has been about democracy in social movements. The yields of activists' efforts to create participatory and egalitarian organizations have been more substantial than is often thought, I have argued, and the obstacles that they have confronted more complicated than simply their willful naïveté before the demands of instrumental action in a political environment. But what about organizations and institutions outside social movements? Can participatory democracy as I have described it work in them? Can innovatory, solidary, and developmental benefits be derived from participatory democracy in political parties? In schools and workplaces? In the political governance of nation-states? As I noted, democratic theorists have paid much more attention to these sorts of institutions than to social movements. Certainly, one can understand their reluctance to see in movements models for democracy writ large. Movements are historically rare, short-lived conflagrations of events, made up of people who are united and enthusiastic in their political commitments and often freed of the everyday responsibilities of family, home, and career. If George Bernard Shaw's complaint that socialism would take up too many evenings can be made also of participatory democracy, then it is hard to imagine anyone but movement activists having the requisite number of evenings.

Yet, despite their detachment from everyday life, or perhaps because of it, social movements have historically been the source of ideas, identities, practices, and organizational forms that endured long after they ended. Identities like *feminist* and *Chicano/a* came from movements; now they influence the lives of people who have nothing to do with those movements. The union, the interest group, the public-interest law firm, the food cooperative, and the alternative health center: these familiar organizational forms all have their origins in social movements. The conditions in which movement groups operate have freed them—and forced them—to experiment with new strategies, tactics, organizational forms, and deliberative styles. Innovations forged in the crucible of necessity have then been adopted by groups and institutions outside movements. In these concluding paragraphs, I offer some thoughts on what might be added to the balance sheet on participatory democracy broadly by taking into account movement groups' experience with the form.

Social movements operate on a much larger scale than do most voluntary groups, although on a smaller scale than nation-states. The challenge for participatory democratic movement groups is to coordinate actions and programs across decentralized units. The lesson of the movements that I have treated here is that, absent such coordination, not only is regional or national action hampered; so too is local action. Connections among units provide mechanisms for comparing results and trading information. When groups are isolated, the experimental, innovatory functions of participatory decisionmaking suffer. Turn participatory democracy into a vision of decentralized units of governance, and the lesson from social movements is that such units must be in regular and, in some ways, ritualized contact with each other. That is, their members should be able to share information and assessments, and they should *meet* periodically to reaffirm their vision and solidarity.

Generally, assertions of principle are more prominent in movements than they are elsewhere in social life. The fact that movements offer few material rewards for participation means that acting in service to one's beliefs is exceedingly important. But the prominence of normative discourse in social movements also means that a variety of conflicts inevitable in group life may be experienced as conflicts of principle. Battles between democratic purists and political pragmatists in the organizations that I studied were often actually about other things: activists' uncertainty about where to go next; some people's sense that their organization was being taken over by newcomers; newcomers' intimidation by veterans. Insofar as battles over the appropriate rigor of the participatory democratic process are fought out also in parent-teacher groups, block clubs, and third parties, there too such battles may obscure the problems of group interaction that they implicitly engage. In particular, I worry that activists' concern with democratic process may substitute for the work of negotiating goals. Behind participatory democracy's appeal as an eschatological vision and as a preoccupation in the here and now may be discomfort with talking about longer-term agendas. Participatory democracy may lead activists to defer the hard choices that they need to make.

Movement organizations are often made up of people with little experience of politics. To work effectively as well as fairly, democratic movement organizations should enact what feminists have called an *ethic of care*, in which members are treated equally but also with concern for each one's self-development. But, since self-development takes place at different tempos and usually involves some teaching and learning, can it be pursued in a system that treats people as equals? A history of activism reveals that numerous relationships have made it possible to maximize equality and joint learning. Activists have modeled participatory democracies on friendship, tutelage, and religious fellowship in ways that have insisted on members' fundamental or potential equality without requiring that such equality be measurable in identical responsibilities and formal power. And, in recent years, activists have wrestled with the downsides of such relationships—variously, their exclusivity, resistance to rules, and emotional volatility—by working out new kinds of democratic relationships. The lesson for polities is that the associational forms that people have depended on and forged anew in movements offer rich materials for new understandings of equality and care.

Finally, social movements are temporary. Of course, some movement organizations last longer than many civic associations—think, for example, of the National Association for the Advancement of Colored People. But movements in which numerous organizations cooperate in a bid to secure political changes not achievable through normal political processes are usually dependent on short-lived windows of opportunity, when it is possible for activists to leverage their apparent numbers and the worthiness of their claims into concessions from those in power. This means that acting expeditiously is of the essence. Social movement organizations that strive to operate democratically must confront the charge that their time-consuming processes torpedo coordinated action. Democracy in social movements makes glaring a tension that probably operates in some form even in organizations that are less dependent for their survival on temporary opportunities for mass action. While not denying that tension, I have argued that, in conditions of uncertainty, few incentives to participate, and participants' inexperience with the rules of the political game, participatory democracy's costs in time are counterbalanced by its innovatory, solidary, and developmental benefits. The latter, especially, should resonate with contemporary concerns about the thin character of citizenship in modern Western democracies. As a number of political theorists have argued, participatory democratic deliberation helps people bring diverse sources of information to bear on common problems and reassess their interests and preoccupations in the light of the common good. It helps nurture an engaged and active citizenry.

But the experience of social movements adds something important to those conclusions. The most progressive democratic changes in this country have come, not from block clubs, PTAs, and the other groups that make up civil society, but from social movements—for racial and gender equality, civil liberties, consumer protection, and workers' rights. These movements have been oppositional, disruptive, and sometimes downright *un*civil. They are the unruly mobs that Athenians worried about and that contemporary champions of participatory democracy have sometimes ignored altogether, counting rather on the joint action of civil society and the state to bring about reform.[25]

We should be wary of such omissions. Democracy in social movements does not produce dutiful citizens. It produces people who question the conventional categories and responsibilities of citizenship—and who question the boundaries of the political, the limits of equality, and the line between the people and their representatives. Just as a movement that is democratic but without internal conflict sacrifices political creativity to stability, so a democracy without movements would foreclose critical avenues of progressive change.

Notes

Documents cited are from personal collections, archival collections, and microfilm collections. Microfilm references are to reel number and, where available, frame number; otherwise, the series number is noted.

The following microfilm/microform collections have been used:
Southern Regional Council Papers (SRC Papers), 1944–68. Ann Arbor, Mich.: University
     Microfilms, 1984. Microfilm.
Stanford University Project South Oral History Collection (Project South), 1965. Glen Rock,
     N.J.: Microfilming Corp. of America. Microform.
Student Nonviolent Coordinating Committee Papers (SNCC Papers), 1959–72. Sanford, N.C.:
     Microfilming Corp. of America, 1982. Microfilm.
Students for a Democratic Society Papers (SDS Papers), 1958–70. Glen Rock, N.J.:
     Microfilming Corp. of America, 1977. Microfilm.

The following abbreviations have been used throughout the notes:

CHS	Chicago Historical Society
CNVA	Committee for Nonviolent Action
CNVR	Committee for Non-Violent Revolution
COHC	Columbia Oral History Collection, Columbia University
CWLU	Chicago Women's Liberation Union
FOR	Fellowship of Reconciliation
KLA	King Library and Archives, Martin Luther King Jr. Center for Nonviolent Social Change, Atlanta
MLKPP	Martin Luther King Jr. Papers Project, Stanford University
MOHP	Mississippi Oral History Project
Project South	Stanford University Project South Oral History Collection
RBOHC	Ralph Bunche Oral History Collection, Moorland-Spingarn Research Center, Howard University
SCPC	Swarthmore College Peace Collection
SDS	Students for a Democratic Society
SHSW	State Historical Society of Wisconsin, Madison
SNCC	Student Nonviolent Coordinating Committee
SOHP	Southern Oral History Program
SRC	Southern Regional Council

PREFACE

1. Plato's *Protagoras* is quoted in Anthony Arblaster, *Democracy* (Milton Keynes: Open University Press, 1987), 21.

2. Lawrence Goodwyn, "Organizing Democracy: The Limits of Theory and Practice," *Democracy* 1 (January 1981): 41–60.

3. Joseph Kahn, "Seattle Protesters Are Back, with a New Target," *New York Times*, 9 April 2000, sec. 1, p. 6, col. 3.

CHAPTER 1

1. C. Wayne Gordon and Nicholas Babchuk contrast instrumental and expressive aims in "A Typology of Voluntary Organizations," *American Sociological Review* 24 (1959): 22–29; see also Russell L. Curtis Jr. and Louis A. Zurcher Jr., "Social Movements: An Analytical Exploration of Organizational Forms," *Social Problems* 21 (1974): 356–70. Wini Breines (*Community and Organization in the New Left* [New Brunswick, N.J.: Rutgers University Press, 1989]) contrasts prefigurative and strategic aims; Emily Stoper ("The Student Non-Violent Coordinating Committee: Rise and Fall of a Redemptive Organization," in *Social Movements of the Sixties and Seventies*, ed. Jo Freeman [New York: Longman, 1983]) contrasts purposive and redemptive aims; Paul Starr ("The Phantom Community," in *Co-Ops, Communes, and Collectives: Social Experiments from the 1960s and 1970s*, ed. John Case and Rosemary Taylor [New York: Pantheon, 1979]) contrasts exemplary and adversary aims. Analyses relying on similar oppositions include Todd Gitlin, *The Sixties: Years of Hope, Days of Rage* (New York: Bantam, 1987); Peter Clecak, *Radical Paradoxes: Dilemmas of the American Left, 1945–1970* (New York: Harper & Row, 1973); Gary L. Downey, "Ideology and the Clamshell Identity: Organizational Dilemmas in the Anti-Nuclear Power Movement," *Social Problems* 33 (1986): 357–71; Barbara Epstein, *Political Protest and Cultural Revolution* (Berkeley and Los Angeles: University of California Press, 1991); and Edward Morgen, *The 60's Experience: Hard Lessons about Modern America* (Philadelphia: Temple University Press, 1991).

2. Tom Hayden, interview by author, New York, 21 September 2000.

3. For an instrumentalist approach, see Doug McAdam, John D. McCarthy, and Mayer N. Zald, "Social Movements," in *Handbook of Sociology*, ed. Neil Smelser (Newbury Park, Calif.: Sage, 1988); and Steven Barkan, "Strategic, Tactical, and Organizational Dilemmas in the Protest Movement against Nuclear Power," *Social Problems* 27 (1979): 19–37. Bert Klandermans, among others, has drawn attention to the paucity of research on movement decisionmaking (see his *The Social Psychology of Protest* [Cambridge, Mass.: Blackwell, 1997]).

4. In a welcome exception, Elisabeth Clemens has theorized movement groups' adoption of strategies, tactics, and organizational forms in terms both of what their members have had experience with and of what seems to work (see her "Organizational Form as Frame," in *Comparative Perspectives on Social Movements*, ed. Doug McAdam, John D. McCarthy, and Mayer N. Zald [New York: Cambridge University Press, 1996]).

5. Irving Howe described students' "romantic primitivism" in his "The Agony of the Campus," in *The University Crisis*, ed. Immanuel Wallerstein and Paul Starr (New York: Vintage, 1971). Edward Shils criticized their desire for perfection in "Dreams of Plenitude, Nightmares of Scarcity," in *Students in Revolt*, ed. Philip Altbach and S. M. Lipset (Boston: Houghton Mifflin, 1969), 12. Clecak, *Radical Paradoxes*, 117. See also Starr, "Phantom Community." Starr does note that some adversary organizations operated on a more communitarian model. But he attributes the participatory democratic practices of the one that he cites

in this regard—SDS—to members' inability to defer egalitarian and communal ideals, likening it to the broader culture's inability to defer gratification.

6. The term *participatory democracy* has been used to describe a macropolitical vision of political and economic institutions governed by their constituents, an organizational form characterized by decentralization, a minimal division of labor, and an egalitarian ethos, and a mode of decisionmaking that is direct rather than representative and relies on consensus rather than on majority rule. This is potentially confusing because members of a participatory democratic organization may make decisions by majority votes, consensus decisionmaking can be used within departments in bureaucracies, and one can believe that bureaucratic movement organizations are necessary to force authorities to grant citizens a role in governance. Perhaps I would be better off using a different term, but I like the historical resonance of *participatory democracy* and its emphasis on participation. When I talk about participatory democracy, I alternate among all three referents—polity, organizational form, and decision mode—but refer mainly to the latter two. In addition to the authors cited in n. 1 above, those who have described participatory democratic organizations include John Lofland, *Social Movement Organizations* (New York: Aldine, 1996); Joyce Rothschild and J. Allen Whitt, *The Cooperative Workplace: Potentials and Dilemmas of Organizational Democracy and Participation* (Cambridge: Cambridge University Press, 1986); Randy Stoecker, *Defending Community* (Philadelphia: Temple University Press, 1994); and Ralph H. Turner and Lewis M. Killian, *Collective Behavior*, 3d ed. (Englewood Cliffs, N.J.: Prentice-Hall, 1987).

7. For example, in a characterization by no means uncommon, Breines (*Community and Organization*, 54) describes the contradiction at the heart of SNCC's self-understanding as an instance of the perennial conflict between "prefigurative" aims and "strategic" ones: "On the one hand it sought to make itself an efficient organization, which meant growing, making decisions quickly, carrying out its stated purposes effectively; on the other hand it sought to make as many people as possible competent to decide on policy, to de-emphasize elite control, to overcome specialization which led to hierarchy, and to extend power to everyone affected by the organization." But are those two sets of goals necessarily at odds? As I will show, developing the political competencies of ordinary people and extending power *were* two of SNCC's "stated purposes," not in tension with them, and were seen as critical to building the organizations that could wrest concessions from those in power. Accomplishing these aims was a measure of SNCC's political effectiveness.

In his account of the demise of the antinuclear Clamshell Alliance, Downey ("Ideology and the Clamshell Identity," 370) describes a split between "egalitarians" committed to consensus decisionmaking and "instrumentalists" willing to relax strict consensus in the interests of political efficacy. During one debate over an action at a proposed nuclear power plant site, he writes, "others implicitly emphasized egalitarianism [at the expense of instrumentalism]... by arguing that a plant occupation was not successful if it did not produce a 'grassroots movement.' " But what does Downey mean by a "grassroots movement"? Why was galvanizing local activism not viewed as an instrumental means of effecting political change? In fact, Downey, tells us, initially it *was* viewed as politically effective. The conflict between instrumentalists focused on stopping the construction of the Seabrook nuclear power plant and egalitarians committed first to eradicating domination within their own ranks was "developing" rather than intrinsic. But labeling the competing commitments *instrumental* and *egalitarian* makes it difficult to see the latter as instrumental. This, then, obscures the ideological shift through which the practices associated with an egalitarian commitment came to be seen as at odds with an instrumental one. What we need, and Downey fails to provide, are activists' changing understandings of what counted as instrumentally rational.

8. See Suzanne Staggenborg, "Stability and Innovation in the Women's Movement: A Comparison of Two Movement Organizations," *Social Problems* 36 (1989): 75–92, and "Can Feminist Organizations Be Effective?" in *Feminist Organizations: Harvest of the Women's Movement*, ed. Myra Marx Ferree and Patricia Yancey Martin (Philadelphia: Temple University Press, 1995); see also Stoecker, *Defending Community*.

While arguing that nonhierarchical, consensus-based, and decentralized decisionmaking compromises what is required for maneuvering within the political arena—namely, clearly identified leaders and chains of commands, expertise, and a capacity to mobilize quickly—most scholars of the form have also recognized circumstances where such costs can be borne by a movement group. When it is aiming, not to effect institutional political reform, but to make changes in the personal lives of participants, time-consuming participatory democratic forms do not impede action. When the group is small, consensus-based decisionmaking is more manageable, and, when the group can generate its own funding, its unconventional structure probably does not threaten its survival. Certain kinds of activities may demand less in the way of centralized coordination, expertise, and a formal division of labor, e.g., service projects rather than action campaigns.

These conclusions are somewhat inconsistent, however. Estimates of how small is small enough vary. When researcher Joyce Rothschild-Whitt ("Conditions Facilitating Participatory-Democratic Organizations," *Sociological Inquiry* 46 [1976]: 75–86) asked members of collectives themselves about the optimal size for collectives in general, almost all of them gave about the number currently in their own group—and the numbers that they gave differed substantially. While some analysts argue that education and service projects demand a high level of expertise and are therefore ill served by participatory democratic organizations, others argue that service projects *are* compatible with such organizations but not with action campaigns. Still others argue that it is precisely in direct action that such forms are viable. For different estimates of how small is small enough, see Si Kahn, *Organizing: A Guide for Grassroots Leaders* (Silver Spring, Md.: National Association of Social Workers, 1991); and John Gastil, *Democracy in Small Groups* (Philadelphia: New Society, 1993). Terry L. Cooper ("Bureaucracy and Community Organization," *Administration and Society* 2 [1980]: 411–44) and Andrew McFarland ("'Third Forces' in American Politics," in *Parties and Elections in an Anti-Party Age*, ed. Jeff Fishel [Bloomington: Indiana University Press, 1978]) both argue that lobbying, service provision, and information exchange demand technical and legal expertise. Staggenborg ("Stability and Innovation") argues, in contrast, that service and educational projects were effectively served by the participatory democratic Chicago Women's Liberation Union.

9. Compare the characterizations made by Rothschild and Whitt, *The Cooperative Workplace*; Rebecca L. Bordt, *The Structure of Women's Nonprofit Organizations* (Bloomington: Indiana University Press, 1997); and Helena Catt, *Democracy in Practice* (London: Routledge, 1999).

A number of political theorists have recently drawn attention to the discursive and deliberative elements of democracy. See, among others, Benjamin Barber, *Strong Democracy* (Berkeley and Los Angeles: University of California Press, 1984); Jurgen Habermas, *Legitimation Crisis*, trans. Thomas McCarthy (Boston: Beacon, 1975); Hannah Pitkin and Sarah Shumer, "On Participation," *Democracy* 2 (1982): 43–54; John S. Dryzek, *Discursive Democracy: Politics, Policy, and Political Science* (Cambridge: Cambridge University Press, 1990); Joshua Cohen, "Deliberation and Democratic Legitimacy," in *The Good Polity: Normative Analysis of the State*, ed. Alan Hamlin and Philip Pettit (London: Blackwell, 1989); and Joshua Cohen and Charles Sabel, "Directly Deliberative Polyarchy," *European Law Journal* 3 (1997): 313–40.

Michael Schudson ("Why Conversation Is Not the Soul of Democracy," *Critical Studies in Mass Communication* 14 [1997]: 297–309) points out that talk for talk's sake is by no means an adequate basis for democratic deliberation. The kind of conversation that we admire in some situations—witty and provocative, allusive, unfocused—may not further the problem solving that is the essence of governance. Conversation, moreover, is potentially rife with exclusions and silences that make, not for democracy, but for its abrogation: "Not the fact of conversation but the norms that govern it make it serviceable for democratic self-government" (ibid., 301).

See also Bernard Manin's critique of Rousseau's deliberative model: "On Legitimacy and Deliberation," trans. Elly Stein and Jane Mansbridge, *Political Theory* 15 (1987): 338–68.

10. On the optimal structure of movement organizations during periods of political quiescence, see Verta Taylor, "Social Movement Continuity: The Women's Movement in Abeyance," *American Sociological Review* 54 (1989): 761–75; and Staggenborg, "Can Feminist Organizations Be Effective?"

11. In this respect, Charles Tilly ("From Interactions to Outcomes in Social Movements," in *How Social Movements Matter: Theoretical and Comparative Studies on the Consequences of Social Movements*, ed. Marco Giugni, Doug McAdam, and Charles Tilly [Minneapolis: University of Minnesota Press, 1999]) argues that all movements seek to demonstrate their worthiness, unity, numbers, and commitment. While a movement must demonstrate all four qualities to at least some degree, larger amounts of one can compensate for deficits in another.

12. On the importance of tactical innovation, see Doug McAdam, "Tactical Innovation and the Pace of Insurgency," *American Sociological Review* 48 (1983): 735–54. On the importance of multiple points of view, see Staggenborg, "Stability and Innovation"; Barbara A. Misztal, *Informality: Social Theory and Contemporary Practice* (New York: Routledge, 2000); and Gerald Zaltman, Robert Duncan, and Jonny Holbeck, *Innovations and Organizations* (Malabar: Robert E. Krieger, 1984).

13. James Scott, *Domination and the Arts of Resistance: Hidden Transcripts* (New Haven, Conn.: Yale University Press, 1990). On the training function of participatory decisionmaking, see Si Kahn, *How People Get Power* (Washington D.C.: National Association of Social Workers, 1994), 51–52.

14. On the developmental aspects of decisionmaking, see, among others, John Stuart Mill, *Representative Government*, in *Collected Works* (Toronto: University of Toronto Press, 1963–91), vol. 9; Jean-Jacques Rousseau, *The Social Contract and Discourses*, trans. G. D. H. Cole (New York: Dutton, 1950); John Dewey, *The Public and Its Problems* (1927; reprint, Athens: Swallow/Ohio University Press, 1991), and *Liberalism and Social Action* (Amherst, N.Y.: Prometheus, 2000); Barber, *Strong Democracy*; Carole Pateman, *Participation and Democratic Theory* (Cambridge: Cambridge University Press, 1970); C. B. Macpherson, *The Life and Times of Liberal Democracy* (Oxford: Oxford University Press, 1977); Joshua Cohen and Joel Rogers, "Secondary Associations," in *Associations and Democracy*, ed. Joshua Cohen and Joel Rogers (London: Verso, 1989); Carol Gould, *Rethinking Democracy: Freedom and Social Cooperation in Politics, Economy, and Society* (Cambridge: Cambridge University Press, 1988); and Thomas Spragens, *Civic Liberalism* (Lanham, Md: Rowman & Littlefield, 1999).

Liberal democrats are not opposed to the idea of politics as contributing to self-development, but they see self-development as a by-product of political participation and, thus, inadequate as an argument for it (see, e.g., Jon Elster, *Sour Grapes: Studies in the Subversion of Rationality* [Cambridge: Cambridge University Press, 1983]). However, as Jane Mansbridge points out (personal communication, 20 April 2000), an assessment of the value of participation depends on a calculation of its accumulated benefits and costs; it does not really matter if some of its benefits are a by-product.

That people turned to protest because they were unable to secure remedies through conventional political means was the insight behind political-process theorists' challenge to earlier collective behaviorist models, and it led to a focus on the conditions making it possible for powerless groups to leverage their meager resources into a collective challenge. For influential political-process works, see Doug McAdam, *Political Process and the Development of Black Insurgency* (Chicago: University of Chicago Press, 1982); William Gamson, *The Strategy of Social Protest* (Homewood, Ill.: Dorsey, 1975); and Charles Tilly, *From Mobilization to Revolution* (Reading, Mass.: Addison-Wesley, 1978).

15. On the inadequacy of formal representation as a measure of movement impact, see Gamson, *The Strategy of Social Protest*; and Edwin Amenta and Michael P. Young, "Making an Impact: The Conceptual and Methodological Implications of the Collective Benefits Criterion," in Giugni, McAdam, and Tilly, eds., *How Social Movements Matter*.

16. Organizational theorists argue in this regard that, if multiple lines of input generate creativity, a more bureaucratic structure can avoid role conflict in a "second stage" of innovation and make it easier to implement innovations (see Stephanie Riger, "Challenges of Success: Stages of Growth in Feminist Organizations," *Feminist Studies* 20 [1994]: 275–300; and James March, *Decisions and Organizations* [New York: Blackwell, 1988]). Staggenborg ("Stability and Innovation") shows that a minimal division of labor can make it difficult to pursue members' projects. On "mimetic isomorphism," see Walter W. Powell and Paul DiMaggio, "The Iron Cage Revisited: Institutional Isomorphism and Collective Rationality in Organizational Fields," *American Sociological Review* 48 (1983): 147–60.

17. Rosabeth Moss Kanter, *Commitment and Community: Communes and Utopias in Sociological Perspective* (Cambridge, Mass.: Harvard University Press, 1972). I take the notion of "complex equality" from Michael Walzer, *Spheres of Justice* (New York: Basic, 1983).

18. I refer to organizational *crises* when disputes over organizational structure and decisionmaking occupied so much time that the group's existing programs were brought to a standstill, or prevented the group from capitalizing on political opportunities that all members recognized as important, or led a substantial portion of the organization's membership to leave.

19. See Jane Mansbridge, *Beyond Adversary Democracy*, with a rev. preface (Chicago: University of Chicago Press, 1983), "Time, Emotion, and Inequality: Three Problems of Participatory Groups," *Journal of Applied Behavioral Science* 9 (1973): 351–68, and "Feminism and Democratic Community," in *NOMOS XXXV: Democratic Community*, ed. John W. Chapman and Ian Shapiro (New York: New York University Press, 1993).

20. Mansbridge, *Beyond Adversary Democracy*, 25.

21. In fact, Mansbridge ("Using Power/Fighting Power: The Polity," in *Democracy and Difference: Contesting the Boundaries of the Political*, ed. Seyla Benhabib [Princeton, N.J.: Princeton University Press, 1996], 47) does also rely on an operational definition of interests. We can say that interests diverge, she argues, "when conflict remains after good deliberation." This more procedural definition of interests—as subjective preferences after good deliberation—raises several questions. What is "good" deliberation, and how much of it is required? Scholars of consensus decisionmaking argue that the most important requirement for reaching consensus is confidence that consensus can be reached. The assumption that a group *has* common interests makes it easier to arrive at a mutually satisfactory agreement. Confidence in the possibility of consensus may simply give participants the patience to work through superficial differences to their more deeply held preferences. On Quaker consensus, see Francis E. Pollard, Beatrice E. Pollard, and Robert S. W. Pollard, *Democracy and the Quaker Method* (London: Ballinsdale, 1949); and Darcy Leach, "Breaking the Iron Law of

Oligarchy: Participatory Democracy in the Religious Society of Friends" (University of Michigan, 1998, typescript).

22. Jean Baker Miller (*Toward a New Psychology of Women*, 2d ed. [Boston: Beacon, 1986]) talks about an "etiquette of conflict" that prevents differences from exploding into debilitating conflict. See also Riger, "Challenges of Success"; and Catt, *Democracy in Practice*, 52. For a discussion of the diverse institutional templates that shape how groups make decisions, see Marshall Scott Poole, David R. Siebold, and Robert D. McPhee, "A Structurational Approach to Theory-Building in Group Decision-Making Research," in *Communication and Group Decision-Making*, ed. Randy Y. Hirokawa and Marshall Scott Poole (Beverly Hills, Calif.: Sage, 1986). There is a substantial literature on the importance of trust in decisionmaking as well as in economic exchange and governance. For interesting treatments, see Barbara Misztal, *Trust in Modern Societies* (Cambridge: Blackwell/Polity, 1996); Charles Tilly, "Processes and Mechanisms of Democratization," *Sociological Theory* 18 (2000): 1–16; Susan P. Shapiro, "The Social Control of Impersonal Trust," *American Journal of Sociology* 93 (1987): 623–58; and Ronald A. Heifetz, *Leadership without Easy Answers* (Cambridge, Mass.: Belknap, 1994).

23. Goodwyn, "Organizing Democracy," 42.

24. I conducted the largest number of interviews with former SNCC staffers and volunteers and interviewed a smaller number of people who were active in the pacifist Fellowship of Reconciliation and the Committee for Nonviolent Action, in SDS, in the feminist New York Radical Women, the Chicago Westside group, and Columbia Women's Liberation, and in the Direct Action Network. I also drew extensively on published and unpublished interviews with activists in all these groups. Retrospective interviews are always tricky sources of data. Memories are filtered through current political preoccupations and commitments as well as being plainly spotty. I responded to these problems by focusing interviews on routine movement activities and interactions more than on often-recounted major events (as much as there ever is a movement "routine") and by discussing particular decisions, sometimes showing interviewees portions of meeting minutes. In addition to the individual interviews, I conducted a number of group interviews with two to six people, all with histories in the same organizations. Far from diminishing interviewees' candor, the group setting allowed people to jog each other's memories and to push each other to give unvarnished accounts of the internal dynamics of their organizations.

This book also draws extensively on records of group deliberations, some tape-recorded or transcribed, and on activists' contemporaneous correspondence and personal writings. Much of the material that I used is available from university archival and microfilm collections. Many documents were also made available to me by activists from their personal collections, and I thank them for their generosity.

25. Notes of Council Meeting of FOR, 16 December 1933, SCPC, FOR Papers, series A-2, box 2.

26. For a fascinating historical analysis of friendship, see Allan Silver, "Friendship and Trust as Moral Ideals: An Historical Approach," *Archives Europeenes de Sociologie* 30 (1989): 274–97. Sociologists have shown that activists can turn people's preexisting relationships into a valuable recruitment tool, using potential joiners' loyalties to each other to counter their predilection to free ride. The point that I want to make here is that people's preexisting social relationships may also shape the organizational structures that they create and the deliberative styles that they use. On "bloc recruitment" through solidaristic networks, see Roger V. Gould, *Insurgent Identities: Class, Community, and Protest in Paris from 1848 to the Commune* (Chicago: University of Chicago Press, 1995); Gerald Marwell and Pamela Oliver,

The Critical Mass in Collective Action: A Micro-Social Theory (Cambridge: Cambridge University Press, 1993); Doug McAdam and Ronelle Paulsen, "Specifying the Relationship between Social Ties and Activism," *American Journal of Sociology* 99 (1993): 640–67; and David A. Snow, Louis A. Zurcher Jr., and Sheldon Ekland-Olson, "Social Networks and Social Movements: A Microstructural Approach to Differential Recruitment," *American Sociological Review* 45 (1980): 787–801. For examples of activists putting old associational forms to new uses, see Emily Honig, "Burning Incense, Pledging Sisterhood," *Signs* 10 (summer 1985): 700–714; Mary Field Belenky, Lynne A. Bond, and Jacqueline S. Weinstock, *A Tradition That Has No Name: Nurturing the Development of People, Families, and Communities* (New York: Basic, 1997); and Elisabeth Clemens, *The People's Lobby: Organizational Innovation and the Rise of Interest Group Politics in the United States* (Chicago: University of Chicago Press, 1997). See also Clemens's discussion of the constraints that activists face in adapting organizational forms in "Organizational Form as Frame." See Paul Lichterman's study of the understandings of commitment animating three antitoxics activist groups, *The Search for Political Community: American Activists Reinventing Commitment* (New York: Cambridge University Press, 1996). Although all three groups saw themselves making decisions by "consensus," Lichterman shows that they meant very different things by that, and he traces the differences to group members' associational backgrounds.

27. In *Beyond Adversary Democracy*, Mansbridge begins to get at this when she observes that participatory democratic groups have often begun as groups of friends. Indeed, she argues that unitary democracy is really the political ideal of friendship, with its values of mutual respect, equality, and affection. She also notes that friendship can shape individual interests or trump them. But, to explain the weakening of group solidarity, Mansbridge relies exclusively on the effects of diversifying interests, in the end reducing friendship to common interests. She misses the ways in which dynamics peculiar to friendship can undermine solidarity.

Two fascinating case studies explore the ways in which preexisting organizational forms—which provide recipes for action as well as resources—may work against effective collective action. In *Congregations in Conflict: Cultural Models of Local Religious Life* (Cambridge: Cambridge University Press, 1999), Penny Edgell Becker argues that the conflicts experienced by contemporary American congregations can be traced to tensions in the models of worship on which congregations operate, variously, *house of worship, family, community,* and *leader* models. Carol Conell and Kim Voss ("Formal Organizations and the Fate of Social Movements: Craft Association and Class Alliance in the Knights of Labor," *American Sociological Review* 55 [1990]: 255–69) trace the Knights of Labor's attempt to organize less-skilled iron- and steelworkers, showing that channeling those workers into the sectional forms with which they were familiar rather than into broad-based organizations limited the Knights' potential for growth.

28. As neoinstitutionalist theorists of organization have pointed out, organizations operate, not on the basis of objective criteria of efficiency, but in tune with the routines, rituals, and myths that stipulate appropriate organizational forms and practices (see Frank Dobbin, "Cultural Models of Organization," in *The Sociology of Culture: Emerging Theoretical Perspectives,* ed. Diana Crane [Oxford: Blackwell, 1994]; John W. Meyer and Richard W. Scott, eds., *Institutionalized Environments and Organizations: Essays and Studies* [Newbury Park, Calif.: Sage, 1994]; Walter K. Powell and Paul J. DiMaggio, eds., *The New Institutionalism in Organizational Analysis* [Chicago: University of Chicago Press, 1991]; and Lynne G. Zucker, ed., *Institutional Patterns and Organizations: Culture and Environment* [Cambridge, Mass.: Ballinger, 1988]). On post-Communist Eastern European feminists' distrust of bureaucratic organizations and parties, see Slavenka Drakulic, "Women and the

New Democracy in the Former Yugoslavia," and Malgorzata Fuszara, "Abortion and the Formation of the Public Sphere in Poland," both in *Gender Politics and Post-Communism*, ed. Nanette Funk and Magda Mueller (New York: Routledge, 1993).

29. Treatments of the symbolic underpinnings of instrumental rationality and other privileged criteria in deliberation include Jeffrey C. Alexander and Philip Smith, "The Discourse of American Civil Society: A New Proposal for Cultural Studies," *Theory and Society* 22 (1993): 151–207; Joan W. Scott, "On Language, Gender, and Working-Class History," *International Labor and Working-Class History* 31 (1987): 1–13; and Michael J. Shapiro, *The Politics of Representation: Writing Practices in Biography, Photography, and Policy Analysis* (Madison: University of Wisconsin Press, 1988). On the feminist challenge to bureaucracy, see Kathy Ferguson, *The Feminist Case against Bureaucracy* (Philadelphia: Temple University Press, 1984); Bordt, *The Structure of Women's Nonprofit Organizations*; and Patricia Yancey Martin, "Rethinking Feminist Organizations," *Gender and Society* 4 (1990): 182–206.

CHAPTER 2

1. The Port Huron Statement was the new left manifesto, drafted in 1962 by Students for a Democratic Society. It is reprinted in *Democracy Is in the Streets*, by James Miller (New York: Simon & Schuster, 1987), appendix. The concept of the "beloved community"— a society in which love, justice, and brotherhood are actualized in everyday life—runs through all Martin Luther King Jr.'s writings and speeches. See, e.g., Martin Luther King Jr., *Stride toward Freedom* (New York: Harper & Row, 1958).

2. On utopian communalist experiments, see Kanter, *Commitment and Community*. On socialist and anarchist communities, see George Woodcock, "Democracy, Heretical and Radical," in *The Case for Participatory Democracy*, ed. C. George Bennello and Dimitrios Roussopoulos (New York: Grossman, 1971). On agrarian populists, see Lawrence Goodwyn, *Democratic Promise* (New York: Oxford University Press, 1976).

3. Pacifists' belief that the "means must reflect the ends" has numerous theological sources. Christian pacifists argue that followers of Jesus must heed his example by showing love toward all men and seeking reconciliation in every situation. War, even when waged for an end that is moral, violates that calling. See, e.g., David A. Hoekema, "A Practical Christian Pacifism," *Christian Century*, 22 October 1986, 917–19; and Paul Jones, "The Meaning of Pacifism," *The World Tomorrow*, April 1928, 164. The injunction to "do now what thou wouldst do then" comes from Thomas à Kempis's *Imitatio Christi* (The imitation of Christ) and is quoted in John Nevin Sayre, "Twenty Years of the F.O.R.," *Fellowship* 1 (October 1935): 3–8. On cooperative experiments as part of the "here-and-now revolution," see David Dellinger, "The Here-and-Now Revolution," *Liberation* 1 (June 1956): 17.

4. On the connections, personal and ideological, between pacifists and the new left, see Penina Migdal Glazer, "From the Old Left to the New," *American Quarterly* 24 (1972): 584–603, and "A Decade of Transition: A Study of Radical Journals of the 1940s" (Ph.D. diss., Rutgers University, 1970); Cristina Scatamacchia, "Politics, Liberation, and Intellectual Radicalism" (Ph.D. diss., University of Missouri, 1990); Staughton Lynd, "Towards a History of the New Left," in *The New Left*, ed. Priscilla Long (Boston: Porter Sargent, 1969); Maurice Isserman, *If I Had a Hammer: The Death of the Old Left and the Birth of the New Left* (New York: Basic, 1987), and "You Don't Need a Weatherman but a Postman Can Be Helpful: Thoughts on the History of SDS and the Antiwar Movement," in *Give Peace a Chance: Exploring the Vietnam Antiwar Movement*, ed. Melvin Small and William D. Hoover (Syracuse, N.Y.: Syracuse University Press, 1992), 22–34; and James Tracy, *Direct Action:*

Radical Pacifism from the Union Eight to the Chicago Seven (Chicago: University of Chicago Press, 1996).

5. "The new society within the shell of the old" appeared in the 1906 preamble to the constitution of the Industrial Workers of the World (quoted in *Rebel Voices: An I.W.W. Anthology*, ed. Joyce Kornbluh [Ann Arbor: University of Michigan Press, 1964], 12). Gompers quoted in Seymour Martin Lipset and Gary Marks, *It Didn't Happen Here: Why Socialism Failed in the United States* (New York: Norton, 2000), 23. On Gompers's managerial style, see Julie Greene, *Pure and Simple Politics: The American Federation of Labor and Political Activism, 1881–1917* (New York: Cambridge University Press, 1998).

6. Lewis's 1936 UMW convention speech quoted in Joel Seidman, *Democracy in the Labor Movement*, 2d ed. (Ithaca, N.Y.: Cornell University, New York State School of Industrial and Labor Relations, 1969). A. J. Muste makes the army–town meeting argument in "Factional Fights in Trade Unions," in *American Labor Dynamics*, ed. J. B. S. Hardman (New York: Harcourt, Brace, 1928).

"Factional Fights in Trade Unions," written for a textbook on labor relations, is fascinating given Muste's own political trajectory. Having helped found the pacifist movement, Muste shifted his allegiance to the labor movement in the late 1910s, becoming the director of Brookwood Labor College and eventually the leader of the Trotskyite American Workers Party. Eight years after the publication of this essay, however, and after a spiritual conversion experience, he reembraced his earlier Christian faith, renounced labor violence, and retook the helm of the pacifist movement. On Muste's career, see Jo Ann Robinson, *Abraham Went Out: A Biography of A. J. Muste* (Philadelphia: Temple University Press, 1981).

7. On Gompers in the Cigar Makers International Union, see Greene, *Pure and Simple Politics*; Philip S. Foner, *History of the Labor Movement in the United States*, 10 vols. (New York: International, 1947–91), vol. 1. Unions had originally been almost completely autonomous, with their first joint bodies, citywide trades associations, given very little power. It would take some time for the AFL to destroy those associations. (See Joel Seidman, *Democracy in the Labor Movement*.) On the IWW, see Vincent St. John, "The I.W.W.—Its History, Structure, and Methods" (http://digital.library.arizona.edu/bisbee/docs/019.php).

8. On the structure of the Knights of Labor, see Gerald N. Grob, *Workers and Utopia* (Evanston, Ill.: Northwestern University Press, 1961), chap. 3; Robert E. Weir, *Beyond Labor's Veil: The Culture of the Knights of Labor* (University Park: Pennsylvania State University Press, 1996), introduction; and Foner, *History of the Labor Movement*, vol. 3. On the conflicts between inclusive and exclusive unionism, see Lipset and Marx, *It Didn't Happen Here*.

9. When Communists fought for control of the International Ladies Garment Workers Union (ILGWU) in the early 1920s, they drew the support of thousands of members, not on account of the appeal of their political line, but in response to the undemocratic suspension of three Communist-dominated locals by the ILGWU leadership (see Irving Howe and Lewis Coser, *The American Communist Party: A Critical History* [New York: Da Capo, 1974]; and Richard Altenbaugh, *Education for Struggle: The American Labor Colleges of the 1920s and 1930s* [Philadelphia: Temple University Press, 1990]). On decisionmaking in the Communist Party, see Harvey Klehr, *The Heyday of American Communism: The Depression Decade* (New York: Basic, 1984). On 1930s alternative unionism, see the essays in Staughton Lynd, ed., *"We Are All Leaders": The Alternative Unionism of the Early 1930s* (Urbana: University of Illinois Press, 1996), esp. Peter Rachleff, "Organizing 'Wall to Wall': The Independent Union of All Workers, 1933–1937," on the IUAW's internally democratic character.

10. On the views of organization held by the CIO's founders, see Robert H. Zieger, *The CIO, 1935–1955* (Chapel Hill: University of North Carolina Press, 1995). Patterson is quoted in

Lizabeth Cohen, *Making a New Deal: Industrial Workers in Chicago, 1919–1939* (New York: Cambridge University Press, 1990), 358.

11. On the virtues of hierarchical organization in this context, see Melvyn Dubovsky, "Not So 'Turbulent Years': A New Look at the American 1930s," in *Life and Labor: Dimensions of American Working-Class History*, ed. Charles Stephenson and Robert Asher (Albany: State University of New York Press, 1986); and Robert H. Zieger, "The Old New Labor History," Roger Edsforth, "Can We All Be Leaders?" and Roger Horowitz, "What Did Workers Want in the 1930's, Anyway?" all in " 'We Are All Leaders': A Symposium on a Collection of Essays Dealing with Alternative Unionism in the Early 1930s," *Labor History* 38 (1997): 165–68, 173–79, and 169–72.

12. Pesotta quoted in Robert Bussel, " 'A Love of Unionism and Democracy': Rose Pesotta, Powers Hapgood, and the Industrial Union Movement, 1933–1949," *Labor History* 38 (1997): 217. Organizers elsewhere struggled with the narrow solidarities that seemed to preclude worker militancy. Indeed, in *Making a New Deal*, Cohen argues that workers who did engage in radical action tended to have participated in an emerging mass culture that gave them access to broader identities and solidarities. Pesotta's belief that union democracy required *social* solidarity among workers jibes with one of the conclusions of a famous study by Seymour Martin Lipset, Martin A. Trow, and James S. Coleman, *Union Democracy* (Glencoe, Ill.: Free Press, 1956). The authors attributed the vibrant internal democracy of the International Typographical Union to the existence of an "occupational community" among printers—essentially, bonds of friendship that extended beyond work hours and both socialized printers into union politics and lifted rank and file to union leaders. Where Lipset, Trow, and Coleman saw these bonds, and the possibility of internal democracy, as a function of printers' isolation from other social networks (on account of their nighttime schedule) and their relative status equality, other analysts have argued that such bonds can be created by and within unions. See Philip W. Nyden, "Democratizing Organizations: A Case Study of a Union Reform Movement," *American Journal of Sociology* 90 (1985): 1179–1203.

13. Workers quoted in Bussel, "A Love of Unionism and Democracy," 220.

14. See Judith Stepan-Norris and Maurice Zeitlin, "Union Democracy, Radical Leadership, and the Hegemony of Capital," *American Sociological Review* 60 (1995): 829–50. Stepan-Norris and Zeitlin defined *democratic* unions as those with a constitution guaranteeing substantial civil liberties and political rights and with institutionalized opposition in the form of freely contested elections and internal debate.

15. See Judith Stepan-Norris and Maurice Zeitlin, "Insurgency, Radicalism, and Democracy in America's Industrial Unions," *Social Forces* 75 (1996): 1–32.

16. C. Wright Mills, *The New Men of Power* (New York: Harcourt, Brace, 1948). On the ILGWU Education Department, see Altenbaugh, *Education for Struggle*.

17. On Bryn Mawr, see Rita Heller, "Blue Collars and Bluestockings: The Bryn Mawr Summer School for Women Workers, 1921–1938," in *Sisterhood and Solidarity: Workers' Education for Women, 1914–1984*, ed. Joyce L. Kornbluh and Mary Frederickson (Philadelphia: Temple University Press, 1984), 109–45. Esther Peterson, interview, in Lyn Goldfarb, "Memories of a Movement: A Conversation," in Kornbluh and Frederickson, eds., *Sisterhood and Solidarity*, 332–33.

18. "Serve American labor . . . " (originally from "Plan Workers' College," *New York Times*, 1 April 1921, p. 8, col. 3) and Saposs both quoted in Altenbaugh, *Education for Struggle*, 79–80, 156, respectively. Mitchell, quoted in Jonathan Bloom, "Brookwood Labor College and the Progressive Labor Network of the Interwar United States, 1921–1937" (Ph.D. diss., New York University, 1992), 48.

19. Paul Wander, "The Function of Education in the Labor Movement," *American Labor Monthly*, May 1923, 86, quoted in Bloom, "Brookwood Labor College," 45; see also Altenbaugh, *Education for Struggle*. On New Deal education programs, see Joyce L. Kornbluh, *A New Deal for Workers' Education: The Workers' Service Program, 1933–1942* (Urbana: University of Illinois Press, 1987).

20. On Bryn Mawr graduates, see Heller, "Blue Collars and Bluestockings." On Brookwood graduates, see Altenbaugh, *Education for Struggle*; and Bloom, "Brookwood Labor College." On Horton's view of Brookwood, see Aimee Isrig Horton, *The Highlander Folk School: A History of Its Major Programs* (Brooklyn: Carlson, 1989); and John M. Glen, *Highlander: No Ordinary School*, 2d ed. (Knoxville: University of Tennessee Press, 1996). On Baker at Brookwood, see Joanne Grant, *Ella Baker: Freedom Bound* (New York: Wiley, 1998).

21. SDS, "The Port Huron Statement," 344, 331.

22. "Tract for the Times" (editorial), *Liberation* 1 (July 1956): 5; Arnold Kamiat, "Idealisms, Real and Counterfeit," *Liberation* 1 (July 1956): 11. On post–World War II radical pacifism, see Tracy, *Direct Action*; Neil Katz, "Radical Pacifism and the Contemporary American Peace Movement: The Committee for Nonviolent Action, 1957–1967" (Ph.D. diss., University of Maryland, 1974); and Isserman, *If I Had a Hammer*.

23. Kamiat, "Idealisms, Real and Counterfeit," 11. On pacifists' intentional communities in the United States, see Rubin Abramowitz, "A Specific Experiment," *Alternative* 1 (March–April 1949): 3; and Staughton Lynd, "The Individual Was Made for Community," and Dave Dellinger, "The Community Was Made for Man," *Liberation* 1 (January 1957): 15–18, 18–19. On those in Britain, see George Woodcock, "Democracy, Heretical and Radical," in *From the Ground Up: Essays on Grassroots and Workplace Democracy*, ed. George C. Bennello (Boston: South End, 1992).

24. Staughton Lynd, phone interview by author, 23 April 2001; Tom Hayden, interview by author, New York, 21 September 2000.

25. George Lakey, phone interview by author, 27 February 2001. Dick Flacks discusses the influence of pacifists on his own view of organization in his "A. J. Muste," *Social Policy* 30 (1999): 7–112; Dick Flacks, personal communication, 30 August 2000. On Ann Arbor SDS, see Bret Eynon, "Community, Democracy, and the Reconstruction of Political Life: The Civil Rights Influence on New Left Political Culture" (Ph.D. diss., New York University, 1993). On Lawson, see David Halberstam, *The Children* (New York: Random House, 1998). Maurice Isserman ("You Don't Need a Weatherman") has argued that pacifists were more of an influence for SDS chapters outside the New York–Chicago–Ann Arbor–Berkeley axis, an influence that extended to chapters' organizational forms.

26. Charles Chatfield makes this argument persuasively in his *For Peace and Justice: Pacifism in America, 1914–1941* (Knoxville: University of Tennessee Press, 1971).

27. The best source on CORE is August Meier and Elliott Rudwick, *CORE: A Study in the Civil Rights Movement* (Urbana: University of Illinois Press, 1975). On Smiley and Rustin in Montgomery, see David Garrow, *Bearing the Cross* (New York: Morrow, 1986); and Tracy, *Direct Action*. On Smiley's work in the South for FOR, see documents in SCPC, Records of the Fellowship of Reconciliation, series E. For examples of his conciliatory work, see Glenn [Smiley] to Al [Hasler], 1 January 1957, SCPC, FOR Papers, series E, box 16, Institutes folder; and Glenn Smiley, "Birmingham and Its Recent Protest," 18 November 1958, SCPC, FOR Papers, series E, box 17, Birmingham folder.

28. Glenn Smiley, "Report from the South, Number 2," 15 August 1956, SCPC, FOR Papers, quoted in Tracy, *Direct Action*, 96. Bayard Rustin, *Strategies for Freedom: The Changing Patterns of Black Protest* (New York: Columbia University Press, 1976), 39. On

Baker's complaint, see Grant, *Ella Baker*. On the founding of the SCLC, see Aldon D. Morris, *The Origins of the Civil Rights Movement: Black Communities Organizing for Change* (New York: Free Press, 1984); and Adam Fairclough, "The Preachers and the People: The Origins and Early Years of the Southern Christian Leadership Conference, 1955–1959," *Journal of Southern History* 52 (1986): 403–40.

29. Jessie Wallace Hughan, "The Early Days," *Fellowship* 1 (December 1935): 9.

30. Poll cited in Lawrence S. Wittner, *Rebels against War* (Philadelphia: Temple University Press, 1984), 3. On "crisis strategy," see Frank Olmstead, "Crisis Strategy," *Fellowship* 1 (September 1935): 10–11. Report of conference in "Pacifist Preparedness: Why Not a 4-Year Plan?" *Fellowship* 3 (February 1937): 6.

31. Quotations from "Commission #3—History and Evaluation of Committee for Non-Violent Revolution," [1946], SCPC, Records of the Committee for Democratic Control, CNVR folder; and Katz, "Radical Pacifism," 10–11.

32. Richard Gregg, *The Power of Nonviolence* (Philadelphia: Lippincott, 1984). Krishnalal Shridharani, *War without Violence: A Study of Gandhi's Method and Its Accomplishments* (New York: Harcourt, Brace, 1939). George Lakey, phone interview by author, 27 February 2001. On Gandhi's belief in leadership, see Gene Sharp, *The Politics of Nonviolent Action* (Boston: Porter Sargent, 1973), pt. 3, p. 463; see also William Robert Miller, *Nonviolence: A Christian Interpretation* (New York: Association Press, 1964).

33. Analogy to Gandhian satyagraphis appears in Continuation Committee of Chicago Conference, 20–22 April 1948, SCPC, Records of the Peacemakers, Minutes folder. "The February Conference on Non-Violent Revolutionary Socialism," [November 1945], SCPC, Records of the Committee for Democratic Control, CNVR folder.

34. On the sit-ins, see Morris, *Origins of the Civil Rights Movement*; Clayborne Carson, *In Struggle: SNCC and the Black Awakening of the 1960s* (Cambridge, Mass.: Harvard University Press, 1981); and Martin Oppenheimer, *The Sit-In Movement of 1960* (Brooklyn, N.Y.: Carlson, 1989).

35. On the Nashville movement, see Halberstam, *The Children*; John Lewis, *Walking with the Wind: A Memoir of the Movement* (New York: Simon & Schuster, 1998); and Morris, *Origins of the Civil Rights Movement*. For a fascinating discussion of the Nashville nonviolence workshop, see Wesley Hogan, " 'Radical Manners': The Student Nonviolent Coordinating Committee and the New Left in the 1960s" (Ph.D. diss., Duke University, 2000).

36. Halberstam describes Lawson's view of consensus decisionmaking in *The Children*. The quote comes from remarks delivered by James Lawson at the "We Who Believe in Freedom" conference, Shaw University, Raleigh, N.C., 14 April 2000.

37. Raleigh sit-in leader quoted in Glenford E. Mitchell, "College Students Take Over," in *The Angry Black South*, ed. Glenford E. Mitchell and William H. Peace III (New York: Corinth, 1962), 79, 80. James Laue, *Direct Action and Desegregation, 1960–1962* (Brooklyn: Carlson, 1989), 116. The Portsmouth sit-inner was Edward Rodman, "Portsmouth: A Lesson in Nonviolence," in *Sit-Ins: The Students Report*, CORE, May 1960, SCPC, FOR Papers, series E, box 20. On Atlanta, see C. Eric Lincoln, "The Strategy of a Sit-In," in *The Quiet Battle*, ed. Mulford Q. Sibley (Boston: Beacon, 1968), 297–98.

38. Constance Curry, interview by author, Raleigh, N.C., 15 April 2000.

39. Bond quoted in Eliot Wigginton, *Refuse to Stand Silently By: An Oral History of Grassroots Social Activism in America, 1921–1964* (New York: Doubleday, 1991), 331. Minutes of SNCC Meeting, 25–27 November 1960, SNCC Papers (microfilm), reel 1, frame 780. On SNCC's early structure, see Carson, *In Struggle*. Shortly before the April 1960 student conference, the Highlander Folk School sponsored a college workshop at which seventy-five

students discussed "the spontaneous origin and spread of the sit-ins" and complained about adults' interference: "When we inform them of what we are going to do, they immediately try to tell us that this is not the time and we get in a long argument." Urging the formation of a Southwide movement organization, they agreed that its function should be "not to direct activities but to coordinate them [and] discuss future activities for consideration by local bodies." (Horton, *The Highlander Folk School*, 242; "Excerpts from Tape of College Workshop—April 1–2, 1960," SHSW, Highlander Research and Education Center Records, 1917–1987, box 78, folder 9; Horton, *The Highlander Folk School*, 245.) On SNCC's formation, see Halberstam, *The Children*; Carson, *In Struggle*; and Garrow, *Bearing the Cross*. On students' insistence on local autonomy, see also "For the Student Peace Union: Report on the Conference on Nonviolent Action and the Achievement of Desegregation, the Student Nonviolent Coordinating Committee," by Charles Jones, October 1960, SCPC, FOR Papers, series E, box 30.

40. Lawson, remarks delivered at the "We Who Believe in Freedom" conference. Ella Baker, interview by Sue Thrasher and Casey Hayden, 19 April 1977, SOHP, 67.

41. Quotations from Notes of Council Meeting of FOR, 16 December 1933, SCPC, FOR Papers, series A-2, box 2. An FOR secretary said in 1949, "The Fellowship from its earliest days has always contained a very strong Quaker element, and for this reason the Quaker method of getting the sense of the meeting without resort to voting has been used since its inception" (quoted in Pollard, Pollard, and Pollard, *Democracy and the Quaker Method*, 77). Reinhold Niebuhr called the organization "a kind of Quaker conventicle inside of the traditional church" (quoted in Peter Brock and Nigel Young, *Pacifism in the Twentieth Century* [Syracuse, N.Y.: Syracuse University Press, 1999], 141). On decisionmaking in the Society of Friends, see Barry Morley, *Beyond Consensus: Salvaging Sense of Meeting*, Pendle Hill Pamphlet no. 307 (Wallingford, Pa.: Pendle Hill, 1993); and Howard H. Brinton, *Guide to Quaker Practice*, Pendle Hill Pamphlet no. 20 (Philadelphia: Pendle Hill, 1955). For other characterizations of FOR leaders and proceedings, see John Ormerod Greenwood, *Henry Hodgkin: The Road to Pendle Hill*, Pendle Hill Pamphlet no. 229 (Wallingford, Pa.: Pendle Hill, 1980), 8; Nat Hentoff, *Peace Agitator* (New York: Macmillan, 1963), 115 (on Muste); and Jervis Anderson, *Bayard Rustin: Troubles I've Seen* (New York: Harper Collins, 1997), 73–74 (on Bayard Rustin).

42. Quotations from Notes on Council Meeting of FOR, 16 December 1933, SCPC, FOR Papers, series A-2, box 2; Minutes of the Council Meeting, 3 March 1933, SCPC, FOR Papers, series A-2, box 2. See also Chatfield, *For Peace and Justice*.

43. Continuation Committee of Chicago Conference, 20–22 April, and Proceedings of National Conference of Peacemakers, 1–3 April 1949, both in SCPC, Records of the Peacemakers, Minutes folder; Theodore Olson, "Discipline in a Nonviolent Action Movement," February 1961, SCPC, Records of the Committee for Nonviolent Action, series XII, box 39, CNVA Conference folder.

44. Theodore Olson, "Discipline in a Nonviolent Action Movement" (see n. 43 above). On the "holier than thou" attitude, see Katz, "Radical Pacifism," 48 (quoting CNVA member Robert Pickus).

45. The statement on discipline is taken from "Workshop on Race and Non-Violence," 9 October 1943, SCPC, FOR Papers, series E, box 19, Institutes folder (see similar statements for FOR workshops in folder). James Lawson, "Evaluation: Institute on Nonviolence," 22–24 July 1959, SCPC, FOR Papers, series E, box 20, "FOR Projects."

46. Brookwood educator David Saposs described the pedagogical foundation of an "effective" labor movement; he is quoted in Altenbaugh, *Education for Struggle*, 157.

CHAPTER 3

1. Among the many accounts tracing participatory democracy to SNCC, see Breines, *Community and Organization*; Lichterman, *The Search for Political Community*; Michael Kazin, *The Populist Persuasion* (Ithaca, N.Y.: Cornell University Press, 1998); and Carmen Sirianni, "Learning Pluralism: Democracy and Diversity in Feminist Organizations," in Chapman and Shapiro, eds., *NOMOS XXXV*, 283–312.

2. Martha Prescod Norman, interview by Bret Eynon, 26 October 1984, COHC.

3. Robert Moses, phone interview by author, 29 December 1992. In the hundreds of field reports submitted by Mississippi projects in 1962 and 1963, I found only one reference to the "beloved community": when James Bevel, a Nashville sit-inner who had gone to work for the SCLC, called on organizers and residents to be scrupulously honest in distributing donated food and clothing as a way to create a beloved community. See [Frank] Smith, Report of Voter Registration in Greenwood, [March 1968], SRC Papers (microfilm), reel 177, frame 1805.

4. Charles Cobb, interview by author, Washington, D.C., 7 February 1992. Since my interview with Cobb, several rich accounts of organizing in the Deep South have begun to fill the gap that he identified. See Charles Payne, *I've Got the Light of Freedom* (Berkeley and Los Angeles: University of California Press, 1995); John Dittmer, *Local People* (Urbana: University of Illinois Press, 1994); and Belinda Robnett, *How Long? How Long? African American Women in the Struggle for Civil Rights* (New York: Oxford University Press, 1997).

5. On the freedom rides, see Halberstam, *The Children*; Carson, *In Struggle*; and Meier and Rudwick, *CORE*.

6. For debate over the proposal, see Garrow, *Bearing the Cross*, 162; Carson, *In Struggle*, 39; and Lewis, *Walking with the Wind*, 181.

7. Amzie Moore, interview by Michael Garvey, 29 March 1977, MOHP. Bob Moses to Jane Stembridge, [August 1960], SNCC Papers (microfilm), reel 4, frames 836–37. Stembridge to Moses, 25 August 1960, ibid., reel 4, frame 835.

8. Plan quoted in Pat Watters and Reese Cleghorn, *Climbing Jacob's Ladder: The Arrival of Negroes in Southern Politics* (New York: Harcourt, Brace & World, 1967), 294. On SNCC's early efforts in McComb, see Payne, *I've Got the Light of Freedom*. In late 1961, the Taconic Foundation committed $250,000 to the Voter Education Project (VEP), which was a new entity operating under the auspices of the Southern Regional Council (see Louis Lomax, *Negro Revolt* [New York: Harper & Row, 1962], 234). The VEP allocated funds to Mississippi, southwest Georgia, Arkansas, and South Carolina as part of its larger voter-education and -registration project. Although SNCC had the largest staff working on voter registration of any of the groups funded by the VEP, it received less than $24,000 of a total of $500,000. (See Carson, *In Struggle*, 70; James Forman, *The Making of Black Revolutionaries* [Seattle: University of Washington Press, 1997], 264; and Ivanhoe Donaldson, field report, 30 October–5 November 1963, SNCC Papers (microfilm), reel 7, frame 1090.)

9. Figures from "Voter Education Project, Participating Programs as of November 1, 1962," SRC Papers (microfilm), reel 179, frames 1045–49. Quotation from Jack Chatfield to SNCC, 20–21 December 1962, SRC Papers, reel 178, frames 516–17. See SNCC organizers' fascinating accounts of organizing contained in the SRC Papers.

10. "Psychological freedom" in Minutes of the SNCC Executive Committee, 29–31 December 1963, MLKPP, Clayborne Carson Papers. John O'Neal, interview by Ronald J. Grele and Bret Eynon, 26 October 1984, COHC. Selma Workshop, 13–16 December 1963, SNCC Papers (microfilm), reel 9, frame 382. On differences between organizing in Mississippi and organizing in southwest Georgia, see also Judy Richardson, interview by

Adele Ottman, 10 October, 8 December 1986, COHC; and Ivanhoe Donaldson, remarks delivered at the "We Who Believe in Freedom" conference, Shaw University, Raleigh, N.C., 13 April 2000.

11. Hollis Watkins, interview by author, Jackson, Miss., 22 November 1996. Bob Moses, phone interview by author, 29 December 1992. "Report on Voter Registration in Washington County, from Curtis Elmer Hayes," 28 January–4 February 1963, SRC Papers (microfilm), reel 177, frame 1670.

12. My account draws on Payne's superb analysis (in *I've Got the Light of Freedom*) of the organizing tradition behind the Mississippi movement. However, I focus more closely than Payne does on Baker's, Clark's, and Horton's views of the relations between movement decisionmaking and radical change and on how these views were taken up by SNCC workers.

13. Ella Baker, "Developing Community Leadership," in *Black Women in White America*, ed. Gerda Lerner (New York: Pantheon Books, 1972), 347; Ella Baker, interview by Sue Thrasher and Casey Hayden, 19 April 1977, SOHP; Baker on King quoted in Grant, *Ella Baker*, 107–8.

14. Baker, "Developing Community Leadership," 352. Grant, *Ella Baker*, 140. Curtis Hayes Muhammad, remarks delivered at the "We Who Believe in Freedom" conference, Shaw University, Raleigh, N.C., 15 April 2000. For an account tracing participatory democracy to Baker, see Carol Mueller, "Ella Baker and the Origins of Participatory Democracy," in *Women in the Civil Rights Movement: Trailblazers and Torchbearers, 1941–1965*, ed. Vicki Crawford, Jacqueline Rouse, and Barbara Woods (Brooklyn, N.Y.: Carlson, 1990). For Baker's views of leadership and organization, see also Ella Baker, interview by Sue Thrasher and Casey Hayden, 19 April 1977, SOHP, 51. On her early role in SNCC, see Ella Baker, interview by John Britton, 19 June 1968, RBOHC.

To refer to people *in* SNCC risks confusion. SNCC was not a membership organization. It had a small staff and a number of people who volunteered with it, sometimes paid by other organizations, sometimes not. In any case, say former SNCC workers, no one got paid very often. I refer to SNCC *staffers*, *workers* (staffers and volunteers), and *organizers* (those who worked on local projects rather than in SNCC's Atlanta headquarters or offices elsewhere).

15. On Horton and the founding of the Highlander Folk School, see Horton, *The Highlander Folk School*; and Payne, *I've Got the Light of Freedom*.

16. Lewis, *Walking with the Wind*, 89. Horton quoted in Morris, *Origins of the Civil Rights Movement*, 143. On Highlander's involvement with SNCC's voter-registration efforts, see "Highlander and Education for SNCC and COFO," *Highlander Reports*, 28 August 1961–31 December 1964, SHSW, Highlander Papers; "Mississippi Voter-Education Report by Bernice Robinson of Highlander Center," 19 July 1962, SHSW, Highlander Papers, box 1, folder 7; and Horton, *The Highlander Folk School*.

17. Horton, *Highlander Folk School*, 46; Myles Horton and Paulo Freire, *We Make the Road by Walking: Conversations on Education and Social Change* (Philadelphia: Temple University Press, 1990), 129, 65; Frank Adams, *Unearthing Seeds of Fire* (Winston-Salem, N.C.: John F. Blair, 1986), 16, 517.

18. Horton on "big ideas" etc. is quoted in Morris, *Origins of the Civil Rights Movement*, 151. On the citizenship schools project, see also Adams, *Unearthing Seeds of Fire*; Horton and Freire, *We Make the Road by Walking*; Payne, *I've Got the Light of Freedom*; and Septima Clark, *Ready from Within* (Navarro, Calif.: Wild Trees, 1986), 78.

19. Figures on citizenship schools from Adams, *Unearthing Seeds of Fire*, 118. Septima Clark, "Literacy and Liberation," in *Black Protest*, ed. Joanne Grant (New York: Fawcett World Library, 1968), 297, and *Ready from Within*, 78.

20. Selma Workshop, 13–16 December 1963, SNCC Papers (microfilm), reel 9, frame 382.

21. "Community Organizations" [1963], SNCC Papers (microfilm), reel 41, frame 76; Transcribed Interviews [with John Buffington] nos. 162 and 165, 1965, Project South (microform).

22. Memorandum to SNCC from Willie Blue, Panola County Project, Batesville, Miss., 2 October 1963, SNCC Papers (microfilm), reel 17, frames 132–33. The differences between rural and urban Southern ministries are discussed in Morris, *Origins of the Civil Rights Movement.*

23. "Report from Charlie Cobb on Voter Registration Activities in Leland Miss.," 31 January–4 February 1963, SRC Papers (microfilm), reel 177, frame 1668. Hollis Watkins, interview by author, Jackson, Miss., 22 November 1996. On ministers' anonymous support, see Wazir (Willie) Peacock, interview by author, San Francisco, 29 September 1996; and Robert Mants, interview by author, Jackson, Miss., 25–29 July 1996.

24. Memo from Charles Cobb to Staff Coordinator, SNCC, "Re: Greenville Mississippi," 8 November 1963, SNCC Papers (microfilm), reel 17, frames 125–28; Charles McLaurin, "Report on Activity in Ruleville and Sunflower County from August 19th to December 28th (1962)," SRC Papers (microfilm), reel 177, frames 1528–31. On women as "bridge leaders," see Robnett, *How Long? How Long?* On those who took the front line in the struggle generally, see Payne, *I've Got the Light of Freedom.*

25. Robert P. Moses and Charles E. Cobb Jr., *Radical Equations: Math Literacy and Civil Rights* (Boston: Beacon, 2001), 81, 87.

26. "Moses of Mississippi Raises Some Universal Questions," *Pacific Scene*, February 1965, 3. Minutes of SNCC Executive Committee Meeting, 27–31 December 1963, MLKPP, Clayborne Carson Papers.

27. On the Summer Project, see Carson, *In Struggle*; Doug McAdam, *Freedom Summer* (New York: Oxford University Press, 1988); Mary King, *Freedom Song* (New York: Morrow, 1987); Forman, *The Making of Black Revolutionaries*; Paul Cowan, *The Making of an Un-American* (New York: Viking, 1970); and Sally Belfrage, *Freedom Summer* (Charlottesville: University Press of Virginia, 1965).

28. Staughton Lynd, "The New Radicals and 'Participatory Democracy,' " *Dissent* 12 (summer 1965): 325. MFDP precinct minutes in County Reports, SNCC Papers (microfilm), reels 65, 66. "Mr. Giles" quote from Sunflower County Meeting, 1 August 1964, ibid., reel 69, frames 327–30. On the MFDP, see Dittmer, *Local People*; Payne, *I've Got the Light of Freedom*; King, *Freedom Song*; and Carson, *In Struggle.*

29. Mike Miller, "The Mississippi Freedom Democratic Party," in *The New Left*, ed. M. Teodori (Indianapolis: Bobbs-Merrill, 1970), 109–11; "Interview with Anonymous White Female Volunteer," July 1965, Transcribed Interview no. 405, Project South (microform); Adaton Area Precinct Meeting, *The Voice of Oktibbeha County*, 7 June 1965, SNCC Papers (microfilm), reel 66, frame no. 109; "The Election in McComb: A Report," SNCC Papers (microfilm), reel 66, frame 287.

30. Tom Hayden, "The Ability to Face Whatever Comes," in *Thoughts of the Young Radicals; and Four Critical Comments on Their Views of America: A Collection of Essays from the New Republic* (n.p.: *New Republic* and Harrison-Blaine, 1966), 118.

31. Casey Hayden, phone interview by author, 22 May 1995. On the pedagogical purposes of SNCC meetings, see Daniel Peter Hinman-Smith, " 'Does the Word Freedom Have a Meaning?' The Mississippi Freedom Schools, the Berkeley Free Speech Movement, and the Search for Freedom through Education" (Ph.D. diss., University of North Carolina, 1993). On SNCC workers' view of the political purposes of participatory decisionmaking, see Executive

Committee Meeting, 10 June 1964, handwritten notes taken by Mary E. King, SHSW, Mary E. King Papers; Michael Thelwell, interview by author, Amherst, Mass., 10 December 1992; and Joanne Grant, interview by author, New York, 28 January 1999.

32. Robert Moses, interview by Clayborne Carson, 29 March 1982, MLKPP, Clayborne Carson Papers.

33. See Ella Baker, interview by Sue Thrasher and Casey Hayden, 19 April 1977, SOHP.

34. Horton and Freire, *We Make the Road by Walking*, 103. On prefigurative organizations' determination to be "opposite," see Downey, "Ideology and the Clamshell Identity." On organizations in organizing, see Kahn, *How People Get Power*; and Paul David Wellstone, *How the Rural Poor Got Power* (Amherst: University of Massachusetts Press, 1978).

35. Some theorists of education refer to the optimal form of adult learning as *andragogy* rather than *pedagogy*. Learners are assumed to be increasingly self-directed rather than dependent, rich in prior experience, and capable of formulating their needs and objectives. The style of teaching, accordingly, is collaborative and informal. Activities are problem centered, and evaluation is conducted jointly. This is the kind of learning on which a developmental project of democracy is based. (See Malcolm Knowles, *The Modern Practice of Adult Education: Andragogy versus Pedagogy* [New York: Association Press, 1970].) The concept has spurred considerable debate in the education literature since it was introduced; this debate is summarized in K. Patricia Cross, *Adults as Learners* (San Francisco: Jossey-Bass, 1981). In arguing that authority is not at odds with equality where it is limited in domain, I am drawing on Walzer's (*Spheres of Justice*, 134–35) case for "complex equality," in which monopolies of a good in one sphere do not translate into power and privilege in other spheres. Thanks to Charlotte Ryan for suggesting the notion of *transparency* to describe leaders' responsibility to make known the sources and components of their expertise.

36. Horton quoted in Morris, *Origins of the Civil Rights Movement*, 145. The organizer Saul Alinsky wrote that "when the people know that the educational leader has the same formal educational background (although his experience has been greater and he has already demonstrated a curiosity as to the meaning of his experiences and acquired certain insights into various patterns of life far beyond that achieved by graduation from a college) . . . [e]veryone joins in to keep the pot boiling and see what kind of stew emerges" (quoted in Carl Tjerandsen, *Education for Citizenship: A Foundation's Experience* [Santa Cruz, Calif.: Emil Schwarzhaupt Foundation, 1980], 102).

37. Horton quotations from Horton and Freire, *We Make the Road by Walking*, 146, 149, 127; Sherrod quoted in Fred Powledge, *Free at Last?* (New York: Harper Perennial, 1991). See also Robert Fisher's discussion of leading and organizing in *Let the People Decide* (Boston: Twayne, 1984).

38. Horton and Freire, *We Make the Road*, 162, 161.

39. See Paul David Wellstone, "Notes on Community Organizing," *Journal of Ethnic Studies* 4 (1997): 73–89; Robert Alford and Roger Friedland, "Political Participation and Public Policy," *Annual Review of Sociology* 1 (1975): 429–79; Gary Delgado, *Organizing the Movement: The Roots and Growth of ACORN* (Philadelphia: Temple University Press, 1986); Harry Boyte, *The Backyard Revolution* (Philadelphia: Temple University Press, 1980); and Fisher, *Let the People Decide*.

40. Minutes of SNCC Executive Committee Meeting, 10 April 1964, MLKPP, Clayborne Carson Papers; Forman, *The Making of Black Revolutionaries*, 235, 419.

41. Muriel Tillinghast, interview by author, New York, 5 June 1996. See also Casey Hayden, "Fields of Blue," in *Deep in Our Hearts: Nine White Women in the Freedom Movement*, by Constance Curry, Joan C. Browning, Dorothy Dawson Burlage, Penny Patch,

Theresa del Pozzo, Sue Thrasher, Elaine DeLott Baker, Emmie Schrader Adams, and Casey Hayden (Athens: University of Georgia Press, 2000); Payne, *I've Got the Light of Freedom*; and Howard Zinn, *SNCC: The New Abolitionists* (Boston: Beacon, 1964).

42. Hollis Watkins, interview by author, Jackson, Miss., 22 November 1996; Staff Meeting Minutes, 9–11 June 1964, SNCC Papers (microfilm), reel 3, frames 975–92; Hayden, "Fields of Blue," 351.

43. These quotations and those in subsequent paragraphs from the June 1964 SNCC staff meeting are taken from Staff Executive Meeting, 10 June 1964, handwritten notes taken by Mary E. King, SHSW, Mary E. King Papers; and SNCC Meeting Minutes, 9–11 June 1964, SNCC Papers (microfilm), reel 3, frames 975–92.

44. Judy Richardson, interview by author, Boston, 10 September 1992. On SNCC's meeting format and its orientation toward group problem solving, see Casey Hayden, interview by author, Raleigh, N.C., 14 April 2000.

45. John O'Neal, interview by Ron Grele and Bret Eynon, 26 October 1984, COHC; Betty Garman Robinson, interview by author, Baltimore, 29 June 1996.

46. King, *Freedom Song*, 405. The notion of SNCC as a "band of brothers" appears frequently in SNCC workers' discussions and writings. For example, see the record of a SNCC staff meeting, 28 November 1964, SNCC Papers (microfilm), frames 744–49, in which Lawrence Guyot criticized the "political immaturity" of some members of the group and declared, "Some folks think SNCC [is] militant and should be solid to the cause—[the] key is 'band of brothers.'" Casey Hayden, personal communication, 21 April 2001. Martha Prescod Norman, interview by Bret Eynon, 26 October 1984, COHC. On SNCC's internal diversity, see Zoharah Simmons (Gwendolyn Robinson), interview by author, Philadelphia, 16 July 1992.

47. Penny Patch, interview by author, Lyndonville, Vt., 10 August 1996; Dorothy Miller Zellner, interview by James M. Mosby, 27 May 1970, RBOHC. See also Constancia Romilly, interview by author, New York, 16 March 1992; Mendy Samstein, interview by author, New York, 5 March 1993; Mike Sayer, interview by author, New York, 19 December 1996; and Casey Hayden, interview by author, 9–11 March 1996.

48. Horton quoted in Adams, *Unearthing Seeds of Fire*, 45; Moses quoted in Robert Penn Warren, *Who Speaks for the Negro?* (New York: Random House, 1965), 98.

CHAPTER 4

1. On the debate over decisionmaking in SNCC and its causes, see Carson, *In Struggle*; McAdam, *Freedom Summer*; Nicolaus Mills, *Like a Holy Crusade* (Chicago: Dee, 1992); Emily Stoper, *The Student Nonviolent Coordinating Committee* (Brooklyn, N.Y.: Carlson, 1989); Gitlin, *The Sixties*; Sara Evans, *Personal Politics* (New York: Knopf, 1979); Cleveland Sellers with Robert Terrell, *The River of No Return* (Jackson: University of Mississippi Press, 1990); Richard King, *Civil Rights and the Idea of Freedom* (New York: Oxford University Press, 1992); Robnett, *How Long? How Long?* Morgen, *The 60's Experience*; and Allen J. Matusow, "From Civil Rights to Black Power: The Case of SNCC, 1960–1966," in *Twentieth Century America: Recent Interpretations*, ed. Barton J. Bernstein and Allen J. Matusow (New York: Harcourt, Brace & World, 1969).

2. On SNCC's expansion, see note 30 below; and Stoper, *The Student Nonviolent Coordinating Committee*, 71.

3. In this chapter, I rely on a much closer analysis of movement deliberations—and of people's commentary about their deliberations—than I have in previous ones. I examined

154 recordings, transcriptions, and minutes of SNCC and Council of Federated Organizations (COFO) meetings, 60 of which were between September 1964 and November 1965. I also drew on hundreds of project reports, memos, and position papers, personal and organizational correspondence, and people's private journals. And I discussed continuities and shifts in SNCC workers' substantive concerns and deliberative styles in over a hundred interviews with former SNCC activists.

4. For accounts of the Challenge, see Belfrage, *Freedom Summer*, 236–46; Carson, *In Struggle*, 123–28; Forman, *The Making of Black Revolutionaries*, 386–96; Gitlin, *The Sixties*, 151–61; Dittmer, *Local People*; and King, *Freedom Song*, 343–49.

5. Blackwell quoted in Dittmer, *Local People*, 87. See also ibid., 17–18; Kenneth O'Reilly, *Racial Matters: The FBI's Secret File on Black America, 1960–1972* (New York: Free Press, 1989), 186–90; King, *Freedom Song*, 347; and Richard Weisbrot, *Freedom Bound: A History of America's Civil Rights Movement* (New York: Norton, 1990), 120.

6. MFDP decides to endorse Johnson in Minutes of the Executive Committee of the Mississippi Freedom Democratic Party, Sunday, 13 September 1964, SNCC Papers (microfilm), reel 69, frame 364; Stanley Wise, phone interview by author, 19 June 1992; "put their point over" in Transcribed Interview [with Fannie Lou Hamer] no. 491, 1965, Project South (microform); "follow leadership" in Charles Sherrod, "It was a cool day in August . . . " (report on the Democratic National Convention), SNCC Papers, reel 62, frames 689–92; MFDP letter quoted in Miller, "The Mississippi Freedom Democratic Party," 110; Julian Bond, interview by author, Washington, D.C., 23 March 1992. On the effect of the Atlantic City debacle on SNCC, see also Emmie Schrader Adams, interview by author, St. Johnsbury, Vt., 8–9 August 1996; Judy Richardson, interview by author, Boston, 10 September 1992; and Dorothy Zellner, interview by author, New York, 4 March 1992.

7. Forman, *The Making of Black Revolutionaries*, 417, 413.

8. "Hattiesburg Report from Barbara Schwartzbaum," [November 1964], SNCC Papers (microfilm), reel 66, frame 1270; Forman, *The Making of Black Revolutionaries*, 424; Minutes of Staff Meeting, 11 October 1964, MLKPP, Clayborne Carson Papers.

9. "Introduction: Semi-Introspective," position paper prepared for the November 1964 staff retreat, SNCC Papers (microfilm), reel 3, frames 440–43; "Ivanhoe opened the session . . . ," [7–12 November 1964], Betty Garman Robinson Papers, private collection; Hattiesburg, Miss., Staff Meeting, 23–24 November 1964, SNCC Papers, reel 3, frame 1025–29.

10. Mike Miller Notes, [1964], SNCC Papers (microfilm), reel 33, frame 124; proposal for decentralized structure in [Casey Hayden], "Memorandum on Structure," [November 1964], Casey Hayden Papers, private collection.

11. King, *Freedom Song*, 450; Mike Miller Notes, SNCC Papers (microfilm), reel 33, frame 124.

12. Edward Brown, interview by Harold O. Lewis, 1967, RBOHC. On Panola County organizing, see Louis Grant, "Panola Freedom Center," 17 October 1964, SNCC Papers (microfilm), reel 66, frame 248; and Penny Patch, interview by author, St. Johnsbury, Vt., 9 August 1996. For a typical report of project problems, see Cliff Vaughs, "Field Report," [June 1965], SNCC Papers, reel 34, frame 28.

13. SNCC Staff Meeting, [fall 1964], notes taken by Mike Miller, Mike Miller Papers, private collection; Nancy and Gene Turvitz to Dear Friends, 10–14 July 1965, SNCC Papers (microfilm), reel 61, frames 1071–72; "Memorandum to: Everybody interested in or working in the community center program," [November 1964], SHSW, Samuel Walker Papers; "Report for Monroe County," 3 March 1965, SNCC Papers, reel 65, frame 976; Staff Meeting,

1 April 1965, SHSW, Jo Ann Robinson Papers; Neshoba Project Report, 1 February 1965, SNCC Papers, reel 66, frame 184; Mary Brumder Report, [fall 1964], ibid., reel 66, frame 1265.

14. On the possible repercussions of the Challenge, see Executive Committee Minutes, 10 April 1964, SNCC Papers, reel 3, frames 334–38.

15. Hollis Watkins, interview by author, Jackson, Miss., 22 November 1996; Transcribed Interview [with summer volunteer] no. 408, 1965, Project South (microform).

16. "Hattiesburg Report from Barbara Schwartzbaum," [November 1964], SNCC Papers (microfilm), reel 66, frame 1270; "Ivanhoe opened the session . . . ," [7–12 November 1964], Betty Garman Robinson Papers, private collection; "November 28, 1964—Dick Kelley," SHSW, Walker Papers; Fourth District Staff Meeting, 15–17 January 1965, SHSW, Jo Ann Robinson Papers; Second Congressional Staff Meeting, 30 November 1964, SHSW, Jo Ann Robinson Papers; "November 28, 1964—Dick Kelley"; Meeting Notes, [April 1965], SHSW, Mary E. King Papers; Nancy and Gene Turvitz to Dear Friends, 4 July [1965], SNCC Papers, reel 61, frames 1092–94.

17. Meeting Notes, [fall 1964], SHSW, Mary E. King Papers; and "Tuesday—July 27, 1965, Meeting of Civil Rights Workers, Tougaloo College," SHSW, Walker Papers. On vacillating leadership, see To: Richard Haley, From: Jo Ann Ooiman, 6 June 1965, SHSW, Jo Ann Robinson Papers. For further examples of SNCC organizers' questioning style, see "Many of you will say after looking at these some 200 questions . . . ," SHSW, Stuart Ewen Papers; "Problems Facing COFO," [October 1964], MLKPP, Clayborne Carson Papers.

18. Liz Fusco, "To Blur the Focus of What You Came Here to Know," [1965], SNCC Papers (microfilm), reel 20, frames 46–54.

19. Canton Staff Meeting, 6 January 1965, SHSW, Jo Ann Robinson Papers, box 2; "To the Freedom Democratic Party from the Fifth District COFO Staff," 14–16 April 1965, SHSW, Harry Bowie Papers.

20. "Cleveland Project Report," [February 1965], SNCC Papers (microfilm), reel 63, frame 438. The Challenge's defeat was probably a result of the successful passage of the Voting Rights Bill, combined with confusion over whether the Freedom Democrats were pressing to be seated rather than solely to remove the Mississippi congressmen, the political fallout from an anti–Vietnam War statement published in a local MFDP newspaper, and the president's opposition. For discussions of the effects on organizing of the Challenge, see Leslie Burl McLemore, "The Mississippi Freedom Democratic Party: A Case Study of Grass-Roots Politics" (Ph.D. diss., University of Massachusetts, Department of Political Science, 1971); Dittmer, Local People; and Francesca Polletta, "The Structural Context of Novel Rights Claims," Law and Society Review 34 (2000): 367–406.

21. Fourth District Staff Meeting, 15–17 January 1965, SHSW, Jo Ann Robinson Papers.

22. Meeting Fragment, [spring 1965], SHSW, Mary E. King Papers.

23. Minutes of Steering Committee Meeting, 23 February 1965, SNCC Papers (microfilm), reel 34, frames 395–96; Sellers with Terrell, The River of No Return.

24. Stokely Carmichael in Executive Committee Meeting Minutes, 12–14 April 1965, SNCC Papers (microfilm), reel 3, frames 410–26; Judy Richardson, interview by author, Boston, 10 September 1992; Casey Hayden, personal communication, 29 August 2001; Dorothy Zellner, interview by author, New York, 4 March 1992. Halfway through a staff meeting in early 1965, Courtland Cox complained that "a lot of people got up and began to discuss their [programmatic] needs . . . and we cut them off to talk of structure." In spite of Cox's intervention, the discussion remained fixed on structure. (Meeting Notes, [February 1965], SHSW, Mary E. King Papers.) Alabama project worker Silas Norman broke into another

discussion to say, "It seems to me that the last six months I have been coming to meetings, everyone always leaves before we get around to discussing programs." The meeting ended almost immediately after; programs were apparently not discussed. (Executive Committee Meeting Minutes, 12–14 April 1965, SNCC Papers, reel 3, frames 410–26.)

25. Mike [Kenney] to Brun, 3 February 1965, SNCC Papers (microfilm), reel 71, frame 387; Minutes of Staff Meeting in Hattiesburg, 22 December 1964, Elaine DeLott Baker Papers, private collection; Fusco, "To Blur the Focus of What You Came Here to Know"; John Perdew quoted in King, *Freedom Song*, 492; Elaine DeLott Baker to Gail and Robert, [1965], Elaine DeLott Baker Papers.

26. Sellers with Terrell, *The River of No Return*, 131.

27. [Mike Thelwell], "Mississippi's Metaphysical Mystics—a Sect Wrapped Up in a Clique within a Cult," [November 1964], SHSW, Mary E. King Papers; Forman, *The Making of Black Revolutionaries*; Elizabeth (Sutherland) Martinez, phone interview by author, 29 June 1995; Muriel Tillinghast, interview by author, New York, 5 June 1996.

28. Charlie Cobb, "On Snick/Revolution/and Freedom," [April 1965], SNCC Papers (microfilm), reel 33, frames 269–72.

29. Julian Bond, interview by author, Washington, D.C., 23 March 1992. See also Betty Garman Robinson, interview by author, Baltimore, 29 June 1996; Fred Mangrum, interview by Robert Wright, 8 July 1969, RBOHC; Minutes, Fifth District Meeting, 25 November 1964, SHSW, Mary E. King Papers; and Julian Bond, interview by John Britton, 28 January 1968, RBOHC.

30. "Tougaloo Mtg., Aug. 64" (handwritten notes), SNCC Papers, reel 39, frame 877; Donald Harris, interview, in Stoper, *The Student Nonviolent Coordinating Committee*; Minutes of Staff Meeting in Hattiesburg, 22 December 1964, Elaine DeLott Baker Papers, private collection; Elayne DeLott, diary entry, [December 1964], Elaine DeLott Baker Papers. Most accounts attribute SNCC's internal turmoil in 1964 and 1965 to the decision, allegedly made without discussion, to add eighty-five mainly white summer volunteers to the staff, a move that made consensus impossible and upset the group's delicate racial balance (see, e.g., Carson, *In Struggle*; Stoper, *The Student Nonviolent Coordinating Committee*; Evans, *Personal Politics*; and McAdam, *Freedom Summer*). In fact, records of SNCC discussions show that the decision to add volunteers who had applied for staff status was made with sensitivity to just these issues. Project directors had been surveyed about their needs for workers, so the decision was not made without consultation. Most of the volunteers who petitioned for subsistence, and especially whites, were added, not to the SNCC staff, but to a separate, newly created Freedom Core (later renamed Freedom Force) that was supported directly by Northern groups and operated until the following spring. (On procedures for handling the volunteers, see "Barbara Jones Re: Subsistence for Volunteers in Mississippi," [fall 1964], SNCC Papers [microfilm], reel 25, frame 259; "The Freedom Force," [spring 1965,] ibid., reel 24, frame 870; "List of People on Staff," [September 1964], ibid., reel 12, frame 647; Untitled list of SNCC staff, ibid., reel 12, frames 648–55; "SNCC Freedom Force," 17 November 1964, ibid., reel 12, frames 634–35; Executive Committee Minutes, 4 September 1964, ibid., reel 3, frames 351–97; and Minutes of Staff Meeting, 11 October 1964, MLKPP, Clayborne Carson Papers; see also King, *Freedom Song*.)

31. Project director to complaining worker in Minutes, Fifth District Meeting, 24 November 1964, SHSW, Mary E. King Papers; complaints about project directors and COFO in Minutes of Fourth District Staff Meeting, Harmony, Miss., 15–17 January 1965, SHSW, Jo Ann Robinson Papers; Elayne DeLott, diary entry, [December 1964], Elaine DeLott Baker Papers, private collection.

32. All quotations from Minutes, Fifth District Meeting, 25 November 1964, SHSW, Mary E. King Papers. Cathy Cade, "COFO in Gulfport—Summer '64," [1965], Cathy Cade Papers, private collection.

33. All quotations from Canton Valley View Staff Meeting, 2 December 1964, SHSW, Jo Ann Robinson Papers, box 2.

34. Carmichael quoted in SNCC Staff Meeting, [fall 1964], notes taken by Mike Miller, Mike Miller Papers, private collection. Moses quoted in Warren, *Who Speaks for the Negro?* 95–96.

35. Minutes, Fifth District Meeting, 25 November 1964, SHSW, Mary E. King Papers; Sellers with Terrell, *The River of No Return*, 157; Bob Moses, interview by Clayborne Carson, MLKPP, Clayborne Carson Papers; "Freedom Schools" (Hattiesburg project discussion), [fall 1964], SHSW, Mike Lipsky Papers, box 1; Minutes, Fifth District Meeting, 25 November 1964, SHSW, Mary E. King Papers.

36. Bond quoted in Stoper, *The Student Nonviolent Coordinating Committee*, 276. On references to the black-white problem, see SNCC Staff Meeting, [fall 1964], notes taken by Mike Miller, Mike Miller Papers, private collection.

37. "Anarchists" in Mary King to Julian Bond, [spring 1965], SNCC Papers (microfilm), reel 36, frame 14; "obstructionist" in "Personal. M. to Jim Forman," [spring 1965], ibid., reel 12, frames 512–13. Staffers quoted in King, *Freedom Song*, 484; and in Meeting Notes, [February 1965], SHSW, Mary E. King Papers.

38. On strong organizations and people, see "A Short Summary of the Executive Committee Meeting," 5–6 March 1965, MLKPP, Clayborne Carson Papers; Minutes of Steering Committee Meeting, 23 February 1965, SNCC Papers (microfilm), reel 34, frames 395–96: Cobb, "On Snick/Revolution/Freedom"; and Executive Committee Meeting, 12–14 April 1965, Clayborne Carson Papers. Defender of loose structure in Staff Meeting, 2 February 1965, transcription of handwritten notes taken by Mary E. King, SHSW, Mary E. King Papers.

39. Meeting Fragment, [February 1965], SHSW, Mary E. King Papers.

40. "Self-appointed troikas" in King, *Freedom Song*, 514. Quotations about "tightening up" and "mov[ing] from morality to reality" in Recommendations from Staff Conference, 5 December 1966, SNCC Papers (microfilm), reel 3, frame 1087–1090; Fact Sheet—Lowndes County, 5 February 1966, SNCC Papers (microfilm), reel 18, frame 672; and State Executive Meeting, 13 November 1965, Mississippi Freedom Democratic Party papers, Quitman County box, SHSW. Not letting people "stand in our way" and "anyone who doesn't like things … " in "To Doug Smith … From Muriel Tillinghast," 20 July 1965, SNCC Papers (microfilm), reel 40, frame 95. "If a person refuses to abide … " quoted in Executive Committee Meeting, 12–13 July 1965, ibid., reel 3, frame 427. "What's happening in SNCC" in Dear Ruby et al. [Executive Committee], 23 April 1965, ibid., reel 1, frame 746. Mike [Miller] to Cyn[thia Washington], October 1965, ibid., reel 24, frames 116–17. "We're not individuals anymore" in "Personal. M. to Jim Forman," [spring 1965], ibid., reel 12, frames 512–13.

41. Sellers with Terrell, *The River of No Return*, 132.

42. SNCC Staff Institute, 10–15 May 1965, transcription of handwritten notes taken by Mary E. King, SHSW, Mary E. King Papers; Nancy and Gene Turvitz to Dear Friends, 10–14 July 1965, SNCC Papers (microfilm), reel 61, frames 1071–72; see also Mike [Kenney] to Gordo, 6 March 1965, ibid., reel 71, frame 469 ("Stokely left for Alabama to recapture the old days and keep from facing the new problems").

43. Guyot quoted in Carson, *In Struggle*, 149; Sellers with Terrell, *The River of No Return*, 147. On the challenges that SNCC faced in Mississippi after the mid-1960s, see Dittmer, *Local*

People; and Polly Greenberg, *The Devil Has Slippery Shoes* (New York: Macmillan, 1969).

44. SNCC Staff Conference, "Assumptions Made by SNCC," 11 May 1966, SNCC Papers (microfilm), reel 3, frames 1053–58. See also Staff Conference, 8–13 May 1966, KLA, James Forman Collection, audiotapes 151, 153, 180.

45. New York SNCC Meeting, June 1966, KLA, James Forman Collection, audiotape 199. On SNCC's development of Black Power, see Forman, *The Making of Black Revolutionaries*; Sellers with Terrell, *The River of No Return*; and Carson, *In Struggle*.

46. Wise's comment in Central Committee Meeting Notes, 22 September 1967, SNCC Papers (microfilm), reel 72, frames 173–205; Stokely Carmichael, "Integration Is Completely Irrelevant to Us: What We Want Is Power for People Who Don't Have It," *The Movement*, June 1966, 127. See also Kwame Ture (Stokely Carmichael), interview by author, Williamstown, Mass., 6 February 1995. And see generally Ruby Doris S. Robinson, "To: SNCC Central Committee, Organizational Report," 21 October 1966, MLKPP, Clayborne Carson Papers; Julian Bond, interview by author, Washington, D.C., 23 March 1992; Jennifer Lawson, phone interview by author, 18 September 1992; and Stanley Wise, interview by author, Atlanta, 9 June 1992.

47. "Black Power: The Widening Dialogue" (discussion between Carmichael and Randolph Blackwell of the SCLC), *New South*, summer 1966, 74. "Break open the chains" and "awaken . . . the black community" in "Motions, Recommendations, Mandates of Central Committee Meeting, May 14–17, 1966," SNCC Papers (microfilm), reel 3, frames 585–89; "educate the black people" in "Report from the Chairman" Stokely Carmichael, 7 May 1967, ibid., reel 3, frames 1129–32; Forman in Central Committee Meeting Notes, 22 September 1967, ibid., reel 72, frames 173–205. Carmichael made similar statements about SNCC's role of ideological vanguard in "What We Want," *New York Review of Books*, 22 September 1966, 5–8, and "SNCC's Path? Carmichael Answers," *National Guardian*, 4 June 1966, 8.

48. On this rendering of leadership, see Adolph Reed Jr., "The 'Black Revolution' and the Reconstitution of Domination," in *Race, Politics, and Culture: Critical Essays on the Radicalism of the 1960s*, ed. Adolph Reed Jr. (Westport, Conn.: Greenwood, 1986). As Robnett (*How Long? How Long?*) points out, it was also a distinctively masculinist notion of leadership.

49. Stone in Central Committee Meeting Notes, 22 September 1967, SNCC Papers (microfilm), reel 72, frames 173–205.

50. Central Committee Meeting, 20 January 1967, SNCC Papers (microfilm), reel 72, frames 130–52; Central Committee Meeting, 4–7 March 1967, ibid., reel 3, frames 631–722.

51. Stanley Wise, phone interview by author, 19 June 1992. On SNCC's last years, see Carson, *In Struggle*; and Forman, *The Making of Black Revolutionaries*.

52. Courtland Cox, interview by author, Washington, D.C., 20 July 1992. By contrast, when McAdam (*Freedom Summer*, 125) says that those arguing for decentralized decision-making held to an "improvisational politics of moral suasion" in which "a band of existential radicals . . . , by force of their example, would catalyze people into action," he reflects a common misperception of loose structurists' arguments. Organizing did not operate chiefly through a politics of example; it worked by helping people launch programs, develop leadership, recruit members, and gain power. McAdam's characterization depends on equating power with conventional bureaucratic organization and moral suasion with nonorganization.

CHAPTER 5

1. Norm Fruchter, "Mississippi: Notes on SNCC," *Studies on the Left* 5 (1965): 76, 78, 76, 77.
2. Victor Rabinowitz, "An Exchange on SNCC," *Studies on the Left* 5 (1965): 87–88, 88, 88.

3. Mike Miller to the Editors of *Studies on the Left*, 20 August 1965 (typescript), Mike Miller Papers, private collection.

4. Breines (*Community and Organization*, 6, 54) describes SNCC and the new left as inspired by a "prefigurative" commitment and notes the "dilemma inherited from SNCC." Epstein (*Political Protest and Cultural Revolution*, 264) describes such movements as aimed at "cultural revolution." On the new left's prefigurative/strategic or expressive/instrumental tension, see Peter Clecak, "The Movement and Its Legacy," *Social Research* 48 (1981): 521–56; Stoper, *The Student Nonviolent Coordinating Committee*; King, *Civil Rights and the Idea of Freedom*; Morgen, *The 60's Experience*; and Starr, "The Phantom Community."

5. On SDS's founding, see Miller, *Democracy Is in the Streets*; Kirkpatrick Sale, *SDS* (New York: Vintage, 1973); Robert Ross, phone interview by author, 3, 4 October 2000; Eynon, "Community, Democracy"; and Hogan, " 'Radical Manners.' "

6. Robert Alan Haber to Charles Jones, Charles McDew, et al., 14 October 1961, SNCC Papers (microfilm), reel 4, frame 1150; Tom Hayden, *Reunion: A Memoir* (New York: Collier, 1988); Casey Hayden, "Fields of Blue," in *Deep in Our Hearts*, by Curry et al.

7. Barbara Haber quoted in Rebecca E. Klatch, *A Generation Divided: The New Left, the New Right, and the 1960s* (Berkeley and Los Angeles: University of California Press, 1999), 24.

8. Betty Garman Robinson, interview by author, Baltimore, 29 June 1996; [Tom] Hayden to [Robert] Haber, SNCC Papers (microfilm), reel 4, frames 1138–40.

9. On Port Huron, see "Proposed Agenda for Spring Conference," 29–31 December 1961, SNCC Papers (microfilm), reel 44, frame 900; Miller, *Democracy Is in the Streets*; and Richard Flacks, "Port Huron: Twenty-Five Years After," *Socialist Review* 93/94 (1987): 143.

10. SDS, "The Port Huron Statement," 333.

11. Robert Ross, "Primary Groups in Social Movements: A Memoir and Interpretation," *Journal of Voluntary Action Research* 6 (July–October 1977) 143; Flacks quoted in Miller, *Democracy Is in the Streets*, 143.

12. Miller, *Democracy Is in the Streets*, 16, 102–3.

13. Hayden, *Reunion*, 79 (on potency of individual action); Tom Hayden, interview by Bret Eynon, 29 September 1978, Bentley Library, quoted in Hogan, " 'Radical Manners,' " 216; Booth quoted in Miller, *Democracy Is in the Streets*, 144. See also Steve Max, interview by author, New York, 23 February 2001.

14. Dick Flacks, personal communication, 28 August 2000; Tom Hayden, interview by author, New York, 21 September 2000; and Barbara Haber, "A Manifesto of Hope," *Socialist Review* 93/94 (1987): 162. On SDS's organizational models, see Richard Rothstein, "Representative Democracy in SDS," *Liberation* 16 (February 1972): 10–17. On the influence of pacifists and Quakers, see Flacks, "A. J. Muste"; Todd Gitlin, interview by author, New York, 10 April 2000; and Miller, *Democracy Is in the Streets*. In *Democracy Is in the Streets*, Miller argues that the Quaker Kenneth Boulding was influential in Hayden's view of democracy, but Hayden himself now denies this. Bret Eynon describes the early 1960s activist scene in Ann Arbor in "Community, Democracy." See also Maurice Isserman, "The Not-So-Dark and Bloody Ground: New Works on the 1960s," *American Historical Review* 94 (1989): 990–1010.

15. The SDS founders were impressed also by Southern activists' receptiveness to anyone who was willing to court the same dangers that they were. The contrast with the closed ranks of old leftists was, for SDS members who were familiar with them, striking. Indeed, those responsible for the Port Huron Statement's anti-anti-Communist plank were not red-diaper babies like Flacks and Steve Max but Al Haber and Tom Hayden, both indignant at old leftists' dismissal of Southern protest leaders as authoritarian and "Stalinist." "I cannot explain to you how exasperating this became to people who were full of life and itching to get

going," Hayden recalled. (Hayden quoted in Miller, *Democracy Is in the Streets*, 121; see also Richard Flacks, interview with author, Washington, D.C., 11 August 1999; and Flacks, "Port Huron," 145.)

16. Norm Fruchter, "SDS: In and Out of Context," *Liberation* 16 (February 1972): 26; James Monsonis, interview by author, Great Barrington, Mass., 14 March 1995; the exchanges are from National Council Meeting, Pine Hill, N.Y., 15–16 June 1964, SDS Papers (microfilm), series 2a, no. 10.

17. Robert Ross, phone interview by author, 3, 4 October 2000; first two sets of quotations from National Council Meeting, Pine Hill, N.Y., 15–16 June 1964, SDS Papers (microfilm), series 2a, no. 10; third set of quotations from Minutes of the SDS National Council Meeting, 5–7 September 1964, ibid., series 2a, no. 11. See also Gitlin, *The Sixties*, 106.

18. Helen Garvy, SDS, phone interview by author, 25 October 2000; Richard Flacks, interview by author, Washington, D.C., 11 August 1999.

19. Garvy quoted in Hogan, " 'Radical Manners,' " 262; [Don] McKelvey to Athan Theokaris, College Station, Tex., 21 May 1964, SDS Papers (microfilm), series 2a, no. 92; Don McKelvey, Ass't Nat'l Sec'y, to Toni Mester, Albany, N.Y., 20 June 1964, ibid., series 2a, no. 84; Don McKelvey to Ned McClennen, 22 June 1964, ibid., series 2a, no. 7.

20. Robert Ross, phone interview by author, 3, 4 October 2000; Barbara Jacobs quoted in Sale, *SDS*, 81; Tom Hayden to Steve Johnson, 10 May 1963, SDS Papers (microfilm), series 2a, no. 25; Mike Zweig quoted in Eynon, "Community, Democracy," 322.

21. On VOICE's experiments with participatory democracy, see Eynon, "Community, Democracy," 333.

22. Hayden, *Reunion*, 106; Hayden in March/April 1962 *SDS Bulletin* quoted in Sale, *SDS*, 97.

23. SDS's rationale for ERAP appeared in "America and the New Era," SDS National Convention Statement, 1963. An "interracial movement of the poor" is from Tom Hayden and Carl Wittman's influential "An Interracial Movement of the Poor?" SDS working paper, winter 1963, reprinted in *The New Student Left*, ed. Mitchell Cohen and Dennis Hale (Boston: Beacon, 1966), 202. Gitlin quoted in Eynon, "Community, Democracy," 351. Stanley Aronowitz observes that *poor* was distinguished from *working class*—the purview of big labor—in his "When the New Left Was New," in *The Sixties without Apology*, ed. Sohyna Sayres, Anders Stephanson, Stanley Aronowitz, and Fredric Jameson (Minneapolis: University of Minnesota Press, 1984), 22. Carl Wittman outlined a new role for white students in his "Students and Economic Action," SDS pamphlet, April 1964, reprinted in Teodori, ed., *The New Left*, 128–33. For treatments of ERAP, see Breines, *Community and Organization*; Miller, *Democracy Is in the Streets*; Hayden, *Reunion*; and esp. Jennifer Frost, *An Interracial Movement of the Poor: Community Organizing and the New Left in the 1960s* (New York: New York University Press, 2001). Hogan's " 'Radical Manners' " traces the influence of SDS activists' prior involvement in the Cambridge, Md., and Chester, Pa., movements on the emerging ERAP plan.

24. Paul Potter, *A Name for Ourselves* (Boston: Little, Brown, 1971), 145. On early problems confronted by ERAP projects, see "Project Problems," Meeting of the Economic Committee of the National Council, Ann Arbor, 16 January [1965; the date noted is 1964, but this is probably mistaken], SDS Papers (microfilm), series 2b, no. 1; as well as Sale, *SDS*; Ann Withorn, *Serving the People* (New York: Columbia University Press, 1984); and Richard Rothstein, "Evolution of the ERAP Organizers," in Long, ed., *The New Left*.

25. Jeffrey quoted in Miller, *Democracy Is in the Streets*, 206; "Memo to all the guys on ERAP from Tom [Hayden]," [1964], SDS Papers (microfilm), series 2b, no. 1. On "keepers,"

see Sharon Jeffrey to Ohio Region Campus Keeper, 4 October 1964, Helen to Kenny the Region Keeper, Great Ohio Region, 7 October 1964, and Ken[neth McEldowney] to Helen the Keeper of the Region Keepers, NYC, NY, USA, UN, 10 October 1964, all in SDS Papers (microfilm), series 2a, no. 27. See also Tom Hayden and Carl Wittman, "Summer Report, Newark Community Union," reprinted in *The New Radicals*, ed. Paul Jacobs and Saul Landau (New York: Random House, 1966), 170; and Richard Rothstein, "A Short History of ERAP," SDS Papers, series 2b, no. 21.

26. Lynd, "The New Radicals and Participatory Democracy," 327–28; Thurman quoted in Studs Terkel, *Race: How Blacks and Whites Think and Feel about the American Obsession* (New York: New Press, 1992), 58.

27. Todd Gitlin, "The Battlefields and the War," SDS working paper, April 1964, reprinted in *The New Student Left*, 127–34; Carol McEldowney, "I will try in this letter," 19 May 1965, SDS Papers (microfilm), series 2b, no. 18. See also "Memo to all the guys on ERAP."

28. Report on meeting with SNCC organizers, 1965, quoted in Sale, *SDS*, 137. In 1966, Rothstein ("A Short History of ERAP") wrote that the problem was eventually solved: "Today, ERAP students are afraid neither to teach nor to learn. The word 'organizer' carries no paternalistic overtones—an organizer is one (student or resident) who spends time telling people about what can be achieved by working together." But that happy resolution was actually less than obvious. In his later writings (the "Short History" had been used as an ERAP recruiting pamphlet), Rothstein said as much (see his "Evolution of the ERAP Organizers").

29. Rothstein, "Representative Democracy in SDS," 17, and "A Short History of ERAP," 284.

30. Hogan, " 'Radical Manners' "; Helen Garvy, phone interview by author, 25 October 2000.

31. Dick Flacks, "Some Problems, Issues, Proposals," 1965 SDS National Convention working paper, SDS Papers (microfilm), series 2a, no. 16; "To ERAP staff and friends from Cleveland project," 5 May 1965, ibid., series 2b, no. 18.

32. Flacks, "Some Problems, Issues, Proposals"; Todd Gitlin, interview by author, New York, 10 April 2000. Greg Calvert, who would become SDS national secretary in 1966, first encountered SDS when he took a group of his students from Iowa State University to the Chicago ERAP project. Organizers' dedication reminded him of the French Worker Priests movement, but he was also worried that they "risked engaging in self-denial and even self-flagellation" as they strove "to become something other than who they were—to live and become like poor people." Determined not to lead, organizers disallowed themselves any role at all (Greg Calvert, *Democracy from the Heart: Spiritual Values, Decentralism, and Democratic Idealism in the Movement of the 1960s* [Eugene, Oreg.: Communitas, 1991], 118). In a *New York Herald Tribune* article about the "new Narodniks," Michael Harrington worried the same thing (see his *Fragments of the Century* [New York: *Saturday Review* Press, 1973], 154–55).

33. C. Clark Kissinger to John Zimmerman, Shimer College, Mt. Carroll, Ill., 12 January 1965, SDS Papers (microfilm), series 2a, no. 73; Carl Oglesby, interview by Bret Eynon, 12 December 1984, COHC.

34. For assessments of ERAP's relative success or failure, see Breines, *Community and Organization*; Withorn, *Serving the People*; Eynon, "Community, Democracy"; Frost, *An Interracial Movement of the Poor*; and Hogan, " 'Radical Manners.' " On the NWRO in the Cleveland, see Lawrence Neil Bailis, "Bread or Justice" (Ph.D. diss., Harvard University, 1972).

35. Carl Oglesby, interview by Bret Eynon, 12 December 1984, COHC.

36. Sale, *SDS*, 168; Todd Gitlin, *The Whole World Is Watching* (Berkeley and Los Angeles: University of California Press, 1980), 25.

37. Steve Max, "The 1965 Convention: From Port Huron to Maplehurst," summer 1965, SDS Papers (microfilm), series 3, no. 3.

38. Robert Pardun, *Prairie Radical: A Journey through the Sixties* (Los Gatos, Calif.: Shire, 2001), 115, 115–16.

39. Nightbyrd quoted in Doug Rossinow, *The Politics of Authenticity: Liberalism, Christianity, and the New Left in America* (New York: Columbia University Press, 1998), 169; Jeffrey Shero to Helen [Garvy], 28 November 1964, SDS Papers (microfilm), series 2a, no. 92; H[elen Garvy] to Barry Goldstein, 20 October 1964, ibid., series 2a, no. 79; Barry Goldstein to Helen Garvy, 16 October 1964, ibid., series 2a, no. 79; [Helen Garvy] to Mary Ellen Chisholm [Emmanuel chapter], 13 September 1964, ibid., series 2a, no. 79; "To Worklist and friends from Helen Garvy, National Office, National Council Meeting," 18–20 April 1965, ibid., series 2a, no. 13.

40. On friendship's exclusivity, see Rebecca Adams and Rachel Torr, "Factors Underlying the Structure of Older Adult Friendship Networks," *Social Networks* 20 (1998): 53; Verta Taylor, "An Elite-Sustained Movement: Women's Rights in the Post–World War II Decades," in *Disasters, Collective Behavior, and Social Organization*, ed. Russell Rowe Dynes and Kathleen Tierney (Newark: University of Delaware Press, 1994). On the threat posed to existing friendship ties by new ones, see Barry Wellman, Ove Frank, Vicente Espinoza, Steffan Lundquist, and Craig Wilson, "Integrating Individual, Relational, and Structural Analysis," *Social Networks* 13 (1991): 233–49; and Evelien Zeggelink, "Evolving Friendship Networks: An Individual-Oriented Approach Implementing Similarity," *Social Networks* 17 (1995): 83–110. On friends' tendency to similarity, see Paul Lazarsfeld and Robert Merton, "Friendship as Social Process," in *Freedom and Control in Modern Society*, ed. M. Berger, T. Abel, and C. Page (New York: Van Nostrand, 1954); and Roger Leenders, "Evolution of Friendship and Best Friendship Choices," *Journal of Mathematical Sociology* 211 (1996): 133–48. On friends' competing pulls to openness and self-protection, see William K. Rawlins, "Openness as Problematic in Ongoing Friendships: Two Conversational Dilemmas," *Communication Monographs* 50 (1983): 1–19. SDS founder Robert Ross examined friendship dynamics in SDS (see his "Generational Change and Primary Groups in a Social Movement," in Freeman, ed., *Social Movements of the Sixties and Seventies*).

41. Fruchter, "SDS"; Robert Pardun, phone interview by author, 3 November 2000; Helen Garvy, phone interview by author, 25 October 2000. On the Kewadin convention, see Sale, *SDS*; Miller, *Democracy Is in the Streets*; and Pardun, *Prairie Radical*.

42. Rossinow, *The Politics of Authenticity*; Jeffrey Shero, "SDS, Organization, and the South," 1964, SDS Papers (microfilm), series 2a, no. 130; Ross, "Generational Change," 185.

43. Tom Hayden, interview by author, New York, 21 September 2000; Gitlin, *The Sixties*, 186.

44. Robert Pardun, phone interview by author, 3 November 2000.

45. Paul Booth, "National Secretary's Report," *New Left Notes* 1, no. 22 (17 June 1966): 1–4; Ken McEldowney to Paul Booth, 21 November 1965, SDS Papers (microfilm), series 3, no. 1; Helen Garvy, personal communication, 5 April 2001.

46. Jeff Shero, "The S.D.S. National Office: Bureaucracy, Democracy, and Decentralization," [December 1965], SDS Papers (microfilm), series 3, no. 3; Robert Ross, phone interview by author, 3, 4 October 2000; Helen Garvy, phone interview by author, 25 October 2000.

47. Robb Burlage to Clark, Helen, NO-ers, et al., 25 April 1965, SDS Papers (microfilm), series 2a, no. 14; Robert Ross, phone interview by author, 3, 4 October 2000; Helen Garvy, phone interview by author, 25 October 2000.

48. Hayden quoted in Miller, *Democracy Is in the Streets*, 270; Robert Pardun, *Prairie Radical*, 115; Todd Gitlin, "Notes on the Pathology of the N.C. [National Council]," *New Left Notes* 1, no. 3 (4 February 1966): 4.

49. On the conference, see Gitlin, *The Sixties*; and Sale, *SDS*.

50. Max, "The 1965 Convention."

51. Winifred Breines, "Whose New Left?" *Journal of American History* 75, no. 2 (September 1988): 528–45.

52. Ibid., 542. See also Richard Flacks, "What Happened to the New Left?" *Socialist Review* 19 (1989): 92–110; Alice Echols, " 'We Gotta Get Out of This Place': Notes toward a Remapping of the Sixties," *Socialist Review* 22 (1989): 9–33; and Steve Max, interview by author, New York, 23 February 2001.

53. Potter to Worklist, [1965], SDS Papers (microfilm), series 2a, no. 29.

CHAPTER 6

1. For analyses of splits in the women's liberation movement, see, among others, Alice Echols, *Daring to Be Bad: Radical Feminism in America* (Minneapolis: University of Minnesota Press, 1989); Ellen Willis, "Radical Feminism and Feminist Radicalism," in *No More Nice Girls* (Hanover, N.H.: Wesleyan University Press, 1992); Barbara Ryan, "Ideological Purity and Feminism: The U.S. Women's Movement from 1966 to 1975," *Gender and Society* 3 (1989): 239–57; and Judith Hole and Ellen Levine, *Rebirth of Feminism* (New York: Quadrangle, 1971).

2. Naomi Weisstein and Heather Booth, "Will the Women's Movement Survive?" *Sister* 4 (1975): 3; Willis, "Radical Feminism," 139; Verta Taylor, "Bringing Emotions into the Study of Feminist Organizations," in Ferree and Martin, eds., *Feminist Organizations*, 232. For more on repression in the movement, see Ruth Rosen, *The World Split Open* (New York: Viking, 2000). Anne Phillips makes the argument about high expectations in *Engendering Democracy* (Cambridge: Polity, 1991).

3. Barbara Winslow, phone interview by author, 9 October 2000. On divisions between politicos and feminists, see Echols, *Daring to Be Bad*; and Willis, "Radical Feminism."

4. Virginia Held, *Feminist Morality: Transforming Culture, Society, and Politics* (Chicago: University of Chicago Press, 1993), 173. On an ethic of care, see Carol Gilligan, *In a Different Voice* (Cambridge, Mass.: Harvard University Press, 1982), 134.

5. Ferguson, *The Feminist Case against Bureaucracy*, 173. Communitarians, like feminists, have been critical of the contractualism at the heart of liberalism. However, they have also seen radically democratic possibilities in indigenous institutions like churches, block clubs, and families—"free spaces" within a landscape of social and ideological control—and, here, feminists have been warier. They have been much more attentive than communitarians to the ways that traditional forms like the family restrain women's individual freedom, development, and equality and thwart democratic possibilities. (See Penny A. Weiss, "Feminism and Communitarianism: Comparing Critiques of Liberalism," in Weiss and Friedman, eds., *Feminism and Community*.) On friendship as a normative ideal, see, inter alia, the essays in Weiss and Friedman, eds., *Feminism and Community*. See also Martha Ackelsberg's argument that friendship can serve as a better basis than can family for reconstituted notions of support, solidarity, self-development, and sexuality (" 'Sisters' or 'Comrades'? The Politics of Friends and Families," in *Families, Politics, and Public Policy*, ed. Irene Diamond [New York: Longman, 1983]). Marilyn Friedman argues that friendship has been "the basis of the bond that is (ironically) called 'sisterhood' " in her *What Are Friends For? Feminist Perspectives*

on Personal Relationships and Moral Theory (Ithaca, N.Y.: Cornell University Press, 1993), 200.

6. Friedman, *What Are Friends For?* 189; Ackelsberg, " 'Sisters' or 'Comrades'?" 346. See also Robert R. Bell, *Worlds of Friendship* (Beverly Hills, Calif.: Sage, 1981); Misztal, *Trust in Modern Societies*; and Silver, "Friendship and Trust as Moral Ideals." Heifetz (*Leadership without Easy Answers*, 187–88) argues that friendship provides a *holding environment* of trust and care—the term is from psychoanalysis—that makes it possible for people to learn new ways of seeing problems and priorities and new ways of behaving.

7. For research findings on friendship and decisionmaking, see n. 40, chap. 5 above. Carol Gould is one of the few political theorists who have addressed directly the limits of friendship as a model for political cooperation (see her "Feminism and Democratic Community Revisited," in Chapman and Shapiro, eds., *NOMOS XXXV*, 396–422).

8. Echols, " 'We Gotta Get Out of This Place.' " Labels for the wing of the women's movement that emerged in the late 1960s are disputed: it is referred to variously as *women's liberation, radical feminism, radical* (in contrast to *moderate* groups like the National Organization for Women [NOW], although, as Jo Freeman points out, some of the legal remedies that NOW was seeking would have radically transformed society), and *younger* (although only a year separated the movement wings' founding and, as Barbara Ryan notes, *younger* tends to connote "more radical"). (See Jo Freeman, "On the Origins of the Women's Liberation Movement," in *The Feminist Memoir Project*, ed. Rachel Blau DuPlessis and Ann Snitow [New York: Three Rivers, 1998], 171–96; and Ryan, "Ideological Purity and Feminism.")

On the sources of feminist activism, another point is important to make. While, for some women, a feminist consciousness emerged from their experience of sexism within the student left and the civil rights movements, other women responded rather to the discrimination and marginality that they experienced once they had graduated from student movements into the worlds of work, marriage, and motherhood. Newly denied the political agency that they had earlier possessed, they turned to feminism to regain it. (See Deborah Gerson, "Practice from Pain: Building a Women's Movement through Consciousness Raising" [Ph.D. diss., University of California, Berkeley, 1996]; and Chude Pamela Allen, personal communication, 23 February 2001.)

9. The paper, "SNCC Position Paper (Women in the Movement)," is reprinted in Evans, *Personal Politics*, 233–35.

10. Evans, *Personal Politics*. "A Kind of Memo" is reprinted in ibid., 235–38.

11. Casey Hayden, interview by author, Denver, 9–11 March 1996; Mary King, interview by author, Washington, D.C., 2 May 1998. See also Hayden, "Fields of Blue." Mary King details her reasons for writing the memo in *Freedom Song*, 459, 445. Hayden and King did not write the memo alone: their coauthors included Elaine Baker (then DeLott), Emmie Adams (then Schrader), and Theresa del Pozzo, all white women (Casey Hayden, interview by author, Denver, 9–11 March 1996; Elaine DeLott Baker, interview by author, Denver, 9–11 March 1996, and Boston, 17–18 June 1996; Emmie Schrader Adams, interview by author, St. Johnsbury, Vt., 8–9 August 1996).

12. Jeffrey quoted in Miller, *Democracy Is in the Streets*, 144. In outlining the summer 1965 ERAP institute, Assistant National Secretary Helen Garvy wrote under the heading "Democracy in ERAP": "Why is there a tendency to think about women as filling certain 'slots' in the movement, and why do many men deny that that problem exists in ERAP?" ("ERAP Institute," 19 May 1965, SDS Papers (microfilm), series 2B, no. 18). On a feminist consciousness in SDS, see Harriet to Hiya Baby, 4 May 1965, ibid., series 2a, no. 13; and Susan

Sutheim, "Women Shake Up SDS Session" (1968), in *Dear Sisters: Dispatches from the Women's Liberation Movement*, ed. Rosalyn Baxandall and Linda Gordon (New York: Basic, 2000), 48–49.

13. Carol McEldowney, "Lystrata" [December 1965], SDS Papers (microfilm), series 3, no. 3; "On Roles in SDS," *New Left Notes* 1, no. 2 (28 January 1966): 4.

14. Chude Pamela Allen, interview by author, San Francisco, 22 July 2000; Booth quoted in Echols, *Daring to Be Bad*, 38.

15. Marge Piercy, "The Grand Coolie Dam," in *Sisterhood Is Powerful*, ed. Robin Morgan (New York: Vintage, 1970), 422.

16. Greg Calvert, "A Left Wing Alternative," quoted in Echols, *Daring to Be Bad*, 42; Freeman, "On the Origins," 183. See also Chude Pamela Allen, interview by author, San Francisco, 22 July 2000; and Cathy Cade, interview by author, San Francisco, 22 July 2000. SNCC workers' call on whites to "work in the white community" could be interpreted in several ways. Did it mean organizing poor whites, with white students renouncing their own privilege in order to build the agency and leadership of the economically oppressed? Did it mean doing support work for the black movement among liberal whites: raising funds, countering negative media coverage, and so on? Or did it mean middle-class white students mobilizing around their own issues, like the draft, university policies, and, for women, sexism?

17. Freeman, "On the Origins," 180.

18. Chude Pamela Allen, personal communication, 1 October 1996; Meredith Tax, "The Sound of One Hand Clapping: Women's Liberation and the Left," *Dissent* 35 (fall 1988): 457; Freeman, "On the Origins," 181.

19. Figures from Maren Lockwood Carden, *The New Feminist Movement* (New York: Sage, 1974), 64; Cathy Cade, interview by author, San Francisco, 22 July 2000; Chude Pamela Allen, interview by author, San Francisco, 22 July 2000; Heather Booth, phone interview by author, 7 July 2000; Vivian Rothstein in Amy Kesselman with Heather Booth, Vivian Rothstein, and Naomi Weisstein, "Our Gang of Four: Friendship and Women's Liberation," in DuPlessis and Snitow, eds., *The Feminist Memoir Project*, 43.

20. Carden, *The New Feminist Movement*, 86. See also Echols, *Daring to Be Bad*; the essays in DuPlessis and Snitow, eds., *The Feminist Memoir Project*; Evans, *Personal Politics*; and Sirianni, "Learning Pluralism."

21. Ann Sutherland Harris, phone interview by author, 29 September 2000; CWLU Chapter Reports and Summary from 1971 and 1972, CHS, CWLU Papers, box 1, "Admin. Files" folder.

22. According to Kathie Sarachild ("Consciousness-Raising: A Radical Weapon," in *Feminist Revolution*, ed. Redstockings [New York: Random House, 1978]), NYRW member Anne Foror came up with the term *consciousness raising*. William Hinton, *Fanshen: A Documentary of Revolution in a Chinese Village* (New York: Vintage, 1966). On the role of consciousness raising in the life of women's liberation groups, see Echols, *Daring to Be Bad*; Gerson, "Practice from Pain"; Carden, *The New Feminist Movement*; Carol Williams Payne, "Consciousness Raising: A Dead End?" in *Radical Feminism*, ed. Anne Koedt, Ellen Levine, and Anita Rapone (New York: Quadrangle, 1973); and Pamela Allen, *Free Space* (New York: Times Change, 1970).

23. Freeman, "On the Origins." On decisionmaking in NYRW, see Ros Baxandall, "Catching the Fire," in DuPlessis and Snitow, eds., *The Feminist Memoir Project*, 208–24; Carol Hanisch, "Struggles over Leadership in the Women's Liberation Movement," in *Leadership and Social Movements*, ed. Colin Barker, Alan Johnson, and Michael Lavalette (New York: University of Manchester Press, 2001); and Chude Pamela Allen, interview by

author, San Francisco, 22 July 2000. Allen remembers NYRW not as a circle of friends but rather as a collection of friendship cliques of two and three people.

24. Chude Pamela Allen, personal communication, 1 October 1996, 31 March 2001.

25. Miller, *Democracy Is in the Streets*, 146.

26. Already in 1970, black feminist Florynce Kennedy objected to what she called the "sisterhood mystique" for denying the fact that some women oppressed others (see her "Institutionalized Oppression vs. the Female," in Morgan, ed., *Sisterhood Is Powerful*, 492–500; see also bell hooks, *Feminist Theory: From Margin to Center* [Boston: South End, 1984]; and Riger, "Challenges of Success," 292). Lise Vogel argues that, contrary to later accounts, the term *sisterhood* was initially used both to encompass all women and to acknowledge their diversity. For Vogel's critique of contemporary histories of radical feminism that see issues of race and class emerging only in the 1980s, see her *Woman Questions: Essays for a Materialist Feminism* (London: Pluto, 1995), esp. chap. 8. See also Annie Popkin's discussion of the ideology of sisterhood in Bread and Roses ("The Social Experience of Bread and Roses: Building a Community and Creating a Culture," in *Women, Class, and the Feminist Imagination: A Socialist-Feminist Reader*, ed. Karen V. Hansen and Ilene J. Philipson [Philadelphia: Temple University Press, 1990]).

27. Kesselman with Booth, Rothstein, and Weisstein, "Our Gang of Four," 25, 37, 38, 39.

28. Ibid., 30, 39, 42. Naomi Weisstein, "Psychology Constructs the Female," in *Readings in the Philosophy of Social Science*, ed. Michael Martin and Lee McIntyre (Cambridge, Mass.: MIT Press, 1994), 597–609.

29. Freeman, "On the Origins," 186; Jo Freeman, phone interview by author, 6 September 2000.

30. Joreen, "The Tyranny of Structurelessness," in Koedt, Levine, and Rapone, eds., *Radical Feminism*.

31. Although "The Tyranny of Structurelessness" is often taken as a brief for hierarchical decisionmaking, in fact it argued for experimenting with ways to better structure egalitarian decisionmaking and, especially, to maximize the developmental benefits of decisionmaking. Distributing authority widely "gives many people the opportunity to have responsibility for specific tasks and thereby to learn different skills"; tasks cannot be rotated too speedily lest "the individual does not have time to learn her job well and acquire the sense of satisfaction of doing a good job." Allocation of tasks should balance ability and interest: "People should be given an opportunity to learn skills they do not have, but this is best done through some sort of 'apprenticeship' program rather than the 'sink or swim' method. Being blacklisted from doing what one can do well does not encourage one to develop one's skills. Women have been punished for being competent throughout most of human history; the movement does not need to repeat this process." Access to resources should be equal: "Members' skills can be equitably available only when members are willing to teach what they know to others" (298–99).

32. See Joan Cassell, *A Group Called Women: Sisterhood and Symbolism in the Feminist Movement* (New York: David McKay, 1977), 135.

33. Ibid. 134.

34. Ibid. 145; Joan Cassell, phone interview by author, 3 October 2000.

35. Cassell, *A Group Called Women*, 145–46.

36. Nancy Whittier, *Feminist Generations: The Persistence of the Radical Women's Movement* (Philadelphia: Temple University Press, 1995), 68.

37. Cassell, *A Group Called Women*, 146; Forer quoted in Echols, *Daring to Be Bad*, 100. See also Hanisch, "Struggles over Leadership"; Willis, "Radical Feminism"; and Rosalyn Baxandall, interview by Ron Grele, 8 May 1989, COHC.

38. Robin Morgan, introduction to Morgan, ed., *Sisterhood Is Powerful*, xxviii.

39. Chude Pamela Allen, interview by author, San Francisco, 22 July 2000.

40. Joan Cassell, phone interview by author, 3 October 2000; Cassell, *A Group Called Women*, 128.

41. "The Feminists: A Political Organization to Annihilate Sex Roles," in Koedt, Levine, and Rapone, eds., *Radical Feminism*, 371–72. For an account of Atkinson's resignation from NOW, see Flora Davis, *Moving the Mountain* (New York: Simon & Schuster, 1991), chap. 5; and Hanisch, "Struggles over Leadership," 88.

42. Barbara Winslow, "Primary and Secondary Contradictions in Seattle, 1967–1969," in DuPlessis and Snitow, eds., *Feminist Memoir Project*, 242; Barbara Winslow, phone interview by author, 9, 26 October 2000.

43. Allen, *Free Space*, 23. On consciousness-raising groups and feminist households, see Gerson, "Practice from Pain."

44. See CWLU Chapter Reports and Summary from 1971 and 1972, CHS, CWLU Papers, box 1, "Admin. Files" folder; the CWLU Hyde Park Chapter's proposal for more formalized structure, "Socialist Feminism: A Strategy for the Women's Movement," [1972], CWLU Papers, box 1; and Margaret Strobel, "Organizational Learning in the Chicago Women's Liberation Union," in Ferree and Martin, eds., *Feminist Organizations*, 145–64. The National Women's Studies Association (NWSA) added yet another element to a mix of participatory and representative structures. Recognizing that majority vote might be persistently unresponsive to the interests of minorities, it combined regional representation with representation by caucus groups: women of color, lesbians, students, community college students, and others. The official policymaking body operated by majority rule, and the Coordinating Council, responsible for implementing decisions, made decisions mainly by consensus. Groups like this have seen themselves as participatory democratic even as they have sought to implement more traditionally adversarial forms. (Robin Leidner, "Stretching the Boundaries of Liberalism: Democratic Innovation in a Feminist Organization," *Signs* 16 [1991]: 263–89.) As Leidner's article went to press in 1990, the NWSA was riven by a battle over its deliberative process and, specifically, its responsiveness to women of color (see Robin Leidner, "Constituency, Accountability, and Deliberation: Reshaping Democracy in the National Women's Studies Association," *National Women's Studies Association Journal* 5, no. 1 [1993]: 4–27; and Carmen Sirianni, "Feminist Pluralism and Democratic Learning: The Politics of Citizenship in the National Women's Studies Association," *National Women's Studies Association Journal* 5 [1993]: 369–84).

45. Kathleen P. Iannello, *Decisions without Hierarchy* (New York: Routledge, 1992), 67. On feminist organizations' relationships with state funders, see Nancy Mathews, "Feminist Clashes with the State: Tactical Choices by State-Funded Rape Crisis Centers," in Ferree and Martin, eds., *Feminist Organizations*, 291–305, and *Confronting Rape: The Feminist Anti-Rape Movement and the State* (London: Routledge, 1994). On the metamorphosis of women's service and support organizations, see Riger, "Challenges of Success."

46. Bordt, *The Structure of Women's Nonprofit Organizations*, 44–45; Jennifer Leigh Disney and Joyce Gelb, "Feminist Organizational 'Success': The State of U.S. Women's Movement Organizations in the 1990s," *Women and Politics* 21 (2000): 39–76.

47. Meredith Tax on "rule by friendship clique" quoted in Strobel, "Organizational Learning in the Chicago Women's Liberation Union," 155. On "pluralist friendship," see Maria C. Lugones with Pat Alake Rosezelle, "Sisterhood and Friendship as Feminist Models," in Weiss and Friedman, eds., *Feminism and Community*, 135–45.

48. Lugones with Rosezelle, "Sisterhood and Friendship as Feminist Models," 138. Chude Pamela Allen (personal communication, 23 February 2001) points out that women's liberationists in the late 1960s and early 1970s would not have liked the word *compañera*— even though, for Allen, Lugones's description does capture the kind of political relationship that she and others wanted. But, Allen says, "we needed a word that was specifically a woman-only word and in my experience of that time, 'compañera' among activists meant being part of the anti-imperialist Left, [working] specifically [on] Cuba and [being part of] the Venceremos Brigade." Allen points to a dynamic that occurred repeatedly in the history of participatory democracy—and, presumably, the histories of any number of movement strategies, tactics, and organizational forms. Options have had negative or positive value in part through the groups with which they have been associated. This is not always a bad thing. The fact is that people outside the movement often make the same associations that activists do. Like activists, the public may see marches as more middle class than strikes and bureaucratic organizations as both slow and efficient. To try to defy those associations may mean losing potential recruits, supporters, or allies. But, in general, to rule out options a priori on account of their political associations forecloses the opportunity to compare their likely costs and benefits.

49. Bordt, *The Structure of Women's Nonprofit Organizations*. Interestingly, Ackelsberg ("'Sisters' or 'Comrades'?") argues that friendship can be an effective model for political relationships and then concludes by calling on activists to consider *comrade* and *companion* as terms to describe their solidary relations—not *friend*.

CHAPTER 7

1. Virginia Ramirez is profiled in Mark Warren, *Dry Bones Rattling* (Princeton, N.J.: Princeton University Press, 2001), 217; Miriam Bearse, interview by author, New York, 26 September 2000.

2. To assign DAN to the direct action movement and COPS to community organizing is to impose a potentially misleading distinction. Like much of today's community organizing, COPS relies on techniques of direct action, and DAN has become increasingly interested in community organizing. I distinguish them nevertheless because COPS and other community-organizing groups define themselves principally by their community base and orientation. To complicate issues further, IAF organizers explicitly distinguish the organizing that they do from the work of a *movement*. They see movements as dominated by charismatic leaders (which they see as at odds with popular power) and as single rather than multi-issue. Nevertheless, it seems legitimate to consider IAF organizing as one strand of contemporary activism or one contemporary activist choice. (Mark Warren, personal communication, 7 November 2000; see also Stephen Hart, *Cultural Dilemmas of Progressive Politics: Styles of Engagement among Grassroots Activists* [Chicago: University of Chicago Press, 2001], 27–28, esp. n. 2.)

3. On the ascendance of professional advocacy groups, see Theda Skocpol, "Associations without Members," *American Prospect* 45 (July–August 1999): 66–73. For list of DAN locals, see the organization's website (http://www.cdan.org). Figures on participation in anti–corporate globalization direct action compiled from Kim Murphy, "WTO Summit Protest in Seattle," *Los Angeles Times*, 1 December 1999, A1; Jane Bussey, "Protests Block DC Streets," *Miami Herald*, 17 April 2000, A1; James Toedtman, "Trade Talks on Track," *Newsday: Nassau and Suffolk Edition*, 16 August 2000, A07; and Kate Jaimet and Karina Roman, "Graffiti, Litter Last Vestiges of Protest," *Ottawa Citizen*, 23 April 2001, A4. Thanks

to Lesley Wood for this information. Figures on community organizing are from Mark R. Warren and Richard L. Wood, *Faith-Based Community Organizing: The State of the Field* (Jericho, N.Y.: Interfaith Funders, 2001).

4. Booth quoted in Fisher, *Let the People Decide*, 129. My account of community organizing in the Alinsky tradition draws on interviews with longtime organizers Mike Miller, Janice Fine, Jennifer Gordon, Richard Healey, and Marshall Ganz and with sociologist Mark Warren in addition to the published and unpublished works cited in this chapter.

5. Saul Alinsky, *Reveille for Radicals* (New York: Vintage, 1946). On Alinsky's views of 1960s activists, see Sanford D. Horwitt, *Let Them Call Me Rebel: Saul Alinsky—His Life and Legacy* (New York: Knopf, 1989), 508, 525. See also Mike Miller, "The Student Movement and Saul Alinsky: An Alliance That Never Happened and Why" (San Francisco: Organize Training Center, 2001, typescript). On Alinsky's organizing efforts, see Horwitt, *Let Them Call Me Rebel*; and Fisher, *Let the People Decide*.

6. On Texas IAF organizing, see Warren, *Dry Bones Rattling*; Mary Beth Rogers, *Cold Anger* (Denton: University of North Texas Press, 1990); and Dennis Shirley, *Community Organizing for Urban School Reform* (Austin: University of Texas Press, 1997). Figures from Warren and Wood, *Faith-Based Community Organizing*. There are other models of community organizing, among them the individual-based rather than institution-based one of the Association of Communities Organized for Reform Now. People are canvassed door-to-door on issues of toxic waste, electricity rates, health care, and so on, and campaigns are organized around those issues. Although there are similarities in style between faith- and institution-based organizing and secular and individual-based organizing, I concentrate on the former. For discussions of the latter, see Fisher, *Let the People Decide*; Delgado, *Organizing the Movement*; and Mark Hanna and Buddy Robinson, *Strategies for Community Empowerment* (Lewiston, N.Y.: Mellen, 1994).

7. On the organizing process, see Warren, *Dry Bones Rattling*; Hanna and Robinson, *Strategies for Community Empowerment*; Shirley, *Urban Organizing for School Reform*; and Ernesto Cortes Jr., "Reweaving the Fabric: The Iron Rule and the IAF Strategy for Power and Politics," in *Interwoven Destinies: Cities and the Nation*, ed. Henry G. Cisneros (New York: Norton, 1993). On faith-based organizing's reliance on political clout and ethical appeal, see Hart, *Cultural Dilemmas*.

8. Figures are from Warren and Wood, *Faith-Based Community Organizing*.

9. Edward Chambers, *Organizing for Family and Congregation* (New York: Industrial Areas Foundation, 1978), 20. On leadership development, see Hart, *Cultural Dilemmas*, 40, 64–65; and Jacqueline B. Mondros and Scott M. Wilson, *Organizing for Power and Empowerment* (New York: Columbia University Press, 1994).

10. This practice was observed in meetings of the Milwaukee Inner-City Congregations Allied for Hope (see Hart, *Cultural Dilemmas*, 105).

11. Warren, *Dry Bones Rattling*, chap. 8. See also Rogers, *Cold Anger*.

12. Warren, *Dry Bones Rattling*; Hart, *Cultural Dilemmas*.

13. Cortes quoted in Warren, *Dry Bones Rattling*, 224. On the meanings of "self-interest," see ibid.; Hart, *Cultural Dilemmas*; and Harry C. Boyte, *Commonwealth* (New York: Free Press, 1989). For an understanding of self-interest as the epitaph one would choose for oneself, see Hart, *Cultural Dilemmas*, 66.

14. COPS leader quoted in Boyte, *Commonwealth*, 98; Stephens quoted in Warren, *Dry Bones Rattling*, 228.

15. Hart, *Cultural Dilemmas*, 63; Cortes quoted in Rogers, *Cold Anger*, 186.

16. Richard L. Wood, *Faith in Action* (Chicago: University of Chicago Press, 2002). See also Hart, *Cultural Dilemmas*; and Warren, *Dry Bones Rattling*.

17. On the effects of pastors' opposition to community organizing, see Wood, *Faith in Action*; Hanna and Robinson, *Strategies for Community Empowerment*; and the essays in Peg Knoepfle, ed., *After Alinsky: Community Organizing in Illinois* (Springfield, Ill.: Sangamon State University Press, 1990). The essays in *After Alinsky* also discuss the danger of projects' dependence on organizers. Mike Miller treats leader co-optation in his "Community Organizing" (San Francisco: Organize Training Center, May 1997, typescript).

18. On recent efforts to expand into statewide and regional organizing, see Warren and Wood, *Faith-Based Community Organizing*. Warren discusses Cortes's regional organizing in *Dry Bones Rattling*.

19. Hart, *Cultural Dilemmas*, 114. For discussions of the place of ideology in faith-based organizing, see Wood, *Faith in Action*; Warren, *Dry Bones Rattling*; Hart, *Cultural Dilemmas*; and Fisher, *Let the People Decide*.

20. Mike Miller, "Organizing and Education: Saul Alinsky, Paulo Freire, and Myles Horton," *Social Policy* 24 (fall 1993): 51–63. Midwest Training Academy organizing director Steve Max argues that committees formed as parts of an organizing campaign are places where people can participate intensively from the start, and learn that way, without bogging the rest of the organization down in long discussions among novices (Steve Max, interview by author, New York, 23 February 2001; see also Kim Bobo, Jackie Kendall, and Steve Max, *Organize! Organizing for Social Change* [Washington, D.C.: Seven Locks, 1991]). Organizers might also work on identifying some kinds of decisions that, made collectively, are more likely than others to generate political learning among participants. In that respect, longtime organizer Jennifer Gordon argues that, where a decision's consequences will be known almost immediately, and where the consequences are for people's lives outside the organization rather than only for the organization, decisionmaking by the group as a whole rather than by its leadership can be an important learning tool. Where that is not the case, Gordon worries that the main lesson for participants will be the tedium of decisionmaking and that the main lesson for leaders will be that their long-standing stake in the organization can be outweighed by the preferences of people who rarely participate. (Jennifer Gordon, personal communication, 21 April 2001.)

21. Katherine Sciacchitano, "Unions, Organizing, and Democracy," *Dissent* 47 (spring 2000): 75–81, and "The Union Is Forever" (paper presented at the UCLEA/AFL-CIO annual conference, San Jose, Calif., 1 May 1998).

22. Hart, *Cultural Dilemmas*; Warren, *Dry Bones Rattling*; Shirley, *Community Organizing for Urban School Reform*. Longtime organizer Kim Fellner criticizes the archetype of the IAF organizer: "the macho maniac dangling a cigarette and a broken marriage" in her "Hearts and Crafts: Powering the Movement," National Housing Institute: Shelterforce Online (http://www.nhi.org/online/issues/101/fellner.html).

23. On "women's ways of organizing," see Randy Stoecker and Susan Stall, "Community Organizing or Organizing Community? Gender and the Crafts of Empowerment," 1997 COMM-ORG working paper (http://comm-org.utoledo.edu/papers.htm); the essays collected in *Women and the Politics of Empowerment*, ed. Ann Bookman and Sandra Morgen (Philadelphia: Temple University Press, 1989), esp. Karen Brodkin Sacks, "Gender and Grassroots Leadership," and Martha Ackelsberg, "Communities, Resistance, and Women's Activism: Some Implications for a Democratic Polity"; the essays collected in *Community Activism and Feminist Politics: Organizing across Race, Class, and Gender*, ed. Nancy A. Naples (New York: Routledge, 1998); and Terry L. Haywoode, "Working-Class Women and Local

Politics: Styles of Community Organizing," *Research in Politics and Society* 7 (1999): 111–34.

24. Mac Scott, interview by author, New York, 26 September 2000.

25. See the DAN website (http://www.cdan.org). On new direct action movements, see Leslie Kaufman, "The New Unrest," *Free Radical*, vol. 1 (February 2000) (http://www.free-radical.org/issue1.shtml).

26. On the consensus process, see War Resisters League, *Handbook for Nonviolent Direct Action* (www.nonviolence.org/wrl), 10, 11.

27. These and subsequent quotations are from Miriam Bearse, Isabell Moore, Mac Scott, and Lesley Wood, interview by author, New York, 26 September 2000.

28. This view of equality is not uncontested in DAN. When Miriam and others noticed that women's participation in meetings was declining, they proposed that a third facilitator or "vibes watcher" monitor the participation of underrepresented groups in meetings and prioritize those groups' interventions in the speakers' queue. The proposal met with strong objections. Opponents claimed that the group could monitor itself without a "cop" and that not to allow itself to do so was simply unfair. Equality demanded that people be treated as equals. Those making such arguments tended to be older white men, several DAN activists tell me. Whether reality or perception, opponents of more expansive notions of equality are associated with an older liberal tradition.

29. "Spokescouncils," n.d. (handout used to train demonstrators at the 2000 Republican National Convention, in author's possession).

30. Epstein, *Political Protest and Cultural Revolution*.

31. Jeremy Varon, David Graeber, Brooke Lehman, and José Lugo, interview by author, New York, 5 March 2001.

32. Epstein, *Political Protest and Cultural Revolution*.

33. For treatments of the Clamshell Alliance and the antinuclear movement generally, see ibid.; and James Jasper, *The Art of Moral Protest* (Chicago: University of Chicago Press, 1998). On the early Clamshell Alliance, see Etahn Cohen, *Ideology, Interest Group Formation, and the New Left: The Case of the Clamshell Alliance* (New York: Garland, 1988). On Quakers' role in the movement, see George Lakey, phone interview by author, 27 February 2001; and Bill Moyer, phone interview by author, 3 May 2001. On the Movement for a New Society, see George Lakey, "'Catching Up and Moving On': What Can We Learn for the Future from the Movement for a New Society" (1989, typescript, in the author's possession). On the Movement for a New Society's split with the Friends, see Allen Smith, "The Renewal Movement: The Peace Movement and Modern Quakerism," *Quaker History* 85 (fall 1996): 1–23. For a sample of Murray Bookchin's writings, see his *Post-Scarcity Anarchism* (Berkeley: Ramparts, 1971).

34. Epstein, *Political Protest and Cultural Revolution*; Jasper, *The Art of Moral Protest*, 192.

35. Lichterman, *The Search for Political Community*, 6, 49 (former new left activist quoted). The Green Party—officially the Committees of Correspondence—was launched in the United States in 1984, shortly after German Greens won seats in Parliament. American Greens, who would eventually run candidates for local, state, and national office, formed independent local groups around values of "decentralization," "grassroots democracy," "respect for diversity," and "postpatriarchal values" (see Association of State Green Parties, "History of ASGP and the Green Party" [www.green-party.org/history.html]).

36. "The '60s Talk to the '00s—and the '00s Talk Back," panel discussion, Columbia University, Sociology Department and Graduate History Association, 14 November 2001.

37. Naomi Klein, "Were the DC and Seattle Protests Unfocused, or Are the Critics Missing the Point?" *The Nation*, 10 July 2000, 18–20; Bill Moyer, phone interview by author, 3 May 2001.

CHAPTER 8

1. For an exception to the dearth of work on the organizational structures that facilitate the gains of organizing, see Kenneth T. Andrews, "Social Movements and Policy Implementation: The Mississippi Civil Rights Movement and the War on Poverty, 1965–1971," *American Sociological Review* 66 (2001): 71–95.

2. Dwight Macdonald, "The Root Is Man," *Politics* 3 (April 1946): 115; SDS, "Port Huron Statement," 332.

3. SDS member quoted in Miller, *Democracy Is in the Streets*, 399.

4. Tax, "One Hand Clapping," 458.

5. As an example of the kind of deliberative system of decisionmaking that I have in mind, consider how the Florida Supreme Court operates. Decisions are made by a majority of the justices, but the task of writing the majority opinion is rotated. The opinion writer may also write a dissenting opinion if she chooses. But the presumption is that she will understand and respect the arguments made by the majority well enough to render them fairly, even when she disagrees with them. What makes this system possible is the fact that the justices talk to each other directly during the deliberative process rather than communicating through clerks or memos. A former chief justice described a "lot of politicking"—but, he specified, politicking of "a different kind.... [I]t's very common to say, 'I can't wait to ask this person this question.'" Justices aim both to persuade and to learn from each other. And they strive to recognize the validity of the other side's reasoning, even if not accepting its ranking of priorities. Of course, there are many things that make the Florida Supreme Court unlike a social movement organization: there are only seven justices; they are restricted to interpreting existing law and judicial precedent; they proceed on a case-by-case basis with plenty of time for deliberation; their decisions are backed by coercion. But the justices' commitment to deliberating together with the expectation, not of unanimity, but of reaching an acceptance of each other's arguments is certainly transportable to movement organizations. Indeed, it has often been a feature of successful movement democracies. (Jo Becker, "'Results-Oriented' Court Gets Down to Business," *Washington Post*, 21 November 2000, A16.)

6. Robert Michels, *Political Parties*, trans. Eden Paul and Cedar Paul (Glencoe, Ill.: Free Press, 1958); Joreen, "The Tyranny of Structurelessness." On the effects of diverging interests, see Mansbridge, *Beyond Adversary Democracy*.

7. Theodore Lowi, *The End of Liberalism: The Second Republic of the United States* (New York: Norton, 1979), 56, 226.

8. On Americans' discomfort with talk of political goals, see Nina Eliasoph, *Avoiding Politics: How Americans Produce Apathy in Everyday Life* (Cambridge: Cambridge University Press, 1998); and Hart, *Cultural Dilemmas*.

9. José Lugo, Jeremy Varon, Brooke Lehman, and David Graeber, interview by author, New York, 5 March 2001; Anonymous DAN member, interview by author, March 2001.

10. Sherryl Kleinman, *Opposing Ambitions: Gender and Identity in an Alternative Organization* (Chicago: University of Chicago Press, 1996), 38–39.

11. See Rebecca Bordt, "How Alternative Ideas Become Institutions: The Case of Feminist Collectives," *Nonprofit Voluntary Sector Quarterly* 26 (1997): 132–55; and Stoecker, *Defending Community*.

12. On internal democracy as a learning process, see Sirianni, "Learning Pluralism"; and Strobel, "Organizational Learning in the Chicago Women's Liberation Union."

13. Bordt, *The Structure of Women's Nonprofit Organizations*; Disney and Gelb, "Feminist Organizational 'Success.'"

14. Iannello (*Decisions without Hierarchy*, 20) distinguishes between *routine* and *critical* decisions. Bordt (*The Structure of Women's Nonprofit Organizations*) uses a similar distinction. Heifetz (*Leadership without Easy Answers*, 121–22) distinguishes between *technical* and *adaptive* decisions.

15. Mansbridge, "Using Power/Fighting Power," 47; Cohen and Sabel, "Directly Deliberative Polyarchy," 329.

16. For a political-theoretical defense of this system, see Mark E. Warren, "Deliberative Democracy and Authority," *American Political Science Review* 90 (1996): 46–60. To give some people more weight than others in making decisions is similar in some sense to a proportional system, in which some people's votes count more because the larger group believes that the subgroup's interests should be represented but are unlikely to be in a system that relies either on majoritarian voting or on consensus. But, in the system that I have in mind, there would be multiple bases for deliberative authority.

17. On the importance of mutual concern to trust and, thence, effective decisionmaking, see Aneil K. Mishra, "Organizational Responses to Crisis: The Centrality of Trust," in *Trust in Organizations: Frontiers of Theory and Research*, ed. Roderick M. Kramer and Tom R. Tyler (Thousand Oaks, Calif.: Sage, 1996); and M. Audrey Korsgaard, Bruce M. Meglino, and Scott W. Lester, "The Effect of Other-Oriented Values on Decision Making: A Test of Propositions of a Theory of Concern for Others in Organizations," *Organizational Behavior and Human Decision Processes* 68 (1996): 234–45.

18. See Horst Hutter, *Politics as Friendship* (Waterloo, Ont.: Wilfred Laurier University Press, 1978).

19. Certain kinds of demographic difference may, on their own, discourage the mutual trust that makes it possible for members of a group to discover common interests. Given a history of inequality between whites and blacks and between men and women, just to name two cases, it is probably not enough for a group in which men predominate simply to open the discussion to women or for groups in which whites predominate simply to open the discussion to blacks. The likely wariness of the process on the part of women and people of color reflects a historically well grounded fear that their input will be ignored, misconstrued, or manipulated. Their interests in a whole range of issues may in the end be similar to those of white people and men in the group (likewise, lesbians' interests may be similar to those of straight women, Latinos' interests to those of Anglos, and so on). But long histories in which maintaining status differences has *been* the chief interest of those on the dominant side of each dyad have made people on the other side rightly tentative about assuming a commonality of interest. DAN activists recognize this when they argue that equality against a backdrop of long-standing inequalities requires formal procedures designed to compensate for previous imbalances of power. Just eliminating obvious inequalities in insufficient. Caucuses and various forms of proportional representation may be important in contexts where communication is likely to be impaired by long-standing inequalities.

Jane Mansbridge describes the problem and evaluates remedies in her "Should Blacks Represent Blacks, and Women Represent Women? A Contingent 'Yes,'" Kennedy School of Government paper (2000) (www.ksg.harvard.edu/prg/mansb/should.html). See also Leidner's analysis of the National Women's Studies Association in "Stretching the Boundaries of Liberalism" and "Constituency, Accountability, and Deliberation."

20. Lakey, " 'Catching Up and Moving On.' "

21. This, I believe, is part of what students of social movements have been trying to get at in talking about the role of "free spaces" in protest. Elsewhere, I have criticized those using the concept for their failure to specify what free spaces actually do. The argument that certain institutions within dominated communities—e.g., the black church in the pre–civil rights movement South or social clubs in Communist Eastern Europe—are somehow empty of ideological assumptions, making it possible for participants to penetrate and begin to challenge dominant ideologies, does not seem to me supportable. However, one might more persuasively argue that such institutions preserve counterhegemonic normative traditions and interactional styles tolerated (or unnoticed) by the powerful. Likewise, the "free spaces" created deliberately within movements may begin to institutionalize alternative ways of interacting. (See Francesca Polletta, "Free Spaces in Collective Action," *Theory and Society* 28 [1999]: 1–38.)

22. Ernesto Cortes Jr., "Reflections on the Catholic Tradition of Family Rights," in *One Hundred Years of Catholic Social Thought*, ed. John Coleman (New York: Orbis, 1991). On comradeship, see Ackelsberg, " 'Sisters' or 'Comrades'?" On pluralistic friendship, see Lugones with Rosezelle, "Sisterhood and Friendship as Feminist Models." On the city as a model of politics, see Iris Marion Young, "The Ideal of Community and the Politics of Difference," in Weiss and Friedman, eds., *Feminism and Community*. On covenant as an alternative to contract, see Marshall Ganz, personal communication, 20 February 2000.

More generally, study of the interactive norms animating episodes of collective action may reveal the existence of diverse standards of equality, autonomy, and fairness. For example, in her study of a hospital union organizing drive, Sacks ("Gender and Grassroots Leadership") found that women invoked notions of family to describe their relations with fellow activists and invoked the relations between parents and grown children to describe what they believed they were entitled to from management. Hierarchy was acceptable provided that it was combined with respect and with an acknowledgment of the individual's capacity to grow, learn, and take increasing responsibility. Far from conservative, familial norms provided an oppositional language, says Sacks, as well as a set of interactional norms.

On women's diverse relationships, see also Ann Ferguson, "Feminist Communities and Moral Revolution," in Weiss and Friedman, eds., *Feminism and Community*. On the parent-child relationship as a model for democratic reciprocity, see Held, *Feminist Morality*. On the possibility of a norm of trust, i.e., a behavioral disposition to engage in trusting behavior that may well inspire trustworthy behavior in others, and one that can be taught, see Jonathan Baron, "Trust: Beliefs and Morality," in *Economics, Values, and Organization*, ed. Avner Ben-Ner and Louis Putterman (New York: Cambridge University Press, 1998).

23. For social-psychological evidence on groups' tendency toward "rigid" responses in the face of increasingly severe environmental threats, see C. D. Batson, "Altruism and Prosocial Behavior," in *The Handbook of Social Psychology*, ed. D. T. Gilbert, S. T. Fiske, and G. Lindzey (Boston: McGraw-Hill, 1998).

24. Mills, "Situated Actions and Vocabularies of Motive."

25. Similar criticisms of democratic theorists' failure to consider social movements have been made by Friedman, "Feminism and Modern Friendship"; and Andrew Szasz, "Progress through Mischief: The Social Movement Alternative to Secondary Associations," in Cohen and Rogers, eds., *Associations and Democracy*. See also Debra Minkoff's argument for the importance of social movements as distinct from the institutions of civil society ("Producing Social Capital: National Social Movements and Civil Society," *American Behavioral Scientist* 40 [1997]: 606–19).

Index